Revolution with a Human Face

Revolution with a Human Face

*Politics, Culture, and Community in
Czechoslovakia, 1989–1992*

James Krapfl

Cornell University Press
Ithaca and London

First published 2013 by Cornell University Press

Printed in the United States of America

Library of Congress Cataloging-in-Publication Data

Krapfl, James, 1971– author.
   Revolution with a human face : politics, culture, and community in
Czechoslovakia, 1989–1992 / James Krapfl.
      pages cm
   Includes bibliographical references and index.
   ISBN 978-0-8014-5205-5 (cloth : alk. paper)
   1. Czechoslovakia—Politics and government—1989–1992.
2. Czechoslovakia—History—Velvet Revolution, 1989. 3. Political
culture—Czechoslovakià. I. Title.
   DB2238.7.K735   2013
   943.704'3—dc23   2013012349

Cornell University Press strives to use environmentally responsible
suppliers and materials to the fullest extent possible in the publishing
of its books. Such materials include vegetable-based, low-VOC inks
and acid-free papers that are recycled, totally chlorine-free, or partly
composed of nonwood fibers. For further information visit our website
at www.cornellpress.cornell.edu.

Cloth printing   10 9 8 7 6 5 4 3 2 1

To my parents

Contents

Figures, Maps, and Tables

Figures

Maps

Tables

Acknowledgments

"So you're going to write about what fools we were?" my friend Ivan asked after I explained to him the nature of the research that had brought me back to Slovakia in 2004. It was a better response than I had expected. Over the years, I had grown accustomed to Czechs and Slovaks responding to my interest in 1989 not with polite curiosity but with awkward discomfiture, hysterical laughter, or angry derision. Evidently it was not a topic one could discuss dispassionately. Ivan's ironic question probably explains why: history has not unfolded the way most citizens of Czechoslovakia expected it would in 1989. Indeed, the contrast between their faith in humanity then and the many deceptions and disappointments that have followed—dare one say as a result?—tends to make 1989 either embarrassing or a cruel reminder of how easily people can be manipulated.

Though readers of this book will see that I do not share Ivan's satirical interpretation of 1989, I am grateful to him and many other conversation partners over the years for ensuring that I take that interpretation seriously. I am equally grateful to those who have dissented from the standard view to argue that 1989 has a meaning which is worth trying to discern and who have encouraged me in my efforts to do so. This book is as much the product of conversation as of solitary reflection, and it is a pleasure at last to acknowledge my debts to those whose intellectual interventions have helped bring the book into being, as well as to those who have in countless other ways provided necessary support.

Let me first thank those citizens of what was once Czechoslovakia who have directly influenced my thinking and who have brought both passion and insight to discussions of their contemporary history. It is indeed a unique advantage of contemporary historians that we can check our evidence and interpretations against the experience of living witnesses, and this book has gained much as a result. For conversations—both amiable and antagonistic—that have been particularly fruitful, I would like to thank Iva Bartová, Václav Bartuška, Ján Budaj, Martin Chmel, Elena Ciprianová, Marcela Čekalová, Peter Daňo, Jozef Fabo, Martin Franc, Dalibor Frončák, Adéla Gjuričová, Jozef Grebač, Stanislav Güttner, Miroslava Holubová, Ján Jezný, István Jobbagy, Marián Kišš, Michal Kopeček, Igor Kubálek, Ladislav Kupčík, Zuzana Kusá, Věra Lišková, Viera Majbová, Juraj Mihalík, Tatiana Mihalíková, Mária Mistríková, Ivo Mludek, Barbora Morávková, Karel Müller, Eva Nekolová, Marc Niubò, Libora Oates-Indruchová, Vladimír Ondruš, Ivan Orság, Michal Pullmann, Bohumil Roedl, Martin Růžička, Tadeusz Siwek, Ivan Solovič, Zdeněk Stuchlík, Ján Suchán, Jiří Suk, Josef Škarban, Mária Škarbanová, Daniel Škobla, Kateřina Šuranská, Jozef Tancer, Barbora Tancerová, Miroslav Tížik, Marcel Tomášek, Jaroslav Tomiczek, Petr Vojtal, Lenka Wünschová, Peter Zajac, František Znebejánek, Pavel Žáček, and Jozef Žatkuliak. Every one of these individuals has made a unique contribution, which if I were to describe them all would go on for many pages, so perhaps I will be forgiven if I single out three who have especially impacted my approach to this project. Jaroslav Tomiczek, whom I met while he was a student in Olomouc in 1997, alerted me to the importance of flyers in the revolution and suggested that I use them as the basis of my study. Jiří Suk has provided with his monumental study of Civic Forum's coordinating center, *Labyrintem revoluce* (Through the labyrinth of revolution), an inspiring model of historical scholarship and a support against which my own work can lean. Mária Mistríková, finally, not only has been extraordinarily generous with her time but has motivated me, with her personal devotion to the Gentle Revolution and her confidence in my ability to tell its story, to work through inevitable spasms of writer's block.

If this book inclines toward an emic perspective (anthropological jargon for "the native's point of view"), it is because an understanding of how a cultural historian's subjects themselves made sense of their experiences is a necessary preliminary step to making sense of these experiences through the "foreign" idiom of scholarship. This scholarly, "etic" perspective is essential to the project, of course, and I would like to thank the many scholars outside the Czech and Slovak republics who have helped me synthesize my etic interpretation. Thanks go first of all to my incredibly supportive dissertation committee at the University of California, Berkeley, chaired by John Connelly and including Victoria Bonnell and Carla Hesse. A more perfect combination of perspective, expertise, and personality could not be imagined. Also at Berkeley, Margaret Anderson, Michael Dean, Jeanne Grant, Simon Grote, Tim Jenks, Blake Johnson, Mark Keck-Szajbel, Anne MacLachlan, Jelani Mahiri, Andrej Milivojević, Daniel Orlovsky, Dana Sherry, Johan Vanderzelde, Edward Walker, and participants in the seminars of the Berkeley Program in Soviet and Post-Soviet Studies and the Working Group on the History and Culture of East

Central Europe all helped to shape my thinking on the Gentle Revolution and my approach to studying it.

My interest in 1989 predated doctoral study, and I would like to thank John Burney and Joan Skurnowicz for courses they taught on comparative revolution and modern European history during my freshman year in college (in 1989–90), that helped set my thinking on its initial path. Elizabeth Beck helped ensure that I got the most out of a 1992 semester in Czechoslovakia, organized by the National Collegiate Honors Council in cooperation with Charles University in Prague and Palacký University in Olomouc, where my general interest in 1989 became a specific interest in a country on the verge of dissolution. Later, Leonard Hochberg and Carol Skalnik Leff helped me devise a research project that I was able to pursue in the Czech Republic from 1996 to 1997. This research provided the basis for a controversial master's thesis at the Central European University in Budapest in 1999, and I am grateful to Roumen Daskalov, László Kontler, and Mónika Mátay for comprising a tolerant and helpfully critical thesis committee.

In the course of conducting research in the Czech and Slovak republics I have benefited intellectually from conversation and in some cases collaboration with other foreign researchers, including Dennis Beck, Richard Grainer, Magdalena Hadjiisky, Karen Kapusta-Pofahl, Jennifer Larson, Mark Lovas, Yordanka Madzharova, Alexander Maxwell, Catriona Menzies, Lisa Peschel, Anna Socrates, James Ward, Julia White, and especially Deanna Wooley, whose emic understanding of the Czech students of 1989 and etic awareness of Anglo-American scholarship have made her an ideal sounding board for many of my ideas. I thank all these individuals, as well as the many others whose comments over the years have contributed to the etic perspective presented here, including Kevin Adamson, Tim Beasley-Murray, Paul Caringella, Dessislava Dragneva, Barbara Falk, Timothy Garton Ash, René Girard, Judith Hegedus, Brian Hodson, Ken Horne, Erin Jenne, Gwen Jones, Padraic Kenney, Sandra Leake, Heather Nehring, Susan Pearce, Robert Pynsent, Marci Shore, Marsha Siefert, Roberto Solarte, Don Sparling, Veronika Šimánková, Vladimir Tismaneanu, Aviezer Tucker, John Unruh, Kieran Williams, and Ryan Wilson.

When I first conceived of this project in its present form as a response to Lynn Hunt's study of politics, culture, and class in the French Revolution, I planned to focus on the flyers and bulletins of 1989, simply extending my original source base in Moravia and Silesia to encompass all of Czechoslovakia. That the book has grown to consider a more massive corpus of ephemeral literature from 1989 to 1992 is thanks largely to the advice and breathtaking goodwill of the many archivists, librarians, and museum workers who have assisted me in my various research trips. Linda Bernard, Jana Boťková, Helena Hollá, Jiří Hoppe, Bohdan Kaňák, Oľga Kvasnicová, Viera Majbová, Mária Mistríková, Martin Molnár, Linda Osyková, Jiří Pulec, Bohumil Roedl, Jiří Suk, Peter Tesák, and Eliška Travníčková have been extraordinarily helpful in this regard. Sincerest thanks go to Peter Zajac for granting me permission to peruse a small part of the Milan Šimecka Foundation's VPN archive, now housed in the Slovak National Archive, and to Michaela Borunská, Marcela Čekalová, István Jobbagy, Michael Kukral, Carol Skalnik Leff, Kevin McDermott, Mária Mistríková, Marc Niubò, and Lenka Wünschová for sharing with me documents from their personal collections. Karel Asha, Corina Manole, Jan Náplava, Alexander Noran, Luke Ryder, Laura Saavedra, Steven Schwartzhoff, Martina Vidláková, and Martin Vostřel provided research assistance, for which I am most appreciative. Valerián Bystrický, Marcela Čekalová, Jitka Herynková, Helena Rozlívková, Oldřich Tůma, and the staffs of the Fulbright Commissions in Prague and Bratislava all magically ensured that practical aspects of my research sojourns were smoothly and competently addressed, and I am grateful to the Historical Institute in Bratislava, the Institute for Contemporary History in Prague, and Palacký University in Olomouc for the institutional affiliation they provided.

The writing of books does not depend on research and intellectual conversation alone; this one would not have come into being without the practical support of many people in several countries. I would like to thank in particular Barbara Voytek and the supremely competent staff of the Institute of Slavic, East European, and Eurasian Studies at Berkeley for deftly administering various aspects of my funding and making the institute a warm and stimulating academic environment. My equally sincere thanks go to Mabel Lee, who capably guides graduate students in Berkeley's history department through the university's labyrinthine bureaucracy and makes miracles commonplace. I cannot begin to express my gratitude to Robert and Rosl Krapfl and their family, who practically made their Bavarian farm a second home to me and who certainly displayed generosity that transcends what one normally expects of sixth cousins one and two generations removed. For additional practical support over the years, ranging from advice on what digital camera to use in my research to free lodging in the course of my travels, I thank Stephanie Ballenger, Ariane Baudhuin, Dennis Beck, Thomas Connolly, Nicholas Dew, Dessislava Dragneva, Nicole Eaton, Božena Fabová, Barbara Falk, Michael and Jennifer Fronda, Michal Grebač, Simon Grote, Carol Harrington, István Jobbagy, Marián Kišš, Pavel Knápek, Habib Krit, Mitch Laipple and his family, Anne MacLachlan, Yordanka Madzharova, Catriona Menzies, Andrej Milivojević, Leonard Moore, Marc Niubò, Alice Palen, Glenn Parado, Michal Pullmann, Johanna Ransmeier, César Rodriguez, Milan Růžička, Steven Schwartzhoff and Eva Schwartzhoffová, Dana Sherry, Jeannette Sherwin, Anna Socrates, Ivan Solovič, Gordon Sweet, Mária Škarbanová, Daniel Škobla, Rastislav Tancár, Jozef Tancer and Barbora Tancerová, Marcel Tomášek, George and Lydia Vandermuehll, Paul Vanoverloop, James Ward and Martina Wardová, Anne Whitaker, Brent White, Julia White, Ryan Wilson, and Deanna Wooley.

For the generous financial support that made this book possible I must thank a variety of institutions and individuals. Initial research was funded by Fulbright and

Fulbright-Hays Fellowships from the U.S. Departments of State and Education, with supplemental funding from the Czech government. Writing and additional research were supported by the American Council of Learned Societies, the Andrew J. Mellon Foundation, the Institute of International Studies at Berkeley, the McGill University Faculty of Arts, the Quebec Fund for Research on Society and Culture, the Social Sciences and Humanities Research Council of Canada, and Paul Hertelendy. Time is often more valuable than money, and this book has benefited immeasurably from the kindness of Catherine LeGrand, who as chair of the History Department at McGill allowed me a year free of teaching responsibilities.

It is unusual for a scholarly monograph in English, written by an American, to be published first in Slovak, but this one has been. Since many of those who have helped make this book possible cannot read English, and since I wanted to know their reaction to my interpretation before inflicting potential errors on readers without the experience to defend themselves, I took advantage of the opportunity to publish a slightly shorter version in Slovakia on the occasion of the twentieth anniversary. My thanks go to Ingrid Hrubaničová and László Szigeti of the Kalligram publishing house for making this possible and to the reviewers of the book, particularly the sociologist Miroslav Tížik and the historians Miloš Řezník, Vítězslav Sommer, and Jiří Suk, for confirming that I have represented the history of their revolution accurately. The changes to this version, therefore, are primarily of the sort necessary to provide context to readers who did not live through the events in question, although some detail has been added and some luxurious digressions have been removed.

The final English text has benefited from the sagacious advice of anonymous reviewers as well as colleagues and students at McGill whom I am happy to name. Readers who value euphony and cogency must share my gratitude to Sami Ahmad, Johanna Beil, Lochin Brouillard, Gabriella Coleman, Grégory Kerr, Jean-Robert Lalancette, Becky Lentz, Jocelyn Pâquet, Nancy Partner, Matthew Signer, Andrea Tam, and the students in my seminars on revolution in central Europe for their thoughtful and detailed critiques. At Cornell University Press my thanks go first to John Ackerman, who has proven himself a marvelously supportive, attentive, and helpfully old-fashioned editor. Ange Romeo-Hall patiently and cheerfully managed the transformation from manuscript to book, Jamie Fuller did the best copyediting I have ever encountered, and Scott Levine tastefully designed the final product. Sincere thanks to all of them. Readers of Kevin McDermott's and Matthew Stibbe's 2006 edited volume *Revolution and Resistance in Eastern Europe* will note that an earlier version of this book's first chapter appeared there, and I am grateful to Berg Publishers in Oxford for permission to reuse this material.

Finally, I would like to thank my parents for what they have unknowingly done to make this book possible. As a farmer, my father raised me to think that ceaseless toil for uncertain reward was somehow normal. My mother, by taking me with her on genealogical expeditions to America's courthouses, trained me at an early age in methods of historical research. By letting me help prepare for precinct caucuses and county conventions of their political party, dragging me along to central committee meetings, and sending me as a "junior delegate" to state conventions, they gave me insight into the practical functioning of democratic politics that has informed my thinking about democracy in Czechoslovakia. The book is dedicated to them.

Abbreviations

Institutions in Possession of Archival Sources

BB	Štátny archív v Banskej Bystrici, pobočka Banská Bystrica
BE	Státní okresní archiv Beroun
BN	Státní okresní archiv Benešov
BV	Státní okresní archiv Břeclav, Mikulov
BZ	Státní okresní archiv Brno-venkov, Rajhrad
CB	Státní okresní archiv České Budějovice
CK	Státní okresní archiv Český Krumlov
DO	Státní okresní archiv Domažlice, Horšovský Týn
DÚ	Divadelní ústav, Prague
GA	Štátny archív v Bratislave, pobočka Šaľa
HIA	Hoover Institution Archives, Stanford, California
HM	Historický múzeum Národného múzea, Bratislava
JN	Státní okresní archiv Jablonec nad Nisou
KN	Štátny archív v Bratislave, pobočka Komárno
KO	Státní okresní archiv Kolín
KS	Štátny archív v Košiciach, pobočka Košice
LN	Státní okresní archiv Louny
MI	Štátny archív v Košiciach, pobočka Michalovce

MU	Archiv Masarykovy univerzity, Brno
OL	Státní okresní archiv Olomouc
OP	Státní okresní archiv Opava
OV	Archiv města Ostravy
PA	Státní okresní archiv Pardubice
PP	Štátny archív v Levoči, pobočka Poprad, Spišská Sobota
PR	Státní okresní archiv Přerov
PV	Státní okresní archiv Prostějov
PX	Štátny archív v Bytči, pobočka Považská Bystrica
SNA	Slovenský národný archív, Bratislava
SV	Štátny archív v Košiciach, pobočka Svidník
TA	Státní okresní archiv Tábor
TN	Štátny archív v Bratislave, pobočka Trenčín
TO	Štátny archív v Bratislave, pobočka Topoľčany
TU	Státní okresní archiv Trutnov
UH	Státní okresní archiv Uherské Hradiště
ÚSD	Ústav pro soudobé dějiny, Prague
ZL	Státní okresní archiv Zlín
ZM	Zemplínske múzeum, Michalovce

Other Abbreviations

(N. B. Where Czech and Slovak differ, the Slovak word or ending is given first.)

AV	akčný/í výbor (action committee)
BAZ	Bratislavské automobilové závody (Bratislava Automotive Works)
CHZ	Chemické závody (chemical works)
ČKD	Českomoravská Kolben Daněk
ČNR	Česká národní rada (Czech National Council)
ČR	Česká republika (Czech Republic)
ČSAD	Československá autobusová doprava (Czechoslovak Bus Lines)
ČSČK	Československý červený kríž/kříž (Czechoslovak Red Cross)
ČSFR	Česká a Slovenská Federatívna/í Republika (Czech and Slovak Federative Republic)
ČSĽA	Československá ľudová armada (Czechoslovak People's Army)
ČSPD	Československá plavba dunajská (Czechoslovak Danube Navigation)

ČSR	Česká socialistická republika (Czech Socialist Republic)
	Česko-Slovenská republika (Czecho-Slovak Republic)
ČSSR	Československá socialistická republika (Czechoslovak Socialist Republic)
ČTK	Československá tisková kancelář (Czechoslovak Press Agency)
DAMU	Divadelní akademie múzických umění (Theatrical Academy of Fine Arts)
DÚM	Diagnostický ústav pre/pro mládež (Diagnostic Institute for Youth)
FF	filozofická fakulta (philosophical faculty)
FMK	Független Magyar Kezdeményezés (Independent Hungarian Initiative)
FS	Federální shromáždění (Federal Assembly)
HZDS	Hnutie za demokratické Slovensko (Movement for a Democratic Slovakia)
Ing.	inžinier/enýr (Engineer)
JRD	Jednotné roľnícke družstvo (United Agricultural Cooperative)
JUDr.	JURIS UTRIUSQUE DOCTOR (Doctor of Law)
JZD	Jednotné zemědělské družstvo (United Agricultural Cooperative)
KC	koordinačné/í centrum (coordinating center)
KDS	Kresťanskodemokratická strana (Christian Democratic Party)
KNV	krajský národný/í výbor (regional national committee)
k.p.	koncernový podnik (syndicated enterprise)
KSČ	Komunistická strana Československa (Communist Party of Czechoslovakia)
KSS	Komunistická strana Slovenska (Communist Party of Slovakia)
KSV	koordinační stávkový výbor (coordinating strike committee)
KV	koordinačný/í výbor (coordinating committee)
LI	Liberecká iniciatíva (Liberec Initiative)
MěNV	městský národní výbor (municipal national committee)
MKV	mestský/městský koordinačný/í výbor (municipal coordinating committee)
MS	Matica slovenská
MsNV	mestský národný výbor (municipal national committee)
MSS	Mezinárodní svaz studentstva (International Students' Association)
MŠ	materská/mateřská škola (nursery school)
NF	Národný/í front/a (National Front)

NRzOS   Národná rada za oslobodenie Slovenska (National Council for the Liberation of Slovakia)

ODS   Občianska/Občanská demokratická strana (Civic Democratic Party)

OF   Občianske/Občanské fórum (Civic Forum)

OH   Občanské hnutí (Civic Movement)

OI   občianska iniciatíva (civic initiative)

OkSS   Okresná/í správa spojov/ů (district communications administration)

OKV   okresný/í koordinačný/í výbor (district coordinating committee)

ONV   okresný/í národný/í výbor (district national committee)

OV   okresný/í výbor (district committee)

OZ   odštepný/odštěpný závod (detached factory)

PdF   pedagogická fakulta (pedagogical faculty)

PF   právnická fakulta (law faculty)

PKO   Park kultúry a oddychu (Park of Culture and Rest)

POV   plénum okresného/ího výboru (district committee plenum)

PR   podnikové riaditeľstvo (enterprise secretariat)

PZDS   Platforma za demokratické Slovensko (Platform for a Democratic Slovakia)

ROH   Revolučné/í odborové hnutie/í (Revolutionary Union Movement)

SAV   Slovenská akadémia vied (Slovak Academy of Sciences)

SKNV   Stredoslovenský krajský národný výbor (Central Slovakian Regional National Committee)

SND   Slovenské národné divadlo (Slovak National Theater)

SNP   Slovenské národné povstanie (Slovak National Uprising)

SNR   Slovenská národná rada (Slovak National Council)

SOU   stredné/střední odborné učilište/ě (specialized secondary training institution)

s.p.   státní podnik (state enterprise)

SPŠS   stredná/střední priemyselná/průmyslová škola stavebná/í (secondary school oriented toward the construction industry)

SR   Slovenská republika (Slovak Republic)

SSM   Socialistický svaz mládeže (Socialist Youth Association)

SSR   Slovenská socialistická republika (Slovak Socialist Republic)

SSSR   Svaz sovětských socialistických republik (Union of Soviet Socialist Republics)

SzF   Szabad Fórum (Free Forum)

SZM	Socialistický zväz mládeže (Socialist Youth Association)
ŠBČS	Štátna banka Československá (Czechoslovak State Bank)
ŠS	šľachtiteľská/šlechtitelská stanica/e (agricultural station)
ŠtB	Štátna bezpečnosť (State Security)
UJEP	Univerzita Jana Evangelisty Purkyně (Jan Evangelista Purkyně University)
UK	Univerzita Karlova (Charles University)
UP	Univerzita Palackého (Palacký University)
UPJŠ	Univerzita Pavla Jozefa Šafárika (Pavol Jozef Šafárik University)
ÚRO	Ústredná/Ústřední rada odborov/ů (Central Council of Trade Unions)
ÚV	ústredný/ústřední výbor (central committee)
VaK	Voda a kanalizácia/ace (Waterworks)
VB	Verejná/Veřejná bezpečnosť/t (Public Security)
VD	výrobné/í družstvo (production cooperative)
VPN	Verejnosť proti násiliu (Public against Violence)
VŠ	vysoká škola (institution of higher education)
VŠCHT	Vysoká škola chemicko-technologická (Higher School of Chemistry and Technology)
VŠMU	Vysoká škola múzických umení (Higher School of Fine Arts)
ZDS	Za demokratické Slovensko (For a Democratic Slovakia)
ZNB	Zbor národnej bezpečnosti (National Security Forces)
ZZN	Zemědělské zásobování a nákup (Agricultural Supply and Purchase)
ZO	základná/í organizácia/ace (basic organization)
ZŠ	základná/í škola (elementary school)
ZV	základný/í výbor (basic committee)

Revolution with a Human Face

Introduction

It is a strange thing that most studies of the Czechoslovak revolution of 1989 ignore or marginalize its most important actor: Czechoslovak citizens. If, after all, the revolution of 1989 was a *democratic* revolution, then it follows that the *demos*—the people—should be at the center of our attention. Instead, most of the historical, political, and even sociological analyses that have been published in the successor states and abroad focus on elites. While some of these studies are superlative, the unsettling implication of the collective reticence surrounding popular engagement in 1989 is that this engagement was not very important. The published memoirs and the interviews printed and broadcast every November in the mainstream Czech and Slovak media do nothing to challenge this conclusion because publishers and journalists as a rule lend their platforms only to recognized "leaders," such that the number of "witnesses" who are authorized to remember the revolution in public has steadily dwindled over the years to perhaps two dozen. As a result, though a casual glance at photographs and film footage from 1989 is enough to remind us that millions of Czechoslovak citizens in that year consciously chose to engage in concerted action, there is no serious public discussion of this engagement to which individuals might relate their personal experiences. This silence leads to forgetting, and if it does not undermine democratic political culture in Czechoslovakia's successor states, it certainly does not strengthen it.

Michelet once defined the aim of history as "resurrection," and this is a fitting description of what the present work must do.[1] This book is a history of the "Gentle

---

[1] Jules Michelet, *Du Prêtre, de la femme, de la famille*, 4th ed. (Paris: Comptoire des Imprimeurs-Unis, 1845), p. 37.

Revolution," as Czechs used to and Slovaks still call it, from below, foregrounding the experiences of the citizens of Czechoslovakia—ordinary and otherwise—on the basis of a systematic analysis of relevant primary evidence. The aim of the book is "resurrection" insofar as most of the evidence presented here has been forgotten, and in bringing this buried material out of its archival "tombs" and into the public light, the book restores voices to historical actors who have hitherto been denied the power to speak. It aims not just to reveal, however, but also to analyze the revolution's central question: that of its meaning. That this was a question is reflected even today in the ambiguity over the revolution's name (should we even call it a revolution, or would "regime change," "the fall of Communism," or simply "events" be more precise?).[2] As we shall see, this ambiguity emerged as early as December 1989, and to a significant extent the history of the revolution was (and has been) the history of efforts to determine its meaning. In contrast to studies that treat 1989 as a mere boundary—a colorful bridge from Communism to post-Communism—this book argues that the revolutionary period was an epoch of meaning-formation in and of itself. It seeks to identify the meanings that Czechoslovak citizens gave the revolution and explain why these meanings came about. It seeks further to explain how Czechs and Slovaks struggled in and after 1989 to defend particular meanings and to impose them on society at large. Ultimately, it is concerned with the implications of these meanings for the establishment and development of a democratic political culture in Czechoslovakia and its successor states.

One of the remarkable consequences of 1989 was that it supplanted 1789 as a practical model for democratic revolution in the modern world. From Ukraine in 2004 to Tunisia and Egypt in 2011, citizens mobilizing against insufferable regimes have looked to the examples set in Eastern Europe at the end of the twentieth century. It is therefore important to understand what East European citizens actually did in 1989 and to what extent they were successful in achieving their goals. While a detailed examination of popular engagement throughout the region would be desirable, the time and skills required to study the thoughts and deeds of a hundred million people in five countries (speaking six languages) place such an undertaking beyond the capacity of a solitary researcher.[3] A careful investigation of a single country, however, with only three major languages and fifteen million people, can challenge global generalizations about 1989 and raise questions that might be worth asking in other national contexts. For the purpose of understanding the

[2] In this book, "Communist" always refers to a Leninist party (usually the Communist Party of Czechoslovakia) and "Communism" refers to a system of rule by such a party; hence the words are always capitalized.
[3] The most accurate general treatment of the revolutionary process throughout Eastern Europe, by a historian who reads all the languages of the region and with balanced coverage of both elites and ordinary citizens, is Robin Okey's *The Demise of Communist East Europe: 1989 in Context* (London: Hodder Arnold, 2004).

revolutionary process, moreover, the Czechoslovak case is particularly interest-ing. Whether or not one agrees with Charles Tilly's theory of revolution in ev-ery respect, his distinction between "revolutionary situations" and "revolutionary outcomes" provides a suggestive way of thinking about 1989.[4] While Poland, Hun-gary, East Germany, Czechoslovakia, and Romania all experienced revolutionary events in that year, the case for a revolutionary situation was marginal in Poland and Hungary, and the case for a revolutionary outcome doubtful in Romania. In Poland and Hungary, while the people were important as a referent that roundtable participants could invoke, it is generally accepted that power never left the hands of the old and new elites.[5] Though in both cases there was a revolutionary outcome, where power was transferred from an old elite to a new one, there was never a revolutionary situation involving a multiplicity of effective but incompatible claims to sovereignty. Only in East Germany, Czechoslovakia, and Romania did popular mobilization force the hands of elites—both old and new—such that the people were a powerful revolutionary actor in their own right, and only in these countries were there episodes of "multiple sovereignty" that Tilly takes to be the defining fea-tures of revolutionary situations. In Romania, however, the popular revolution was essentially usurped by Communist apparatchiks in the National Salvation Front.[6] Only East Germany and Czechoslovakia experienced both revolutionary situations and revolutionary outcomes, but in East Germany the outcome was quickly modi-fied by absorption into West Germany. Czechoslovakia was comparatively freer to determine the outcome of its revolution. Whereas many of the popular revolution-ary dynamics that began in East Germany in the fall of 1989 were truncated by unification, in Czechoslovakia they were able to run their course.[7] It is by studying Czechoslovakia, therefore, that we can learn most about the revolutionary potential of 1989.

[4] Charles Tilly, *European Revolutions, 1492–1992* (Oxford: Basil Blackwell, 1993), pp. 1–16, 233–36.

[5] Practically the only accounts of the 1989–90 period in Poland and Hungary from a grassroots perspec-tive are Tomek Grabowski, "The Party That Never Was: The Rise and Fall of the Solidarity Citizens' Com-mittees in Poland," *East European Politics and Societies* 10, no. 2 (Spring 1996): 214–54; and Alan Renwick, "The Role of Non-Elite Forces in the Regime Change," in *The Roundtable Talks of 1989: The Genesis of Hungarian Democracy*, ed. András Bozóki (Budapest: Central European University Press, 2001), 191–210. For accounts emphasizing the roundtable negotiations between old and new elites, see Marjorie Castle, *Trig-gering Communism's Collapse: Perceptions and Power in Poland's Transition* (Lanham, Md.: Rowman & Littlefield, 2003); and Rudolf Tőkés, *Hungary's Negotiated Revolution: Economic Reform, Social Change, and Political Succession, 1957–1990* (Cambridge: Cambridge University Press, 1996).

[6] This process is elegantly explained in Kevin Adamson and Sergiu Florean, "Discourse and Power: The FSN and the Mythologisation of the Romanian Revolution," in *The 1989 Revolutions in Central and East-ern Europe: From Communism to Pluralism*, ed. Kevin McDermott and Matthew Stibbe (Manchester, U.K.: Manchester University Press, 2013), 172–91. The best book-length account of the Romanian revolution is Peter Siani-Davies, *The Romanian Revolution of 1989* (Ithaca, N.Y.: Cornell University Press, 2005).

[7] Charles S. Maier provides a thorough account of the East German revolution from 1989 to beyond unification in *Dissolution: The Crisis of Communism and the End of East Germany* (Princeton, N.J.: Princeton University Press, 1997); but Gareth Dale provides a more grassroots perspective in his well-researched *The East German Revolution of 1989* (Manchester: Manchester University Press, 2006).

How can we write the history of fifteen million people? How can we determine what meaning—if any—the revolution had for ordinary citizens assembled on town squares and active in grassroots political associations in 1989 and subsequent years? The best place to begin is the words and actions of these citizens themselves. Beginning in November 1989, striking students and workers churned out tens of thousands of declarations, flysheets, bulletins, posters, and open letters—documents that speak eloquently to the assumptions, expectations, and motivations of their popular authors. Since most documents are dated, moreover, it is possible to trace the day-by-day evolution of these assumptions, expectations, and motivations. Together with video recordings, newspapers, and the minutes of Party and administrative organs as well as the new citizens' associations, these documents reveal the complex symbolism of collective action in 1989, replete with festivals, happenings, and pilgrimages that accomplished—in addition to or in lieu of any explicit political purpose—the sacralization of a revolutionary community. While the most intense collective effervescence took place in November and December 1989, citizens continued to produce flyers, declarations, bulletins, and letters in exceptionally large quantities during the early 1990s—a stream of discourse that was quickly supplemented by an explosion of unregulated print. These later documents allow us to trace the evolution of revolutionary mentalities to some of their logical conclusions.

Some may wonder that sources for such a study are accessible to historians so relatively recently after the period in question. The standard thirty-year waiting period for the release of documents has, after all, not yet expired. There are two reasons why these documents are available. First, the revolutionary demands of 1989 for truth and accessibility of information have been reflected in Czech and Slovak laws regulating state archives, such that nearly all government documents and documents relating to political organizations produced prior to 1 January 1990 can be made accessible to the public as soon as archivists have succeeded in acquiring them and putting them in order. Second and more important, most of the documents necessary for the study of popular political culture have been public from the beginning, never subject to a waiting period. Though researchers have (with a single exception) ignored them, the flyers and bulletins that were the primary means of information exchange in 1989 have always been available for study.[8] Records of non-state organizations, such as the civic initiatives that sprang up during the revolution, are open as long as their owners wish to make them so. In all, at least seventy archives, museums, and libraries in the Czech and Slovak republics and abroad have open collections that can be used for the study of revolutionary *mentalités* on the basis of primary documents besides newspapers.

[8] Prior to this book, the only systematic attention any of these documents received was in Bohuslav Beneš and Václav Hrníčko, *Nápisy v ulicích* (Brno: Masarykova univerzita, 1993), a study concerned with slogans.

Studies of the Czechoslovak revolution have thus far tended to focus exclusively on Prague, seldom transcending the bounds of the former federal capital to investigate even Bratislava and Brno on the basis of more than hearsay. Many different communities lived in Czechoslovakia, however, and to understand the meaning of 1989 in any systematic fashion, the experiences of these distinct communities must be compared. The revolution did not mean the same to Slovaks as it did to Czechs, and Slovakia's Hungarian-speaking minority interpreted it still differently. Administrative divisions among Czechoslovakia's 112 districts resulted in a spectrum of diverse experiences in the popular quest for the democratization of local government and industry, ranging from the mass resignation of district officials in Topoľčany to the physical repression of would-be demonstrators in Ostrava. Hopes for the reconstitution of political community varied among the historic regions of Czechoslovakia, and naturally the possibilities for collective action differed between large cities and small villages. In short, to understand the meaning of revolution in Czechoslovakia and the ways in which this meaning was contested and evolved, it is necessary to compare revolutionary rhetoric and action at multiple levels and to recognize that the capitals may have been more exceptional than emblematic.

Since the breakup of Czechoslovakia, there has been a tendency among scholars in both successor states to "nationalize" their history—to investigate only the Czech or the Slovak dimensions of historical phenomena during the period of the common state. While in some cases this methodology may be appropriate, when applied to the revolution of 1989 it is a distorting anachronism. The actors of 1989, from striking farmers in the remotest village to students negotiating with Communist officials in the capitals, thought in terms of a Czechoslovak community and acted accordingly. Events in one republic influenced developments in the other in ways that cannot be ignored without falsifying the past. Some historians, noting this problem, have suggested that the revolution in Slovakia was a related but "different revolution" from the one in the Czech lands, but even this representation is not quite accurate.[9] If we are to use the trope of difference, then a close examination of the evidence reveals that the revolution in Brno was different from the one in Prague, and that was different again from the one in Klatovy, which of course was different from the one in Kráľovský Chlmec, and quite soon we are forced to acknowledge that there were thousands of distinctly "different" revolutions. Czechoslovakia in 1989 consisted simultaneously of one nation and two, of one community and many, and an accurate investigation of the politics and culture of the revolution must acknowledge this sometimes tense, often complicated, but always concurrent unity and multiplicity.

[9] See, for example, *Labyrintem revoluce*, part 3, *Slovensko, jiná revoluce*, directed by Petr Jančárek in cooperation with Jiří Suk, Česká televize, 2006.

An apposite method for studying the history of fifteen million people is what was called the "new" cultural history when it became established in French- and English-language historiography in the 1980s. Informed by cultural anthropology, this now mainstream school of cultural history seeks to understand the mentalities of societies and social groups and the transformation of these mentalities over time. In contrast to traditional social history, which tends to break society down into classes and assume that social behavior is a reflection of social class, cultural history considers that perceptions, beliefs, and methods of determining meaning are more directly related to decision making and historical action. By "culture," cultural historians have in mind "webs of significance," as the anthropologist Clifford Geertz once defined the term.[10] They are concerned with the production of meaning and the social sharing of meaning via signs, symbols, rituals, and other bearers of significance. In the same way that a language is meaningful to those who more or less agree on the correct interpretation of certain patterns of sound or a certain arrangement of scratches on paper, so gestures, clothing, images, places, and practices can convey certain meanings in one culture but other meanings or no meaning in another. Cultural historians, therefore, seek to "read" these patterns in the same way they might read a language, in order to determine how particular people in particular places make sense of their world and how these symbolic systems constrain and channel human action and the unfolding of history. By analyzing in this fashion the surviving evidence of popular political engagement in 1989 and the early 1990s, we can learn how Czechoslovak citizens made sense of the revolution and how this sense influenced their behavior.

Historians of the eighteenth century will note that the subtitle of this book recalls Lynn Hunt's pathbreaking analysis of politics, culture, and class in the French Revolution.[11] The present book aims to accomplish for the revolution of 1989 what hers did for that of 1789. The purpose is not to understand 1989 in terms of 1789 but to come to a new understanding of 1989 by asking questions and applying methods that have enriched our understanding of phenomena that the actors of 1989 themselves identified as comparable. Like their French predecessors, Czechs and Slovaks faced the need to reconstitute political community, to devise new rules of political practice, and to resolve questions of symbolic and political representation. Czechs and Slovaks saw themselves as carrying on the revolutionary tradition that had begun in France in 1789, even as they consciously innovated upon this tradition to meet the requirements of the late twentieth century. By closely examining revolutionary rhetoric, symbolic forms of political practice, and the sociology of politics in diverse geographical settings, Hunt was able to show how the revolutionary experience gave rise to a new political culture, understood as "the values, expectations, and implicit

[10] Clifford Geertz, *The Interpretation of Cultures* (New York: Basic Books, 1973), p. 5.

[11] Lynn Hunt, *Politics, Culture, and Class in the French Revolution* (Berkeley: University of California Press, 1984).

rules" that provide the logic of political action.[12] The present book demonstrates that these methods, developed for the study of early modern European history, can be applied with equal effectiveness to contemporary phenomena.

The picture that emerges is that of a surprisingly idealistic revolution that was at once social, political, and even religious. The French historian François Furet once wrote that "with all the fuss and noise, not a single new idea has come out of Eastern Europe in 1989."[13] The evidence, however, shows that while new ideas may not have come *out* of Eastern Europe, they were certainly there. Perhaps most intriguing was the idea of "humanness," to which other revolutionary principles like nonviolence and democracy were logically related. Czechs and Slovaks did not reject the Communist regime because it was socialist but because it was unresponsively bureaucratic and "inhumane." Demands for nonviolence, democracy, and humanness, moreover, were not made only on the governments in Prague and Bratislava but on political and economic administration at all levels; discussion of the meaning of these ideas further established them as blueprints for the refashioning of quotidian human relations and the "rebirth" of the self. Human relations were thus at the heart of the popular revolution, which can be interpreted as a kind of reformation, or transference of sacrality.

It must be emphasized that this book is not concerned with the academic question of what caused the revolution. Rather, it investigates the practical question of what people do when they find themselves in a revolutionary situation. In the debates about causes and outcomes that have preoccupied social scientists since 1989, the revolutionary experience itself has been taken for granted. It has been assumed that journalists' and other impressionistic accounts of temporary eyewitnesses tell us all we need to know about what ordinary citizens thought and did in 1989 and subsequent years, but systematic investigation demonstrates that these accounts provide a very inaccurate representation of reality.[14] Remarkably, over twenty years after the revolutions of 1989, we still do not know basic facts about what happened, how the citizens who constituted East European societies behaved, and what motivated their behavior. This book is intended to help set the record straight and, more important, to analyze the character of the revolutionary experience. Its purpose is to uncover the logic that informed popular political activity in Czechoslovakia from the beginning of the revolution, when citizens claimed for themselves new roles in public space, to the closure of opportunities for popular political engagement in 1991–92.

---

[12] Ibid., p. 10.

[13] Quoted in Ralf Dahrendorf, *Reflections on the Revolution in Europe* (New York: Times Books, 1990), p. 27.

[14] Tony Judt's *Postwar*, for example, while marvelous in many respects, is highly inaccurate in its portrayal of the Czechoslovak revolution of 1989, despite the fact that Judt "was in Prague at this time." *Postwar: A History of Europe since 1945* (New York: Penguin, 2005), pp. 616–22.

Students of civil society will find this book relevant to their interests, though the term itself appears seldom in its pages. Czechs and Slovaks in 1989 spoke constantly of "citizens" and eagerly joined "civic initiatives," but the term "civil society" was entirely absent from their discourse. This book's methodology is based on the premise that, to understand the mentality of these citizens, it makes more sense to examine concepts they used than those they did not. Academic definitions of civil society, moreover, are legion, and it is not necessary to stake a claim in that minefield in order to show how Czechoslovak citizens established a democratic political culture. The debates about civil society in relation to 1989 have mostly hinged on the question of whether civil society was a cause or product of the revolutions, rather than on the nature of the revolutionary experience itself.[15] Those who argue the former usually insist that dissident associations under Communism constituted at least a rudimentary civil society that could exert pressure on their governments and mobilize fellow citizens in 1989, while those who argue the latter claim that they did not. The evidence that informs this book has been used elsewhere to demonstrate that, in Czechoslovakia, dissident associational frameworks played a vital role in structuring civic activity during the revolution, though citizens' motives for mobilization usually had other roots.[16] This is similar to Gareth Dale's argument (for East Germany) that opposition groups "planted a flag" around which independently mobilizing citizens could organize.[17] Be that as it may, it is clear that however civil society is defined, citizens in 1989 became massively involved in it, effectively reconstituting it if it did not already exist. Insofar as civil society can be regarded as a component of democratic political culture, this book sheds light on that reconstitution.

The book has six substantive chapters. The first serves as a prologue, setting the stage for the main argument by taking us deeply into the mind-set of Czechoslovak citizens who, beginning in 1989, perceived themselves to be participants in an unfolding revolution. By December of that year, Czechoslovak citizens were in practically universal agreement that a revolution was taking place, with even Communist apparatchiks rushing to embrace the term. Later, debates emerged about just what kind of a revolution it was, whether it was over, and whether any revolution had in fact occurred. Drawing on the narrative theories of Hayden White and Northrop

---

[15] Arguments that civil society existed in Czechoslovakia before 1989 and played a causative role in the revolution can be found in Vladimir Tismaneanu, *Reinventing Politics: Eastern Europe from Stalin to Havel* (New York: Free Press, 1992); and Barbara Falk, *The Dilemmas of Dissidence in East Central Europe* (Budapest: Central European University Press, 2003). Contrary arguments are formulated in John K. Glenn, *Framing Democracy: Civil Society and Civic Movements in Eastern Europe* (Stanford, Calif.: Stanford University Press, 2001); and Stephen Kotkin with Jan T. Gross, *Uncivil Society: 1989 and the Implosion of the Communist Establishment* (New York: Modern Library, 2009).

[16] James Krapfl, "The Diffusion of 'Dissident' Political Theory in the Czechoslovak Revolution of 1989," *Slovo* (London) 19, no. 2 (Autumn 2007): 83–101.

[17] Dale, *East German Revolution*, pp. 101–28.

Frye, this chapter demonstrates that successive and rival interpretations of unfolding history not only reflected participants' perceptions; they were political instruments by means of which participants strove to shape the course of history. The chapter aims to restore the sense of what was at stake for historical actors and argues for the validity of the term *revolution* as a means of appreciating their experience.

Chapters 2 and 3 develop the main argument: that citizens experienced the revolution first and foremost as the genesis of a transcendent new sense of community, which they then sought to represent to one another first semiotically, then in durable institutions. Chapter 2 demonstrates that a new sense of community came into being in Czechoslovakia after 17 November and that this new community— whether or not it "really" existed—was experienced as sacred. As a transcendent signifier, this sacralized community served as the first principle in an expanding universe of signifiers by means of which citizens sought to express their collective ideals and map them onto social, political, and economic institutions. The result, within a very short space of time, was a distinctly new, revolutionary culture, complete with its own rituals, prohibitions, and myths, but harboring an inner tension between a commitment to nonviolence and the imperative of confronting violence effectively.

The third chapter interrogates the flyers, bulletins, and declarations of 1989 on the basis of both quantitative and qualitative analysis to ascertain what the genuinely popular ideals of November and December were and how citizens understood them at the time. It discusses five core ideals in depth, arguing that *humanness* was the logically central ideal, and it shows that *socialism* was not as universally discredited an ideal as many scholars and politicians have claimed it to be. The chapter notes that belief in the advent of a "new society" was extremely widespread in 1989; it therefore concludes with reflections on the reasons behind this remarkable idealism and considers the extent to which "the ideals of November" were, in fact, genuinely new.

Chapters 4 through 6 examine the "constitutional moment" that the communal revolution of 1989 opened up, asking how Czechoslovak citizens at grassroots levels sought to institutionalize the "ideals of November" in their collective social, economic, and political life. Chapter 4 discusses the erection of internal boundaries within a revolutionary Czechoslovak community that originally perceived itself as united. It argues that inroads of nationalist sentiment among more than a fringe of the population led first through local patriotism, then through regionalism, with each new form of community identification a means of achieving the demands of the previous one. Taking the hitherto unknown history of Civic Forum in Slovakia as a case study, the chapter shows that urban rivalry lay behind conflicts over regional and national representation, with motives of empire trumping impulses toward federation.

The fifth chapter examines popular efforts in December 1989 and January 1990 to harmonize local circumstances with the constitutional abolition of the

Communist Party's leading role. It focuses on the democratization from below of workplaces, unions, and local government, demonstrating that the revolution by no means ended with Václav Havel's election as president in December 1989. The chapter assesses the successes and failures of this democratization movement and investigates the conflict that resulted between a still revolutionary populace and new elites who sought to bring the revolution to a close.

Chapter 6, finally, profiles the local-level spokespersons of the revolutionary associations Civic Forum and Public against Violence and chronicles their struggle to discern and implement "the will of the people" from 1989 to 1991. The chapter demonstrates how local activists found themselves increasingly caught between the demands of their citizenries and the policies of the associations' leaders in Prague and Bratislava. This led to center-periphery conflicts about the nature of representation and the fate of the revolution, which culminated in the dissolution of the civic movements and the concomitant rise of the radical, partisan successors that engineered the dissolution of the Czech and Slovak Federative Republic against the will of a majority of its people in 1992.

A single book can only begin to tell the story of popular political culture in revolutionary Czechoslovakia. Any one of the chapters in this book could easily be expanded into a volume by itself, so rich and varied is the evidence. Additional themes, too—such as the evolution of political festivity between 1990 and 1992 and the diffusion of new ideologies in the same period—have had to be omitted for reasons of time and space. This book, therefore, does not pretend to be definitive. Rather, it seeks to contribute to the continuing debate about the meaning of 1989 and to open up new, fruitful fields for both scholarly and public inquiry. Though it may be the first cultural history of the Czechoslovak (or any other) revolution of 1989, it is to be hoped that it will not be the last.

Chapter 1

The Rhetoric of Revolution

"So, this is probably a revolution."[1]

If only because some label is required to discuss what happened in Czechoslovakia in 1989, the question incessantly arises, Was it, properly speaking, a revolution? Charles Tilly, a prominent theorist of revolutions, argues that it was, because the case satisfies his definition of *revolution* as a "revolutionary situation" (contested sovereignty) followed by a "revolutionary outcome" (transfer of power).[2] Jaroslav Krejčí, a rival theorist, insists it was not, because the case fails to meet his definitional requirement that change be accomplished by means of illegitimate violence.[3] One reason that the question has never been settled, of course, is that there is no universal agreement on definitions. Rather than arbitrarily choosing a definition and asking whether the evidence fits, however, we can gain new insight into what was historically at stake by adopting a new point of departure: the rhetoric of historical actors themselves. In 1989 and well into the 1990s, many Czechoslovak citizens identified what was happening in their country as a revolution, and for them the term reflected an important aspect of their experience. Rather than trying to decide whether they were "right" or "wrong," we can ask what they meant by the term and how this meaning changed over time. We can consider, moreover, the

---

[1] A girl in the procession of 17 November 1989 in Prague, quoted by Jaroslav Richter in Petr Holubec, ed., *Kronika sametové revoluce* (Prague: ČTK, 1990), p. 2.

[2] Charles Tilly, *European Revolutions, 1492–1992* (Oxford: Blackwell, 1993).

[3] Jaroslav Krejčí, *Great Revolutions Compared: The Outline of a Theory* (New York: Harvester Wheatsheaf, 1994).

political motivations that individuals may have had at different points in the history of their "revolution" for speaking of *revolution* in certain ways or for avoiding the term altogether.

Narrative theory provides an excellent means of apprehending the way Czechs and Slovaks made sense of their experience. They began narrating the history of their revolution as soon as they perceived it to have begun, for this enabled them to make sense of their experience and to influence how others interpreted what was happening. Narratives, in other words, were efforts to fix the meaning of events as they unfolded. As such, they necessarily had political implications, for in a context where human action or inaction could have decisive consequences, the final outcome of events depended very much on how human agents interpreted their meaning. If, after the events of 17 November, the citizens of Czechoslovakia had accepted the official narrative that "forces of order" had intervened to prevent hooligans from disrupting "public order," subsequent history would not have unfolded as it did. By accepting the counternarrative that riot police had brutally "massacred" innocent young students during their peaceful observance of a state holiday, Czechoslovak citizens found the motivation necessary to mobilize en masse and constitute themselves as a new force with which the Communist regime had to reckon.[4]

The narrative theorist Hayden White observes that historical narratives are necessarily verbal structures that purport to explain events, structures, or processes by representing them in the form of stories with discernible beginnings, middles, and ends.[5] We can add that in the case of "unfinished" history, the end may be implied rather than stated, and indeed the narrative may be a call for participants in the story to achieve a particular end. These formal properties mean that historical narratives, like all stories, must have a plot structure; language forces narrators to highlight certain details while ignoring others and to impose on multidimensional and continuous human experience a linear arrangement that identifies a discrete beginning and end. Drawing on the literary theory of Northrop Frye, White suggests that despite the infinite variety of particular narratives that can be created to explain a given historical phenomenon, the underlying plot structures in which narratives can be cast are generally limited to what Frye calls the "generic" plots of romance, comedy, tragedy, and irony/satire.[6] (There are other possibilities, though they do not

---

[4] John K. Glenn has examined the Czechoslovak revolution using frame theory, which in many ways overlaps with narrative theory. Glenn, however, is concerned with the framing strategy only of Civic Forum elites and allied theater professionals whom he credits as the primary mobilizers of passive fellow citizens. The account presented here considers a broader sample of the Czechoslovak population and accepts the claims of mobilizing citizens that it was primarily students who mobilized them. *Framing Democracy: Civil Society and Civic Movements in Eastern Europe* (Stanford, Calif.: Stanford University Press, 2001).

[5] Hayden White, *Metahistory: The Historical Imagination in Nineteenth-Century Europe* (Baltimore: Johns Hopkins University Press, 1973), p. 2.

[6] Northrop Frye, *The Anatomy of Criticism: Four Essays* (Princeton, N.J.: Princeton University Press, 1957), pp. 158–238.

usually lend themselves to historical narrativization; we will discuss one of them—myth—in the next chapter.) It should be pointed out that the technical definitions of these terms do not necessarily correspond with popular understandings (e.g., a comedy in the literary critical sense need not be funny), but these distinctions will be clarified in the course of our discussion. It should also be pointed out that though language forces on narrators a "choice" of plot structure, this choice is not usually conscious; more often it reflects preexisting moral or political commitments that determine how a narrator interprets history to begin with. As we will see, each plot structure is consonant with a particular assumption about human agency: romantic plots, for instance, posit that their characters have the power to effect significant transformations on their environment, whereas satirical plots deny this. As a result of narrators' preexisting beliefs about the potential of human action, some ways of "emplotting" history inevitably seem more natural or honest than others. Nonetheless, the choice of plot structure can be productive as well as reflective. Particularly in the case of unfolding history, where the end is yet to be determined, the *kind* of story in which narrators and listeners perceive themselves to be participating may motivate them to particular kinds of action—or inaction.

This chapter examines what might be called "the discourse of the Gentle Revolution about itself" by means of narrative theory.[7] The chapter does not set out a methodology that the rest of the book follows, though the rest of the book is informed by it. Rather, this chapter lays the foundation for later chapters by unhinging preconceptions, demonstrating that the revolution of 1989 was about more than just "the fall of Communism," and outlining what was at stake for Czechoslovak citizens as they themselves expressed it. The chapter takes inspiration from Lynn Hunt's pioneering study of French rhetoric in the 1790s, wherein she argued that comedic narratives of revolution were supplanted by romantic and ultimately tragic narratives, but the analysis presented here is synchronic as well as diachronic, examining conflict among rival, contemporaneous interpretations as well as general evolution over time.[8] It will be shown that while all protagonists began interpreting the Czechoslovak revolution within the framework of romance, successive attempts to cast the story comedically, tragically, and ultimately satirically were linked to specific groups, none of whose perspectives achieved hegemony. Inescapably, each emplotment implicitly articulated a program for future action, upon which Czechoslovak citizens could not agree. Each narrative shift marked nothing less than a revolt against a particular understanding of revolution, or against revolution per se.

---

[7] Cf. Mona Ozouf, "De Thermidor à Brumaire: Le Discours de la Révolution sur elle-même," *Revue historique* 243 (1970): 31–66.

[8] Lynn Hunt, *Politics, Culture, and Class in the French Revolution* (Berkeley: University of California Press, 1984), pp. 34–39.

Revolution as Romance

> Everyone knows that there has been a battle between good and evil since
> time immemorial. Our students have now intervened in this awful battle
> on the side of good—and achieved an utter triumph.
>
> —Michal Horáček, November 1989[9]

The revolution began, by nearly all accounts, on 17 November 1989, when special police forces brutally suppressed a peaceful, student-led manifestation in Prague.[10] Accounts of the "massacre" were the first historical narratives the revolution produced about itself, and they set the tone for romantic interpretation of subsequent events.[11] Initially these accounts were presented orally, as when drama students burst into Prague theaters on the night of 17 November to tell colleagues what was happening, but in subsequent days witnesses put their recollections into simple, direct texts that circulated throughout Czechoslovakia:

> Special units of the Interior Ministry succeeded in dividing the crowd. I was in the part closed off between the Na Perštýně intersection and Voršilská street. The side street, Mikulandská, was also cut off. . . . The police called us to disperse, but there was nowhere to go. We were closed in.[12]

> Policemen ran among the demonstrators and cruelly beat them. The assault intensified and units joined with police dogs. Armored transports drove into

---

[9] Quoted in Tomáš Drábek, "Amerika pláče," *EM '89*, no. 9, p. 4. In 1989 Michal Horáček was an editor for the Socialist Youth Association's magazine *Mladý svět* (Young World), and was instrumental in coordinating the first meeting of Civic Forum with government representatives.

[10] Some Bratislava students later dated the revolution from 16 November 1989, when they had demonstrated for higher education reform. "Revolučný kalendár," *Zmena*, no. 11 (6 December 1989), p. 4. This event, however, achieved only local significance and did not influence developments outside circles of Bratislava university students. For this reason it belongs among the many student efforts following the statewide conference of the Socialist Youth Association (SZM/SSM) on 11 and 12 November to express dissatisfaction with conditions in education and the SZM, together with similarly isolated events in Olomouc and Prague. "Z monologu dialog," *Stráž lidu* (Olomouc), 18 November 1989, p. 4; "Jaký je tvůj názor na průběh jednání a závěry celostátní konference SSM?" *Coproto*, no. 5 (16 November 1989). It was also just one of a series of prerevolutionary protests, including the ecological demonstrations in Teplice from 11 to 13 November. This Bratislava interpretation of the revolution's beginnings, moreover, appeared very much ex post facto; in the beginning all students, including those in Bratislava, cited the events of 17 November as the reason for their strikes.

[11] In their choice of the word *massacre*, students were evidently influenced by the events of 4 June on Tiananmen Square, for the victims of which they observed a moment of silence during their manifestation of 17 November. See, for example, "Kdo? ne-li my. Kdy? ne-li teď!!!!" *Proto*, no. 7 (20 November 1989), p. 1; and "Pamatuj: Peking!!!!!" (LN: fond 569, box 1, folder 13).

[12] "Byla jsem 17. listopadu na Albertově, Vyšehradě a na Národní třídě," Prague, 19 November 1989 (PX: súčasná dokumentácia, folder "Nežná revolúcia—1989").

the crowd. Everywhere there were cries for help and the hysterical shrieks of girls and women, drowning amid the barking of dogs. . . . Blood was visible everywhere.[13]

Fragments of clothing, shoes, and underwear lay about. Some were dragged to doorsteps, stripped naked and beaten.[14]

When a policeman raised his truncheon against this girl I put myself in his way without thinking. For this I was dragged away. . . . A storm of blows rained on my head, back, and genitals. I heard men with hatred in their voices shout "give it to the mother f—ker!" "On his face!"[15]

Another girl in tears wailed . . . that they had beaten and dragged away her husband. . . . Policemen beat her, too, though she was pregnant.[16]

Romantic plots, according to Frye, narrate the story of a quest, a heroic struggle between good and evil, where either protagonist or antagonist stands to achieve decisive victory. They take place in a world where extraordinary things can happen and where humans are capable of extraordinary deeds.[17] The texts of witness established this framework by contrasting the nonviolence of the marchers and their humane attempts to help one another with the gratuitous violence and vulgarity of their attackers. The violence they had witnessed was beyond the ordinary experience of most participants as well as of compatriots who heard their story; it stimulated an urgent desire for extraordinary action "to overcome government by violence" once and for all.[18]

Students and actors made such action possible by inviting all citizens to participate in a general strike on 27 November, setting examples with their own full-time strikes, which they inaugurated on 18 November. They were conscious of taking a great risk. Should their initiative fail, actors could expect to lose their jobs, and university administrators threatened not only to expel students but to punish their families and "rinse their hands in students' blood."[19] Despite the peaceful capitulation of Communist regimes in neighboring countries, there was no guarantee that Czechoslovak hardliners would follow suit, and the years following 1968 had shown what manner of reprisal could befall individuals who openly defied

[13] Radim and Jakub Kalivoda, "Svědectví" (LN: fond 569, box 1, folder 11).
[14] "Svedectvo" (PX: súčasná dokumentácia, folder "Nežná revolúcia—1989").
[15] "Svědectví účastníků" (OV: sbírka soudobé dokumentace, box "Revoluce 1989: Materiály 1989–90").
[16] "Svědectví" (KO: sbírka 1989), p. 2.
[17] Frye, Anatomy of Criticism, p. 33.
[18] "17. listopad" (PX: súčasná dokumentácia, folder "Nežná revolúcia—1989").
[19] Jiří Ceral, in Milan Otáhal and Miroslav Vaněk, Sto studentských revolucí: Studenti v období pádu komunismu—životopisná vyprávění (Prague: Lidové noviny, 1999), p. 245.

the regime. (Many people looked on this historical experience as a better guide to action than current events abroad.)[20] Nonetheless, strike initiators felt they had no choice, and as they "wrote" the revolution, they emplotted it as a romance.[21] "I don't give a damn whether other schools join or whether you join," a drama student in Prague exclaimed, "I can't continue like this any longer, I'm going on strike now, IMMEDIATELY!!!"[22] Such headlong movement and disregard for consequences are characteristic of romantic protagonists. Students vowed to continue their strike until several demands had been fulfilled: (1) a thorough investigation of the massacre and punishment of its perpetrators, (2) free and honest reporting in the media, (3) release of all political prisoners, (4) freedom of assembly, and (5) a "consequential dialogue with all segments of society without exception."[23] Realizing that their efforts would be fruitless without the support of society at large, students and actors countered media censorship by personally visiting factories, farms, and workplaces and by covering walls and shop windows across the country with typewritten flyers and hand-produced posters.[24] They testified to the violence of 17 November, explained that their demands were in everyone's interest, and helped establish workplace strike committees. Most important, they gave citizens the sense that their action could be meaningful.

At the same time, broadly based citizens' initiatives began springing up, from the Independent Hungarian Initiative in southern Slovakia to the Liberec Initiative in northern Bohemia. The most important of these were Public against Violence (Verejnosť proti násiliu, or VPN), established on 19 November in Bratislava, and Civic Forum (Občanské/Občianske fórum, or OF), created simultaneously in Prague.[25] Given their location in the capitals, they immediately came to orchestrate much of the popular movement and assume the role of negotiators with the regime; chapters of VPN and OF were soon established in municipalities, workplaces, and among interest groups throughout Czechoslovakia. In addition to supporting the students' demands, they called for the resignation of leading political figures.[26]

Even before the General Strike, in the face of massive demonstrations, the regime began to consider concessions, and armed forces, though mobilized, did not

---

[20] See, for example, Jiří Křečan, "V pátek 17.11.1989 . . . ," Olomouc, 1990 (private collection of Carol Skalnik Leff, Urbana, Ill.), p. 1; and Otáhal and Vaněk, *Sto studentských revolucí*, pp. 333, 417, 420.

[21] The metaphor is taken from Marek Benda et al., *Studenti psali revoluce* (Prague: Univerzum, 1990).

[22] Michal Dočekal, quoted ibid., p. 31.

[23] "Prohlášení studentů pražských VŠ," Prague, 18 November 1989, in Milan Otáhal and Zdeněk Sládek, eds., *Deset pražských dnů (17.–27. listopad 1989): Dokumentace* (Prague: Academia, 1990), p. 32.

[24] Authorities, of course, tore down flyers and posters, whereupon students and their supporters would replace them. This became known as "the poster war."

[25] Throughout this book, where it is appropriate to provide both Slovak and Czech variants of a word, the Slovak is given first except in cases (such as this one) where context logically dictates otherwise.

[26] "Na setkání v hledišti . . . ," Prague, 19 November 1989, in Otáhal and Sládek, *Deset pražských dnů*, pp. 47–48; "Stanovisko združenia Verejnosť proti násiliu . . . ," Bratislava, 21 November 1989, in Ľubomir Feldek, ed., *Keď sme brali do rúk budúcnosť* (Bratislava: Archa, 1990), pp. 14–15.

intervene. On 27 November it is estimated that one half of Czechoslovakia's labor force took active part in the General Strike, and another quarter (health care workers, elementary school teachers, and others who felt that their responsibilities precluded active participation) expressed symbolic solidarity.[27] The regime offered significant concessions as a result, most importantly repealing the constitutional clause guaranteeing the Communist Party a "leading role" in society. Subsequent weeks followed in the spirit of a quest. While OF in Prague and VPN in Bratislava entered negotiations with federal and republican governments, chapters of these associations elsewhere (together with students in university towns and church representatives in some localities) negotiated with local officials and workplace directors to achieve dramatic changes. Demonstrations and political-theatrical "happenings" continued in tandem with political events at local, national, and international levels.[28] When federal leaders proposed a new government that allotted Communists a majority of ministerial seats, citizens threatened another general strike, compelling Civic Forum leaders to press the Communists for a government with a non-Communist majority by 10 December. When Nicolae Ceaușescu's regime massacred peaceful demonstrators in Romania, Czechoslovak citizens mobilized again, sending trains and trucks full of humanitarian aid donated by individuals, businesses, and hospitals.

The central theme of romance is transcendence, and reflections on the revolution in 1989 were replete with this idea.[29] Widespread metaphors of cleansing and rebirth expressed a perception of ontological transformation, as did representations of students as knights, Václav Havel as a saint, and the people as gods.[30] Many spoke of a "new society," and some even declared that Czechs and Slovaks were ushering in a new civilization.[31] Intrinsic to this sense of transcendence was a perceived

---

[27] Holubec, *Kronika*, p. 18.

[28] On the origins of happenings in the 1960s as partially improvised theater blurring the distinction between actors and audience, see Michael Kirby, "Happenings: An Introduction," in *Happenings and Other Acts*, ed. Mariellen R. Sandford (London: Routledge, 1995), 1–28. On the development of happenings as a politically charged participatory art form in east central Europe in the 1980s, see Padraic Kenney, *A Carnival of Revolution: Central Europe 1989* (Princeton, N.J.: Princeton University Press, 2002).

[29] White, *Metahistory*, p. 8.

[30] See, for example, koordinačný stávkový výbor VŠ, "Pane premiére, žasneme!" Prague, 3 December 1989, reprinted in *Přetlak*, no. 9 (5 December 1989), p. 5; Boris Pentějelev, "Občané, my všichni jsme se narodili 17. listopadu 1989" (private collection of Lenka Wünschová, Olomouc); "Svatý Václav drží koně" (TU: fond "KC OF Trutnov," box 2); "Jede se do Prahy," *Přetlak*, no. 18 (15 December 1989), p. 1; Milan Hanuš, "Ples národního porozumění," *Přetlak*, no. 28 (2 January 1990), p. 3; "Budiž světlo—řekli lidé," *Jiskra* (Český Krumlov), 22 December 1989, p. 2; and posters in HM. The seal of the Professional Union of Students, as printed in the header of every issue of *Informační bulletin celostátního koordinačního výboru vysokých škol*, represented students as knights.

[31] Bohuslav Blažek, "Stará moc a nová civilizace," Prague, 26 November 1989 (ÚSD: archiv KC OF, box 160); Blažek, "Výraz nové civilizace," Prague, 29 November 1989 (LN: fond 569, box 2). See also "Od něžné revoluce k nové civilizaci," *Profórum*, no. 12 (21 April 1990), pp. 3–5.

transformation of human relations. People marveled that money lost in crowds was returned and that vehicles left unlocked were not stolen.[32] Strangers kissed one another on Wenceslas Square, and happenings throughout the country connected people both physically and emotionally. Recalling one such event in Olomouc, the student Milan Hanuš described "a feeling of stupendous wholeness and rightness. . . . Around me dozens of unknown and nonetheless intimately familiar faces. And, I believe, even the same feeling within."[33]

The word *revolution* was first heard in the student demonstration of 17 November and began percolating in popular discourse at least as early as 21 November.[34] Many names were given the revolution in the beginning, including "Joyful," "Students'," "Cleansing," and "Children's," but "Gentle Revolution" was the most common. (In the Czech lands the name "Velvet Revolution" later achieved preeminence.)[35] These appellations signaled, on one hand, a metaphorical identification of processes unfolding in Czechoslovakia with processes perceived as parallel in other revolutions in European history.[36] On the other hand they signified a revolt against a revolutionary tradition perceived as violent and disorderly. By using means that were "as clean as the goal," Czechoslovak citizens hoped that their revolution would succeed in preserving the democracy and transcendence that had been ephemeral in other revolutions, avoiding degeneration into violence and chaos.[37]

The only alternative to the romantic interpretation of unfolding history, initially, was the ironic official narrative, which held that students had attacked security forces on 17 November.[38] For those who rejected this official narrative, the choice of a framework that posited a simple opposition between truth and lies, good and evil, was not experienced as a choice so much as a moral obligation. As with all revolutionary rhetoric, however, romantic discourse had political implications. This plot structure trusted people, as individual moral subjects, to act in the interests of the common good and called on them to do so. Indeed, casting the revolution in the romantic mode gave it implications that were, in the strict sense, anarchic and would quickly generate a more "sober" reaction.[39]

---

[32] See, for example, Verejnosť proti násiliu and Študentské hnutie, *Nežná revolúcia* (Bratislava: Opus, 1990), sound recording.

[33] Milan Hanuš, "Happening," *Přetlak*, no. 9 (5 December 1989), p. 8.

[34] Holubec, *Kronika*, p. 2; "Pracující ŠS Stupice!" Stupice, 22 November 1989 (ÚSD: archiv KC OF, box 91). See also Otáhal and Vaněk, *Sto studentských revolucí*, p. 359.

[35] According to Jan Měchýř, it was a French journalist who invented this term, but Měchýř does not support the claim with any evidence. *Velký převrat či snad revoluce sametová? Několik informací, poznámek a komentářů o naší takřečené něžné revoluci a jejich osudech (1989–1992)* (Prague: Československý spisovatel, 1999), p. 13.

[36] Seventeen eighty-nine (France) was by far the most common reference in the romantic interpretation of the revolution. Advocates of the comedic interpretation cited 1787 (America) as a model to emulate and 1792 (France) or 1948 (Czechoslovakia) as examples to avoid.

[37] Josef Jařab, "Nedělní zamyšlení," *Přetlak*, no. 21 (18 December 1989), p. 3.

[38] Aleš V. Poledne, *Jak šly dějiny*, Česká televize, 16 November 2004.

[39] White, *Metahistory*, p. 29.

Revolution as Comedy

> A million and seven hundred thousand Communists do not comprise
> some different biological or moral species from the rest of us.
> —Václav Havel, December 1989[40]

Comedy is a qualification of romance's quest for transcendence, centering on the theme of reconciliation. It emphasizes the common humanity of both protagonist and antagonist, portraying their conflict more as a clash of interests than a struggle between good and evil. The archetypal comedy tells the story of a rising new society struggling against an old; the old eventually accommodates the new and a fresh harmony is created. "The tendency of comedy is to include as many characters as possible in its final society; the blocking characters are more often reconciled or converted than simply repudiated."[41] Comedy was the second generic plot chosen to frame the revolution's history, and it was chosen primarily by new elites for the purpose of ending the revolution. On four occasions Havel and those around him tried to present a comedic resolution as having occurred, but only the last two attempts achieved widespread, if transitory, acceptance.

Following an informational meeting on 21 November, Prime Minister Ladislav Adamec agreed to open negotiations with Civic Forum on 26 November. OF invited Adamec to address demonstrators that day as a sign of good will, and he agreed. At the gathering of half a million, Havel proclaimed that "the dialogue of power with the public has begun. . . . From this moment we shall *all* take part in the government of this land and *all* of us therefore bear responsibility for its fate." Havel's words clearly suggested an inclusive, comedic strategy for interpreting the present as part of history, and Adamec initially played along by saying he favored a common solution. Then he proposed that the General Strike be shortened to just a few minutes and that strike committees disband, and he noted that he must consult the Party about OF's demands.[42] Applause turned to whistles, and Civic Forum leaders reluctantly had to call for Adamec's resignation if he did not agree to reconstitute the federal government.[43] Nevertheless, OF leaders tried to demobilize the populace after the General Strike, calling for an end to mass demonstrations; together with VPN in Bratislava, they encouraged strike committees to metamorphose

[40] Jiří Suk, ed., *Občanské fórum: Listopad-prosinec 1989*, vol. 2, *Dokumenty* (Brno: Doplněk, 1998), p. 245.
[41] Frye, *Anatomy of Criticism*, p. 165.
[42] Quoted in "Chorál přísahy nad Prahou," *Svobodné slovo*, 27 November 1989, p. 1 (emphasis added).
[43] Jiří Suk, *Labyrintem revoluce: Aktéři, zápletky a křížovatky jedné politické krize (od listopadu 1989 do června 1990)* (Prague: Prostor, 2003), p. 46.

into Civic Fora or branches of Public against Violence for the purpose of negotiating with local leaders.[44]

Civic Forum's next attempt to present the public with a comedic resolution culminated on 3 December, when Adamec was supposed to name the new government. In anticipation, OF leaders encouraged students to discontinue their strike, arguing that the government would need a chance to work in peace. The most radical students resisted, and it was just hours before Adamec's announcement that all student leaders empowered to make such a decision finally agreed. When the announcement came, featuring a government in which Communists occupied fifteen of twenty ministerial chairs, OF leaders were inclined to welcome it.[45] Again, however, the public reacted antagonistically. The ratio "15:5" was not what people envisioned by the end of the Party's leading role, and in protest they took to the streets once more. Students resumed their strike and in some cases intensified it; OF and VPN had to demand that Adamec form yet another government by 10 December.[46]

Adamec resigned on 7 December, to be replaced by his vice premier, Marián Čalfa. Civic Forum, having refused the Communists' invitation to roundtable talks based on Polish and Hungarian models, consented nonetheless to a meeting of "decisive political forces" across an oblong table. OF and VPN were to sit on one side, the Communists opposite; lesser parties and other organizations in the National Front—hitherto vassals of the Communists—were to choose which side to support.[47] Together these forces agreed on the composition of a new federal government, which Havel dubbed "the Government of National Understanding." In subsequent speeches Havel emphasized that Communists were to be included in the new society as equal partners. "The Communist Party guaranteed the totalitarian system and therefore all Communists without exception carry heightened responsibility for the marasmus in which our country finds itself. This obliges them," he continued, "to work harder than everyone else today for a free future for us all." Havel noted that OF and VPN had themselves nominated two Communists to the government, and he praised Adamec and Čalfa for their willingness to cooperate.[48] A comedic reconciliation seemed to be at hand.

Bowing to popular demands, President Gustáv Husák resigned after swearing in the new government on 10 December. Later that day, Civic Forum

[44] "Stanovisko OF ke dni 27. listopadu 1989," Prague, 27 November 1989, in Suk, Občanské fórum, vol. 2, pp. 32–33; "Slovo k dnešku robotníkom a nielen im," Bratislava, 29 November 1989 (PX: súčasná dokumentácia, folder "Nežná revolúcia—1989").

[45] Suk, Labyrintem, pp. 57–58.

[46] "Nepřehlédněte!" Přetlak, no. 8 (4 December 1989), p. 10; Koordinační stávkový výbor VŠ, "Strategie stávky VŠ (pro pokračování stávky)," Prague, 4 December 1989, reprinted in Přetlak, no. 9 (5 December 1989), p. 5.

[47] Suk, Labyrintem, pp. 155–66.

[48] Suk, Občanské fórum, vol. 2, p. 245.

proposed that his replacement be none other than Václav Havel. To compli-
cate matters, however, four other candidates declared themselves, including
Alexander Dubček, rightly or wrongly considered a hero of 1968.[49] OF, confident
from its victories thus far, assumed it would be able to convince its partners at the
oblong table to accept Havel and see to it that the Federal Assembly elect him.
The Communists, however, acted as if they had fully adapted to the principles
of the new society and proposed a referendum as the most democratic means
of electing the president. The OF leadership was taken aback; it did not want
a popular vote for the simple reason that Havel might lose. Opinion polls suggested that Dubček was the favorite candidate in both Slovakia and the Czech
lands, and other indicators showed strong popular support for direct elections.[50]
Unwilling to abandon the idea of making Havel president, OF leaders mustered
several reasons why direct elections were not appropriate "at this moment," including their cost, the time campaigns would take, and tradition dating back to
the First Republic that parliament should choose the president. Students, who
had rejected OF's renewed appeal to end their strike on 10 December, nonetheless supported Havel and employed their nationwide network of "agitators" to
turn public opinion around.[51] The problem of parliament, however, was solved
only when Čalfa, in a private conversation with Havel, offered behind the scenes
to rig Dubček's election to the office of Federal Assembly chairman and to cajole
or blackmail deputies into electing Havel president according to existing constitutional provisions.[52]

These arrangements were of course not revealed until years later. All the public
knew at the time was that students descended on Prague from across the country to
demonstrate daily before parliament on Havel's behalf and that Communist representatives at what had by now become a round table ultimately agreed to Civic Forum's demands.[53] It thus seemed, when the Federal Assembly unanimously elected
Havel president on 29 December, that leading figures of the old society had once
again acquiesced to the legitimate demands of the new, and the event could be
celebrated as a further sign of reconciliation. Civic Forum's communiqué praised
the Communists' willingness to participate in "the further development of democracy, humanness, and national understanding."[54] On the evening of 29 December,

---

[49] The other candidates were Ladislav Adamec, Čestmír Císař, and Věra Čáslavská.

[50] Suk, *Labyrintem*, p. 218.

[51] The words *agitator* and *agitation*, despite their Communist connotations, were adopted by students
themselves.

[52] We still do not know exactly what Čalfa said to deputies; thus far he has confessed only to being "really
quite brutal." Suk, *Labyrintem*, pp. 200–201, 216–17, 225–27.

[53] The formerly puppet parties had lobbied from the beginning for a genuinely round table where each
party would have the same weight. Civic Forum consented to this on 11 December, three days after the
"oblong table" meeting. Ibid., pp. 214–15.

[54] "Komuniké k volbě prezidenta," *InForum*, no. 5 (29 December 1989), p. 1.

a crowning festival typical for the conclusion of a comedy was held on Prague's Old Town Square, attended by Havel, popular actors and musicians, and tens of thousands of people from all over Czechoslovakia who had come to Prague to witness the election: the "Ball of National Understanding."[55] Students, at last, ended their strike.

The attempt to emplot the revolution comedically can be seen as a revolt against the continuation of revolution. As in classic revolutions, leaders newly empowered in Czechoslovakia sought to abate the potentially uncontrollable enthusiasm of the mobilized populace and turn it to more routine forms of political engagement.[56] It is not surprising, then, that some leaders questioned whether the term *revolution* should even be used. In a 10 December speech, for example, Havel suggested that while many were calling "this excited and dramatic period" a "peaceful revolution," only historians would be able to tell at some future date what it "really" was.[57] Distancing himself from the concept of revolution was a rhetorical tool for helping to bring about the revolution's end. It was part of a comedic emplotment that incorporated both the mobilized populace and all but the most compromised functionaries of the old regime in what was supposed to be a new consensus. The leaders' insistence on legal continuity was likewise part of this emplotment, accepting change only when it resulted in an orderly fashion from negotiations among recognized social actors. The political implications of the comedic plot were therefore liberal, potentially even conservative, but by no means radical.

Romance and Comedy in Conflict

> Friends, a second revolution has begun, no less exhausting and painful than the first. . . . Let us be wary before the rise of new apparatchiks and toadies of power. Let us patrol who speaks for us and where. Let us be uncompromising in the exposition of injustice. Power can quickly turn against us once again.
>
> —Martin Mejstřík, January 1990[58]

From the comedic perspective, Havel's election marked the revolution's end; for romantics, however, it was merely a brilliant episode in an ongoing quest. In early

[55] Hanuš, "Ples"; *Růžové právo*, 22 December 1989, p. 1. Similar celebrations took place outside Prague; see, for example, "Nezapomeňte!!!," *Přetlak*, no. 26 (27 December 1989), p. 2, and "Prehľad činnosti VPN v Púchove" (PX: súčasná dokumentácia, folder "Nežná revolúcia—1989").

[56] See Mona Ozouf, *Festivals and the French Revolution*, trans. Alan Sheridan (Cambridge, Mass.: Harvard University Press, 1988), p. 42.

[57] Havel later reiterated this ambivalence. Suk, *Občanské fórum*, vol. 2, pp. 202, 244.

[58] "Vážení přátelé," *Informační bulletin celostátního koordinačního výboru vysokých škol*, no. 0 (15 January 1990), p. 1. Mejstřík was one of the most radical members of the student strike committee in Prague; after 3 December he alone was empowered to call off the student strikes.

1990 many loci emerged where popular desire to continue the revolution clashed with elites' insistence that it was over; two of the most important were the question of workplace administration and national or regional political representation.

Logically, the end of the Party's leading role in society meant that Communists should cease dominating decision-making structures not only at the level of federal and republican governments but at the level of school, workplace, and local administration as well. People began democratizing these institutions in December 1989 and continued with increased confidence in January 1990. Students, well-organized and enjoying tremendous prestige, managed to achieve representation in academic senates and changes of university personnel without much trouble. Democratization of local administration proved more difficult, with enormous geographic diversity in the willingness of old apparatchiks to bow to popular pressure, but it was generally facilitated by federal and republican laws on local government reconstruction in the first quarter of 1990. Democratization of workplaces proved the most problematic task. Workers everywhere voted confidence or lack thereof in their directors, nominating replacements in the latter case. Not always, however, did discredited directors agree to leave, nor did local government organs (to which workplace directors in the command economy were generally answerable) always make the necessary arrangements. Strikes thus broke out in numerous places. In some cases, members of the old *nomenklatura* founded their own VPN or OF within a workplace, challenging the legitimacy of the original association.[59] Although most changes probably took place in an orderly fashion, the media naturally highlighted sensational examples, and given the hectic conditions prevailing in the Prague and Bratislava coordinating centers, these were the cases OF and VPN leaders learned most about.[60]

OF and VPN leaders feared economic crisis and loss of political credit as a result of unrest in the workplaces and took dramatic steps to try to eliminate irregularities. Petr Pithart, OF's chief spokesman after Havel became president, went on federal television appealing to workplace OFs to eschew all "pseudorevolutionary" methods. "Continue to call what is happening a revolution if you want. It is after all just a question of taste. But let us act decently—decently and reasonably."[61] Milan Kňažko, a central figure in VPN and one of Havel's advisers, proclaimed on Slovak television three days later that the revolution was over and called on workers to stop

[59] Ingrid Antalová, ed., *Verejnosť proti násiliu 1989–1991: Svedectvá a dokumenty* (Bratislava: Nadácia Milana Šimečku, 1998), p. 42; Petr Pithart, "Projev P. Pitharta v čs. tevizi [sic]," *InForum*, no. 11 (23 January 1990), p. 2; and Suk, *Labyrintem*, p. 298.

[60] KV VPN Bratislava, "Situácia VPN na pracoviskách," *Hornonitrianska verejnosť*, 8 March 1990, p. 4; and Pithart, "Projev," pp. 1–2.

[61] Pithart, "Projev," pp. 2–3. For the Slovak translation, see "Je to revolúcia?" *Telefax VPN*, no. 1 (2 March 1990), pp. 1–3.

the "cadre war."[62] The response of workplace collectives to these appeals was mixed. Some moderated their methods, some continued as before, and some became internally divided and incapable of collective action. The VPN leadership ultimately decided to disband workplace branches in the spring of 1990.[63]

Many Slovaks and Moravians sought to continue the revolution by securing their rights to national and regional self-government. Demands for "a rigorously democratic federation" and the reinstatement of Moravia's political integrity emerged in the first days of the revolution but assumed ever greater intensity in the spring of 1990.[64] When President Havel on 23 January recommended that the Czechoslovak Socialist Republic be officially renamed "the Czechoslovak Republic," a three-month-long debate ensued about whether perhaps "Czecho-Slovak Republic" or "Czecho-Slovak Federation" would be better.[65] "Our gentle revolution . . . has not halted, but marches on!" exclaimed a VPN journalist in Prievidza at the height of this "hyphen war." "Recently it has tested its methods of struggle in the contest over the new name of our state. . . . Even in a gentle revolution we must fight for the identity of our nation, whether other people like it or not."[66] While those Slovaks demanding outright independence at this time were a small minority, they were a loud and flamboyant one; on 1 March Slovak nationalists even invaded the Slovak National Council building in Bratislava.[67] Moravians in Brno also demonstrated (in less insurrectionary fashion) for Moravian territorial integrity. Regarding the Moravian question, OF leaders acknowledged the democratic merits of demands for self-government and thus gave moderate regionalists hope, but they insisted that reforms wait until "questions of federal importance" had been resolved.[68] VPN leaders condemned the radical nationalists as emotional demagogues standing outside the tradition of November and emphasized that VPN stood for the "completion" of Slovak sovereignty via legitimate political channels and negotiation with federal partners.[69]

---

[62] Milan Kňažko, "Vážení priatelia, čas revolúcie na uliciach . . . ," 22 January 1990 (SNA: Archív VPN, fond. odd. II).

[63] Antalová, *Verejnosť*, p. 108. Civic Forum considered this step but ultimately decided against it.

[64] "Programové vyhlásenie občianskej iniciatívy Verejnosť proti násiliu a Kooordinačného výboru slovenských vysokoškolákov," Bratislava, 25 November 1989, in Feldek, *Keď sme brali*, p. 35; and Miroslav Richter, "Provolání Moravského občanského hnutí ze dne 20.11.1989," Brno (UH: sbírky UH, box 7, folder "Letáky a plakáty všeobecné"). Prior to Communist seizure of power, Moravia (in union with Silesia) had been a self-governing jurisdiction alongside Bohemia and Slovakia; in 1948 these jurisdictions were abolished and new regional territories formed that did not respect historic boundaries.

[65] The most thorough account of this debate is Milan Šútovec's *Semióza ako politikum alebo "Pomlčková vojna": Niektoré historické, politické a iné súvislosti jedného sporu, ktorý bol na začiatku zániku československého štátu* (Bratislava: Kalligram, 1999).

[66] Martin Kaniok, "To je ono!" *Hornonitrianska verejnosť*, 12 April 1990, p. 1.

[67] Šútovec, *Semióza*, pp. 217–25.

[68] Minutes of the "0th" republic-wide OF convention (ÚSD: archiv KC OF, "OF—interní písemnosti: Sněmy OF," box 1, folder "Nultý sněm OF [16.12.1989]: Setkání zástupců krajských a okresních OF"); and "Rozhovor s panem Pithartem, tiskovým mluvčím OF a panem Kotrlým, členem koordinačního centra OF," *Přetlak*, no. 28 (2 January 1990), p. 4.

[69] "Komuniké," *Telefax VPN*, no. 5 (3 April 1990), p. 1.

These and other popular impulses perpetuated a romantic emplotment of the revolution against elite attempts to adhere to the comedic storyline. A more complicated rhetorical situation emerged when rank-and-file supporters of OF and VPN sought to democratize these movements themselves. The founders of these citizens' associations in Prague, Bratislava, and other cities were essentially self-chosen; when it became clear that OF and VPN would continue into 1990 as political movements, the question arose as to whether the coordinating councils really represented all those in whose names they claimed to speak. In some localities votes were held to decide this question, but elsewhere—particularly in Prague and Bratislava—the established leaders resisted opening council membership to representatives "from below." Justifying such a stance in movements that claimed to champion democracy was obviously a challenge, which leaders surmounted in this case by invoking the revolutionary principle. "Are we a democratic or a revolutionary institution?" asked the central OF Council member Václav Benda, arguing against regional representation. "I am for the revolutionary."[70] Even as OF and VPN leaders tried to set the terms of debate in other modes, they could not help falling back on the language of revolution.

As elections approached, a variety of circumstances pushed the new elites to adopt ever more overtly romantic rhetoric. First was inability to resolve the question of Communist property in a timely manner, with the resulting fear that the Party's extensive assets would give it an electoral advantage.[71] Compared with the Communists, OF and VPN were extremely poor political formations, able to finance their campaigns only by borrowing money from the students.[72] Both OF and VPN took to portraying Communists as devils and emphasizing the Party's responsibility for all problems that Czechoslovakia faced. To foster a sense of an all-or-nothing struggle against "dark forces," they highlighted examples of provincial Communists who vowed retribution against OF and VPN supporters should the Party win.[73] Though in a consolidated democracy such representations might seem primarily satirical, in a society where daily citizens were demonstrating and signing petitions for the Communist Party to be outlawed, the romantic element cannot be ignored.[74] Inability to push reforms through the federal and republican parliaments and governments was a second romanticizing catalyst. The public loudly demanded a definitive solution to the *nomenklatura* problem in workplaces, a transparent dismantling of the secret police apparatus, and concrete proposals for

---

[70] Suk, *Labyrintem*, p. 306.

[71] "Zápis ze sněmu OF dne 31.3.1990" (ÚSD: archiv KC OF, "OF—interní písemnosti: Sněmy OF," box 1, folder "Sněmy OF: 31.3.1990"), p. 4.

[72] Jiří Hapala, "Jde o volby, nebo ne?" *Fórum* (Prague), 8 May 1990, p. 3. Students had been the primary recipients of public donations in 1989.

[73] See, for example, "Ukaž, kdo jsi," *Občanský deník*, 26 May 1990, p. 2; "Někdo zapálil?" *Občanský deník*, 1 June 1990, p. 2; and *Telefax VPN*, no. 8 (25 April 1990), p. 8.

[74] See Suk, *Labyrintem*, pp. 397–98.

economic reform; Civic Forum and Public against Violence accordingly petitioned the parliaments and governments for action but with minimal success.[75] The civic movements could retain their credibility only by blaming the Communists. A final factor was what might be called a "great fear" of the secret police, intensified when the parliamentary commission investigating 17 November suggested that the secret police had to some extent staged the massacre.[76] The people demanded lustration of candidates for political office as a means of stamping out the possibility of such conspiracy in the future, and, reluctantly, OF and VPN agreed. Far away now was the idea of "national understanding" that would include all the people of Czechoslovakia; to the extent that people still adhered to "the tradition of November," they saw it as a quest.[77]

By the time of the federal and republican elections in June 1990, all attempts at a comedic resolution of the revolutionary narrative had been abandoned. In the face of what was increasingly being called "gentle stagnation," popular antipathy toward the blocking characters mounted, whether these characters were identified as Communists, the secret police, or Pragocentrists. Despite the acuteness of social, political, economic, and ecological problems, however, people remained largely optimistic that now they would finally be solved—that freely elected governments would be able to accomplish what the Government of National Understanding, with its only partially reconstituted parliaments, had been unable to do.[78] Alexander Dubček therefore compared the resounding electoral victory of OF, VPN, and non-Communist parties to the storming of the Bastille.[79] It was a decidedly romantic interpretation of unfolding history.

Revolution as Tragedy

> There still persists a distrust of the market, an unwillingness to leave our fates in the hand of impersonal mechanisms . . . and by contrast a belief in the effectiveness of politics . . . and the possibility of a political solution to economic problems. To overcome this, we need a much deeper revolution than that which occurred after 17 November, a revolution that won't be visible on squares and in mass demonstrations, but which will take place inside all of us, which will last much longer, the results of which will long be binding.
>
> —Václav Klaus, September 1990[80]

---

[75] "Zápis ze sněmu OF dne 31.3.1990," p. 11.

[76] Cf. Georges Lefebvre, *The Great Fear of 1789: Rural Panic in Revolutionary France*, trans. Joan White (New York: Pantheon Books, 1973).

[77] "Pozvánka OF," *Občanský deník*, 24 May 1990, p. 3.

[78] "Vláda 'národní oběti'," *Fórum*, 11 July 1990, p. 6.

[79] Alexander Dubček, "Dobyli sme Bastilu," *Telefax VPN*, no. 16/17 (20 June 1990), p. 5.

[80] "Socializmus je mrtev, ale leviatan žije dál," *Lidové noviny*, 20 September 1990, p. 1.

The tragic frame is prompted by failure to achieve transcendence. Belief in the possibility of transcendence is a characteristic that romance and tragedy share, but while romance can attribute failure only to a diabolical antagonist, tragedy is more introspective, asking what flaw of the protagonist's may have contributed to his fall.[81] Given its concern with identifying the *causes* of failure, together with its implicit faith in the possibility of transcendence, tragedy lends itself to radical political programs.[82] By determining what caused catastrophe in the first instance, witnesses stand a better chance of avoiding it in the second. Tragedy was therefore the emplotment of choice for Czechs and Slovaks who revolted against the revolution's prevailing course in order to promote a more radical one.

Tragic emplotments did not become common until after the elections of June 1990, but isolated individuals had already begun articulating them in December 1989. The ecological activist Ivan Dejmal, for example, became a Cassandra-like figure in Civic Forum's coordinating center early on. At the beginning of December he protested against what he saw as OF leaders' suppression of the movement's original, internal democracy. As the Prague Forum's plenum—which in the beginning had been a decision-making assembly—came to be summoned less and less, with closed committees close to Havel increasingly making all important decisions, Dejmal pointed out that Civic Forum's potential to incarnate a new form of politics was being sacrificed.[83] After Havel accepted Čalfa's offer to rig his election to the presidency, Dejmal—without knowing the details but sensing that something was amiss—wrote Havel a sharp letter chastising him for engaging in "behind-the-scenes machinations" and dissimulation. Dejmal urged Havel to "come to his senses" before it was too late, warning that otherwise this departure from "life in truth" would come back to haunt the democratic movement.[84]

After the elections of June 1990, the decisions of the Federal Assembly and national councils to go on a two-month vacation precipitated a sharp decline in OF's and VPN's popularity. Everywhere citizens complained of continuing uncertainty about what economic reforms the federal government would introduce, together with growing doubts about the future of the federation. More loudly, they protested that the "red nobility" remaining in local leadership positions was taking advantage of the uncertainty to steal public property and that employees who protested were being fired or otherwise persecuted.[85] No one responsible for the

---

[81] Frye, *Anatomy of Criticism*, pp. 210–12.

[82] White, *Metahistory*, p. 29.

[83] Irena Suková, ed., *Proměny politického systému v Československu na přelomu let 1989/1990* (Prague: Nadace Heinricha Bölla, 1995), p. 56. For more on the functioning of the plenum, see Timothy Garton Ash, *We the People: The Revolution of '89 Witnessed in Warsaw, Budapest, Berlin & Prague* (London: Granta, 1990), pp. 87–116.

[84] Suk, *Labyrintem*, pp. 241–44.

[85] See, for example, Marián Sklenka, "Osudy odvažných chlapov," *Verejnost'*, 2 July 1990, p. 2; and Lujza Bakošová, "Prepúšťajú Vás?" *Nitrianska verejnost'*, 6 September 1990, pp. 1–3.

November massacre had yet been punished. People began to suggest that nothing had changed since November, or even that matters were worse. Responding to public pressure, district committees of OF and VPN issued a string of appeals for radical action, most of which met with the indifference or antagonism of the centers. When, amid this crisis, parliament went on vacation, people asked how OF and VPN could allow it. Who had won the elections, after all?[86]

The mood at Civic Forum's August republican convention was imbued with this sense of crisis. "How dare the government and National Council take vacations when so much urgently needs to be done?" raged Bohumil Kubát, the Czech Republic's agriculture minister.

> Let us ask ourselves the basic question: is the outcome of our revolution reversible? I believe that it is, very easily. . . . Our opponent doesn't respect the laws according to which we conduct ourselves. . . . Therefore I believe that we should . . . stick together and stop quarreling, or rather fighting among ourselves. We must realize that we've lost a lot of time. . . . We can't let our movement be debilitated. That would be our absolute end.

The delegates agreed that disunity within their own ranks was a tragic flaw. Some more specifically criticized the "humanitarian" and "legalistic" policies of Dagmar Burešová (chairwoman of the Czech National Council) and Petr Pithart (now Czech premier), which had blocked the punishment of 17 November culprits. A delegate from Chrudim lashed out against Pithart for condemning OF Hodonín's initiative to compile a list of all *nomenklatura* occupying directorships in that district. "Our mafiosi walk the street and laugh in our faces: 'What do you want? After all, your premier protects us!'" While Pithart and other leading figures defended their positions, the delegates generally agreed that the revolution had been too "velvety" and that some kind of radicalization was in order.[87]

District representatives, having daily contact with problems at the grassroots level, came ever more acutely to believe that OF's Prague-based leaders were out of touch; already maddened by the center's resistance to internal democratization, these representatives grew progressively more radical. Václav Klaus—who, unlike his colleagues, did not go on vacation but traveled throughout the districts establishing rapport with local leaders—portrayed the difference between Prague and the districts as one

---

[86] "Druhá fáza revolúcie," *Verejnost*, 24 August 1990, p. 1; Iveta Vrbová, "Dva měsíce prázdnin: Rozhovor s Ivanem Fišerou z KC OF a poslancem FS nejen o práci parlamentu," *Fórum*, 29 August 1990, p. 12; "Kdo vlastně vyhrál volby?" *Fórum*, 12 September 1990, p. 3.

[87] "Zápis ze Sněmu OF dne 18.8.1990" (ÚSD: archiv KC OF, "OF—interní písemnosti: Sněmy OF," box 2, folder "Sněmy OF: 18.8.1990"), pp. 5–6, 8–9; and Vladimír Šuman, "Postupovat radikálněji," *InForum*, no. 36 (21 August 1990), pp. 7–8.

between an incompetent, intellectual, and moderate "Left" and a pragmatic, radical "Right."[88] Most district representatives, desperate for a solution to their increasing powerlessness and isolation, found this interpretation of OF's tragic flaw inspiring. They therefore voted decisively at the October republican convention to make Klaus their chairman. Klaus proceeded to expel from Civic Forum political subgroupings that had "abandoned OF's political line" and began the process of transforming OF into a "right-wing" party.[89] While some lamented the passing of OF's original identity as a forum for all citizens, casting the event in a tragic light, others found in Klaus's election an escape from tragedy and embarked on a new romance.[90] "The Left . . . with its vague humanism led society to insufferable stagnation and demoralizing skepticism," wrote one journalist. Klaus's election, however, marked a "second revolution," the "real revolution," from which could be expected "the definitive completion of systemic changes begun almost a year ago."[91] In February 1991 OF would split officially into a Civic Democratic Party, led by Klaus and enjoying great popularity among Czech voters, and a Civic Movement, destined for oblivion.

A sense that the revolution had taken a tragic turn similarly shook VPN. At its September 1990 republican convention the outgoing chairman, Ján Budaj, observed that "people . . . are returning to the apathy and cynicism that served them so well in previous decades. With respect to the people, we face the same atmosphere that existed before 17 November."[92] The Slovak premier, Vladimír Mečiar, opined that "No one in Slovakia but VPN has a realistic economic program, but we don't know how to sell it. We don't know how to impart our perspective to the public and present ourselves as a movement that realizes the national interest."[93] Delegates pointed out specific problems that they claimed had contributed to the public's loss of faith—notably lustration scandals and the *nomenklatura*'s growing power—and complained that formation of VPN policy was excessively concentrated among Bratislava elites. VPN leaders dismissed these criticisms as "natural" and "emotional," leaving discontent to simmer in the coming weeks.[94] Is it good or bad that "we are not like them"? district leaders began to ask, referring to a distinction made in 1989 between "the people" and the Communists.[95] "Today we can be embarrassed only by the fact that we have not sufficiently taken up the Jacobin movement as a great, optimistic revolutionary tradition of our past."[96]

[88] See Suk, *Labyrintem*, p. 459.
[89] Měchýř, *Velký převrat*, p. 212; see also Jan Vávra, "Pravidla hry," *Fórum*, 14 November 1990, p. 2.
[90] Jan Vávra, "Začátek nové kapitoly," *Fórum*, 17 October 1990, p. 2.
[91] Bohumil Pečinka, "Skutečná revoluce," *Studentské listy*, vol. 1, no. 20 (November 1990), p. 2.
[92] Quoted in Peter Schutz, "Rozlučka s Jánom Budajom," *Akcia*, 1 October 1990, p. 1.
[93] Vladimír Mečiar, "Prispôsobiť sa novým požiadavkám," *Telefax VPN*, no. 20 (19 September 1990), p. 6.
[94] "Stretnutia s médiami," *Telefax VPN*, no. 21 (21 September 1990), p. 3.
[95] Peter Schutz, "Večergate," *Akcia*, 20 October 1990, p. 6.
[96] Štefan Eliáš, "Slovo k rodákom," *Akcia*, 15 October 1990, p. 8.

A step in this direction was taken when the Trnava district committee called a working meeting of district representatives without informing central VPN organs. This meeting, held on 20 October, sharply criticized the center for its passivity with regard to surviving structures of the old regime, a defensive posture with regard to VPN's national dimension, lack of attention to social problems in workplaces, and resistance to internal democracy. Delegates demanded reconstruction of central VPN organs and expressed full support for Mečiar and his government, which they saw as a counterweight to VPN's coordinating center.[97] Juraj Flamik, chairman of that body, condemned the Trnava Initiative as "conspiratorial."[98] Following another convention in February 1991, where motions to make VPN chairmanship elective did not carry, district representatives again acted independently to establish "VPN-For a Democratic Slovakia" (VPN-ZDS), claiming to defend the movement's "original platform" and condemning the policies and practices of "certain leading figures" in VPN.[99] At a VPN-ZDS rally in March, Mečiar claimed that "the central leadership . . . has betrayed part of the sense of the revolution." He criticized the center for closing workplace branches and being out of touch with the people on social and national policy, and he proposed a new type of organization where districts would "transmit the will of the people, not follow orders from a center."[100] In April ZDS would officially split from VPN, becoming the Movement for a Democratic Slovakia (HZDS) and Slovakia's most popular political formation. In VPN as in OF, tragic perception provided the necessary basis for a new romantic endeavor.

Tragic interpretations also came to dominate among the group that had started the revolution: the students. In Bratislava, students greeted the first anniversary of 17 November with an appeal for the "defense of democracy," warning that "the Nation" was becoming "a manipulated mass in the hands of new Leaders."[101] Students and other civic groups organized a public commemoration of 17 November under the banner "humanness, decency, tolerance," but symptomatically, nationalists usurped it, turning Bratislava's SNP Square into a site of conflict. In Prague, students observed the anniversary by officially refusing to celebrate it, arguing that basic demands from the previous year remained unfulfilled. "There is no longer reason to call our revolution 'velvet'," they proclaimed. "Rather, it is a *stolen* revolution!"

[97] "Závery z pracovného rokovania zástupcov okresných a mestských rád a koordinačných výborov VPN, zvolaného na základe podnetov z jednotlivých regiónov Slovenska," *Telefax VPN*, no. 24 (24 October 1990), p. 3.

[98] Juraj Flamik, "Stanovisko k stretnutiu v Trnave," *Telefax VPN*, no. 24 (24 October 1990), p. 3. VPN had one chairman for its coordinating committee and another for the organization as a whole. It is worth noting that neither was elected by republic-wide assemblies, as was the case with OF after October.

[99] "Vyhlásenie zástupcov OR VPN pri konštituovaní pôvodnej platformy VPN zo dňa 5.3.1991 v Bratislave," *Smena*, 6 March 1991, p. 3.

[100] Vladimír Mečiar, "Aby ľudia mali komu veriť (Vystúpenie Vladimíra Mečiara na stretnutí PZDS v Martine dňa 23.3.1991)," *Telefax VPN*, no. 4/91 (26 March 1991), p. 6.

[101] "Iniciatíva na obranu demokracie: Vyhlásenie členov novembrového Koordinačného výboru vysokých škôl Slovenska," Bratislava, 28 October 1990, in *Echo*, vol. 1, no. 10, p. 1.

The tragic flaws responsible for this were, first, "our lack of follow-through and that of our leaders, who are for the most part sinking in self-satisfaction, complacency, and dangerous softness," and second, the politics of compromise and "the sad experience we have with left-wing ideas, which take society to be an irresponsible, nameless herd." The students presented the president and government with thirteen demands, ranging from purges of state institutions to a rigorous transition to a market economy, and they repeated their call from the previous year for a thorough investigation of 17 November and punishment of the massacre's perpetrators. The students appealed to the public to abandon flaws that had led to a state of universal disappointment, mistrust, unease, and tension, calling on citizens to "Join us, that we may create a common strength. The voice of one will fail. But the voice of the majority will become the genuine expression of the will of the people." "We want to become an inspired society," they entreated, which would live in synergy with "that force or thought, which exists like a mysterious order over all our earthly life."[102] Nothing significant came of the appeal.[103]

Revolution as Satire

> There was no revolution in Czechoslovakia in November 1989, because a revolution would have brought new institutions and new ideas to power. But if we want to call it a revolution, then we have to add that that revolution, from inexperience, committed suicide.
>
> —Jan Urban, November 1992[104]

Irony is a name given to both a trope (which can be used for effect in any of the generic plots) and a distinct plot structure. Satire is the militant form of ironic emplotment.[105] The central theme here is the disappearance of the heroic. While tragedy is still concerned with the hero's failings, the ironic plot allots virtually no freedom to the hero, and seeks explanations (if any) only in social structures. "*Sparagmos*, or the sense that heroism and effective action are absent, disorganized, and foredoomed to defeat and that confusion and anarchy reign over the world, is the archetypal theme of irony and satire."[106] Irony destroys all faith in both the ideal good of man and any quest for transcendence; extreme irony raises fatalism to the level of metaphysical belief.

---

[102] "Provolání VŠ studentů k vyroči 17. listopadu," *Studentské listy*, vol. 1, special issue (Autumn 1990), pp. 1–2 (emphasis added).

[103] Bohuslav Fic, "Ke druhému výroči 17. listopadu," *Studentské listy*, vol. 2, no. 23 (November 1991), p. 5; and Jan Kavan and Libor Konvička, "Youth Movements and the Velvet Revolution," *Communist and Post-Communist Studies* 27, no. 2 (1994): 168.

[104] Jan Urban, "Bezmocnost mocných," *Listy* 23, no. 5 (1993): 7.

[105] Frye, *Anatomy of Criticism*, p. 223.

[106] Ibid., p. 192.

We have already encountered irony as a trope in such formulations as "gentle stagnation," or when students drew attention to the fact that their 1990 demands repeated those of 1989. None of these expressions, as yet, were components of ironic emplotments because their authors still attributed agency to the people, suggesting that it was possible to learn from errors and correct them. The growing use of irony was natural, however, because the tragic hero's "fall is involved both with a sense of his relation to society and with a sense of the supremacy of natural law, both of which are ironic in reference."[107]

In satirical emplotments, human agency is an illusion and political action is therefore pointless, a view that tends to support a conservative, even reactionary stance. The quintessential satires of the Gentle Revolution are those that interpret it as a conspiracy, drawing attention not only to the thesis that the secret police orchestrated the so-called revolution but to the folly of ordinary people for thinking their engagement in it could possibly have been meaningful. Such interpretations began to appear in the spring of 1990, following the 17 November commission's reports on secret police involvement, and they grew to a flood with the emergence of a tabloid press in October 1990.[108] More poignant than satirical interpretations in the gutter press, however, was militant irony among individuals who had previously identified themselves as protagonists of the revolution. While some students on the first anniversary attempted desperately to recapture lost transcendence, others insisted that there had been no revolution and mocked people who naively thought otherwise. One student journalist condemned Charles University's plan to erect a monument to the students at the spot where the 17 November march had commenced, arguing that "it is clear today that the 'hegemon' of our 'revolution' was already on 16 November the highest bosses of the Interior Ministry and State Security."[109] Following the demise of OF and VPN in 1991, former activists in these associations also began to articulate satirical interpretations of the "revolution," invoking ostensibly objective definitions of the term rather than the metaphors that had dominated in 1989. "We're lying to ourselves," said one former member of OF's executive council. "Revolution, as every little child knows, is an upheaval, often violent—something that interrupts continuity and liquidates the old system. This, however, played no role in what happened in November or in the things in which we took particular pride thereafter: velvetiness and legal continuity."[110] Jan Urban, who had been Civic Forum's chief spokesman from March to June 1990, not only denied in 1992 that any revolution had occurred but questioned whether what had happened possessed any meaning at all.[111]

[107] Ibid., p. 37.
[108] See *Fórum*, 12 December 1990, p. 3; and Měchýř, *Velký převrat*, p. 213.
[109] Martin Bartůněk, "Mládí vpřed!," *Studentské listy*, vol. 1, special issue (Autumn 1990), p. 2.
[110] Pavla Grünthalová, "Requiem za 17. listopad: Rozhovor s Pavlem Naumannem," *Necenzurované noviny*, no. 27 (1992), p. 5.
[111] Urban, "Bezmocnost mocných," p. 3.

If the transition to a comedic emplotment marked a revolt against romantic conceptions of revolution, the transition to satire marked a revolt against the idea of revolution itself. In Czech discourse the events of 1989 came increasingly to be called a *převrat* (reversal), or "the so-called revolution." Even the Civic Forum Foundation, established in 1989 as an institution that continues to support Czech culture, started referring to the revolution in its brochures as "the November events," and *Lidové noviny*, an originally samizdat newspaper that the revolution made one of the Czech Republic's best-selling dailies, commemorated the fifteenth anniversary of 17 November with a cartoon depicting the revolution as nothing but a conspiracy between Havel and the Communists.[112] Slovak discourse long remained perceptibly less ironic, with Gentle Revolution remaining the standard name for the events of 1989 both in the media and in popular discourse, but militant irony became a powerful undercurrent there as well.

At various junctures between 1989 and 1992, Czechs and Slovaks revolted either against particular aspects of revolution or against the course they saw the revolution taking. Proponents of the romantic interpretation, with their concern for transcendence, revolted against a revolutionary tradition they saw as bloody and self-destructive. Advocates of the comedic interpretation revolted against the revolutionary enthusiasm of the romantics, fearing its latent anarchy and seeking as quickly as possible to end the revolution. Supporters of the tragic interpretation revolted against directions in which they saw the revolution heading—directions they perceived to be leading to disastrous, or at least undesirable, results. Sages of the ironic interpretation, finally, revolted against the idea that there had ever been a revolution. Each new emplotment served as a blueprint for its appurtenant revolt, a plan of action or inaction that ultimately served political or moral purposes.

Czechs and Slovaks were not the first to use the term *revolution* as an instrument in political struggle. The seventeenth-century English Roundheads, perhaps the first historical actors to apply the term to their own experience, did so because the astronomical metaphor implied that Providence had ordained their victories, just as He governed the revolutions of celestial spheres. It placed their legitimacy beyond question. The Cavaliers, for their part, rejected the term for this very reason, insisting that a "rebellion" (by definition illegitimate) was occurring instead.[113] In 1789, deputies to the National Assembly initially condemned crowd actions at the Bastille as an illegitimate "riot," but once they perceived that this event had secured them a victory over the Crown, they reinterpreted it as a legitimate act of "revolution" authored by the French people.[114]

---

[112] *Lidové noviny*, 15 November 2004, p. 12.

[113] Ilan Rachum, "The Meaning of 'Revolution' in the English Revolution (1648–1660)," *Journal of the History of Ideas* 56, no. 2 (April 1995): 195–215.

[114] William H. Sewell, Jr., "Historical Events as Transformations of Structures: Inventing Revolution at the Bastille," *Theory and Society* 25, no. 6 (December 1996): 841–81.

The Bolsheviks after 1917 took pains to narrate their occupation of the Winter Palace as a popular insurrection, the first act in "the Great October Socialist Revolution," in order to legitimate their seizure of power.[115] More examples could be given. The point is that from the beginning, historical actors have embraced or rejected the term *revolution* primarily because of its political implications in particular historical contexts. The meaning of the word has varied, but its narrative usage has always been motivated by the need to legitimate accomplished or potential courses of action.

Was there a revolution in Czechoslovakia in 1989? The answer to this question depends entirely on how the facts of history are narrated. There are no objective reasons for choosing one plot structure over another; the choice is ultimately moral. Consequently, it is less interesting that the events of 1989 fit or depart from any particular definition of revolution than that Czechs and Slovaks—to an extent and for a time—experienced these events as revolution. They were neither more nor less justified in doing so than the seventeenth-century Europeans who first compared complex sociopolitical upheavals to the circular motions of the heavens.

[115] James Von Geldern, *Bolshevik Festivals, 1917–1920* (Berkeley: University of California Press, 1993).

Chapter 2

The Big Bang of the Signifiers

"That is not how I see our gentle revolution. . . . I don't see her in any
human form, though it is clear to me that she was of the feminine gender,
and therefore velvet and gentle: one thing, though, I know surely, that
she came with empty hands—she carried nothing in them, neither gifts
nor weapons. For at her beginning was neither the Bastille nor Aurora,
but instead that old biblical WORD, which supposedly was also at the
beginning of the world, only that this time this word was not God, but
man: his thoughts and desires, his dreams—of freedom and happiness, of
a dignified life, and of democracy."[1]

We have seen how the general lines of Czech and Slovak discourse shifted
from nearly unanimous discussion of "revolution" in 1989 to later invocation of
terms considered more neutral, such as "upheaval" and "events." Scholarly inquiry into the "events" has followed a similar progression. Whereas between 1990
and 1992, the word *revolution* figured most commonly in monographs devoted to
1989 and its aftermath, in subsequent years terms such as *collapse* and *fall* have become more standard. The change in emphasis is not merely rhetorical, reflecting
an attempt to provide sober, scientific correctives to the enthusiastic, triumphalist
narratives of the early 1990s; it reflects a change in the object of inquiry as well.
Specifically, focusing on the *collapse* of Communist authority in 1989 neglects the
phenomenon of *creation* which also characterized that year—and which contem-
poraries experienced as more relevant to their futures.

Stephen Kotkin has articulated a particularly extreme version of this trend in
scholarship with his avowedly revisionist account of the "implosion" of Communist

[1] Albert Marenčín, *Kultúrny život*, 1 August 1990, p. 3.

regimes in Eastern Europe. In Kotkin's view, mass mobilization merely took the form of disorganized "bank runs" on bankrupt regimes everywhere except Poland, where an organized opposition (Solidarity) predated the regime change of 1989, and the only thing about 1989 that requires explanation is how the regimes collapsed without organized opposition.[2] This characterization does not fit Czechoslovakia, however (and it is questionable whether it applies anywhere else). Not only was the Czechoslovak state not economically bankrupt (though morally it may have been) but Czechoslovak citizens achieved a high degree of organization in a matter of days, consciously influencing the way the Communist leadership surrendered political power and giving rise to forms of political practice that would set lasting precedents. Kotkin would have profited from considering the understanding of democratic revolution that his collaborator, Jan Gross, articulated just prior to the birth of Solidarity: the process whereby communities (creatively) reassert themselves against governments.[3]

In Czechoslovakia, this creative aspect of the revolution was coeval with its perceived onset. The violence of 17 November led immediately to the formation of new patterns of social interaction and a new sense of community, concomitant with new ways of thinking and communicating. This was directly related to the rise of romantic forms of discourse discussed in the previous chapter and the attendant belief in the meaningfulness of individual human action that made mobilization possible. The intensity of this social interaction was experienced as something surprising and unexpected, something that transcended ordinary human experience and left few participants unmoved, something semidivine. To describe it, the prominent economist Valtr Komárek resorted to the language of the sacred, referring to a "'holy' emotion" on which it was necessary "to found the future Czechoslovak Socialist Republic."[4] He was by no means alone. If we accept Durkheim's argument that the sacred is at least to some extent society's image of itself—a representation of society's collective ideals that expresses and dramatizes social relationships in a manner conducive to social solidarity—such metaphors are

[2] Stephen Kotkin with Jan T. Gross, *Uncivil Society: 1989 and the Implosion of the Communist Establishment* (New York: Modern Library, 2009). Central to Kotkin's argument is the premise that Czechoslovakia was, like Romania, a totalitarian (or "would-be totalitarian") state up to November 1989 in the sense Jan Gross has given the term. As Michal Pullmann has shown, however, this assertion does not hold up to scrutiny. Czechoslovakia in the late 1980s more closely matched the characterization of a "posttotalitarian" state as Václav Havel described it. Jan T. Gross, *Revolution from Abroad: The Soviet Conquest of Poland's Western Ukraine and Western Belorussia*, rev. ed. (Princeton, N.J.: Princeton University Press, 2002; Michal Pullmann, *Konec experimentu: Přestavba a pád komunismu v Československu* (Prague: Scriptorium, 2011); Václav Havel, "The Power of the Powerless," in *Open Letters: Selected Writings, 1965–1990*, ed. Paul Wilson (New York: Vintage Books, 1992), pp. 125–214.
[3] Jan T. Gross, *Polish Society under German Occupation: The Generalgouvernement, 1939–1944* (Princeton, N.J.: Princeton University Press, 1979), p. 306.
[4] Quoted in "Tisková beseda s Valtrem Komárkem: Neváhejme zlomit moc mafie," *Přetlak*, no. 6 (2 December 1989), p. 2.

telling.[5] Sociologically, the revolution can be described as the sacralization of a new sense of community.[6]

Likewise, the revolution can be regarded as a "big bang" of signifiers.[7] The value of "the sacred" as a sociological concept is that it serves as a first principle in symbolic systems, parallel to the role that postulates play in geometry. In geometry, once five basic and unprovable principles are accepted, all the rest can be logically derived. Cultural systems are of course messier and far more inconsistent than mathematical ones, yet nonetheless uncontested assumptions—sacred principles—lie at the foundation of social and cognitive systems.[8] In 1989, Czechoslovak citizens reconsidered these givens and formulated new axioms and theorems to represent a reimagined community and map out its contours.[9] The elaboration of a symbolic system with respect to this reimagined community took place in such extraordinary forms of collective political action as public manifestations, happenings, and pilgrimages, as well as in images and rhetoric. Assembled citizens created new symbols to represent themselves and transformed through collective action the meaning of old ones. Language itself changed in the process. The sacralization of a new sense of community in Czechoslovakia necessitated myriad efforts to articulate representations of that community, first symbolically and then in political, social, and economic institutions (the function of which is to stabilize relationships between signifiers and signified).[10]

An example of this semiotic creativity was an "allegorical procession" that students in Olomouc prepared for the enjoyment and edification of their fellow citizens on 15 December 1989. Boys dressed as policemen, with mock shields and truncheons, pretended to beat "demonstrators" who proclaimed, "We have empty hands," clearly alluding to the events of 17 November in Prague. Stylized administrators marched with filing binders, calling "for the renewal of bureaucracy," while students, tied together and wearing red blindfolds, were led through the streets,

[5] See Steven Lukes, *Emile Durkheim: His Life and Work* (New York: Harper & Row, 1972), pp. 482–84.

[6] I am informed here by Mona Ozouf's argument that French revolutionary festivals accomplished a "transfer of sacrality" from the monarch to the revolutionary community. *Festivals and the French Revolution*, trans. Alan Sheridan (Cambridge, Mass.: Harvard University Press, 1988).

[7] My thanks to Carla Hesse for suggesting this phrase. The cosmological metaphor was current in the revolution itself; see, for example, "Co s nimi?! Vysoké školy půl roku po velkém třesku," *Moravské noviny*, 19 July 1990, p. 1.

[8] See Clifford Geertz, "Centers, Kings, and Charisma: Reflections on the Symbolics of Power," in *Culture and Its Creators: Essays in Honor of Edward Shils*, ed. Joseph Ben-David and Terry Nichols Clark (Chicago: University of Chicago Press, 1977), pp.150–71. For a critique and vindication of Geertz, see William H. Sewell, Jr., *Logics of History: Social Theory and Social Transformation* (Chicago: University of Chicago Press, 2005), pp. 175–96.

[9] Cf. Benedict Anderson, *Imagined Communities: Reflections on the Origins and Spread of Nationalism* (London: Verso, 1983).

[10] On the semiotic function of institutions, see Mary Douglas, *How Institutions Think* (Syracuse, N.Y.: Syracuse University Press, 1986).

crying, "Long live the Communist Party of Czechoslovakia!" A youth costumed as a red star with the mask of a human skull bore a sickle like the grim reaper, and behind him pallbearers carried a coffin. The procession paused in front of the district court building, where students draped tricolor sashes over two stone lions and solemnly crowned them, and then it continued to the spot where, until just recently, statues of Lenin and Stalin had stood. There, "Comrade Totalitarianism" was ceremoniously "interred," and three women—dressed to represent Freedom, Justice, and Democracy—waved to onlookers following their release from a cage.[11]

This "happening," as it was called, was a collective act of signification. By reenacting the "massacre," students reminded participants and onlookers of what had brought them together as a community; they affirmed and reiterated the sacred foundations of the revolutionary community's self-definition. The "bureaucrats" and the blindfolded "party members" represented what the community was struggling against, while the three women represented ideals with which the community identified. The lions heraldically symbolized the national community, now reasserting its sovereignty. The star with the face of death represented an entire system of human relations, which now people believed they were collectively expunging from their midst.

Theorists of "contentious politics" have emphasized the importance of culturally distinctive "repertoires" as the means by which participants in contentious politics make their claims known, and it might be tempting to identify the Olomouc procession as an exemplary item in such a repertoire.[12] The problem, however, is that there is not much contention to be seen. Though the manifold ways in which the students mocked the (allegedly departed) Communist regime may have seemed offensive to those who still cherished their party cards, the student gestures were not really addressed to them. The procession was meant primarily for the benefit of those taking part, reinforcing their sense of unity and articulating their collective ideals.[13] Similarly, though the procession bore a genealogical relationship to what Padraic Kenney calls the "carnivalesque" repertoire of central European social movements in the late 1980s, it took on dimensions that transcended the framework of a carnival.[14] Rather than merely suspending the rules that usually govern society,

[11] Ivan Langer and Zdeněk Zukal, *Happening* (Olomouc: Univerzita Palackého, 1990), video recording; Jan Marek, "Včera mělo opět celé město možnost . . . ," *Přetlak*, no. 19 (16 December 1989), p. 1; *Stráž lidu* (Olomouc), 23 December 1989, p. 2.

[12] Doug McAdam, Sidney Tarrow, and Charles Tilly, *Dynamics of Contention* (Cambridge: Cambridge University Press, 2001), pp. 16, 18. See also Charles Tilly, *Regimes and Repertoires* (Chicago: University of Chicago Press, 2006).

[13] One of the organizers has explicitly confirmed this. Ivan Langer, quoted in Milan Otáhal and Miroslav Vaněk, *Sto studentských revolucí: Studenti v období pádu komunismu—životopisná vyprávění* (Prague: Lidové noviny, 1999), p. 521.

[14] Padraic Kenney, *A Carnival of Revolution: Central Europe 1989* (Princeton, N.J.: Princeton University Press, 2002). Kenney sees the revolution as ending in 1989 (his narrative ends on 17 November 1989), but

the procession articulated new principles of governance; the goal was no longer to challenge an existing order so much as to create a new one. To make sense of collective action in revolutionary Czechoslovakia, therefore, we need to expand the notion of a repertoire to encompass more than just contentious claim-making, allowing it to include any collective act of signification that articulates collective ideals and aims to make social reality harmonize with them. We will see that, in keeping with deeply rooted traditions of political activism in central Europe, the purpose of much collective action in 1989 was to transform society, not just the regime. As striking students in Olomouc insisted, the revolution was first of all a moral, not a political revolution.[15]

This chapter examines the repertoire of politically relevant signifying practice in which Czechoslovak citizens engaged in 1989. It demonstrates that a new sense of community came into being among Czechoslovakia's citizens after 17 November and argues that this imagined community became the sacred center of an expanding universe of signifiers meant to represent it. It will be shown that the clash between violence and nonviolence on 17 November was experienced as a mythic moment of foundation, forging community and catapulting perception of unfolding history from the ironic mode to the romantic. In the process of symbolic differentiation that followed, Czechoslovak citizens created a new political culture, complete with its own rituals, moral codes, and myths. We will consider in the next chapter the specific "thoughts, desires, and dreams" that citizens articulated—the system of collective ideals with which they expressed identification and which they hoped to see incarnated in social, political, and economic institutions. In this chapter, our concern is with the collective effervescence that made such articulation both possible and imperative.

A New Community

Czech and Slovak accounts of November and December 1989 are replete with references to a beautiful or inimitable "atmosphere." On the day of the General Strike, television reporters described a "fantastic atmosphere" prevailing across the country.[16] Tomáš Hradílek, a spokesman for the dissident human rights association Charter 77, spoke of a "beautiful fever," which he compared to "falling in love."[17] According to students in Olomouc, "the joyful atmosphere was actually tangible," and the folk singer

---

in the case of Czechoslovakia this is an etic (perhaps Polish) view; most, if not all, Czechs and Slovaks who perceived a revolution saw it as beginning in 1989.

[15] Tomáš Hyjánek, "Cesta k demokracii," Přetlak, no. 11 (7 December 1989), p. 1.

[16] Timothy Garton Ash, We the People: The Revolution of '89 Witnessed in Warsaw, Budapest, Berlin & Prague (London: Granta, 1990), p. 106.

[17] Quoted in Přetlak, no. 4 (30 November 1989), p. 10.

Jaromír Nohavica said it felt like being drunk on new wine.[18] This "atmosphere" was none other than a new quality of human relations, made possible by the sense of solidarity that spread among Czech and Slovak citizens after 17 November and their newfound ability to act in concert. As the student Jiří Křečan recalled after a rally in the Palacký University sports hall on 20 November, "The feeling of unity and strength astounded perhaps everyone."[19]

Social interaction became incredibly intense in November and December 1989. As one Slovak journalist observed, "Suddenly we all want to assemble as much as possible, to listen as much as possible, and to speak as much as possible."[20] Ladislav Adamec spoke of "effervescence" in society; others pointed to an "enormous explosion of energy."[21] They might as well have been quoting Lynn Hunt's account of the origins of the sacred in "a surplus of energy created by an extraordinarily high level of social interaction"[22]—or citing Durkheim himself:

> There are periods of history when, under the influence of some great collective shock, social interactions have become much more frequent and active. Men look for each other and assemble together more than ever. That general effervescence results which is characteristic of revolutionary or creative epochs.[23]

The collective effervescence of 1989 had, like other historical examples of the phenomenon, the power to create a sense of transcendent communal fellowship among participants and to engender a new system of symbols with which this perceived community might be discussed and comprehended. Insofar as the assembled community could be considered representative of Czechoslovak society (an equation made at the time), the intensity and duration of their collective effervescence succeeded in reconfiguring that society's self-definition—that is, what it held to be sacred. It was this reconfiguration of sacrality and the attendant genesis of a new symbolic vocabulary that enabled the VPN activist Ladislav Snopko later to recall, "November awoke the initiative of citizens to communicate."[24]

Czechs and Slovaks caught up in this intense social interaction frequently described ontological transformation as a result. Recalling a happening in Olomouc, the student Milan Hanuš wrote,

[18] Quoted in "Koncert—Hala UP 2.12.1989," *Přetlak*, no. 8 (4 December 1989), p. 5.

[19] Jiří Křečan, "V pátek 17.11.1989 . . . ," Olomouc, 1990 (private collection of Carol Skalnik Leff, Urbana, Ill.), p. 3.

[20] Irena Tomčiaková, "Keď víchor vetrá zatuchnuté kúty," *Kysuce*, 15 December 1989, p. 6.

[21] Vladimír Hanzel, ed., *Zrychlený tep dějin* (Prague: OK Centrum, 1991), p. 15; fragment beginning "změna hospodářského mechanismu . . ." (LN: fond 569, box 2).

[22] Lynn Hunt, "The Sacred and the French Revolution," in *Durkheimian Sociology: Cultural Studies*, ed. Jeffrey Alexander (Cambridge: Cambridge University Press, 1992), p. 27.

[23] Émile Durkheim, *The Elementary Forms of the Religious Life*, trans. Joseph Ward Swain (New York: Macmillan, 1915), p. 241.

[24] Martin Slivka, *Dni nádeje*, Slovenská televízia, 17 November 2004.

Then someone had the idea to make a human chain and in a moment we had the entire town hall encircled. A few songs at the corner and a parade to the rector's office, plenty of singing on the way, *a feeling of stupendous wholeness and rightness*. Another one of the moments from these days, a moment when I am proud that I am a student.[25]

According to the student Boris Pentějelev, "we were all born on 17 November," and editors of the OF-VPN newspaper in Komárno reiterated this idea in January when they wrote that society was "in the state of birth, still without sin."[26] The musician Jaroslav Hutka said that not only he but the whole nation had returned from emigration.[27] Metaphors of awakening, or of the recovery of health after illness, were widespread.[28] All these metaphors expressed the idea that a new state of being had been attained. This sense of ontological transformation was indelibly linked with a weakening of distinctions between self and other. "Around me dozens of *unknown and yet intimately familiar* faces," wrote Hanuš. "And, I believe, even the same feeling within."[29] Even people who did not know each other in any objective sense felt intersubjectively connected.

The revolutionary sense of synergy was a powerful one, capable of modifying behavior. Accounts of 1989 are filled with examples of a crowd taking up a chant in unison and of individuals and groups volunteering time, goods, or experience to the cause. This "awesome" atmosphere can therefore be said to have exerted a moral influence, in the senses both of peer pressure and of deontological obligation.[30] As Durkheim argues,

> While one might perhaps contest the statement that all social facts without exception impose themselves from without upon the individual, the doubt does not seem possible as regards religious beliefs and practices, the rules of morality and the innumerable precepts of law—that is to say, all the most characteristic manifestations of collective life. All are expressly obligatory, and this obligation is the proof that these ways of acting and thinking are not the

---

[25] Milan Hanuš, "Happening," *Přetlak*, no. 9 (5 December 1989), p. 8 (emphasis added).

[26] Boris Pentějelev, "Občané, my všichni se narodili 17. listopadu 1989," Olomouc (private collection of Lenka Wünschová, Olomouc); *Reflex*, 5 January 1990, p. 3.

[27] Quoted in "Koncert—Hala UP 2.12.1989," *Přetlak* 1, no. 8 (4 December 1989), p. 6.

[28] For an example of metaphors of awakening, see "Kolegové, probuďte se!" *Plzeňský student*, no. 10 (12 December 1989), p. 1. Examples of "healing" metaphors can be found in Pracovníci Slovenského národného múzea, "Pre Občianske fórum v Prahe," Bratislava, 23 November 1989 (ÚSD: archiv KC OF, box 93); and *Kladenská záře*, 5 December 1989, p. 1.

[29] Hanuš, "Happening," p. 8 (emphasis added).

[30] Jaroslav Hutka, 2 December 1989, quoted in "Jaroslav Hutka v Olomouci," *Přetlak* 1, no. 9 (5 December 1989), p. 4.

work of the individual but come from a moral power above him, that which the mystic calls God or which can be more scientifically conceived.[31]

Actions after 17 November had to be considered "in the framework of the decency of the present days."[32] The "atmosphere" of 1989 brought people out of the everyday and lent meaning to actions which otherwise would have been inconceivable.

The ontological and moral transformations were accompanied by epistemological shifts. First and foremost, there was a new relationship to truth. "Truth! Truth!" citizens demanded on the squares—and they demanded full knowledge of the truth: the truth about 17 November, the truth about 1968, the truth about relatives who had disappeared in the fifties, the truth about a mining accident in 1988, the truth about the sources of money functionaries had used to build their villas, and so on ad infinitum.[33] Citizens desired not only to know the truth but to live in accordance with it. "Let us henceforth tell each other only the truth," bank tellers in Trnava proposed.[34] Beer brewers in Prague declared, "We want to live in truth."[35] Knowledge of the truth and the ability to live in accordance with it naturally presupposed the ability to discover it, something Czechs and Slovaks believed they could do through open dialogue.[36] This was part of the reason why citizens filled the squares to overflowing, arriving before and staying after any organized program in order to converse in small, spontaneously arising groups.[37] "Even if concrete things are not resolved from day to day at such meetings," commented a participant in Čadca, "they nonetheless have one plus. Yes, even this is good: that people will no longer be afraid to express their thoughts."[38] In other words, they needed no longer fear to seek for truth. The new relationship to "truth" naturally involved linguistic shifts as well. In district newspapers and among flyers circulating in the streets there often appeared "glossaries" explaining words being reintroduced from English, like *míting* or *happening*, and redefining old concepts, like

[31] Émile Durkheim, *Sociology and Philosophy*, trans. D. F. Pocock (Glencoe, Ill.: Free Press, 1953), p. 25.

[32] Václav Procházka, "Jak jsem dělal blba," *Nový život* (České Budějovice), 15 December 1989, p. 3.

[33] For more on the mining accident, see "Provolání zaměstnanců dolu Zd. Nejedlý v Odolově," 30 November 1989 (TU: fond "KC OF Trutnov," box 2).

[34] "Stanovisko pracovníkov pobočky ŠBČS v Trnave k súčasnej vnútropolitickej situácii v našej vlasti" (ÚSD: archiv KC OF, box 98).

[35] "Prohlášení svazáků ZO SSM Staropramen s.p. Pražské pivovary, závod Staropramen" (ÚSD: archiv KC OF, box 97).

[36] This was principle no. 1 of Civic Conversation's "Eight Rules of Dialogue," a ubiquitous flyer of 1989. The original version of the text, which mutated freely in circulation, can be found in *EM'89*, no. 0, p. 9.

[37] See, for example, *Manifestace v Opavě 27.11.1989* (OP: Sbírka dokumentačních materiálů—rok 1989, box "Listopad 1989—leden 1990: OF Opava"), video recording.

[38] Milan Chovanec, quoted in Tomčiaková, "Keď víchor."

abdikovat and *demokracie*.[39] As a journalist in Galanta wrote, "We have restored to many words their time-honored human content."[40]

The magnitude of the ontological, moral, and epistemological transformations led many Czechs and Slovaks to perceive a decisive break in time. Journalists after New Year's wrote articles about Czechoslovakia "in the Year Zero."[41] "It is impossible to return to darkness, now that we have perceived a ray of light," wrote students in Banská Bystrica.[42] One of their colleagues in Bratislava composed a poem about "days of resurrected time."[43] There was a widespread perception that something about the assemblies was unprecedented, that the country was undergoing historic changes, that history had "accelerated."[44] Several people described the period following 17 November as a "holiday," an extended time outside ordinary time.[45] Some were even willing to espouse the break in time with oaths of permanence: "We are with you," wrote one collective farm strike committee to VPN in Bratislava, "and never otherwise."[46]

This complex transformation—the genesis of a new sense of community and identity, a new commitment to morality, and a new way of making sense of the world—provided a powerful referent for future development, and Komárek was not the only one to resort to religious language to describe it. On television, the actor Milan Kňažko called what was happening a miracle, and the political prisoner Ján Čarnogurský described as "heavenly music" the chants he heard through his prison window from crowds outside demanding his release.[47] God stood behind the students, claimed a citizen in Trutnov, and parents of schoolchildren in a Bratislava suburb identified the revolution as "our sacred cause."[48] Students in České Budějovice rewrote the Lord's Prayer to express their revolutionary aspirations, and a Civic Forum activist in Ostrava likened the revolution to the

---

[39] See, for example, "Slovníček aktuálních pojmů" (private collection of Lenka Wünschová).

[40] Judita Púčeková, "Čas vianočný," *Víťazná cesta*, 21 December 1989, p. 1.

[41] See, for example, "Filmová přehlídka v roce nula," *Fórum* (Prague), 25 April 1990, p. 4.

[42] BB: Zbierka plagátov získaných od študentov Pedagogickej fakulty v Bystrici, 1989–1990.

[43] HM: Zbierka plagátov, box "Plagáty: 1989 a ďalej s číslom," poster no. 53840.

[44] See, for example, "To Jičín ještě nezažil," *Předvoj*, 8 December 1989, p. 1; Věřící studenti vysokých a středních škol, "Prohlášení věřících studentů," Prague, 22 November 1989, in Milan Otáhal and Zdeněk Sládek, eds., *Deset pražských dnů (17.–27. listopad 1989): Dokumentace* (Prague: Academia, 1990), p. 240; Studenti DAMU, "Prohlášení ke středoškolským studentům," in Otáhal and Sládek, p. 78; Hanzel, *Zrychlený tep dějin*.

[45] Slivka, *Dni nádeje*.

[46] Letter from Ján Chovančák, chairman of the strike committee of JRD "Goral," Suchá Hora, to KV VPN Bratislava (SNA: Archív VPN, fond. odd. I).

[47] *Štúdio Televíznych novín*, Slovenská televízia, 24 November 1989; Ľubomír Feldek, ed., *Keď sme brali do rúk budúcnosť* (Bratislava: Vydavateľstvo Archa, 1990), p. 36.

[48] Miroslav Mědílek, "Návrh Občanskému fóru v Trutnově a příspěvek redakci *Krkonošské pravdy*" (TU: fond "KC OF Trutnov," box 1, "Kopie různých prohlášení"); "Správa z priebehu štrajku na ZŠ v Lamači dňa 27.11.1989" (SNA: Archív VPN, fond. odd. I).

Exodus.[49] Timothy Garton Ash discusses the symbolism of Agnes Přemyslovna's canonization on 12 November, noting a prophecy that miracles would occur in Bohemia in the event, and close as Garton Ash was to the mentality of the time, his memoir is itself riddled with biblical allusions.[50]

Their experience was real, but Czechs and Slovaks found it difficult to describe using the language of more ordinary times. Those who did not invoke religious language frequently resorted to fairy-tale metaphors to describe what they were experiencing. For one laborer in Trenčianske Jastrabie, the students, artists, and intellectuals were like a collective prince who had unlocked the door of a dungeon and released the people from the dominion of an evil warlock. The laborer compared the sirens that sounded at the beginning of the General Strike to the wedding bells at the end of a fairy tale for the prince and his bride and noted how the sirens, which previously he and other workers had hated, had now become "the most beautiful music."[51] In Bratislava, a poster entitled "A Fairy Tale for Children of the 1990s" pictured a student on horseback riding to rescue "seven dwarfs" (OF, VPN, the KSČ's four satellite parties, and "the people") from the Communist Party, represented as an anthropomorphized red star holding a whip.[52] Czech students identified themselves as the Knights of Blaník, legendary heroes prophesied to waken from their sleep under Bohemia's Mount Blaník in the hour of their country's greatest need.[53] Many more examples could be given.

We thus return to the romantic mode of perception and narration discussed in the previous chapter. The mythic rhetoric of sacrality and the romantic rhetoric of the fairy tale had not been common in Czechoslovak discourse prior to 17 November, yet after 17 November they became the dominant means of describing the momentous shifts taking place in social and mental life. How did it happen that two nations hitherto (and since) renowned for their black humor and generally ironic outlook on life suddenly became full of romantic idealists? Northrop Frye speculates that the evolution from romantic (high mimetic) to ironic (nonmimetic) rhetoric is not linear but circular, with irony growing ever more metaphysically fatalistic and ultimately giving way to romance via the mythic experience of sacrifice.[54]

[49] "Světe náš," *Informační servis* (České Budějovice), no. 13 (20 December 1989), p. 1; "Exodus," *Hlasatel*, no. 2 (17 January 1990), p. 8.

[50] Garton Ash, *We the People*, p. 99. Padraic Kenney criticizes Garton Ash for resorting to the language of the miraculous, though he himself ends up using it (*Carnival of Revolution*, pp. 33, 216). Indeed, religious metaphors are endemic in emic secondary literature about 1989. A further example is Gale Stokes, *The Walls Came Tumbling Down: The Collapse of Communism in Eastern Europe* (New York: Oxford University Press, 1993).

[51] Letter from D. P., Trenčianske Jastrabie, to KV VPN Bratislava, 27 November 1989 (SNA: Archív VPN, fond. odd. I).

[52] HM: Zbierka plagátov, box "Plagáty: 1989 a ďalej s číslom," poster no. 33675.

[53] "Aby blaničtí rytíři mohli zrušit pohotovost" (LN: fond 569, box 2).

[54] Northrop Frye, *The Anatomy of Criticism: Four Essays* (Princeton, N.J.: Princeton University Press, 1957), p. 42.

To explain the dramatic shift in Czechs' and Slovaks' symbolic universe, then, we must take a closer look at 17 November.

Origins of the New Community

There is abundant evidence that Czechs and Slovaks prior to 17 November 1989 interpreted the world (and particularly their country, "Absurdistan") in predominately ironic terms. Student bulletins in Prague in the months leading up to 17 November provide a good illustration, for though their distribution was strictly limited, they were uncensored. The students contributing to these journals expressed despair that while the Soviet Union, Hungary, and Poland were becoming more open and democratic, Czechoslovakia kept company with Romania.[55] They complained of moral crisis and apathy on the part of fellow students and citizens. "No one else cares about the future of our faculty," they bemoaned, when an election to a deanship was actually contested but only eight students showed up for a debate between the candidates.[56] Despite having achieved, within the framework of *prestavba/přestavba* (the Czechoslovak version of *perestroika*), unprecedented opportunities for free discussion in newly created university discussion fora, as well as within the Socialist Youth Association, students still lamented, "We really don't know how to discuss."[57] "We call for pluralism of opinion, but then don't let our opponent say his piece."[58] There was a pervasive sense of stagnation, frustration, and uncertainty. Individual students began moving in the direction of romanticism, identifying themselves as anarchists and enjoining their colleagues to the "Sisyphean endeavor" of fomenting dialogue, but they still identified their position (ironically) as one of "stoic unrest."[59]

Within a few days after 17 November, however, the dominant Czechoslovak mode of interpreting the world was unabashedly romantic; the world had become meaningful and individuals confident of their place in it. The change began during the ceremonies held the afternoon of 17 November at Charles University's campus in Prague's New Town, in memory of ten students the Nazi regime had killed fifty years previously in connection with anti-Protectorate demonstrations.[60] The

[55] "Jednomyslnost ve škole demokracie," *Proto*, no. 5 (June 1989), p. 4; Jana Bryndová, "Londýnská abeceda," *Proto*, no. 6 (September 1989), p. 10; Milan Podobský, "Drobničky ze sovětské kultury," ibid., p. 11; Václav Bartuška, "Vlak do stanice zítra," ibid., p. 22.

[56] Ivan Barvínek, "Chceme změny!" *Proto*, no. 5 (June 1989), p. 2.

[57] Klára Pospíšilová, in "Jaký je tvůj názor na průběh jednání a závěry celostátní konference SSM?" *Coproto*, no. 5 (16 November 1989), p. 1.

[58] Milan Podobský, "Dobrý den, tedy!" *Proto*, no. 4 (March 1989), p. 13.

[59] Lucie Protivanská, "Pierot: Parafráze na stoický neklid," *Proto*, no. 4 (March 1989), p. 14; "Doba fórová," *Proto*, no. 6 (September 1989), p. 2.

[60] Jan Opletal, the most honored of these students, was shot during a demonstration on 28 October 1939, the anniversary of the founding of Czechoslovakia; he died thirteen days later. Opletal's funeral on 15 November became the occasion for another, mainly student, demonstration, which led to the closure of Czech

anniversary commemoration had been permitted by the authorities, "International Students' Day" being a state holiday, but it intersected with student ferment and a widespread sense among Praguers—who not long ago had witnessed the mass flight of East Germans via the West German embassy in Prague—that something might happen; in the event, fifteen thousand people showed up for the ceremonies at Albertov.[61] Banners included the 1968 slogan, ironic in form but romantic in content, "Be realists, demand the impossible!"[62] A veteran of the 1939 events told the assembled students that he was proud they were fighting for the same thing. When a representative of the Socialist Youth Association addressed the crowd, it began speaking as one in antagonistic rejoinder, until the student Martin Mejstřík pointed out that dialogue required listening to all sides and promised that another point of view would soon come. It came from the student Martin Klíma, whose speech was now romantic in both form and content. "Subjugation is worse than death," he proclaimed, trembling. "Today we shall not just piously remember; we are concerned about the present. . . . We students, of course, must above all study and prepare ourselves for society, as we are often reminded. But it should also work the other way: we should prepare this society for ourselves!"[63] After a minute of silence in memory of the victims of "Prague '39 and Peking '89," the crowd set out for the second stop on its approved itinerary: the National Cemetery. There it was estimated that the crowd had grown to fifty thousand.[64] The official ceremony—which few could now see or hear—was overshadowed by the phenomenon of the largest assembly of citizens that Prague had seen since 1969. Amid the sea of souls—most of whom had never participated in a demonstration before—tongues were unleashed, and a sense of common cause came into being. When secret police provocateurs suggested surpassing the original program and marching en masse to Wenceslas Square, members of the crowd had no idea it was provocation, so closely did the movement resonate with their natural desire to relish this new sense of community a little longer.[65] When the foremost marchers entered Národní třída, they found their way blocked by special police units, and after several thousand had entered the boulevard, policemen who had been waiting in a side street cut them off from the multitude behind. The latter were dispersed, while those who had entered the boulevard found there was no way out. There followed a lengthy

universities, the deportation of over a thousand students to the Sachsenhausen concentration camp, and the execution of nine students on 17 November.

[61] Oldřich Tůma, "9:00, Praha-Libeň, horní nádraží: Exodus východních Němců přes Prahu v září 1989," *Soudobé dějiny* 6 (1999): 147–64; Petr Holubec, ed., *Kronika sametové revoluce* (Prague: ČTK, 1990), p. 2.

[62] "Kdo? ne-li my. Kdy? ne-li teď!!!!," *Proto*, no. 7 (20 November 1989), p. 1.

[63] Aleš V. Poledne, *Jak šly dějiny*, Česká televize, 16 November 2004; Otáhal and Sládek, *Deset pražských dnů*, p. 19.

[64] "Kdo? ne-li my," pp. 1–2; Poledne, *Jak šly dějiny.*

[65] *Televizní noviny*, Česká televize, 17 November 1999.

standoff, during which the crowd shouted, "We have empty hands," offered flowers to the security forces, and created what was thereafter described as a "living
altar" of candles between itself and the row of Plexiglas shields blocking its path.[66]
During this standoff, with the threat of violence suddenly acute, the sense of community among the surrounded demonstrators grew acute as well. Earlier chants of
a lighthearted crowd for freedom and the ouster of prominent political figures gave
way to impassioned unison singing of hymns and cries for nonviolence. One of the
students in the throng recalls not having particularly liked the American spiritual
"We Shall Overcome" before, but when the crowd took it up in the tense moments
of its entrapment, he felt that singing it was the most important thing he could do.[67]
In this situation, in other words, individuals' sense of what was important shifted.
An ironic stance was no longer possible; there was now only violence on one hand,
nonviolence on the other—and the difference was meaningful. Nonviolence, moreover, was the ideal that bound the surrounded marchers to one another. Their sense
of solidarity was very real; witnesses later recalled that after the police breached
the "living altar" and commenced an attack that would leave at least 568 people
injured, strangers went out of their way to help strangers, and only by self-discipline
was a rush prevented wherein some members of the dense crowd might have been
trampled or asphyxiated.[68] Apartment dwellers in the neighborhood opened their
doors to fleeing citizens, cramming hundreds of strangers into tiny flats.[69] The next
day, those who could still walk felt united by the need to *do* something; a return to
life as usual seemed to them *immoral.* Thus there assembled in university buildings
and theaters those groups of mostly students and cultural professionals who decided
to go on strike and who called for a general strike on 27 November. A new sense of
community had come into being based on principles different from those that had
governed social interaction previously; in the beginning, it was sufficient simply to
reject the violence of 17 November. The combination of a new sense of community
with a new collective self-definition and a new pattern for determining meaning
amounted to a new sense of what was sacred—the basis of a new symbolic system.

This new sense of community spread (highly mimetically) from the initial
group to encompass the majority of Czechoslovak citizens. Rasma Karklins and
Roger Petersen explain this diffusion using threshold models.[70] A complementary

[66] Lubomír Černý, "Provolání," Prague, 20 November 1989 (PV: sbírka soudobé dokumentace, box
"Občanské fórum: Plakáty a různé").

[67] Pavel Dobrovský, writing in Marek Benda et al., *Studenti psáli revoluce* (Prague: Univerzum, 1990),
p. 56.

[68] Martin Mejstřík, *Deník: Řekněte jim, že sametová . . .* (Brno: Computer Press, 2010), p. 334.

[69] Michael Kukral, *Prague 1989: Theater of Revolution* (Boulder, Colo.: East European Monographs,
1997), pp. 57–58; Jaroslav Bouma, "*Kde jsi byl, když hřmělo?*" Česká televize, 19 November 1999.

[70] Rasma Karklins and Roger Petersen, "Decision Calculus of Protesters and Regimes: Eastern Europe
1989," *Journal of Politics* 55, no. 3 (August 1993): 588–614.

model might invoke the notion of adopter categories or liken the diffusion to the spread of a contagious disease.[71] For many, the force that pushed them to join the groundswell of protest (or the excuse that enabled them finally to justify it) was solidarity with the students beaten on Národní. People who had long been passive said, "We can't let them beat our children."[72] People were visibly shaken after watching amateur videotapes of the "massacre."[73] Later adopters of the innovation to protest may have been motivated more by the dictum "Be not the first by whom the New are try'd, Nor yet the last to lay the Old aside," but initially the spread of revolutionary community involved individuals, one by one or group by group, adopting a posture of empathy with the victims of violence.[74]

In the weeks that followed, Czechs and Slovaks repeatedly emphasized that it was the students' ordeal on Národní that had sparked their newfound unity, and they described the process using the language of sacrifice. Ivan Hoffman, in what became the anthem of the Slovak revolution, insisted, "Those young ones for us raised their empty hands. / For us they were beaten, for our keeping silent." The sacrifice, moreover, was efficacious: "On our streets years have passed since then / and bells have tolled to signal to evil its end."[75] A Vranov nad Topľou man gave blood to the Red Cross, symbolically dedicating it to the students beaten on Národní "as an expression of awe, respect, and thanksgiving that by their efforts the process of renewal has begun in our society."

> The trickling of the blood of innocent Prague students melted the ice and a massive river of the strength and will of the industrious people of our country began to wash away the ice floes of the administrative-directive system. Today we can say that this river cannot be stopped from finding its way to the ocean of freedom and democracy.[76]

Durkheim has been criticized for emphasizing the functioning of the sacred in stable societies, rather than the historical genesis of sacrality, but as Lynn Hunt suggests, we can fill this lacuna by considering the critical theory of René Girard.[77] In Girard's view sacrifice not only reproduces a relationship with the sacred—sacrifice mimics the process by which the sacred is engendered. In a social system that has

---

[71] See Everett Rogers, *Diffusion of Innovations*, 4th ed. (New York: Free Press, 1995), pp. 252–334; and James Krapfl "The Diffusion of 'Dissident' Political Theory in the Czechoslovak Revolution of 1989," *Slovo* (London) 19, no. 2 (Autumn 2007): 85–90.

[72] See, for example, Miloš Macourek, "Významný den" (OV: sbírka soudobé dokumentace, box "Revoluce 1989: Materiály 1989–90").

[73] *Televízny klub mladých*, Slovenská televízia, Bratislava, 8 December 1989.

[74] Alexander Pope, *An Essay on Criticism*, 2nd ed. (London: W. Lewis, 1713), p. 17.

[75] Ivan Hoffman, "Sľúbili sme si lásku," first performed in Bratislava, 26 November 1989, reprinted in Feldek, *Keď sme brali*, pp. 36–37.

[76] M. Jefanov, "Roztopili sa ľady," *Vranovské noviny*, 15 December 1989, p. 3.

[77] Hunt, "Sacred," pp. 37–39.

undergone symbolic dedifferentiation (consonant with irony, which denies the meaning of symbols), Girard argues that symbolic difference (upon which meaning depends)
can be reintroduced when members of a community mimetically join one another
to expel a common victim, a "scapegoat" that represents the violence or disorder
dividing or confounding the community. The difference created is that between a
now-united community and the victim it has united to expel. This fundamental
difference upholds the meaning of an expanding body of signifiers, with the victim
itself becoming a transcendent signifier of the community's existence as a unity. The
victim is thus subsumed within the sacred, such that the sacred can, in Girard's view,
be identified essentially as transfigured human violence.[78]

The important thing here is the unity (the comm-unity) that is formed. According to Girard, this occurs by a process of unanimous exclusion, whereby the
community unites in violence *against* something. What happened on 17 November was an inversion of this process, however, for it was the police attacking the
marchers that cemented the unity of the latter party. The community reborn was
the community of the scapegoats, the community of the sacrificed. They were
aware of a boundary between their symbolic system and that of the state—a
boundary demarcated by violence—but it was not their violence, and in offering
flowers to the policemen they showed that they did not preclude the possibility
of welcoming their persecutors into their community should the persecutors also
renounce violence.

Despite the inversion, the victims of 17 November nonetheless became symbols
of the sacred foundations of the new community. Those who received wounds that
night were later proud of the fact (and their friends jealous).[79] Students, for their
part, gained a prestige unknown since the deaths of Jan Palach and Jan Zajíc in
1969. Though many of those injured on 17 November were actually middle-aged,
popular perception at the time nonetheless focused on students and young people
as the primary victims—partly because it was students who had made the events
of 17 November possible but probably also because young people could more in-
disputably be identified as innocent.[80] Workers joining the strike movement wrote
as if students as a class had been attacked on 17 November (a perception that students themselves shared).[81] In all the significant political events that followed, from

---

[78] René Girard, *Violence and the Sacred*, trans. Patrick Gregory (Baltimore: Johns Hopkins University
Press, 1977); and, with Guy Lefort and Jean-Michel Oughourlian, *Things Hidden since the Foundation of the
World*, trans. Stephen Bann and Michael Metteer (Stanford, Calif.: Stanford University Press, 1987).

[79] Heather Nehring, "Working in the Czech Republic: Exploring Interaction and Communication"
(master's thesis, University of Texas at El Paso, 1995), p. 89.

[80] Oldřich Tůma, *Zítra zase tady! Protirežimní demonstrace v předlistopadové Praze jako politický a sociální
fenomén* (Prague: Maxdorf, 1994).

[81] See, for example, "Všichni pracovníci obvodného zdrav. střediska Čtyři Dvory . . ." (CB: Kronika
města Českých Budějovic, box "Kronika—1989: Dokumentace A1-B48," oddíl A, folder "Výzvy a rezo-
luce českobudějovických závodů a institucí zaslané stávkovému výboru studentů XI.1989"); "Provolání proti
násilí" (CB: sbírka dokumentace K1139).

negotiations with government functionaries to mass meetings on the squares of small towns, savvy organizers were careful to make sure that students were present, even if they had to import them.[82] Construction workers in Prague called for a monument to the "rebelling student."[83] A woman in Chrudim proposed that Czechoslovak students be awarded the Nobel Peace Prize, and citizens throughout the country were soon signing petitions in support of the idea.[84]

Proximate aspects of the "massacre" also became transcendent signifiers of the new community. The site on Národní where the violence occurred became, as the American observer Michael Kukral described it, a "shrine," with candles burning for months afterwards and a sign informing visitors, "It happened here!"[85] Similar sites of reverence sprang up throughout the country. In Olomouc, for example, a blown-up photograph of a student in the crowd on 17 November became the centerpiece of constantly replenished candles and flowers.[86] The date itself took on new meaning. Citizens throughout Czechoslovakia proposed renaming prominent streets and squares after 17 November long before other name changes were suggested.[87] In Hradec Králové, Technical Services promised to plant seventeen trees (come spring) "as an expression of respect and sympathy with students across the republic, who initiated the process of genuine societal renewal, and as a symbol of the massacre of 17 November 1989." The trees were intended "forever to recall our gentle revolution" and to be sites "where students will be able to commemorate 17 November—unforgettable for many reasons—every year."[88] *November* became a term denoting not just the eleventh month but the entire revolution, such that journalists and scholars still write "since November" in reference to events and trends that, strictly speaking, took place or started months or even years later.

The Girardian interpretation of the sacrificial genesis of community and the sacred resonates with one that a number of Czechs and Slovaks—notably signers of Charter 77 and their sympathizers—advocated at the time. The Czech philosopher Jan Patočka, formulating a "heretical" (and Durkheimian) philosophy of history in the 1970s, had argued that history was "the shaken certitude of pre-given

[82] Michal Horáček, *Jak pukaly ledy* (Prague: Ex libris, 1990), pp. 90–91; Ivo Mludek, interview by author, Opava, 20 February 1997, tape recording; notes about planned events in ZL: Sbírka plakátů, box "17. listopad—29. prosinec 1989 Zlín," folder "Divadlo pracujících Gottwaldov: Listopad—prosinec 1989."

[83] "My, pracovníci střediska technických revizí . . . ," Prague, 27 November 1989 (ÚSD: archiv KC OF, box 152).

[84] Z. Ludvíková, "Návrh na udělení Nobelovy ceny" (LN: fond 569, box 2); *Smer* (Banská Bystrica), 6 January 1990, p. 2.

[85] Kukral, *Prague 1989*, p. 67.

[86] Tomáš Piňos, "Ve středu 24.1.1990 . . . ," *Přetlak*, no. 33 (25–26 January 1990), p. 3.

[87] One of the people, for example, who asked to speak on SNP Square in Bratislava proposed to rename that city's downtown Poštová Street "the Street of 17 November" (SNA: Archív VPN, fond. odd. I).

[88] Karel Michal, "Já nic—já muzikant . . . ," *Nové Hradecko*, 19 December 1989, p. 2.

meaning."[89] However meaning might be shaken, though, civilization still demanded it, returning ever and anon to sacrifice in its efforts to restore the differences that made meaning possible. Patočka argued that in the most recent, "technological" phase of history, Western civilization had become an elaborate system of routinized sacrifice, increasingly reducing the meaning of individuals to their roles and concealing (or forgetting) the "truth" of human individuality, thus compelling the vast majority of mankind to "live a lie." Patočka suggested that men and women thus objectified and externalized are victims of a sort, as was evidenced vividly by soldiers sent to the front in World War I in an orgiastic attempt to preserve pregiven meanings. "Peace and the day necessarily rule by sending humans to death in order to assure *others* a day in the future in the form of progress, of a free and increasing expansion, of possibilities they lack today. Of those whom it sacrifices it demands, by contrast, *endurance* in the face of death."[90] As long as men and women remain ruled by "the day"—"by the hope of everydayness, of a profession, of a career, simply possibilities for which they must fear and which feel threatened"—they will not perceive their victimhood. On the threshold of death, however, if "the motives of the day which had evoked the will to war are consumed in the furnace of the front line," the sacrificed may perceive their status and recognize what history is all about.[91] Comparing French and German soldiers' accounts of their experiences on the Great War's western front, Patočka pointed out that beyond an initial experience of profound meaninglessness, an experience of transcendent but nonsacrificial meaningfulness was possible. The "shaken" perceive that the everyday, its life and its "peace" have an end. Everyday life—"mere life"—had been chained by fear. In the experience of "life at the peak," however, human beings cease to be afraid. They cease to plan for the ordinary days of a possible future, for they see that these days have an end; they become free in a way they had not been before. They perceive, moreover, that the so-called adversary on the other side of the front is actually a partner in the same experience; those who had seemed to be opposites are revealed to the shaken as being spiritually united. Thus emerges "the solidarity of the shaken," which Patočka suggested has the potential to become a transforming force in history.[92] It was in this belief that Patočka and his followers founded Charter 77, and Charter 77 signatories turned to the idea again in 1989 as an explanation for the emergence of powerful solidarity among Czechoslovak citizens.[93]

---

[89] Jan Patočka, *Heretical Essays in the Philosophy of History*, trans. Erazim Kohák (Chicago: Open Court, 1996), p. 118. See also Jacques Derrida's essay on Patočka, *The Gift of Death*, trans. David Wills (Chicago: University of Chicago Press, 1995).

[90] Patočka, *Heretical Essays*, p. 129.

[91] Ibid., p. 130.

[92] Ibid., pp. 118–35.

[93] Krapfl, "The Diffusion of 'Dissident' Political Theory," pp. 94–95, 99–100.

To help explain how the reconfiguration of sacrality on 17 November informed the subsequent development of political culture in Czechoslovakia, it is instructive to consider a further aspect of Girard's hypothesis: the "double transference." Violence, Girard notes, can have two valences. As a force that divides, it can cause dedifferentiation and deterioration of meaning. As a force that unites, however, through collective expulsion of a "scapegoat" or representation of disorder, it can restore differentiation as the basis for meaning. Both valences are transferred onto the sacred, such that representations of both forms of violence can become transcendent signifiers of the community. Thus, as we shall see, not only did students and the time and place of the "massacre" come to represent the revolutionary community, but so in their fashion did red stars, portraits of Gustav Husák, and bits of the barbed wire that until December 1989 had demarcated Czechoslovakia's borders with the West. Cultural forms deriving from the foundation of community can also be distinguished by the type of violence they address and the manner in which they do so. Ritual reflects the positive valence of the sacred—the violence that unites. If it was an act of violence that established the community's identity in the first place, then the natural (mimetic) means to preserve this identity is ritually to repeat the original act. Prohibition, on the other hand, seeks to ward off the negative valence of the sacred by preventing the violence that divides. To a large extent, prohibitions seek to regulate human relations so as to keep mimetic rivalry from becoming violent. Myth, finally, is the narrative that the symbolic system creates about its origins, usually structured in such a way as to occlude the community's responsibility for generative violence.

In the weeks following 17 November, we can trace practically day by day how new rituals, prohibitions, and myths came into being. The collective viewings of videotapes of the massacre were one type of community-reinforcing ritual that emerged in these days, as were happenings—many of which re-created the massacre dramatically. The example of the Vranov man giving his blood in symbolic tribute to the students' blood that, he believed, had made the revolution possible is an example of a ritual sacrifice modeled on the original one. The identification of the new community with nonviolence and the need for guidelines for behavior in the newly opened public sphere stimulated the formulation of a corpus of moral codes (i.e., prohibition), from protocols on how to behave when arrested to lists of rules for conducting dialogue. Perhaps the most noteworthy of these documents, originating in Gottwaldov and reprinted throughout Moravia and Slovakia, was the "Ten Commandments of Our Revolution":

1. Don't employ violence and never do anyone harm!
2. Don't settle old scores with anyone!
3. Deal with your adversaries in such a way that they become your friends!
4. Apply the principle that ideas are superior to brute force!
5. Be tolerant, don't offend, don't threaten!

6. Speak with everyone about everything and listen patiently to every opinion!

7. Help everyone who needs your help!

8. Draw attention to those who take recourse to violence and disinformation.

9. Maintain humanness [*lidskost*] in all situations. Do unto others as you would have them do unto you!

10. Let us all meet on the basis of universal human values, which are liberty, equality, fraternity, tolerance, democracy, and humaneness [*lidskost*]![94]

As demonstrated in the previous chapter, Czechs and Slovaks began narrating the history of their revolution almost as soon as it had begun, and this narrativization was itself a form of mythmaking. The past was reinterpreted along with the present to highlight the goodness of the people and the violence of the Communist regime. The nonviolence of the revolution itself assumed mythic proportions, obscuring both resonances of violence on the part of the mobilized populace and real acts of violence perpetrated by stalwarts of the old regime.

In sum, a new, revolutionary culture came into being on 17 November. It could even be called a new religion. The university professor Josef Jařab, for example, later wrote of a "gospel of nonviolence," which students spread like missionaries.[95] Not everyone was a devotee, just as not everyone was fully a participant in the "new community," but a new sense of community did exist, with its own myths, rituals, and codes of behavior, its own symbolic system, its own matrix for the determination of meaning.

Collective Effervescence and Symbolic Differentiation

The period following 17 November was by all accounts an intensely creative one. With great spontaneity and humor, the revolutionary community revised and expanded its symbolic vocabulary. University students on strike in November and December churned out an enormous volume of bulletins and flyers, some serious, some funny, all innovative. Together with striking actors, they turned the streets and squares into theaters where boundaries between stage and spectator dissolved. Hundreds of new associations appeared, from the Army Forum to the ecologically oriented Trend of the Third Millennium.[96] Newspapers were founded, poetry written, and songs composed.

[94] Karel Chrastina, "Desatero naší revoluce," Gottwaldov, 5 December 1989, in *Naše pravda*, 12 December 1989, p. 2. Identical or similar versions can be found in OL, PV, and ZL; a Slovak translation ("Desatoro našej revolúcie") is preserved in BB.

[95] Josef Jařab, "Nedělní zamyšlení," *Přetlak*, no. 21 (18 December 1989), p. 3.

[96] R. Vinklárek et al., "Vojenské fórum," Drhovice, 5 December 1989 (PV: sbírka soudobé dokumentace, box "Občanské fórum: Plakáty a různé," folder "Materiály již neaktuální"); also available in DO, OP, and OV. "Návrh na založenie strany 'Trend tretieho tisícročia'" (LN: fond 569, box 2).

The products of this revolutionary creativity were, above all, representations of the new, sacred sense of community. We have seen already how symbols of 17 November served this function. The weeks following 17 November saw the rapid multiplication of symbolic representations, visible most tellingly in festive forms of collective action.

Forging Community

If 17 November was the birthdate of the new community, the General Strike made that community fully manifest. On the morning of "the historic day," 27 November, a man in the North Bohemian village of Varnsdorf christened his newborn son Viktor, "to symbolize conviction and faith."[97] At the time no one yet knew what proportion of the population would join the two-hour strike at noon. VPN Bratislava did not know, and the list of strike-supporting institutions prepared for OF Prague on 26 November suggests that it was aware of only a tiny fraction.[98] In the end roughly half of Czechoslovakia's working population took part by interrupting work, and another fourth expressed support symbolically. The General Strike thus became the largest and perhaps the most significant of all the revolution's varieties of collective action.

Observance of the General Strike was characterized by simultaneity, dramatic gestures of coming together, concerted action, and most memorably by the visible presence of the assembled community. When the strike began at exactly twelve o'clock, one could often hear not only the sirens and church bells of one's own town or village but those of neighboring settlements as well; the country was effectively covered with a solid blanket of sound, symbolizing a people at one. Methods of observing the strike varied widely. In general, workers on collective farms and in enterprises similarly distant from a town square held meetings in their cafeterias or courtyards, often taking the opportunity to draft proclamations.[99] Workers in Levice watched the videotape from 17 November. Apprentices in Ostrava's Mining Machine Works observed the general strike by taking down "dogmatic slogans."[100] Schoolteachers conducted dialogues on political events with their pupils.[101] The focal point of the event, though, was the mass meetings on town squares. Participation in these meetings frequently began with the singing of the national anthems or the reading of a student text at one's workplace, followed by a festive march to the town

[97] "Plně se stotožňuji s prohlášeními a programem OF . . . ," Varnsdorf, 27 November 1989 (ÚSD: archiv KC OF, box 152).

[98] ÚSD: archiv KC OF, box 160.

[99] See, for example, the letter from collective farmers of JRD "Mier," Mužla, to "Výbor 'Verejnosť proti násiliu'," Bratislava (SNA: Archív VPN, fond. odd. I).

[100] Učňové a mistr odborné výchovy SOU, k.p. Báňské strojírny, "Na podporu požadavků . . . ," Ostrava, 27 November 1989 (ÚSD: archiv KC OF, box 47).

[101] Zdravotnícki pracovníci detských jaslí, "Vyhlásenie," Bratislava, 27 November 1989 (SNA: Archív VPN, fond. odd. I).

square.[102] Secondary school students from Hurbanovo walked the fifteen kilometers to Komárno to participate in the *míting* there; they could have taken trains or buses but chose to walk in order to intensify the experience, effectively turning it into a pilgrimage.[103] In Sereď, people in the crowd held hands while singing the national anthem that concluded the strike *míting*.[104]

In the week prior to the General Strike countless flyers, posters, and speeches had emphasized that it was a symbolic gesture, and accordingly the countless forms of participation were by no means limited to work stoppage.[105] Health care professionals and those who for various reasons felt they had to work through the strike nonetheless wore tricolors, displayed flags, and posted signs expressing their support. A woman in Chminianská Nová Ves wrote that she would "join the general strike of all Czechoslovak students on 27 November" by lighting candles in the windows of her house "because this is an exit from great darkness and this light will shine into the future."[106] In a television debate on 24 November, Milan Kňažko had said that 27 November should be "the day of the tricolor."

> Everyone can express solidarity in his own way. Salesclerks, your general strike can be the smile with which you serve customers on Monday. Doctors and nurses, your general strike will be that people on that day will leave you more satisfied than at other times. Drivers . . . of trains, buses, trams, trolleybuses, let your general strike be ringing, honking, clanging, symbolic halting, the display of flags. Bakers, your strike is the tricolor, and bread more fragrant than at other times. Policemen, let your general strike be truncheons put away. Journalists and filmmakers, let your general strike be to speak the truth. The goal of this general strike is a dignified life.[107]

To strike, in other words, meant to be the best one could be. In keeping with this idea, employees of a school cafeteria in Bratislava—to cite just one example—wrote that they performed their work in "exemplary" fashion during the General Strike.[108] For two hours they lived in a world imagined to be perfect. In effect, the whole country did this, and it set a powerful precedent for judging the future.

[102] Letter from Štrajkový výbor pri PR Stavoindustria, š.p. Bratislava, to "Centrálny koordinačný výbor," VŠMU, Bratislava, 27 November 1989 (SNA: Archív VPN, fond. odd. I).

[103] "Masové vystúpenie za demokraciu," *Dunaj*, 2 December 1989, p. 1.

[104] "Dialógu sa musíme učiť," *Víťazná cesta*, 7 December 1989, p. 1.

[105] "Generálny štrajk—symbol, nie ekonomické oslabenie" (HM: Zbierka plagátov, unlabelled box).

[106] Veronika Antolová, Chminianská Nová Ves, quoted in "Ohlasy," *Prešovské noviny*, 30 November 1989, p. 2.

[107] *Štúdio Televíznych novín*, 24 November 1989.

[108] "Mi [sic], pracovníci školskej jedálne," Bratislava, 27 November 1989 (SNA: Archív VPN, fond. odd. I).

As a phenomenon, the General Strike did not end with the return to work at two o'clock. Most collectives underscored their devotion to the community as a whole by promising to return to the national economy the time they had devoted to the strike, sometimes pledging extra work beyond the two missed hours. "In the interest of not disrupting the fulfillment of our tasks each member of the section will, by the end of the year, work half a shift overtime for free," proclaimed one group of researchers.[109] Students of the military academy in Žilina promised to plant a hundred thousand trees to make up for their participation in the General Strike.[110] Some Hradec Králové workers were *required* to make up the strike time, but in most cases it was voluntary.[111] Though it was widely pointed out that a two-hour strike could do no more damage to the economy than the many hours that had been lost over the years to Party-supervised political meetings in workplaces, workers nonetheless strove to ensure that the General Strike would have no ill effect on national production. This gesture was just as symbolic a testimony of citizens' solidarity as the strike itself.

The General Strike made the new community fully manifest to itself—indeed, cemented the idea that there *was* a new community.

> The general strike of 27 November was like a cathartic surgical intervention to remove embedded fear and widespread civic passivity. The monumental support of the population revealed the strength of public opinion, strengthened civic consciousness, activated interest in public affairs, and brought about a feeling of belonging together. . . . The strike was the expression of a new power and the signal for genuine restructuring [*prestavba*].[112]

After the General Strike, it was clear where power lay, and officials at all levels were inclined to compromise. It was also clear that protests (which had spread to the army) could not be put down without Soviet help, which at this point in the central European autumn was evidently not forthcoming. On 29 November, therefore, the Federal Assembly struck from the constitution the clause guaranteeing the Communist Party a leading role in society. The General Strike was thus a takeoff point, comparable to 14 July 1789. Even if the written constitution was not changed until two days later, on 27 November it was clear that the real constitution of society had shifted and that a new power outside state power had arisen. It was also clear

[109] ROH Výzkumného a vývojového ústavu, "Zápis ze schůze úseku ROH," Stráž pod Ralskem, 23 November 1989 (ÚSD: archiv KC OF, box 157).

[110] Štefan Debnár, "Kronika uplynulých dní," *Cieľ*, 30 November 1989, p. 6.

[111] ZV ROH závodu Ligmet, "Stanovisko ZV ROH k žádosti členů ZO ROH ze dne 23.11.1989," Hradec Králové (ÚSD: archiv KC OF, box 157).

[112] Zdeno Kosáč, "Občianske fórum hnutia Verejnosť proti násiliu," Banská Bystrica (BB: Materiály získané od hnutia Verejnosť proti násiliu v Banskej Bystrici, 1989, box 1), p. 1.

that state power would have to comply with popular power if a potentially violent crisis was to be avoided. Beyond this political significance, the General Strike was a turning point in the development of popular political culture. The first instances of iconoclasm during the strike were but a foretaste of the transformation about to occur as the community now manifest sought to remake the world in its own image.

REMAKING THE WORLD IN THE COMMUNITY'S IMAGE

Though OF in Prague called for an end to mass assemblies after 27 November, civic associations in other towns frequently encouraged them, and they continued to take place spontaneously from time to time. Other forms of collective behavior, however, vied for attention and provided additional means for individuals to relish their newfound communion. Human chains, marches, "trains of the Gentle Revolution," and happenings all made the community constantly manifest and lent themselves to symbolic and even physical transformation of participants and their environment. Citizens used these festive activities to remap symbolic geographies, to enforce justice, to dismantle physical and metaphysical barriers, and to transform themselves and their surroundings in accordance with ideals now perceived to define the community.

One of the most widespread and elementary forms of this rich repertoire of collective action was the human chain. While large chains, such as those connecting cities, required advance planning and coordination, smaller ones could form quite spontaneously and so were within the reach of practically any substantial group of people. Human chains, or "living chains" as they were often called, symbolized first and foremost the community itself, physically united as a single living entity. Sometimes that was their sole purpose, but sometimes they were used to draw attention to a particular cause, as when citizens in Vyškov formed a human chain around the town square on 4 December to encourage townspeople to sign a petition or when secondary school students in Třinec marched in a chain on 14 December under the banner of ecological concerns.[113] Frequently, however, the chains became a way to bring people together across distances, symbolically reducing the distance or dismantling mental barriers between them. Such were the human chains spanning the twenty-six kilometers between the rival towns Pardubice and Hradec Králové on 3 December and the twenty-two kilometers between Banská Bystrica and Zvolen on 9 December.[114] Citizens of Břeclav undertook a symbolically more profound reconfiguration of spatial relationships by forming a human chain to the hitherto inaccessible Austrian village of Reinthal, a mere eight kilometers away, as part of

---

[113] "Lidský řetěz," *Náš život*, 8 December 1989, p. 1; "Živý ekořetěz v Třinci," *Ozvěny-Echo*, 22 December 1989, p. 1.

[114] "Horoucí srdce v mrazivé neděli," *Nové Hradecko*, 5 December 1989, p. 1; "Živá reťaz," *Smer*, 8 December 1989, p. 2; Eva Benčíková and Radomír Vrbovský, "Dvadsať kilometrov priateľstva," *Smer*, 11 December 1989, pp. 1–2.

their "Hands to Europe" happening.[115] Human chains could also be used to change people's relationship to a public site by surrounding it, thereby symbolically repossessing it. Such was the Olomouc chain around the town hall, mentioned above. In České Budějovice, students created a chain that encircled the old town precisely where the city wall had once stood; it was intended to symbolize "unity, solidarity, and resolute refusal to retreat from justified demands."[116]

When combined with movement, human chains could become vehicles of a quest, the setting out of a people to achieve a particular goal through their concerted action. A particularly dramatic event of this kind took place in Brno on 26 November. "It took only a very short time for a chain of human hands to form in Brno, stretching from Freedom Square [in the center, the site of mass demonstrations] to the city's prison in Bohunice. There amid much chanting the liberated political prisoner Petr Cibulka was literally carried from his prison."[117] Students commented that "were it not for the crowd of 5,000, which gathered before his prison on 26 November and enforced his release, Petr Cibulka would probably still be sitting in jail."[118] This incident illustrated the power the community believed it had to act directly on the social order, and participants understood it as an incarnation of democracy.

Perhaps the grandest such expedition involved over one hundred thousand citizens who set out from Bratislava on 10 December 1989. Following arrangements VPN activists had made in advance, most walked through Austrian customs and proceeded jovially toward the small town of Hainburg, some twelve kilometers distant (only, of course, after creating a human chain that wound from central Bratislava to the border). After passing through the village of Wolfsthal, halfway between Bratislava and Hainburg, some turned north toward the Austrian side of the Danube below Slovakia's Devín Castle, while others continued on to Hainburg—where they marveled at how colorful and modern the town seemed and how friendly its inhabitants were. At the Danube, the marchers found a boat floating on the boundary between Austria and Czechoslovakia, with a loudspeaker connecting them with fellow citizens who had gathered on the other side. From the Austrian side, the VPN spokesman Ján Budaj delivered a speech culminating in the words "Hello Europe!" whereupon the previously exiled folk musician Karel Kryl, from the boat, led people on both sides of the river in singing the Czech and Slovak national anthems. Canoeists with Czechoslovak flags paddled in the stream, while beneath the castle people tore down the barbed wire marking the border. Some of the wire was ferried to the Austrian side, where the artist Daniel Brunovský fashioned

[115] "Řetěz lidských rukou" (BV: sbírka fotografie, inv. č. 5878, photo 16).
[116] Nový život (České Budějovice), 1 December 1989, p. 4.
[117] "Během velice krátké doby se v Brně spojil řetěz . . ." (ÚSD: archiv KC OF, box 152).
[118] Petr Koffer, "Za co všechno může být člověk uvězněn . . . ," Přetlak, no. 5 (1 December 1989), p. 7.

it into a colossal sculpture shaped like a heart, around which the crowd erected a mound of stones and lighted candles.[119] A symbol of separation became a symbol of love and communion, and there are still people who keep pieces of the barbed wire they cut on that day—totemic reminders of the "atmosphere," which serve to preserve the transcendent emotions of the moment.[120] While this expedition was less spontaneous than the human chain to Cibulka's prison, it still featured the essential element of collectively setting out on a journey to achieve a reordering of the social environment. Citizens set out with the goal of repossessing space (the previously closed-off border region) and changing the character of the border (physically dismantling the barbed wire, walking across the border to show that it was now just an imaginary line that could easily be crossed). They reclaimed the border region as part of their world.

Another expedition to connect people across space and "to speed up the revolutionary process" was the Train of the Gentle Revolution, which ran from Bratislava to Košice on 6 December.[121] It was inspired by the "magnificent rides" (spanilé jízdy) that students in Prague had begun in the week preceding the General Strike.[122] Thus named in reference to Hussite military excursions of the fifteenth century, the magnificent rides were described as student "missions" to villages and workplaces in the provinces.[123] The religious metaphors were apt, for once "magnificent riders" managed to break through a factory's defenses (doorkeepers and, in some cases, the Party's own armed force—the People's Militia), workers would assemble to listen to the students, as to the traveling preachers of Hussite times.[124] Though the magnificent rides first set out from Prague, students in other university towns immediately adopted the method (which they continued to employ into the spring of 1990). The Train of the Gentle Revolution, however, was to be the most magnificent of magnificent rides.

Though some Nitra students joined in, the Train of the Gentle Revolution was the initiative of Bratislava students, in cooperation with VPN in Czechoslovak Railways, "to connect all of Slovakia."[125] The organizers specifically wanted to reach out

[119] Martin Bútora and Ladislav Snopko, "Hello Europe," trans. Helena Le Sage, in Bratislava Symposium I: Ethics and Politics/Art against Totality, ed. Maria Štefánková and Marta Zisperová (Bratislava: Slovak National Gallery, 1990), pp. 93–95. See also Róbert Lifka, "Hainburg—prvý krok do sveta," Trenčianska verejnosť, no. 1 (December 1989), p. 4.

[120] Peter Zajac, conversation with author, April 2004.

[121] Juraj Johanides and Pavol Korec, Vlak nežnej revolúcie, broadcast as part of Televízny klub mladých, Slovenská televízia, 8 December 1989; V. Knupp, "Vlak nežnej revolúcie," Smer, 7 December 1989, p. 2; Spišské hlasy, 13 December 1989, p. 1; Zora Východu, 13 December 1989, pp. 1–3; Cieľ, 14 December 1989, p. 3; Poddukelské noviny, 14 December 1989, p. 2.

[122] "Vlak nežnej revolúcie," Zmena, no. 11 (6 December 1989), p. 1.

[123] Marika Doležalová, "Mise proti strachu?" Rovnost, 8 December 1989, p. 1.

[124] "Prohlášení občanského fóra s.p. Státní statek Trutnov—závod služeb ze dne 6.12.1989" (TU: fond "KC OF Trutnov," box 1, folder "Kopie různých prohlášení").

[125] Johanides and Korec, Vlak nežnej revolúcie.

to geographically removed countrymen, who they believed were not as engaged as citizens in the Slovak capital. (This perspective later proved to be controversial, with citizens in Košice especially citing the train as yet another example of Bratislava's ignorance about the rest of Slovakia, but at the time no one seems to have argued the point.)[126] In the fifteen towns where the train stopped, students, VPN activists, and actors distributed flyers, bulletins, and posters, while townspeople gave them apples, oranges, and flowers in exchange (one elderly man tried to offer students a mug of beer, but they refused—this was an abstinent revolution).[127] A witness in Poprad recalled that the train, "with its message of determination and faith that the students' sacrifice had not been in vain," enhanced her feelings of belonging to a national community and that many were in tears when the train departed.[128] At its final destination, Košice, the train's passengers became guests of honor at a packed assembly on the town square.[129] The Bratislava undertaking inspired students and civic initiatives in Banská Bystrica and Brno to organize their own trains on 8 and 13 December.[130]

One of the most creative outpourings of the energy produced by this intensified social interaction was the happening, an occasion described as occurring when "a group of people begin something and the rest spontaneously join in."[131] The Palacký University student Milan Hanuš recalls one such event:

I froze the moment I entered the square. I heard a voice distorted by a loud-speaker, icily reciting the caustic sentence: "Citizens disperse! This assembly has not been approved by the national committee [an organ of local govern-ment]." Only after a moment did I realize that a theater full of symbols was being played out before my eyes. I watched how people stripped themselves of the "bandages of the past and of fear" and then lit candles around piles of these bandages.[132]

The important elements of a happening were (1) a gathering of people, (2) ma-nipulation of symbols, usually in a theatrical and often humorous manner, and

---

[126] O. R. Halaga, "Porozumením k stabilite," *Akcia*, no. 9 (15 June 1990), p. 3. It is worth noting that many of the Bratislavans aboard the train had seldom or never been so far east before; see Johanides and Korec, *Vlak nežnej revolúcie.*

[127] Civic initiatives in Slovakia emphasized in their flyers that "alcohol and coarseness are against us." See, for example, "Vyhlásenie martinského výboru občianskej iniciatívy Verejnosť proti násiliu" (BB: Zbierka písomností získaných od študentov Pedagogickej fakulty v Banskej Bystrici, 1989–1990).

[128] *Podtatranské noviny*, 14 December 1989, p. 1.

[129] Zuzana Kostelníková, collage of archival footage from East Slovakia in 1989, broadcast as part of *Regionálny denník*, Slovenská televízia, 17 November 2004.

[130] "Vlak nežnej revolúcie," *Smer*, 9 December 1989, p. 1; *Přetlak*, no. 12 (9 December 1989), p. 9; *Rovnost*, 14 December 1989, p. 1.

[131] Tomáš Roreček, quoted in Hanuš, "Happening," p. 8.

[132] Hanuš, "Happening," p. 8.

(3) spontaneity. Sometimes the gatherings were completely spontaneous—people just assembled with a feeling that "something would happen."[133] More often there was some degree of organization, though the most successful happenings always incorporated on-the-spot improvisation; that was, after all, one of the reasons why people came.[134]

Though incorporating spontaneity, happenings were usually designed to effect some sort of transformation, whether within individuals or a community or on the external environment. The bandage happening in Olomouc was an example of the ontological variety. It took place in a square marked off within the upper town square and surrounded by onlookers on three sides. Into this enclosure a group of students ran, only to find themselves "trapped," and soon to be "beaten" by "forces of public order." The "massacred" students were then taken away from the scene, returning shortly thereafter in bandages. While a choir on the fourth side of the enclosure sang spirituals, the students proceeded to unwrap each other, and as Hanuš wrote they then made piles of bandages and lit candles around them.[135] The happening, obviously, was an allegory of the process by which the revolutionary community had come into being, culminating in a metaphor of convalescence. This metaphor, the recovery of health (purity) after a disease or injury, resonated with a metaphor about the revolution itself that was widespread in the discourse of the time. It was significant, moreover, that individuals could not unwrap themselves; they needed help from others, just as the revolutionary catharsis was possible only in reference to the community as a whole.

Late-December happenings in Brno and Uherské Hradiště were similarly intended "to break down the walls of urban estrangement and for at least a moment eliminate age barriers, to make us realize that we don't live in our country among strangers, but that we are one nation, one big family." The programs provided for an exchange of gifts and the singing of Christmas carols, emphasizing that "absolutely everyone must sing."[136] These were ritualistic attempts to maintain (or create) harmony between individuals and the community's new conception of itself as "one big family," where all members were to be "absolutely" equal and where all members would love one another freely.

Happenings that had external symbols of the community as their object were among the most popular and most humorous. Here is how the Palacký University student Lída Dušková described one such gathering, in Olomouc on 9 December:

---

[133] Marcela Čekalová, interview by author, Opava, 5 December 1996, tape recording.

[134] Speaking of a happening in Prague, one Vladimír Sraier commented, "It was nice, because it was spontaneous." Quoted in John Tagliabue, "Prague's Velvet Revolutionaries Recall John Lennon," *New York Times*, 9 December 1989.

[135] Langer and Zukal, *Happening*. Zdeněk Zukal, interview by author, Olomouc, 24 June 2009.

[136] "Rádi se mějme—dárky si dejme," folder "Letáky a plakáty z Uh. Hradiště" (UH: sbírky UH, box 7); "Rádi se mějme, dárky si dejme" (BZ: sbírka soudobé dokumentace, sign. F-8.04); and *Rovnost*, 19 December 1989, p. 3.

At three o'clock the students and people of Olomouc gathered on the Lower Town Square, ready for another splendid happening. Everyone fingered a couple of inflatable balloons in their pockets, and wondered in vain what they might be for. The crowd's curiosity was amplified as it began to drift toward the Theresian Gate [and down Lenin Boulevard to the Stalin-Lenin monument]. Only a few began to suspect. . . .

On the monument's pedestal two posters appeared. The first depicted a droopy-looking red star, limping forward on crutches. . . . [The second bid Stalin and Lenin] to fly away to warmer regions. Then the curious learned what the balloons were for. With all their strength people began to inflate their balloons and tie them to the ropes which marked off the whole paved area in front of the statues. . . .

The crowd sang, made merry and mostly wondered what would happen next. Student mountain climbers circled around the statues, entwining them with ropes. Suddenly, between the heads of Stalin and Lenin, there appeared a third face—a mountain climber's. He received a resounding acclamation, as did the friend who joined him. "Will they finally begin to remove this awful monument?" the crowd wondered. Soon they learned the truth. Slowly, ropes adorned with countless balloons began to mount the statues. . . . The crowd surrendered itself to buoyant mirth.

At length the statues were entirely covered with balloons . . . and the climbers descended amid vigorous applause. The line holding everything to the ground was cut, and someone shouted "Stalin, let go! It's no good to you now anyway!"

"10, 9, 8 . . . 2, 1, START!" In the eyes of all present the statues broke away from their pedestal and floated up, up—and away. The crowd waved them off . . . and considered that, from this perspective, everyone could at last delight in the statues' beauty and originality.[137]

On one level, Dušková's account was obviously false—the statues did not, of course, fly away (they were later sawed into pieces and removed to a museum warehouse). On another level, however, Dušková's account was profoundly true, for it reflected her and very likely also her peers' perception that, by their collective action, a monster had in fact disappeared from their midst.[138] The "gala shrouding" of a statue of Klement Gottwald (Czechoslovakia's first Communist president) in Opava on 22 December, organized by the Movement for Nonviolence, was a similar event.[139]

---

[137] Lída Dušková, "Další studentský hepening—opět skvělý," Přetlak, no. 13 (10 December 1989), pp. 3–4.

[138] For more on the balloon happening, see Petr Zatloukal, Gaudeamus (Olomouc: Univerzita Palackého, 1990), pp. 40–41, 70–71; and Langer and Zukal, Happening.

[139] "K slavnostnímu zahalování . . ." (ÚSD: archiv KC OF, volný soubor č. 3, folder "Listopad 89: prohlášení, letáky, výzvy").

Many of the red stars, slogans, portraits, and street signs that were taken down in northern Moravia and eastern Bohemia in 1989 were taken to the East Bohemian village of Bezpráví (which means "iniquity"), where on 9 December they were ceremoniously placed in an "Outdoor Museum of Totalitarianism."[140] In all these examples, collective action transformed a symbol of dictatorship and oppression into a symbol of popular power and solidarity. Placed in an incongruous new setting or startlingly redecorated, these old symbols now expressed the values of the revolutionary community. They represented what the community was rejecting—and by inverse logic what it was.

THE OTHER AS SYMBOL OF THE SELF

From collective action that transformed stone emblems of the old regime into symbols of the new community it was a short and natural step to treating human emblems in the same fashion. This step, however, brought participants into an uneasy relationship with the principle of nonviolence on which the community was founded, for it reestablished popular unity on the basis of unanimous exclusion—the standard sacrificial principle rather than its inversion. A few days before the General Strike, for example, students in Prague—who had been denied permission to address delegates to a collective farmers' convention in the Palace of Culture—responded by surrounding the building with a human chain. Just as on 17 November, a symbolic difference was created between those forming the circle and those inside, but now it was the revolutionary community that did the surrounding. Of course, no violence occurred, and we should not be too distressed by the complaints of some delegates that the symbolism was menacing, but nonetheless this incident marked a new departure in the manner by which the revolutionary community expanded its symbolic system.[141]

The human chain in Brno to release Petr Cibulka from prison was an example of the people setting out to enforce their sense of justice. A similar event took place in Bratislava at the end of December, but this time the impulse was one of accusation rather than liberation. At least since the General Strike, popular discourse in Bratislava had made much of Vasil Biľak—a member of the Central Committee who had invited the Warsaw Pact to invade Czechoslovakia in 1968—and particularly his villa. Humorists noted how ironic it was that a self-styled representative of the working class could afford such luxurious accommodations, and it eventually came out that he had bought the place from the state at a nominal price.[142] Czechoslovakia's general procurator had announced on 12 December that Biľak could

[140] Jiří Křečan, "'Jakeš na hrad!' aneb Pokládání základního kamene skanzenu totality v obci Bezpráví," *Přetlak*, no. 14 (11 December 1989), p. 2.

[141] "Po sjezdu družstevních rolníků," *Českolipský nástup*, 7 December 1989, p. 3.

[142] HM: Zbierka plagátov, box "Plagáty: 1989 a ďalej s číslom," poster no. 33583; *Pravda* (Bratislava), 12 December 1989; "Keby šlo len o jedného . . . ," *Smer*, 28 December 1989, p. 5.

not be held accountable for his actions in 1968 because the twenty-year statute of limitations had passed. The procurator added, however, that the public could itself become a court, albeit without power to punish.[143] Posters accordingly appeared in Bratislava that boldly asked, "Do you want to learn the truth about 1968? Let's ask VASIL BIĽAK in person. Meeting on Thursday, Dec. 21 at 16:00 on Peace Square, whence we'll repair to Biľak's villa and pose him a few questions." The invitation caused some alarm, provoking discussions in the press and inspiring one passerby to write on one of the posters, "Don't do it!!! Let him answer these questions before a court!!! You could be misused by the secret police!!!"[144] Nevertheless, at the appointed time, six hundred people of all ages, carrying banners that expressed dissatisfaction with Biľak's politics while in office, set out from the square on foot to his mansion on Timravina Street. The crowd chanted slogans over the fence for a few minutes, and Biľak came out. Following a short rumpus, a student took the initiative to moderate the discussion, in which the assembled citizens asked Biľak about his property and that of other leading functionaries, about his involvement in the Warsaw Pact invasion, and about his role on 17 November and in subsequent developments. Biľak denied any wrongdoing but agreed to meet with the public again. Despite the fear that the confrontation would turn violent, there were only a few insulting outcries, and for the most part the meeting had a peaceful character. The police standing by did not have to intervene.[145]

Students in Olomouc seem to have vied with colleagues in Bratislava for the distinction of inventing the most colorful festivals. On 8 December they convoked a happening that would find imitators in Gottwaldov, Hradec Králové, and Prešov (at least).[146] Inspired by the music of Pink Floyd, students and citizens of Olomouc gathered to erect a wall of cardboard boxes between themselves (the people) and the headquarters of the district Communist Party: "the wall between us." People wrote slogans such as "Boxes of the world, unite" and "Let's vote for snowmen—they know when to leave" on the boxes, and passing automobiles were invited to honk if the scene pleased them.[147] Again the idea of enclosure was at work, the people claiming power over a public site by surrounding it, but in this case they were not making the site their own; instead they were "quarantining" the "carcinogenic structure of the Party." This happening made the unity of the people manifest by their opposition to representatives of danger. As a wall of cardboard boxes, of course, it was only a symbolic barrier that could theoretically be breached if those inside chose to

[143] Jiří Teryngel, "Pred súd verejnosti," *Pravda*, 20 December 1989, p. 4.
[144] HM: Zbierka plagátov, box "Plagáty: 1989 a ďalej s číslom," poster no. 33623.
[145] Peter Ondera, "Prekvapenie pre obe strany," *Pravda*, 22 December 1989, p. 2.
[146] "Studenti se postavili před budovou OV KSČ v Gottwaldově," 11 December 1989 (ZL: Sbírka plakátů, box "17. listopad—29. prosinec 1989 Zlín"); *Nové Hradecko*, 19 December 1989, p. 1; *Prešovské noviny*, 19 December 1989, p. 1.
[147] *Přetlak*, no. 12 (9 December 1989), pp. 1–4; Langer and Zukal, *Happening*.

come out and join the people. It was, however, only natural that some should think to draw gallows on the wall, since surrounding and isolating (a representation of) danger is merely a step away from expelling (the representation of) danger.[148]

Students intervened in this case to stop the "unknown young people" from decorating the wall with gallows, and they kept a permanent watch on the structure for the more than two weeks of its existence to ensure that no similar attempts were made.[149] In this instance, as in countless others, students served as the "National Guard" of the Gentle Revolution, endeavoring—as had their predecessors two hundred years previously—to maintain order and prevent acts of violence on the part of the revolutionary populace. As we shall see, however, it was not always clear even to them where the boundary between violence and nonviolence lay, since violence—real or symbolic—is capable not just of disrupting order but of creating it. The violence that unites can cast out the violence that divides. Many of the symbolic forms of political practice that the revolution engendered reached back to this time-honored, ritualistic method of restoring order or creating a new order by collectively surrounding and expelling a real or perceived cause of disorder. They always stopped short of employing actual violence, but the natural impulse still revealed itself symbolically. This impulse, moreover, was frequently not even perceived as coexisting uneasily with the revolutionary prohibition of violence, for from within a mythological system, ritual violence is experienced not as violence but as purification.

Purity and Danger

All the symbols and symbolic gestures discussed above—and many more—added up to a new system of symbols that revolutionary citizens collectively generated in November and December 1989. What participants were essentially deciding through all these forms of collective interaction was which ideas, objects, structures, and people accurately represented their community and which did not. As the anthropologist Mary Douglas points out, cultural systems involve large-scale schemes of categorization. That which a given culture's scheme is able to make sense of, which fits within its structures and ultimately harmonizes with its ideas about itself, is experienced as "clean," "pure," or "orderly." That which the scheme cannot comprehend or which threatens its ordered system is "dirty," "corrupt," or "dangerous."[150] Since no cognitive scheme is capable of apprehending all truths without

[148] "Dementi," Přetlak, no. 24 (22 December 1989), p. 5.
[149] Ibid.
[150] Mary Douglas, Purity and Danger: An Analysis of the Concepts of Pollution and Taboo (New York: Praeger, 1966), p. 162; and Implicit Meanings: Essays in Anthropology (London: Routledge & Paul, 1975), pp. xi–xxi.

itself being inconsistent, the "dangerous" perpetually exists alongside the "pure," though it may not always be noticed.[151] This is because the categories according to which people think determine to a large extent what they are capable of thinking and even what they are likely to perceive.

The distinction between reality and perception mediated by a categorizational scheme is exquisitely illustrated in the way many Czechoslovak citizens in 1989 interpreted "the West." While Czechoslovakia in 1989 was perceived as a land of "deep moral, spiritual, ecological, social, economic, and political crisis," the West (or its constituent parts) was imagined to be a place of wholeness.[152] "We belong among the developing countries of Europe, to the Third World," proclaimed a group of Olomoucers. "In the morning we go to work, after work we grub for goods, at home there is cooking, washing, minimal time for children . . . , in the evening television and then sleep. It's comparable to the lives of animals." In the West, by contrast, "without any propaganda, all life is oriented so that people may be happy and live their lives satisfactorily."[153] The journalist Michal Horáček argued that only by studying in the West, and especially in the United States, would his countrymen "learn how to take care of themselves." He urged striking students to begin thinking about who would take up the American scholarships he was sure were forthcoming, claiming that

> those Americans are really awfully nice people; every one of them is giving to some hungry child in India—it's completely normal. Here if we try to donate five crowns to Nicaragua people go crazy. But with them it's completely normal. No one advertises anything anywhere; they just send the money. And this is such a pure idea.[154]

These examples illustrate that much of what was believed about the West in 1989 was not based on empirical fact. Rather, the West served as a screen onto which Czechs and Slovaks could project their own images of a pure, ideal society.

Perceptions of danger tended not to be quite so exaggerated, since the examples were more within the realm of experience, but we can still see an inclination to portray dangers as monstrous or even diabolical, rhetorically reflecting the fact that they did not fit categories now considered proper. Though at the beginning the revolutionary movement was explicitly directed against violence (in all its forms) rather

---

[151] Douglas Hofstadter, *Gödel, Escher, Bach: An Eternal Golden Braid* (New York: Basic Books, 1989), pp. 71, 86.

[152] "Co chceme: Programové zásady Občanského fóra," Prague, 26 November 1989, in Otáhal and Sládek, *Deset pražských dnů*, p. 503; reprinted in Jiří Suk, ed., *Občanské fórum: Listopad-prosinec 1989*, vol. 2, *Dokumenty* (Brno: Doplněk, 1998), p. 28.

[153] "Ředitelce základní školy v Kvasicích," 28 November 1989, in *Přetlak*, 2 December 1989, pp. 5–6.

[154] Quoted in Tomáš Drábek, "Amerika pláče," *EM '89*, no. 9, p. 4.

than against the Communist regime as such, as momentum continued through November and December the mobilized populace increasingly reaffirmed its identification of itself as a wholesome and pure category of existence by reference to the regime. "A hydra with a thousand heads and a thousand tentacles," students called it.[155] Even devils were said to distance themselves from the "hellish politics" of the KSČ.[156] The regime was held to have led society into a state of dedifferentiation, reducing Czechoslovakia from its interwar status as a great economic power to the level of "unmodern" Third World countries, to have fostered widespread corruption, and to have no regard for human life—as 17 November made abundantly clear.[157]

It was not long before not just the regime as such but particular human cogs in its machinery came to be seen as dangers as well. Among them were members of the *nomenklatura* who still occupied most key positions in regional and local administrative structures. Turncoats were a particular strain of this impurity. "Not long ago they stood for the regime, [but] now they try to turn around and join Civic Forum," warned a train dispatcher in Olomouc.[158] A rural elementary school teacher complained of a district methodologist, who before the revolution had "zealously served her [Communist Party] superiors" but who now, "afraid for her position, is tirelessly active in Civic Forum." "Beware of such people," the teacher wrote. "They damage the beautiful and clean ideas of the students' revolution and that of all honest people who fight for a democratic society and a better future for us all."[159] At all levels of administration there were people "who for twenty years insisted one thing and overnight learned to say something else," and there was great fear that they might, like wolves in sheep's clothing, manipulate the upcoming free elections in order to reverse the nation's progress.[160]

A more sinister danger was seen in the still-functional state security agency. In a vein typical of many outcries, the student Tomáš Zábranský wrote,

> The past few weeks have called forth in all of us a new, hitherto unknown feeling. A feeling of patriotism, serendipity, pride. A feeling of peculiar pressure in our eyes while singing hymns. A feeling of elation from newly acquired, surprising freedom. Only, this freedom is for now just a temporary state.

---

[155] "Stávka nekončí," *Přetlak*, special issue [30 November 1989], p. 1.

[156] *Přetlak*, no. 12 (9 December 1989), p. 8. Compare Pardubice's *Studentský list*, no. 15 (18 December 1989).

[157] See, for example, OF Olomouc, "Několik vět k Lidovým milicím," 30 November 1989 (PX: súčasná dokumentácia, folder "Nežná revolúcia—1989"); also available in OL and OV.

[158] "Co je v současné době pro Československou revoluci nejnebezpečnější?" *Přetlak*, no. 22 (19 December 1989), p. 2.

[159] P. Hanák, "Tak jak to vlastně myslí teď?" *Přetlak*, no. 22 (19 December 1989), p. 3.

[160] Jan Marek, "Politika kontra poesie," *Přetlak*, no. 26 (27 December 1989), p. 6.

Within us there have also awoken feelings of powerless anger and rage . . . mixed with fear. Fear of an enormous, thousand-headed hydra, defying all attempts at control. The existence of an apparatus which we all know about yet which no one knows how to define, an apparatus which is paradoxically even more dangerous because of its name, an apparatus which has precedents perhaps only in fascist police states or the cannibalistic regime of former President Marcos.[161]

Fear of the secret police intensified as the committee investigating the 17 November massacre continued its search for truth but met with a less-than-transparent response from state security. Fear increased as a result of what was discovered—but even more because of what remained secret.[162]

The question of how to respond to these threats was problematic, given the community's identification with nonviolence. "The road to the goal must be as clean as the goal itself," wrote the popular professor and soon-to-be new rector of Palacký University, Josef Jařab.[163] Some suggested that compromised functionaries should simply "feel the pressure" of public opinion and leave of their own accord.[164] Others proposed to ramp up the pressure by making matters public. Zábranský demanded that the activities of the secret police be mapped and their organizational structure exposed to public scrutiny.[165] His fellow student Tomáš Roreček argued that people should publicly declare their lack of confidence in incapable or discredited individuals by means of petitions or voting.[166] These approaches did not satisfy everyone, however, and some people called for more forceful measures.

One of the time-honored ways in which societies attempt to respond to danger, from primitive sacrifice to modern means of dealing with the homeless, is to expel it. If accomplished collectively, expulsion can intensify the sense of community among those who have united to remove the danger. It can also engender new symbols of community, possibly including the expelled representatives of danger or the instruments of their expulsion. It restores the integrity (purity) of the symbolic system and can even strengthen it. Though there were no public executions in the revolution of 1989, impulses in this direction did manifest themselves on the symbolic plane, both blatantly—as in the attempt to draw gallows on the wall of boxes in Olomouc—and more subtly, as in the many "funerals for totalitarianism" that took place throughout Czechoslovakia.[167] Rhetorically, students insisted

---

[161] Tomáš Zábranský, "Stát ve státě," *Přetlak*, no. 13 (10 December 1989), p. 1.

[162] See Václav Bartuška, *Polojasno: Pátrání po vinících 17. listopadu 1989* (Prague: Ex libris, 1990).

[163] Jařab, "Nedělní zamyšlení," p. 3.

[164] "Tisková beseda s Valtrem Komárkem," p. 2; "Hlasy horníků při setkání zástupců stávkových výborů OKR v sobotu 2. 12. na DOLE HLUBINA," *Přetlak*, no. 10 (6 December 1989), p. 6.

[165] Zábranský, "Stát ve státě," p. 1.

[166] Tomáš Roreček, "Samet bez trhlin!" *Přetlak*, no. 20 (17 December 1989), p. 5.

[167] In addition to the Olomouc example cited at the beginning of this chapter, see "S bolestí v srdci . . ." (DO: sbírka soudobé dokumentace, box "Soudobá dokumentace 1989–1991/Vzhledy 1990–1991");

that "it is necessary to draw a sword and cut off the heads of this hydra one by one."[168] When Nicolae Ceauşescu—who in the second half of December became for Czechs and Slovaks a symbol of Communist murderousness—was killed, students reported the news with the words "Dracula is dead," rhetorically condoning his execution by labeling him a monster.[169] Editors of the official Slovak youth newspaper went further, proclaiming, "What a beautiful day! The devil died on Christmas."[170]

Proposals to deal violently with the community's enemies were labeled "provocation," and provocateurs were presented as yet another threat to the community and its "clean" revolution. Students and spokespersons for the civic initiatives pressed instead for adoption of the other time-honored method of confronting danger: finding a way of incorporating it within society's categorizational scheme by either redeeming it or reconfiguring the scheme itself. Václav Havel, for example, insisted that "there must not be a hunt for Communists. There must be justice but not revenge." As an example of the "dignity" that Havel said the revolution should maintain, he recalled the manifestation on Letná, where "OF invited two of the riot police [who had attacked the crowd on 17 November] onto the platform. It happened that three quarters of a million people, together with Václav Malý, prayed the 'Our Father' that these people might be forgiven. This is a model situation, which should be an example for all others."[171] A similar event took place in Bratislava, where Milan Kňažko brought onto the platform on SNP Square two women—the mother and sister of two young people killed by occupying Soviet forces in 1968. He announced that these women had decided to forgive the soldiers who, on the orders of others, perpetrated this crime, and he invited the entire assembly to join them by repeating in unison the words "All together."[172] In the first example, the symbols of danger were "purified"; in the latter, the means of perception were altered so that the symbols no longer appeared dangerous. It is worth noting, though, that in neither case were the voices in the crowds quite as unanimous as the celebrants of these rites may have desired.[173]

The distinction between justice and revenge is not always clear, and the attempt to separate them into strictly demarcated categories in Czechoslovakia led to considerable confusion. On 15 December, for example, the student bulletin in Olomouc

---

"S hlubokým pocitem štěstí . . ." (BZ: sbírka soudobé dokumentace, sign. F-8.04); "S hlubokým zármutkem v srdci . . ." (OV: sbírka soudobé dokumentace, box "Revoluce 1989: Materiály 1989–90").

[168] "Stávka nekončí."

[169] Přetlak, no. 26 (27 December 1989), p. 1.

[170] Smena (Bratislava), 27 December 1989, p. 1.

[171] Quoted in "Volební program V. Havla," Přetlak, no. 26 (27 December 1989), p. 7.

[172] Verejnosť proti násiliu and Študentské hnutie, Nežná revolúcia (Bratislava: Opus, 1990), sound recording, side 4.

[173] It was not only elites in the civic associations who orchestrated rites of forgiveness. In Bratislava, students made a human chain to Devín Castle in order there to release doves over the Danube as a symbol of forgiveness to the armies that had invaded Czechoslovakia in 1968. Smena, 7 December 1989, p. 1.

carried a cartoon of a tiny man, representing the Communist Party, on the verge of being squashed by the giant foot of Civic Forum.[174] Three Civic Forum members reacted with vigorous opposition to the cartoon, saying that it reminded them of similar drawings they had seen under fascism or in the days of Stalinist show trials. "Civic Forum and all decent people," they wrote, "profess as their creed humanistic ideals and nonviolence, and thus they don't want to nor will they humiliate anyone." They appealed to the students to "be like you were at the beginning, with clean hearts and clean hands, with clean thoughts."[175] The students responded with an apology, explaining that they did not intend to call for the oppression of Communists and that they would not under any circumstances renounce the principles of nonviolence and tolerance.[176] It would not, however, be the last time that such an issue came up.

The tension between a prohibition against violence and collective practices that ran up against it persisted into the 1990s, with citizens increasingly asking whether the revolution had not, after all, been "too velvety." To be successful in maintaining the "purity" of the symbolic system and the social reality that was to mirror it, nonviolent methods required enormous energy and constant vigilance. Such levels of social energy and attention were maintained throughout December 1989 and into the new year, but they would increasingly wane as people turned their attention to private matters. In addition, the fact that the contradiction between prohibition and ritual was *perceived* itself destabilized the symbolic system and people's corresponding ability to determine the meaning of concrete situations. In all cultures, religious rites or the judicial rituals derived from them routinely require members of a community to use violence that is otherwise prohibited, but normally the categorizational scheme filters perception so well that the contradiction is not seen. In the Gentle Revolution, however, it was seen, and this was one of the factors that, in 1990, would cause the demise of consensus about the future of the aging new community.

For the moment, though, the symbolic revolution had achieved much. Building on the sense of nonsacrificial community that developed in response to the violence of 17 November, a new symbolic system had come into being with the community itself as its sacred center. This system of signs and symbols enabled citizens to communicate with one another in new ways and to make sense of the world in ways that had scarcely been imaginable before. As the collective effervescence of 1989 continued, citizens steadily enlarged these "webs of meaning," representing themselves in ever more numerous symbolic forms and articulating in ever-greater detail the defining ideals of their community. With this foundation to draw upon,

---

[174] *Přetlak*, no. 18 (15 December 1989), p. 7.

[175] Milan Hejtmánek, Jaroslav Jezdinský, and Věra Jezdinská, "K jedné botě," *Přetlak*, no. 21 (18 December 1989), p. 2.

[176] "K botě," *Přetlak*, no. 21 (18 December 1989), p. 2.

they were equipped to turn to the next task: representing the community in human institutions.

Though the repertoire of signifying practices that Czechoslovak citizens adopted in 1989 resembled in some respects the forms of collective claim-making used in contentious politics, the context in which the Czechoslovak practices were set—and hence the meaning they produced—transcended the framework of contentious politics. Citizens participating in the assemblies and happenings of the revolution or contributing to the flood of discourse it unleashed did not merely challenge the legitimacy of an existing regime; they established the sacred foundations from which the legitimacy of a new regime (or "new society," as they put it) could be derived.[177]

To borrow from the language of formal mathematics, the sacred corresponds to the unprovable axioms that serve as the foundation of a symbolic system, while legitimacy can be understood as a property of theorems within that system. Legitimacy is thus a form of validation within a symbolic system held in place by something considered sacred. A legitimate theorem is one that is sound and valid within the framework of the system as a whole. A "legitimate axiom," however, is an oxymoron, since axioms ultimately refer to nothing beyond themselves; we can believe in their truthfulness, but we cannot prove it.

Though the concepts of legitimacy and sacrality are distinct, they are nonetheless complementary. As Edward Tiryakian has observed, Weberian conceptions of legitimacy can be contained within a Durkheimian understanding of the sacred. Tiryakian points out that both Weberian "charisma" and Durkheimian "collective effervescence" require an assembled community, but whereas for Weber this "charismatic community" is in the background, for Durkheim the assembly is in the foreground.[178] The relationship between legitimacy and the sacred is parallel to the relationship between a charismatic figure and the community he or she represents. The Durkheimian assembly, via collective effervescence, is the generator of sacrality, which can then be represented by a Weberian charismatic figure or one of the derivative matrices of legitimacy.[179]

Political scientists have argued that the "collapse" of Communist regimes in central and eastern Europe was catalyzed by these regimes' attempts to switch to the legal-rational mode of legitimation. Ken Jowitt argues that Communist parties possessed a kind of corporate charisma from their inception and that a gradual switch

---

[177] The trope of a new society will be examined in greater detail in chapter 3.

[178] Edward Tiryakian, "Collective Effervescence, Social Change and Charisma: Durkheim, Weber and 1989," *International Sociology* 10, no. 3 (September 1995): 274.

[179] The anthropologist Peter Worsley notes that by leaving the community in the background, Weber confuses the charismatic figure with the source of charisma. Worsley demonstrates that this source can only be the community itself, for which the charismatic figure is a representation. Worsley, *The Trumpet Shall Sound: A Study of "Cargo Cults" in Melanesia*, 2nd ed. (London: MacGibbon & Kee, 1968), pp. 266–72.

to legal-rational legitimacy undermined the regimes' raison d'être.[180] Leslie Holmes maintains that Communist power is inherently coercive—that is, not dependent on legitimacy—and that any attempt to switch to the legal-rational mode of domination results in contradictions that must inevitably lead to the regime's collapse.[181] Both agree, though, that the net result in central and eastern Europe was an estrangement between leaders and staffs, which, when coupled with apparent failure to legitimate the system to the "masses," resulted in a legitimation crisis.

While this framework may explain why Communist authority collapsed so easily in 1989, it does not explain the other central dynamic of that momentous year: the spontaneous mobilization of millions of European citizens. It does not explain why they went out onto streets and squares, and it does not explain the significance of their collective behavior once they did. The argument advanced here is that, in Czechoslovakia at least, citizens mobilized in order to participate in the creation of a new world. The weakness that made it possible for Communist authority to crumble certainly had long-term structural causes, and Gorbachev's noninterventionist policy vis-à-vis the satellites obviously created opportunities for radical change (which, indeed, the "staffs" were already exploiting).[182] Rather than passively waiting for change to take place from above, however, citizens took responsibility for their and their children's futures; in Klíma's words, they mobilized to prepare a society for themselves. It was citizens, in their vast numbers, who gave the final push that drove Communist power holders to the negotiating tables. These citizens were not interested merely in elite resignations, moreover; their goal was the creation of a new society.

This process of creation began, in Czechoslovakia, with the "birth" of a new sense of community—a sense of community that was experienced as sacred, such that it became the touchstone to which subsequent representations referred. The signifiers we have considered in this chapter—as well as the abstract ideals we shall examine in the next—were all representations of the new sense of community that came into being with the "big bang" of 17 November, representations that Czechs and Slovaks collectively articulated during the collective effervescence of 1989. Positivists may ask whether a new community really came into existence in Czechoslovakia, but what matters is that Czechs and Slovaks demonstrably believed it did and acted accordingly. In later chapters we will discuss how the revolution inaugurated a "constitutional moment" in which all social, political, and economic institutions—from the local gardening club to the federal state—were open to reconstitution. This development was a natural extension of the collective effervescence of 1989,

---

[180] Kenneth Jowitt, *New World Disorder: The Leninist Extinction* (Berkeley: University of California Press, 1992).

[181] Leslie Holmes, *The End of Communist Power: Anti-Corruption Campaigns and Legitimation Crisis* (New York: Oxford University Press, 1993).

[182] Pullmann, *Konec experimentu.*

and citizens insisted on taking part in order to ensure that the institutions devised accurately represented the sacred sense of community in which they had become so passionately invested. They believed, with Komárek, that the future of their country had to be built on a "holy emotion."

Interpreting the revolution as the sacralization of a new sense of community provides the most effective means of analyzing systematically the *experience* of the revolution, as citizens of Czechoslovakia themselves described it. In this interpretation, the "atmosphere" to which witnesses to this day still raptly refer becomes more than pretty fluff around the edges of supposedly more real social processes; generation of the "atmosphere" becomes itself the crucial social process on which all others depend.

Chapter 3

The Ideals of November

"It is necessary to see what we have written through its sense and not its words and sentences. It should not be dogma."[1]

The collective effervescence discussed in the previous chapter made it possible to believe that a new society was at hand in Czechoslovakia, and citizens of all political persuasions hailed its advent. The revolution, according to a group of Bratislava factory workers, inaugurated a "new epoch," with "new thoughts" and "new feelings."[2] Shipyard workers in the Slovak capital expected "such a development in our country that will bring about a new, socially just society."[3] Students in November and December were said to be "working like bees at the construction of a new society," and by mid-December even Communists acknowledged that a "new society" was in the making.[4] According to hopeful students in Prešov, "The most beautiful world can be ours!"[5]

What were the contours of this heralded new society? What were "the ideals of November"? In the Czech and Slovak republics today these ideals are much invoked, especially on every anniversary of 17 November. Politicians, both in and out of power, make claims about the principles that united Czecholovak citizens

---

[1] Občianska iniciatíva SPŠS Považská Bystrica, "Prevolanie k spoluobčanom!" 4 December 1989 (PX: fond G1, box 1, folder "Gymnázium").

[2] "Pracovníčky Priemyselného kombinátu, š.p. Bratislava str. 460 'Písmomaliarstvo' (Brigáda BSP) týmto vyjadrujeme účasť . . ." (SNA: Archív VPN, fond. odd. I).

[3] "Vyhlásenie pracovníkov závodu Lodenica," Bratislava, 27 November 1989 (SNA: Archív VPN, fond. odd. I).

[4] See, for example, "Nová spoločnosť a naša strana," *Pravda* (Bratislava), 16 December 1989, p. 3.

[5] Daniela Pomajdíková, "Reťaz nádeje je šťastie," *Premeny*, no. 3 (19 January 1990), p. 8.

in 1989, and needless to say these claims—historical interpretations—serve to legitimate potential courses of action or acceptance of the status quo. Students, both those presently matriculated and veterans of 1989, hold commemorations promulgating their interpretations of the revolution's ideals, usually implying protest against current governments or their policies. Elements of the lunatic fringe try to get their say in as well. General agreement about what the "ideals of November" were, however, remains elusive, there being no single document—like the American Declaration of Independence or the French Declaration of the Rights of Man and the Citizen—that might credibly be claimed to encapsulate them. Instead, people tend to extrapolate from their own personal experience, assuming that what they experienced in their particular locality and milieu was typical of the revolution as a whole. There is no reason to assume, however, that the ideas that motivated a salesclerk in Michalovce to take to the streets were the same as those that motivated a dissident intellectual in Prague. Yet insofar as our aim is to understand the ideals of what was an undeniably popular revolution, both perspectives are equally relevant.

The approach that most Western analysts have adopted in discussing the ideas and ideals of 1989 is similarly unsatisfying. In general, this approach has taken the prerevolutionary writings of dissident intellectuals (mostly in Prague) as representative of the ideas of the revolution, perhaps in conjunction with personal experience (usually in Prague) at some point between 1989 and 1992.[6] As has already been suggested, however, personal experience in a given locality is not a reliable guide to understanding revolutionary mentalities as a whole, and it is worth adding that popular mentalities even a few weeks after the strikes ended on 3 January were not what they had been while the strikes were ongoing.[7] There are good reasons, moreover, why dissident or other ideas promulgated before the revolution should not be taken as a congruent image of thinking *in* the revolution. The events following 17 November created a new social context for the circulation, articulation, and discussion of ideas. Texts that had previously been banned now became accessible to a wide audience. Mass media began to report more truthfully, and new platforms emerged for the written and oral exchange of ideas, primarily at the local level. Most important, revolutionary developments stimulated a greater passion for the discussion of public affairs on the part of the general populace than there had been since 1968 (or has been since) and caused fears of open questioning and honest expression of opinion to fall by the wayside. In other words, collective effervescence *preceded* the collective formulation of any

[6] See, for example, Krishan Kumar, *1989: Revolutionary Ideas and Ideals* (Minneapolis: University of Minnesota Press, 2001).
[7] Though students in Prague ended their strike on 30 December, others took up to four days to follow suit. Milan Hanuš, "Jak jsme (ne)stávkovali," *Přetlak*, no. 35 (8–14 February 1990), p. 8.

corpus of ideas that could be taken as "the ideals of November." Moreover, the magnitude and force of change after 17 November compelled people to reprioritize and in many cases reconsider ideas they had held previously, as well as to confront new ones. Even Václav Havel, who for years had preached a lifestyle of "living in truth," was forced by the revolution to consider whether in some instances it might not be better to lie.[8] We cannot simply take a group of ideas that existed before the revolution and assume that these were the ideals of 1989. We must look for these ideals in the discourse of the revolution itself.

One of the names suggested for the Czechoslovak revolution of 1989 was "conversational revolution."[9] The revolution set off an avalanche of discourse, taking place on street corners and in theaters, in small groups that spontaneously formed on the squares before and after *mítings*, and among those gathered in front of walls and shop windows to read the flyers posted there. Much of the talk was concerned with outlining the contours of "the new society." At the beginning of December, OF-VPN Banská Bystrica explicitly posed the question, "What should the new society look like?"

> This question, the answer to which is not simple, is being sought in discussions conducted on television, on the radio, in newspapers, and in cultural houses. Pluralist, tolerant, brighter, more universal, more effective, more blissful, more human, constantly adapting to new circumstances. This is why the Civic Forum of the movement Public against Violence is a platform for open dialogue without regard to citizens' political, social, national, and religious affiliation. In its programmatic declaration it emphasizes the nonviolent solution of existing problems with the help of cultivated dialogue.[10]

In other words, while certain general characteristics of "the new society" were clear, the details could be worked out only through conversation.

The revolution never found time to organize and fully think through its ideas and their implications. The pace of events frequently exceeded the capacity of the human mind to keep up. Nonetheless, everything was laid out in the discourse of 1989, and it is possible for historians to go back and consolidate it. While no single text exists as a reliable statement of revolutionary ideals, several thousand texts do. Scattered in dozens of archives and libraries across the Czech and Slovak republics and in countless private attics and basements, the flyers, proclamations, manifestos, and bulletins of November and December 1989 explain the motivations,

---

[8] Jiří Suk, "K prosazení kandidatury Václava Havla na úřad prezidenta v prosinci 1989: Dokumenty a svědectví," *Soudobé dějiny* 6, no. 2–3 (1999): 355–56.

[9] "O dialogu demokratickém," *Stráž lidu* (Olomouc), 19 December 1989, p. 5.

[10] Zdeno Kosáč, "Občianske fórum hnutia Verejnosť proti násiliu . . . ," Banská Bystrica (BB: Materiály získané od hnutia Verejnosť proti násiliu v Banskej Bystrici, 1989, box 1).

beliefs, and hopes of the citizens of what was then Czechoslovakia in their own words. It was mostly students and the civic initiatives (OF and VPN) that wrote, typed, and circulated the flyers, though some other groups and individuals contributed as well. These documents provide succinct and clear explanations of their authors' aims and the principles they advocated. Flyers were so ubiquitous in 1989, and their contents so varied, that students in Olomouc and national committee deputies in Beroun, at least, held that if an opinion was not expressed in a flyer, it could be assumed not to exist.[11] Perhaps two thousand of these documents survive. In the run-up to the General Strike of 27 November, in its aftermath, and in the run-up to a second general strike (proposed for 11 December but then called off), collectives in workplaces throughout Czechoslovakia drafted proclamations, declarations, and manifestos listing their demands, explaining their reasons for going or not going on strike, and expressing their opinions on everything from the state of the factory canteen to Czechoslovak foreign policy. Collectives sent copies of these documents to striking students as well as to coordinating committees of OF and VPN in their regions or in the capitals. In Bratislava, at least, volunteers in the VPN coordinating committee counted signatures and determined that they had received proclamations endorsing revolutionary changes from a majority of the Slovak workforce; it may be assumed that the corpus of documents sent to Prague was similarly representative.[12] Perhaps ten thousand of these documents have survived. Bulletins, finally, were produced by striking students and civic initiatives throughout Czechoslovakia. Some were produced daily (especially in November and early December); others appeared weekly or sporadically. Unlike the flyers and proclamations, they continued to appear well into 1990 and even 1991 in some cases. While they reflected the opinions primarily of striking students and activists in the civic initiatives, they frequently (and especially in 1989) also provided a platform for citizens from the broader community to express themselves. Over a hundred different bulletins were produced, and over a thousand distinct issues survive. In addition to these documents, the records of many speeches have survived, either on tape or in the form of the speakers' notes, and they provide valuable additional evidence about the discussion of ideas in 1989. Newspapers, too, became increasingly accessible platforms for debate in late November and especially December 1989.

Needless to say, sifting through this amount of material is a daunting task, but it is not an impossible one. In order to gain an appreciation of what ideas in 1989 were truly popular, it is sufficient to read only a large sample of the documents to

---

[11] Studenti UP, "Kdo je krátkozraký," *Přetlak*, no. 7 (3 December 1989), p. 3; "Zápis z 16. plenárního zasedání Okresního národního výboru v Berouně, které se konalo ve středu 6. prosince 1989 . . ." (BE: fond "ONV Beroun," box "ONV Beroun II").

[12] Personal communication with Mária Mistríková, former archivist of the VPN coordinating committee in Bratislava, November 2006.

find that certain themes repeat themselves with predictable regularity and that ideas tend to come in clusters. By reading a majority of the documents, patterns in the presentation of ideas become apparent, as do hints of social and geographic diversity in the attachment to certain ideas. The conclusions presented below are based on such a reading of a majority of revolutionary flyers, proclamations, and bulletins, collected from most of the Czech and Slovak archives and libraries that hold them (including the largest collections in Prague and Bratislava).

This chapter identifies the ideals that Czechoslovak citizens recurrently emphasized in 1989, explains how citizens (sometimes variously) understood these ideas, and examines how ideas were related to one another in citizens' minds. In the course of this discussion it will become apparent that the revolution in Czechoslovakia was a remarkably idealistic one, and it will be argued that this idealism can be attributed directly to the intensity of collective effervescence in Czechoslovakia—an intensity that may have set it apart from other countries of Eastern Europe in 1989.[13] The chapter concludes with suggestions about the origins of the ideals of 1989 and considers the common assertion that there were no "new" ideas in 1989.

Quantity and Quality

Before we plunge into a close reading of the revolutionary texts, a brief quantitative analysis can orient us with regard to what the qualitative reading is likely to reveal. The set of documents that lend themselves most readily to quantitative study are those workplace proclamations that enumerate demands. It is possible to take a random sample of these lists and simply count how often particular types of demands appear. Since workplace proclamations were the most common revolutionary texts, and since citizens from all walks of life were their authors, such an analysis is likely to yield a fairly accurate representation of what ordinary citizens hoped the revolution would achieve.

Figure 1 shows the relative strength of various categories of citizens' demands in a random sample of one hundred demand lists produced across Czechoslovakia in November and December 1989.[14] These lists contain a total of 591 demands, falling

---

[13] While collective effervescence in East Germany seems to have been comparable in intensity to that in Czechoslovakia in 1989, it seems to have been significantly less intense in Poland and Hungary—part of the reason that Germans, Czechs, and Slovaks speak of "peaceful," "velvet," or "gentle" revolutions in 1989, while Poles and Hungarians with only a few singular exceptions do not. Romania remains a mysterious case, for while evidence of collective effervescence comparable to that of East Germany and Czechoslovkia exists for Timişoara and Bucharest, there has been very little systematic analysis of the popular experience of the revolution outside these two cities.

[14] Though random in the sense that the only principle of selection was to obtain an equal number of Czech and Slovak lists, the sample is not geometrically similar to the total set of lists produced in Czechoslovakia in November and December 1989. The Slovak lists are mostly from late November, while the Czech are mostly from the first half of December; Moravian lists, moreover, are underrepresented in the Czech

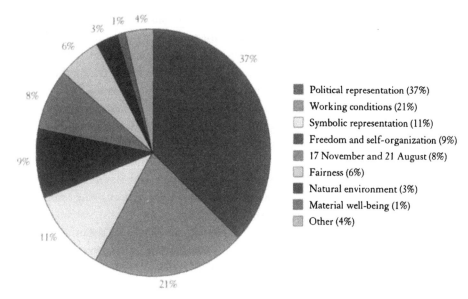

Figure 1. Relative emphasis in demand lists

into thirty-nine specific categories. To facilitate interpretation, these specific categories have been grouped into nine general categories.[15]

Some commentators have claimed that, for ordinary East Europeans, 1989 was
primarily about catching up with the West in terms of living standards—that the

sample. Consequently, it is not possible at this stage to provide more definitive conclusions on the basis of
quantitative analysis than the very general ones here presented. While a small number of the lists were
taken from district newspapers, most come from the archives of the coordinating centers of OF and VPN
in Prague and Bratislava (Moravian underrepresentation is due to the fact that Moravian collectives and
civic associations were more likely to send lists to Brno or Olomouc than to Prague). Within Bohemia and
Slovakia the sample is geographically representative.

[15] The general category "political representation" includes these specific categories: resignations (7.62%),
democracy in the public sphere (7.33%), political representation generally (6.93%), the Party's leading role
(5.37%), dialogue in the public sphere (3.55%), reforming the Party (1.83%), political pluralism (1.78%),
political accountability (1.41%), national rights and representation (0.51%), and the writing of a new constitution (0.37%). "Working conditions" includes eliminating the People's Militia (5.02%), banning the KSČ
from the workplace (4.49%), union representation (3.36%), de-ideologization of the workplace (2.91%),
workplace democracy (2.26%), personnel changes (1.10%), rehabilitation of workers fired because of their
stance in 1968 (0.85%), and other working conditions (0.76%). "Symbolic representation" includes access to
and truthfulness in the media (6.69%), symbols generally (removal of banners and red stars, name changes,
the wording of oaths, etc.) (3.53%), and free speech (presented more as a way of facilitating accurate representation of popular will than as a personal right) (0.93%). "Freedom and self-organization" includes
de-ideologization of education (3.27%), rights to free association or independence from association (1.61%),
rejecting the "administrative-directive system" (1.02%), political prisoners and untarnishing the reputation
of dissidents (1.02%), removal of KSČ influence on the army and police (0.85%), de-ideologization of social life generally (0.49%), religious freedom (0.37%), local control of affairs (0.25%), and other rights and
freedoms (0.48%). "17 November and 21 August" refer to demands for investigation of the Národní třída
massacre and punishment of its perpetrators (5.67%), as well as to similar demands regarding the Warsaw

motivations of ordinary citizens were, in short, materialistic.[16] The evidence from Czechoslovakia does not support this view. In the lists of demands that citizens drew up in November and December 1989, the most common concern was about the quality of political representation. Roughly 37 percent of the entries in these lists focus on some aspect of political representation. Another 62 percent deal with such nonmaterial concerns as human relations in the workplace, investigation of the 17 November massacre or reappraisal of 1968, ecology, and the de-ideologization of social life. Only about 1 percent can, without stretching the imagination, be identified as materialistic.[17] This does not mean, of course, that desire to share in the material prosperity of Western neighbors was absent from Czech and Slovak minds, but it does support the claim that—in November and December, at least—the revolution was primarily about human relations.

It would naturally be a mistake to rely exclusively on written lists of demands for an understanding of what ordinary Czechoslovaks hoped the revolution would achieve. There are other sources indicating that issues figuring low on the ladder of demands were nonetheless prominent in citizens' visions of how the new society should look. Nevertheless, statistical analysis of the demand lists helps to establish certain contours. First, the demands were for the most part principled. Only a very few expressed what might be called "subsistence demands," like lower taxes or better working conditions, without reference to metaphysical principles. Second, the principles invoked were the same as those most commonly discussed in the flyers, bulletins, and speeches of November and December: democracy, freedom, nonviolence, fairness, and humanness. Workers either invoked these principles in their declarations to justify particular demands or argued for their general application in political and social life. It may be possible to dispute the degree of popularity of particular ideas, but not the general emphasis on ethics.

This conclusion resonates with claims that students themselves made in 1989. In the Slovak television debate of 24 November, the student Miloš Lauko insisted that the student strike did not threaten society materially: "It threatens our society *morally*."[18] "Our joyful revolution . . . has not yet become a political revolution," wrote students in Olomouc as late as 7 December. "Thus far it is primarily a revolution

Pact invasion of 1968, including demands for the withdrawal of Soviet troops (2.43%). "Fairness" includes surrender of KSČ property to public use (3.19%), fairness generally (1.44%), corruption and the rule of law (0.76%), and an independent judiciary (0.51%). "Natural environment" (2.73%) and "Material well-being" (0.76%) are self-sufficient categories. "Other" (4.55%) includes diverse demands ranging from the completion of local building projects to universal tolerance.

[16] See, for example, Jonathan Zatlin, "The Vehicle of Desire: The Trabant, the Wartburg, and the End of the GDR," *German History* 15, no. 3 (1997): 358–80.

[17] It is worth noting that East Germans, too, were more likely to cite lack of freedom than to give material considerations as the reason for their decision to emigrate in 1989. Mike Dennis, *The Stasi: Myth and Reality* (Harlow, U.K.: Pearson/Longman, 2003), p. 223.

[18] *Štúdio Televíznych novín*, Slovenská televízia, Bratislava and Košice, 24 November 1989.

of conscience, a moral revolution."[19] These findings also confirm what Ján Budaj claimed in a television debate marking the fifteenth anniversary: "The November revolution was a revolution of ethics. . . . It was not discussed then how particular sectors of the economy should look, or even very much about laws. What was talked about was a new beginning of relationships to this land."[20]

While quantitative analysis can suggest the general contours of the public dialogue that took place in 1989, it is only via qualitative study that we can really come to grips with the ideals that citizens espoused in 1989 and understand the principles according to which they sought to renew society. By what method, however, can we make sense of a dialogue in which so many people participated? As a heuristic device it is possible to identify five core values around which other ideas clustered in the revolutionary discourse of 1989. These values were not necessarily considered more important than others; what distinguishes an idea as "core" is the relatively large number of other ideas to which it was related. Thus the most central of the ideals of 1989, humanness, was rhetorically connected with at least eleven other prominent ideas, nonviolence with eight, and so on. It should be emphasized that this is merely a means of arranging the cacophony of revolutionary discourse in such a way that it can be discussed in a linear fashion. It may be possible to devise different arrangements following different principles of organization, and even following the relational principle, other researchers might discern slightly different patterns. The important thing is that organizing our discussion around the core values allows us to discuss the most common revolutionary ideals in a systematic way.

One popular ideal of 1989—socialism—deserves special attention independently of the clusters surrounding the five "core" ideals. This is because it was the only ideal that was the subject of serious disagreement in 1989. To be sure, some minor differences were expressed regarding other revolutionary values, such as the extent to which nonviolence was practicable, but no one disputed that these ideas were worth pursuing in principle. Socialism was different in that stances both supportive and opposed emerged in the first days of the revolution, marking the first discernible cleavage within otherwise united public opinion. It is also worth dwelling on the concept because many now mistakenly believe that support for socialism was absent in 1989.[21]

The discussion that follows is limited to the discourse of 1989 itself—the period between 17 November and the end of the student strikes following Havel's election

---

[19] Tomáš Hyjánek, "Cesta k demokracii," *Přetlak*, no. 11 (7 December 1989), p. 1.

[20] *Regionálny denník*, Slovenská televízia, 17 November 2004.

[21] See, for example, Timothy Garton Ash, *We the People: The Revolution of '89 Witnessed in Warsaw, Budapest, Berlin & Prague* (London: Granta, 1990), pp. 115, 147; Gale Stokes, *The Walls Came Tumbling Down: The Collapse of Communism in Eastern Europe* (New York: Oxford University Press, 1993), p. 9; and Lonnie Johnson, *Central Europe: Enemies, Neighbors, Friends*, 2nd ed. (New York: Oxford University Press, 2002), p. 259.

as president. During this period popular discussion of ideas and values exhibited a remarkable coherence. Only after the strikes, when the revolutionary community first relinquished power to institutions that were supposed to represent the community, did the unity and certitude of 1989 begin to dissipate.

Nonviolence

Chronologically the first ideal articulated in the revolution was nonviolence. It came to be of primary importance in the standoff between the trapped marchers and the riot police on 17 November and became a principle both justifying the ensuing strike wave and guiding its conduct. "It should not be permitted to govern by violence," wrote students in their texts of witness.[22] The civic movement founded in Bratislava, which ultimately spread throughout Slovakia and gained sympathizers in the Czech lands, expressed the centrality of its commitment to nonviolence in its very name, Public against Violence.

While there are no confirmed reports of anyone being killed in the Gentle Revolution (unless one counts a wave of functionary suicides in January), fears that the regime might resort to violence were real and justified.[23] The army was put on alert, and the Communist Party's own armed forces—the People's Militia—were called up, with some four thousand militiamen arriving in Prague on 22 November.[24] Some students mysteriously disappeared while venturing away from their universities to mobilize support, and many others were beaten.[25] One aspect of the revolutionary elevation of nonviolence was an appeal to power holders and especially to members of the armed forces and police apparatus not to use violence on fellow citizens.

Striking students and their supporters were not just against regime violence, however; they invested much more verbiage in preventing violence from the side of the populace. In the beginning they were particularly wary of provocation to violence by the secret police, which would provide a pretext for the regime to use violence and could discredit the movement. In time, the term *provocation* became practically synonymous with *temptation*, referring to any suggestion that citizens should resort to violence regardless of its source. The nonviolence of the Gentle Revolution was deliberate, and we should not underestimate how difficult it was to maintain it.

[22] "17. listopad" (PX: súčasná dokumentácia, folder "Nežná revolúcia—1989").
[23] There are unconfirmed reports. See Martin Mejstřík, *Deník: Řekněte jim, že sametová . . .* (Brno: Computer Press, 2010); and "Svědectví" (KO: Sbírka 1989), p. 2.
[24] Jiří Suk, *Občanské fórum: Listopad-prosinec 1989*, vol. 1, *Události* (Brno: Doplněk, 1997), p. 65.
[25] See, for example, Filip Ebr, "Ve čtvrtek 23.11.1989 se vypravila . . . ," Prague (ÚSD: archiv KC OF, box 93); *Nový život* (Blansko), 20 December 1989, p. 3; *Nový život*, 10 January 1990, p. 3; Pavel Svoboda, "Akce gymnázium," *Nový život*, 24 January 1990, p. 2; "Prvé kroky na ceste k dialógu," *Prešovské noviny*, 30 November 1989, p. 2; Milan Otáhal and Miroslav Vaněk, eds., *Sto studentských revolucí: Studenti v období pádu komunismu—životopisná vyprávění* (Prague: Nakladatelství Lidové noviny, 1999), p. 313.

The Gentle Revolution's understanding of nonviolence was also quite radical. It was radical, first of all, for challenging the Weberian definition of the state as a necessarily violent institution, insisting that an alternative was possible. The revolution's aspirations were thus nothing short of transcendent—in keeping with the romantic mode of cognition that prevailed at the time. Activists also emphasized that the revolution was against not just physical violence but violence of all kinds, including psychological, social, economic, and ecological.[26] Nonviolence was thus not merely a political program but a way of life.

The ideal of nonviolence led directly to the ideal of love. Citizens in the Bohemian town of Roztoky summarized their program in December 1989 as "Against violence—more love."[27] "As long as we don't betray truth and loving nonviolence," wrote the influential social ecologist Bohuslav Blažek, "nothing can threaten us."[28] The connection between love and nonviolence was perhaps most colorfully emphasized in Bratislava. On 24 November a speech by Ján Budaj on the essential nonviolence of the revolution led directly to the singer Marika Gombitová's being brought onto the platform and leading the assembled thousands, from her wheelchair, in singing "A Land Named Love."[29] Two days later, the folk singer and Charter 77 signatory Ivan Hoffman debuted his freshly composed song, "We Promised One Another Love," which was soon being sung by hand-holding crowds on squares throughout Slovakia and enjoyed some popularity in Moravia as well.[30] The song built on the image of "those young people" in Prague holding up their empty hands and appealing for nonviolence just before being attacked, musically expressing the resolve of their countrymen to raise their empty hands in solidarity, promising to love one another in order to usher in a "a new day" and "to signal to evil its end."[31] The emblem of the Slovak student movement, of course, was a heart.

Self-Organization

Nonviolence was linked to a second cluster of ideals centered around the principle of self-organization. The mass mobilization following 17 November was justified

[26] See, for example, "Ako to je s odmeňovaním umelcov?" (BB: Materiály získané od hnutia Verejnosť proti násiliu v Banskej Bystrici, 1989, box 1); Daniel Brezina and Peter Lebovič, "Prestavbu začala strana?" *Gemerské zvesti*, 7 December 1989, p. 2; Dominik Matušinský, "Úprimný večer s J. Kronerom," *Kysuce*, 8 December 1989, p. 1; "Dialógy, ktoré ste nepočuli v rozhlase," *Kysuce*, 8 December 1989, p. 2.

[27] "Proti násilí—více lásky!" *Roztocké noviny*, no. 11/12 (November/December 1989), p. 17.

[28] Blažek, "Stará moc a nová civilizace," Prague, 26 November 1989 (ÚSD: archiv KC OF, box 160), p. 4.

[29] Verejnosť proti násiliu and Študentské hnutie, *Nežná revolúcia* (Bratislava: Opus, 1990), sound recording, side 2.

[30] It appeared, for example, in the student bulletin *Poslední zvonění*, no. 2 (30 November 1989), p. 1.

[31] Ivan Hoffman, "Sľúbili sme si lásku," first performed in Bratislava, 26 November 1989, reprinted in Ľubomír Feldek, ed., *Keď sme brali do rúk budúcnosť* (Bratislava: Vydavateľstvo Archa, 1990), pp. 36–37.

as a protest against violence in solidarity with the victims of the Prague "massacre." Proclamations from workplaces between 20 November and the General Strike almost always cite moral indignation over the massacre as the reason for workers' decisions to join the strike. Joining the strike movement, however, necessarily meant self-organization. In some cases students advised workers on how to elect strike committees and plan their course of action, but there were no central directives and for the most part people had to organize themselves. The first public demonstrations after 17 November, moreover, took place without any organization; people simply showed up. As Ivo Mludek, a Charter 77 signatory and revolutionary activist in Opava, recalled,

> We didn't believe we'd be able to get people on the square here in Opava. After those years of unbelievable passivity on the part of the people, of their apathy and collaboration and a certain greater or lesser coexistence with the regime, none of us believed that people from here would go out onto the square. Therefore we went to Ostrava for the first demonstration. And to our great surprise, people here gathered on the square and took a stand more or less without any planning, because no one told them anything.[32]

Beyond the nonviolent motives for self-organization, mobilizing citizens were keen to ensure that the course of the revolution remain nonviolent, and this too required self-organization. Commentators marveled that crowds of hundreds of thousands could act in a concerted fashion to guarantee the safety of participants. Stavostroj workers in Nové Město nad Metují thanked participants in the General Strike, "that with their responsible approach they ensured the calm and dignified course of the strike."[33] Secondary school students in Písek explicitly linked their self-organization with the nonviolent course of the General Strike.[34] The Interior Ministry estimated that crime declined during the last week of November by 75 percent.[35] The revolution was frequently characterized as "a revolution of decent people," pointing out a contrast between the consciously nonviolent self-organization of the revolutionary community and the violence of the regime.[36] When a dense crowd in Prague was asked to open a path for an ambulance, it did so, chanting, "We are not like them!"[37] One reason people cooperated in such simple but meaningful gestures was that they emphasized that citizens could order themselves

---

[32] Ivo Mludek, interview by author, Opava, 20 February 1997, tape recording.

[33] "Zpráva o generální stávce v s.p. Stavostroj," Nové Město nad Metují, 28 November 1989 (ÚSD: archiv KC OF, box 47).

[34] "Prohlášení studentů SLŠ Písek ke generální stávce" (ÚSD: archiv KC OF, box 47).

[35] "Kde máte ty živly," Studentský list, no. 5 (1 December 1989), p. 1.

[36] See, for example, OF Gottwaldov, "Revoluce slušných lidí," Naše pravda, 12 December 1989, p. 1.

[37] Garton Ash, We the People, p. 147.

and do so without violence—thereby disproving the regime's insistence that it had to use violence to preserve order.[38]

The principle of self-organization was also understood in opposition to "administrative-directive" methods of management. Calls for the reduction of bureaucracy and unnecessary administration were ubiquitous. Craftsmen in a Hrnčiarske Zalužany cooperative, for example, wanted a "50 percent reduction in administration," and workers frequently supported such demands by arguing that they had to work twice as hard to support all the administrators in their organizations.[39] The bloatedness of bureaucracies, moreover, was frequently identified as a cause of corruption. OF-VPN Banská Bystrica repeatedly condemned what it called in Gorbachevian language the "administrative-directive manner of running society," contrasting it with the "nonviolent resolution of existing problems with the help of cultivated dialogue."[40] A physician in Čadca seconded this notion, insisting that "one must deserve the future. It is necessary to begin with courageous, liberated work, and *without excessive management*."[41]

The opposite of excessive management, in other words, was self-organization, characterized by spontaneity and informality. Civic Forum and Public against Violence were meant and widely taken to be incarnations of spontaneous self-organization and informality on a mass scale, as was the revolution itself. The spirit of the times was such that other associations were compelled to pay at least lip service to this principle. The Socialist Youth Association in Topoľčany, for example, declared that "we are fighting and will fight in the future to ensure that the SZM program be informal and emerge from nothing other than our members' own demands."[42] Spontaneity was identified as the means by which the new community had come into being, making it a sacred principle that could legitimize social phenomena.[43] We may question whether all events that were claimed to be spontaneous in 1989 really were, but if some were not, it would only underscore the value placed on spontaneity. At least part of its value lay in the fact that it seemed most likely to reveal genuine attitudes, feelings, and dispositions; it was the most effective means of guaranteeing accurate representation, or truth. The stress that Czechs and Slovaks placed on spontaneity and informality was reflected, moreover, in language—

---

[38] The first official reports of the events of 17 November in Prague insisted that "units of public order" had to intervene to prevent demonstrators from disturbing the peace. Aleš V. Poledne, *Jak šly dějiny*, Česká televize, 16 November 2004.

[39] "My pracovníci VD-Šamotka . . . ," Hrnčiarske Zalužany, 27 November 1989 (SNA: Archív VPN, fond. odd. I).

[40] "Ako to je s odmeňovaním umelcov?"; Kosáč, "Občianske fórum," pp. 1–2.

[41] V. Pavlík, "Ľudskosť je vlastná človeku," *Kysuce*, 8 December 1989, p. 3 (emphasis added).

[42] "Stanovisko Predsedníctva OV SZM Topoľčany," *Dnešok*, 12 December 1989, p. 1.

[43] For an example of this widespread phenomenon, see OF Tesla Radiospoj, "Zápis ze seznamovací schůze Místního Občanského fóra," Prague, 6 December 1989 (ÚSD: archiv KC OF, nezpracovaná hromada č. 1).

which became refreshingly simple and direct—and in clothing, with revolutionary protagonists ostentatiously wearing sweaters and casual clothing even in formal settings.

A further ideal associated with self-organization was freedom. Though one of the most commonly expressed demands in demonstrations and proclamations, it received relatively little commentary in 1989 itself (there would be more later). Most often freedom was discussed in the same breath as rejection of excessive bureaucracy and administrative formality or glorification of spontaneity and self-organization. To be sure, the virtue of freedom as guarantor of other social goods was emphasized. A Košice poster, for example, claimed that "free people are kinder, more decent, and more considerate toward one another," and VPN Banská Bystrica quoted the exiled Czech philosopher Erazim Kohák, who had written that "democracy begins neither with revolution nor with liberation, but with the growth of free people."[44] Lists of demands also specified some of the particular kinds of freedom that their authors wanted guaranteed—namely freedom of the press, religion, speech, association, assembly, career choice, movement, and enterprise (in that order of frequency). There was, however, little discussion of what freedom might mean at an existential level. Widely demanded though it was, it seems to have been considered a relatively unproblematic concept.

Democracy

The single most common demand to be expressed in November and December 1989 was for free elections, and principles closely related to democracy, such as pluralism and dialogue, figured prominently in revolutionary discussions. Democracy was without question one of the revolution's highest values.

The first proclamations after 17 November, in addition to condemning violence and appealing to citizens to act, called for democratic dialogue and free elections. Many citizens got their first real experience with democracy in the week preceding the General Strike, when students and working people across the country elected strike committees. (A few, scattered free elections to positions within workplaces had taken place earlier in the autumn of 1989, but for the most part the Communist Party still carefully controlled elections right up to the end.)[45] The first free elections in what would soon be post-Communist Czechoslovakia were thus not the parliamentary elections of June 1990, as is usually averred, but the elections to strike committees in November 1989. The democracy of these elections was direct—as was Czechs' and Slovaks' second major experience of democracy: the General Strike

---

[44] KS: zbierka z Nežnej revolúcie, folder "Plagáty: Rôzne"; *Fórum* (Banská Bystrica), no. 2 (3 December 1989), p. 1.

[45] "Anketa OF a VPN pro čs. podniky a organizace" (ÚSD: archiv KC OF, boxes 34–35).

itself. Though the motivation for the strike was first of all to protest the violence the regime had employed on 17 November, in the days preceding the strike students and Civic Forum made explicit what it was becoming: an "informal referendum" on the future of the country.[46] The regime's decision to surrender its leading role two days after the strike was but an admission of what this informal referendum had already made clear: the regime could no longer even pretend to legitimacy. These two experiences of democracy were formative; citizens grew accustomed to participating directly in the government of their affairs and achieving results.

Revolutionary citizens tended to understand democracy in a straightforward Aristotelian manner. This was seen as a radical departure from the interpretation hitherto articulated by Party and state ideologues, who had of course always claimed that Communist Czechoslovakia was democratic. They had navigated between the basic meaning of democracy and Czechoslovak reality by articulating the Leninist theory of democratic centralism, in the face of which revolutionary Czechs and Slovaks demanded "democracy without qualification." Their understanding of democracy therefore tended to a certain fundamentalism—one might be tempted, following François Furet, to call it "direct" or "pure" democracy.[47]

The basic meaning of democracy, as articulated by revolutionary Czechs and Slovaks, was that people should be able to participate meaningfully in the decision-making process. Decisions should not be made—as they had been in the past—"about us without us." Both the leaders of the civic associations in their negotiations with state and party officials and the people in their demonstrations and declarations rejected what they called "cabinet politics," where decisions "about people without people" were made behind closed doors.[48] This complaint about the way decisions had been made in the past was leveled not only against the state apparatus but against workplace management as well, where directors and administrators frequently made decisions and issued statements in the name of employees (as Communist ideology required) without ever consulting them. This experience led collectives like those in the Litomyšl waterworks to declare, "We do not wish that anyone else should speak for us!"[49]

This is not to say that Czechs and Slovaks rejected any idea of representation. While citizens believed that at the level of workplaces and other small communities

[46] "Prohlášení Občanského fóra ze dne 25.11.—4.30 hod.," Prague, 25 November 1989, reprinted in Jiří Suk, ed., *Občanské fórum: Listopad-prosinec 1989*, vol. 2, *Dokumenty* (Brno: Doplněk, 1998), p. 25; Václav Havel's speech on Letenská pláň, Prague, 25 November 1989, ibid., p. 26. See also Michal Horáček, *Jak pukaly ledy* (Prague: Ex libris, 1990), p. 126.

[47] François Furet, *Interpreting the French Revolution*, trans. Elborg Forster (Cambridge: Cambridge University Press, 1981).

[48] See, for example, "19.12.1989—12°° MÍTING . . ." (BB: Materiály získané od hnutia Verejnosť proti násiliu v Banskej Bystrici, 1989, box 2).

[49] Zaměstnanci VaK provoz Litomyšl, "Prohlášení členů ROH—provoz Litomyšl" (ÚSD: archiv KC OF, box 47).

direct democracy might work, they recognized that beyond a certain point, political representation was necessary. The question was how to ensure that this representation be *accurate*. There was some talk of a unitary "general will," but for the most part Czechs and Slovaks accepted that there would be diversity of interest and opinion in society, and they counted on majority vote as the fairest means of decision making in conditions of diversity. "We demand a government that will be representative," wrote agricultural supply workers in Kostelec nad Orlicí, "expressing the interests of the majority of us."[50] The trick was to find ways of translating the pattern of diversity from the population as a whole onto representative institutions. One method was to make representation "proportional," not in the sense used by political scientists of parliamentary democracies, where seats are allotted to parties based proportionally on their electoral results, but more ambitiously in the sense of proportionally representing the forces of society—of which political parties were seen to be only a subset. "We demand by free elections," declared revolutionaries in Banská Bystrica, "to create . . . a parliament . . . in which all parts of our society will have representation."[51] Referring a week or so later to the national committees, Banská Bystrica's civic association explained its conception of representation more specifically: "the pluralist representation of individual political parties, deputies without party affiliation, and civic initiatives."[52] When Ladislav Adamec on 3 December named a new government with fifteen Communists and only five non-Communists, the principle of "proportional" representation was used to argue for the government's inadmissibility. "We cannot discern . . . any acceptable reason," wrote OF Žirovnice, "why in a state with 15 million inhabitants and only 1.5 million KSČ members, the government should again include a majority of Communists."[53] This formulation reveals the true radicalism of the idea, implying that even in pluralist party systems, if a majority of the population is nonpartisan, so too should be the government. The composition of representative institutions, moreover, was to mirror the proportion not only of party to nonparty members in the general population but of other interest groups as well. Several groups of citizens criticized the "15:5" government not just because a majority of its members were Communist but also because it included only one woman.[54] Others argued

[50] "Prohlášení občanského fóra pracujících k.p. ZZN Rychnov nad Kněžnou se sídlem v Kostelci nad Orl. dne 5.12.1989" (ÚSD: archiv KC OF, nezpracovaná hromada č. 1).

[51] "Program Občianskeho fóra hnutia Verejnosť proti násiliu," incorrectly dated 21 November 1989 (BB: Materiály ziskané od hnutia Verejnosť proti násiliu v Banskej Bystrici, 1989, box 2). This was an emendation of the Programové vyhlásenie VPN a KV slovenských vysokoškolákov, Bratislava, 25 November 1989.

[52] KC OI VPN Banská Bystrica, "Je nevyhnutné vysloviť nedôveru aj Rade, Plenu a predsedníctvu SKNV?" (BB: Materiály ziskané od hnutia Verejnosť proti násiliu v Banskej Bystrici, 1989, box 2).

[53] OF Žirovnice, "Provolání," 4 December 1989 (ÚSD: archiv KC OF, nezpracovaná hromada č. 1).

[54] See, for example, "Prohlášení Občanského fóra a stávkového výboru při Středisku bytových služeb a zámečnictví Oblastního podniku služeb v Lounech," 4 December 1989 (ÚSD: archiv KC OF, nezpracovaná hromada č. 4), p. 1.

that "a pluralist political system," understood in this sense, would at last ensure "the participation of working people in the running of the state."[55] Essentially, this was an "estates" model of representation, similar to medieval and early modern systems that allocated seats in representative bodies according to social category, and one that has reappeared from time to time in late modern European history, as when Parisians in 1848 created their "Estates General of Labor."[56] It is worth noting that in creating their candidate lists for the June 1990 elections, OF and VPN tried to act in accordance with this principle, ensuring the presence of students, laborers, ethnic minorities, and women on their lists in electable positions.

Realizing that delegates to representative institutions might, during their term in office, cease to represent their constituents accurately, citizens proposed three popular checks on institutional power. One was to have important debates and votes broadcast live on television, and a second was to have referenda on important issues whenever a certain number of citizens demanded it.[57] The third check was one that the Communist regime had enshrined in law but never allowed to be practiced freely: that voters in a particular district could at any time recall a delegate who "broke his trust." Needless to say, this final check assumed preservation of the formally majoritarian electoral system of the Communist era, where each delegate was answerable to a particular constituency rather than to a party.

The means to achieving accurate representation were to be, of course, free elections. These, it was believed, would "create in practice the points of departure for genuine democracy."[58] Citizens emphasized that free elections should take place "at all levels," "to all representative organs."[59] As workers in Bratislava's Slovnaft refinery explained during the General Strike, "We are for free elections—yes. But for free elections from basic units up (elections of shift leaders, leading economic workers in individual workplaces, directors, and central organs)."[60] The demand that workplaces as well as the various levels of government be democratic was practically universal. First of all, this meant that trade unions should be democratized—that workers should be able to elect union representatives and officials freely rather than merely approving those sanctioned by the same Party that also oversaw nominations

[55] Stávkující studenti VŠ, "Vážení spoluobčané!!! O co nám nyní jde!!!," 27 November 1989 (ZM: zbierka plagátov, č. 1991–00109). Similar versions are preserved in OL.

[56] William Sewell, Work and Revolution in France: The Language of Labor from the Old Regime to 1848 (Cambridge: Cambridge University Press, 1980), pp. 253–54, 267–68.

[57] See, for example, "Vyzýváme vedení a zaměstnance Čs. rozhlasu . . ." (ÚSD: archiv KC OF, box 97) and "Pracovníci odboru hospodaření na své schůzce . . . ," 24 November 1989 (ÚSD: archiv KC OF, box 157, folder "24.11. prohl. jednotl. i institucí").

[58] Kosáč, "Občianske fórum," p. 2.

[59] "Stanovisko č. 2 pracovníkov Archeologického ústavu SAV v Nitre," 27 November 1989 (SNA: Archív VPN, fond. odd. I); "Usnesení občanského fóra pracovníků Mototechna s.p. závod 23 Mladá Boleslav," 7 December 1989 (ÚSD: archiv KC OF, nezpracovaná hromada č. 1).

[60] Speech read during the general strike in Slovnaft, Bratislava, 27 November 1989 (SNA: Archív VPN, fond. odd. I).

to management positions. It was believed that union organs should defend the interests of an enterprise's entire workforce.[61] More radically, workers wanted to elect their managers and directors too. Those with "natural authority"—as determined by the workforce—were to occupy posts at all levels of administration.[62]

The popular understanding of democracy was not limited to elections, referenda, and the ability to recall disappointing representatives. It also featured, centrally, the principle of dialogue, as a means by which citizens, in conversation with one another and with their elected representatives and officials, should reach decisions and form policy. This dialogue was not supposed to be just between leaders and representatives of the public but would be one to which every citizen could contribute. As the students declared in their founding proclamation, "We demand . . . the inauguration of a consequential dialogue with *all* segments of society without exception."[63] Milan Kňažko spelled out the full meaning of this demand in the Slovak television debate of 24 November: "It is necessary . . . to create one enormous round table, around which 15 million people can sit. And we must reckon with absolutely every opinion, so that everyone might freely express himself without fear, that he might express his own substance and vision of our society."[64] On the ground, local activists made honest efforts to see that this really happened. At a December meeting of 611 citizens in the Silesian town of Bílovec, for example, "the floor was given to everyone who wanted to express his opinion or convey the standpoint of existing political parties or initiatives."[65] Whether or not this was entirely true, there was clearly a perception that it should be. It was considered democratic, moreover, to consider every opinion; students invoked this principle as a reason for polemicizing even with provocative flyers, and especially at the district and more local levels, activists involved in coordinating committees took pains to respond to every letter they received.[66] As workers in Valašské Meziříčí emphasized, in unison with the dominant view, "Dialogue is possible only after all active forces have spoken."[67] The

[61] Studenti FF UK, "Využít odbory," Prague, 25 November 1989 (BB: Materiály získané od hnutia Verejnosť proti násiliu v Banskej Bystrici, 1989, box 3); the same or similar versions can also be found in CB, DÚ, KO, KS, LN, MI, MU, OL, OV, PR, PV, and SV.

[62] "Politický program koordinačného výboru slovenských vysokých škôl," Bratislava, 24 November 1989 (ZM: zbierka plagátov, č. 1991–00109); similar or identical versions are also preserved in BB and OL. As we shall see in chapter 5, workers began holding such elections in December 1989 and continued with renewed vigor in the new year.

[63] "Prohlášení studentů pražských VŠ," 18 November 1989, in Milan Otáhal and Zdeněk Sládek, eds., *Deset pražských dnů (17.–27. listopad 1989): Dokumentace* (Prague: Academia, 1990), p. 32 (emphasis added).

[64] *Štúdio Televíznych novín,* 24 November 1989.

[65] "Prohlášení ze shromáždění Občanského fóra města Bílovce konaného dne 7.12.1989" (ÚSD: archiv KC OF, nezpracovaná hromada č. 1).

[66] "Pozor na provokace!" *Přetlak,* no. 5 (1 December 1989), p. 6.

[67] "My, níže podepsaní pracovníci státního podniku Urxovy závody . . . ," Valašské Meziříčí, 23 November 1989 (ÚSD: archiv KC OF, box 93).

only people to whom dialogue should be closed were "those who would introduce violence"—an exception that, obviously, would in time prompt anguished debate.[68]

As students emphasized, dialogue was not only to be open to everyone, but was also to be consequential, informing public decision making. This principle was so sacred to revolutionary Czechoslovaks that reference to it was sufficient to delegitimize state leaders; these were criticized and their resignations demanded precisely because of their unwillingness to hold serious dialogue with the broad public.[69] This has something of the character of an ex post facto judgment and clearly illustrates both the new principles on which public life was supposed to function and the cosmic nature of the shift. "Democracy needs leaders, not lords," people declared, and these leaders should turn, as one Banská Bystrica citizen wrote to Gustáv Husák, "to the entire people with its opinion, demand, or directive."[70]

Revolutionary activists paid considerable attention to how dialogue was conducted. Among the most widely circulated documents of November and December was "The Eight Rules of Dialogue," drawn up by a circle of central Bohemian intellectuals calling themselves Civic Conversation (Občanská beseda) in the summer of 1989. They had envisioned precisely the kind of dialogue that became so prominent during the revolution, calling on citizens in their localities to meet and discuss issues of common concern, writing up conclusions on which the majority agreed, and submitting them to authorities with power to enact them. The only difference between the Civic Conversation program and the revolutionary culture of dialogue that in fact emerged was that Civic Conversation did not really expect many leaders to heed popular demands, while revolutionary citizens expected them to do so without exception. In any case, the Eight Rules became part of the revolution's fundamental moral code, comparable to the "Ten Commandments" discussed in the previous chapter.[71]

1. Your opponent is not an enemy but a partner in search of truth. The goal of our discussion is truth, in no case intellectual competition. Participation in dialogue assumes a triple respect: toward truth, toward the other, and toward the self.

2. Try to understand each other. If you do not correctly understand the opinion of your opponent, you can neither refute his claims nor accept them.

---

[68] Koordinačný výbor slov. vys. škol, "Naše stanovisko," Bratislava, 25 November 1989 (ZM: zbierka plagátov, č. 1991–00109).

[69] See, for example, Úklid, Prague (ÚSD: archiv KC OF, box 157).

[70] "Demokracie potřebuje vůdce ne pány!!!" (BB: Zbierka plagátov získaných od študentov Pedagogickej fakulty v Banskej Bystrici, 1989–1990); "Pán Husák, obraciam sa na Vás otvoreným listom," 1 December 1989 (BB: Materiály získané od hnutia Verejnosť proti násiliu v Banskej Bystrici, 1989, box 1).

[71] Many versions of this document appeared in its diffusion to all corners of the republic. The one reproduced here is the original, published in EM'89, no. 0, p. 9.

Formulate for yourself the objections of your partner, so that it may be clear how you understand him.

3. Don't present insistence without objective reasons as an argument. In such a case it is just a matter of your opinion and your partner need not concede the weight of argument.

4. Don't skirt the issue. Do not avoid unpleasant questions or arguments by directing the discussion elsewhere.

5. Don't try to have the last word at all costs. No quantity of words can make up for a missing argument. Silencing a partner does not mean refutation of his argument or disavowal of his ideas.

6. Don't undercut the personal dignity of your opponent. Whoever attacks the person of his opponent, rather than his thought, loses the right to participate in dialogue.

7. Don't forget that dialogue requires discipline. In the end it is with reason, never with emotion, that we form our claims and judgments. He who is unable intelligibly and calmly to express his opinion cannot conduct a worthwhile conversation with others.

8. Don't confuse dialogue with monologue. Everyone has the same right to express himself. Don't get lost in minor details. Consideration toward everyone else can be expressed by your ability to save time.

There is evidence that these rules were taken quite seriously. Following the Letná manifestation of 25 November, which led many citizens to criticize OF's leadership as being insufficiently democratic, several citizens specifically admonished the Prague coordinating committee for not following the Eight Rules.[72] While the Eight Rules became the most widely accepted guidelines for the practice of dialogue in both republics, they were not, to be sure, the only ones. Bratislava economics students, for example, published a similar list translated from a Swedish handbook on democracy.[73] While it did not come to enjoy the circulation of the Eight Rules, it testifies to the need people felt for some kind of objective principles to guide what was widely perceived as a new social practice. By following these rules, Czechoslovaks believed they could "build a society in which every citizen will be able to have his own opinion, to express it publicly, and not to be persecuted for it in any way if it not be in harmony with official politics."[74]

While some revolutionary citizens may have limited their concern to the democratization of public affairs, many seem to have envisioned something more

[72] Letters from M. L., Pilsen, and A. F., Hradec Králové, to KC OF Prague, 27 November 1989 (ÚSD: archiv KC OF, box 97).

[73] Ekonóm, vol. 19, special issue (December 1989), p. 4.

[74] Pracovníci Stavebného podniku Dolný Kubín, quoted in "Za oprávnené požiadavky," Orava, 29 November 1989, p. 1.

profound. The Red Cross in Dolný Kubín anticipated "the deep democratization of our entire society."[75] A Forum of Women in Považská Bystrica gave a specific example of what such "deep democratization" might entail, demanding "the equal representation of men and women in the process of child rearing, so that the raising of children and youth be conducted in a democratic spirit."[76] To this day, democracy remains a principle according to which not just politics but an entire array of social phenomena is judged.

The Gentle Revolution, of course, was not the first time the slogan "All power to the people" had been heard.[77] In writing of the French Revolution, François Furet makes a distinction between what he calls representative democracy and pure democracy. Representative democracy, for Furet, involves the delegation of decision-making power to representatives elected periodically, with strictly limited powers of citizens to control their representatives between elections. Pure democracy, on the contrary, makes representatives (if any) constantly subject to the popular will, understood to be unitary.[78] In revolutionary Czechoslovakia no one argued for a democracy that would not involve representatives, but there was considerable debate and eventually sharp disagreement about how to ensure the accuracy of representation. Not a few expressed views that could be identified as those of pure democracy. "Let only the most capable win our trust in free elections," wrote basic service soldiers in Banská Bystrica, "and *all of us* will follow them."[79] Some seem to have accepted contested elections only if the outcome were predetermined, as in the slogan of a group of Nitra office workers: "Free elections for socialism with a human face!"[80] Toleration for minorities was sometimes also rejected, as when a participant in a meeting of the Michalovce district national committee proclaimed, "We must first of all be democratic; we can't require national committee chairmen to include citizens of gypsy origin if people are against it."[81] Still, even though most Czechoslovak citizens wanted to exercise far more control over their representatives between elections than Furet would allow, they still for the most part accepted the twin principles of majority vote and protection for dissenting minorities. Between Furet's two democratic extremes, in other words, revolutionary Czechs and Slovaks articulated a third way.

[75] "Stanovisko OV ČSČK," *Orava*, 6 December 1989, p. 2.
[76] "Programové vyhlásenie fóra žien podporujúcich koordinačný výbor Verejnosť proti násiliu" (PX: fond G1, box 1, folder "KDS 1989").
[77] "My podepsaní občané . . . ," *Řičice*, 26 November 1989 (ÚSD: archiv KC OF, box 152).
[78] Furet, *Interpreting the French Revolution*.
[79] Vojáci ASVS Dukla Banská Bystrica, "Prehlásenie," before 27 November 1989 (BB: Materiály získané od hnutia Verejnosť proti násiliu v Banskej Bystrici, 1989, box 3) (emphasis in original).
[80] "Prehlásenie. My pracovníci operatívneho plánu . . . ," Nitra, 27 November 1989 (SNA: Archív VPN, fond. odd. I).
[81] "Zápisnica zo 16. schôdze Rady Okresného národného výboru v Michalovciach, konanej dňa 1. decembra 1989 o 8,00 hodine v zasedacej sieni rady ONV" (MI: fond "ONV Michalovce"), p. 6.

Fairness

A further central value of the revolution was *fairness*. In posters, speeches, and flyers Czechoslovaks widely called for social leveling, but these expressions reflected a desire not so much for equality as for fairness. Inequality itself was not perceived as bad, but inequality achieved in an unjust or unfair manner was.

Citizens expressed indignation over such perks of state and party functionaries as special hospitals and recreational facilities, from which ordinary people were barred. "Where did you get the money for your palaces?" citizens asked.[82] Should there be "spas for the aristocracy?"[83] Aristocratic metaphors abounded. In the context of pervasive Marxist rhetoric about equality, the economic and social distinctiveness of the higher functionaries was identified as hypocritical. When Communists drew attention to the incomes of some of the artists supporting the revolutionary cause in an attempt to discredit them, the strategy backfired.

> Let you functionaries rather justify the reasons why laborers and technicians in factories have such incomes that it is hardly possible to live from them. Try to compare the pay and benefits, for example, of a seamstress in OZ or ZDA, who toils eight hours at the belt, with the pay and benefits of functionaries, directors, and vice directors. . . . This process . . . is aimed against functionarial parasitism, injustice, the arrogance of people who with impunity have endangered the existence of their subordinates.[84]

This perception of hypocritical and therefore unfair inequality informed ubiquitous (and often humorous) visions of social leveling. "Give the palaces to the children," people cried.[85] "We want all hospitals to be turned into State Sanatoria for everyone."[86] Prophecies were made that leading functionaries would soon become streetcar drivers and construction workers. Images of functionaries being sent to shovels or exchanging places with titled intellectuals whom the regime had stoking boilers were everywhere.[87] "Long live the Central Committee! But with laborers' pensions!"[88]

Citizens were careful to emphasize that inequality was not necessarily bad in and of itself, that the problem was inequality established in an unjust or unfair

---

[82] Graffiti written on "Vnitrostranická informace" (LN: fond 569, box 2), p. 2.

[83] "Lázně pro aristokracii?" *Stráž míru*, 27 December 1989, p. 2.

[84] OI VPN Topoľčianskeho okresu, "Členovia občianskych iniciatív VPN!" *Dnešok*, 12 December 1989, p. l.

[85] " 'Dajte palác deťom'," *Prešovské noviny*, 14 December 1989, p. l.

[86] Milan Ferencei, "Vážení priatelia!" (SNA: Archív VPN, fond. odd. I). "State sanatoria" were special health care facilities for the upper levels of the *nomenklatura*.

[87] See, for example, HM: Zbierka plagátov, box "Plagáty: 1989 a ďalej s číslom," poster no. 33628.

[88] HM: Zbierka plagátov, box "Malé plagáty r. 1989 + voľby—l. demokratické," poster no. 33613.

manner. "Actors *make* money because they act," wrote the creator of a Bratislava poster in reaction to the provocative "Actors' Pay" flyers, "but for what have our party and state functionaries *received* (not made) money? Earned money is not a shame, even if it is a lot, but money stolen from us by functionaries is a shame; does it not burn them?"[89]

A form of unfairness against which citizens particularly protested was corruption, widely perceived to be systemic. People complained of bribery and nepotism and argued that laborers had to work in undignified conditions because corrupt officials embezzled the money that was supposed to go toward purchase of new machines.[90] Solutions to the problem were seen in the elevation of the law, insistence upon expert qualifications for occupants of leadership posts, and the publicizing of offenses. Laws existed, of course, to defend workers and citizens against managerial abuses. The problem was their enforcement and lack of public knowledge about them. Law students therefore composed and circulated a series of flyers informing citizens of their rights and advising them how to proceed legally in cases of abuse.[91] Many local OFs and VPNs joined the students in offering free legal consultation.[92] To supplement this renaissance of legal awareness, the public insisted on independent courts to enforce it. To reduce possibilities for corruption people insisted on the staffing of managerial posts either by democratic election or by open competition (*konkurzy*), with hiring committees composed of experts, not

[89] HM: Zbierka plagátov, box "Plagáty: 1989 a ďalej s číslom," poster no. 33622.

[90] Stávkující studenti VŠ, "Vážení spoluobčané!!! O co nám nyní jde!!!"

[91] In their manifold versions, the specific flyers that Charles University law students produced included the following: "Hogyan válható le egy vállalat igazgatója" (private collection of István Jobbagy, Komárno), "Jak odvolat poslance" (BB), "Jak odvolat poslance nejvyšších zastupitelských sborů" (CB), "Jak odvolat poslance z nejvyšších zastupitelských sborů" (PX), "Jak odvolat ředitele podniku" (BB, DÚ, KS, MI, MU, OL, PR, PV, PX, and SV), "Jak odvolat vedoucího vnitřní organizační jednotky" (TA), "Jak pracuje Váš poslanec?" (CB), "K možnosti odvolání poslanců nejvyšších zastupitelských sborů" (KS and ÚSD), "Lidové milice" (OV), "Lidové milice a právo" (OL, PV, and ZL), "Možnost odvolání" (PV), "Možnost odvolání poslance" (KS), "Možnost odvolání poslanců zastupitelských orgánů" (OL), "Možnost odvolání poslanců zastupitelských sborů" (MU), "Možnost odvolání ředitele podniku" (PX), "Možnost pracovně-právních postihů v případě . . ." (OL), "Možnosť pracovnoprávnych postihov v prípade . . ." (BB), "Možnosti odvolání poslanců nejvyšších zastupitelských sborů" (BB, KS, MI, MU, OP, PR, and PV), "Možnosti odvolania poslancov najvyšších zastupiteľských zborov" (BB and ZM), "Poslanci a voliči" (KS, OL, OV, and PV), "Pracovně právní důsledky případného přerušení práce" (BB, BN, DÚ, OL, PR, and PV), "Pracovně právní postihy z pondělní stávky" (UH), "Pracovno právne dôsledky prípadného prerušenia práce" (BB), "Práva a povinnosti člena ROH—ze stanov ROH" (TA), "Práva členské schůze JZD" (TA), "Právní otázky" (ÚSD), "Právní postavení Lidových milicí" (BV and TA), "Právní rozbor ústavní svobody shromážďovací a svobody pouličních průvodu a manifestací a zákonnosti postupů státních orgánů při její realizaci" (ÚSD), "Využít každé příležitosti!!!" (BB and ÚSD), "Využít odbory" (BB, CB, DÚ, KO, KS, LN, MI, MU, OL, OV, PR, PV, and SV), "Zadržení" (OL). These and others were included in such anthologies as "Občané, máte svá práva!!!" (ÚSD), "Občané, seznamte se se svými občanskými právy!" (BB, KO, KS, MU, OL, and OV), "Právna poradňa" (KS), and "Pravní poradna" (BB, KS, MU, and OL).

[92] Studenti pražských VŠ, "Dělníci, obraťte se na poradenské středisko . . . ," before 27 November 1989 (BB: Materiály získané od hnutia Verejnosť proti násiliu v Banskej Bystrici, 1989, box 3).

just administrators. A final method of combating corruption was seen in making offenses public—in the belief that public opinion might place sanctions on offenders. In Košice, for example, a list was published of functionaries who had gained property abandoned by émigrés and how much they had paid for it.[93] As a result of these measures, enthusiastic revolutionaries hailed "the end of corruption, bribery, and nepotism."

Socialism

Related to the principle of fairness was a further popular ideal: socialism. The reader with knowledge of only the scholarly literature on 1989 is surprised to find, in the Czech and Slovak archives from November and December, ubiquitous appraisals of socialism that were overwhelmingly positive, calling for its preservation and renewal, not its dismantling. "We don't want to dismantle socialism, but we want to dismantle everything that stands in socialism's way," wrote Bratislava railway workers.[94] One OF poster called "for a merrier socialism."[95] Many, of course, called for socialism with a human face.

Scholars who have noted this prosocialist rhetoric have tended to dismiss it as strategic rather than sincere. On close examination, however, it seems beyond doubt that most popular expressions of devotion to socialism were sincere. In the first place, support for socialism was expressed even by the most radical revolutionary actors. Banská Bystrica students assured workers that they did not want a return to the labor conditions of the First Republic.[96] Olomouc students explicitly "distanced themselves" from all antisocialist positions, grouping them together with violent ones.[97] Since students had already taken considerable risk upon themselves by speaking openly about other demands, it seems odd that they should revert to subterfuge on this question. If one argues that students had to be careful in discussing socialism with the general public, since support for alternatives to socialism might be less popular than their other demands, this is only to concede the question. Additional evidence for popular attachment to socialism is that the kind of democracy people envisioned—with workplace managers being elected by the workers rather than appointed by owners—was easiest to implement in a socialist system. It was, indeed, exactly the system that reform Communist planners had introduced and that workers had embellished in 1968. As Bratislava students declared, "The

[93] "PhDr. Pavol Kačmar, CSc." (KS: zbierka z Nežnej revolúcie, folder "Rôzne").

[94] "Členovia ZO SZM pri Československých štátnych dráhach, Bratislavská oblasť, Traťová strojova stanica . . . ," Bratislava, 27 November 1989 (SNA: Archív VPN, fond. odd. I), p. 2.

[95] LN: fond 569, box 1, folder 23.

[96] "Robotníci, naši otcovia a starí otcovia . . ." (BB: Materiály získané od hnutia Verejnosť proti násiliu v Banskej Bystrici, 1989, box 1).

[97] "Prohlášení nezávislého svazu studentů UP Olomouc," 23 November 1989 (OL: Sbírka soudobé dokumentace, sign. 148–22).

historical foundation for the solution of our problems is to resume in a positive way the process of reconstruction [*prestavba*] which our society began to undertake in the 1960s."[98]

The most convincing evidence of popular attachment to socialism, however, is the pains taken to argue that true socialism was in harmony with other revolutionary ideals and that the so-called socialism Czechs and Slovaks had been living under had in fact been deformed by their leaders. Citizens in Louny equated socialism with "democracy + nonviolence + each according to his abilities, to each as he deserves (but really)."[99] The pastor of the Czechoslovak Hussite church in Tábor argued that democracy equaled socialism.[100] Shipyard workers on the Danube criticized the Communist Party for deforming socialism.[101] "They are antisocialist," wrote an employee in the headquarters of West Slovakia's grocery distributor, referring to what she called the "red nobility."[102] Vladimír Ondruš, one of VPN's spokesmen at the 24 November television debate, said that "the dispute in our society today is not for or against socialism, but about the form of socialism. . . . Socialism is after all not the heritage of functionaries, who want to preserve their privileges for themselves and their children. Socialism is the heritage of the citizens of this country."[103] It was like the adherents of a religion turning against their clergy for having betrayed the articles of faith.

The reason that so many commentators have gotten this wrong may be that socialism was the only ideal of 1989 not to enjoy practically universal support, and the extent of support varied geographically. There was more support for a radical break from socialism and adoption of Western-style market economies in and around the capitals and in parts of southern Slovakia than elsewhere in Czechoslovakia. In January, the Bratislava student bulletin *Zmena* quickly adopted a pro-free-market stance, and the leadership of the Association of Strike Committees (based initially in Prague's Institute for Economic Forecasting) espoused the view that only a market economy would ensure a productive economy.[104] In Komárno, with its mostly Hungarian population attuned to developments south of the border, editors of the VPN/FMK newspaper spoke favorably of "developed countries with market

---

[98] "Politický program koordinačného výboru slovenských vysokých škôl."

[99] "Prohlášení Občanského fóra a stávkového výboru při Středisku bytových služeb a zámečnictví Oblastního podniku služeb v Lounech," 4 December 1989 (ÚSD: archiv KC OF, nezpracovaná hromada č. 4), p. 2.

[100] Václav Urban, "Socialismus v ekonomické a mravní oblasti," *Palcát*, 13 December 1989, p. 3.

[101] "My, pracovníci ČSPD závod Prístav . . . ," Bratislava, 24 November 1989 (SNA: Archív VPN, fond. odd. I).

[102] Ľudmila Pašková, "Pýtam sa Vás, ktorí ste bez názoru . . . ," Bratislava, 27 November 1989 (SNA: Archív VPN, fond. odd. I), p. 1.

[103] *Štúdio Televíznych novín*, 24 November 1989.

[104] "Strana mladých—Národní liberáli," *Zmena*, no. 17 (January 1990), p. 3; "Jaké jsou programové zásady odborové politiky," *Zpravodaj stávkových výborů*, no. 3 (16 January 1990), p. 3.

economies" and dismissively of "so-called socialist countries."[105] Though more re-search will be necessary to define the cleavage precisely, it would seem to have been primarily geographic—correlated with networks of communication and trade. Age and socioeconomic status do not by themselves appear to have been such significant factors. When Václav Havel carefully stated that the word *socialism* had "lost all meaning in the Czech linguistic context" and articulated support for "social jus-tice" instead, he was trying to change the minds of the majority of his compatriots. Western commentators concentrated in the capital, however, took statements like this as representative of public opinion.[106] They would have done better to consult the results of public opinion polls conducted just before Havel's statement, which showed that 45 percent of Czechoslovak citizens, when asked about future social development, believed that their country should follow "a socialist path," while 47 percent expressed support for something "in between" socialism and capitalism.[107]

We may of course question what Czechs and Slovaks had in mind when they expressed support for socialism in 1989. The VPN spokesman (and sociologist) Fedor Gál did as much in the television debate of 24 November when he said a so-ciological study had demonstrated that ordinary people did not know what social-ism was. This was a dangerous direction for the debate to go and Milan Kňažko (an actor, more sensitive to his audience) quickly changed it.[108] Indeed, whenever OF or VPN leaders in Prague and Bratislava even implicitly suggested the possi-bility of discarding socialism, people expressed reservations.[109] The Communists picked up on the issue of socialism in an attempt to isolate OF and VPN, and it was a smart move, for indeed, dominant portions of the OF and VPN leaderships were prepared to part with something called socialism in a way the general public was not.

In the beginning, when revolutionary protagonists contrasted their hopes for the future with a "period of darkness" in the recent past, no one claimed that that period extended farther back than 1968. To criticize the past twenty years was to condemn the policies of "normalization" and to mourn the possibilities for a re-formed socialism that had been smothered in 1968; it was also to imply that 1968 could serve as the starting point for a new departure. To criticize the past forty years was to condemn the Communist project as a whole and could also (but did

---

[105] Ivan Scholtz, "'Kultúrna politika' KSČ," *Reflex*, 5 January 1990, p. 3. See also "A Magyar Diákszövet-ség nyilatkozata," *Szabad Kapacitás*, no. 1 (10 January 1990), p. 6.

[106] Garton Ash, *We the People*, p. 96.

[107] Dragoslav Slejška et al., *Sondy do veřejného mínění: Jaro 1968, podzim 1989* (Prague: Svoboda, 1990), pp. 51–52, reproduced in Bernard Wheaton and Zdeněk Kavan, *The Velvet Revolution: Czechoslovakia, 1988–1991* (Boulder, Colo.: Westview, 1992), p. 220.

[108] *Štúdio Televíznych novín*, 24 November 1989.

[109] See, for example, "Prehlásenie pracovníkov DÚM Záh. Bystrica," Bratislava, 27 November 1989 (SNA: Archív VPN, fond. odd. I), and "Vážení spoluobčania! Medzi nami nie je v súčasnej dobe asi nikto..." (BB: Materiály získané od hnutia Verejnosť proti násiliu v Banskej Bystrici, 1989, box 1).

not necessarily have to) mean rejection of socialism as such. Even Havel, in his earliest speeches on Wenceslas Square, referred to only twenty years of decline. He spoke of "twenty years outside of time" on 22 November, and a Civic Forum declaration mentioned "twenty years of silence" on 27 November.[110] The switch to "forty years" took place on 28 November, the day after the General Strike.[111] In the timing of this rhetorical shift, we may suspect that strategy did play a role. Another turning point can be seen in the discussions in Prague's Civic Forum coordinating center on 6 December, when the elites of that association discussed whether to support Dubček or Havel for president. To support Dubček would have been to espouse the "twenty years of decline" narrative and concomitantly to support trying "socialism with a human face." To support Havel, however, would mean that "there will be no phase of reform Communism, however enlightened, or *přestavba*; this will instead be a different, categorically different phase."[112] Zdeněk Jičinský—a Dubček supporter—appealed to an opinion poll conducted in Prague the same day and pointed out that whereas the majority gathered in that room might support Havel and the interpretation of the past that went with him, the same could not be said of the majority of the population, which was spontaneously crying "Dubček President" on the squares. Petr Oslzlý—a Havel supporter—replied that most respondents to this latest poll were actually undecided, and he suggested that "people in this neutral category do not yet have a name in their heads. We will put that name in their heads and they will follow that name, which we say."[113] This campaign to put Havel's name in people's heads, incidentally, went out of its way to emphasize that while Havel came from a "bourgeois" family, he did not want to restore an exploitative bourgeois order, and that he had even married a proletarian.[114]

The explicit popular support for something called socialism did not mean that people simply wanted to preserve the mechanisms that existed. OF Banská Bystrica proclaimed that socialism should be renewed.[115] Collective farmers in Jaslovské

---

[110] Speech on Wenceslas Square, 22 November, in Suk, *Občanské fórum*, vol. 2, p. 17; "Občanské fórum k pražským manifestacím," 27 November 1989, ibid., p. 32. The latter has also been reprinted in Otáhal and Sládek, *Deset pražských dnů*, p. 537; similar or identical versions can be found in BB, DÚ, HIA, and PV.

[111] "Vnitřní organizace Občanského fóra," Prague, 28 November 1989, in Otáhal and Sládek, *Deset pražských dnů*, p. 553, and as "Co jsme" in Suk, *Občanské fórum*, vol. 2, p. 35. Identical or similar versions can be found in BB, BE, CK, DÚ, HIA, KS, OL, OV, PR, and PV; Slovak translations can be found in KS and ZM.

[112] Michal Kocáb, quoted in Jiří Suk, *Labyrintem revoluce: Aktéři, zápletky a křížovatky jedné politické krize (od listopadu 1989 do června 1990)* (Prague: Prostor, 2003), p. 199.

[113] Ibid., pp. 200–201.

[114] Informační centrum Českomoravské divadelní obce, "Kdo je Václav Havel" (BV: fond "ONV Břeclav," box "Listopadová revoluce/1989–90 ONV Břeclav"). See also James Krapfl, "The Diffusion of 'Dissident' Political Theory in the Czechoslovak Revolution of 1989," *Slovo* (London) 19, no. 2 (Autumn 2007): 92–93.

[115] "Slovo socializmus dajme konkrétny obsah," *Smer*, 29 November 1989, p. 5.

Bohunice echoed Vladimír Ondruš in appealing "for a new, modern face of socialism."[116] Though according to the previously cited poll only 3 percent of the population expressed support for "capitalism," 47 percent wanted to alloy socialism with market mechanisms. Students in Olomouc explicitly called for a socialist market.[117] Such schemes had existed in Hungary since 1968, and some forms of private enterprise had already been legalized in Czechoslovakia in 1988 under pressure from Soviet *perestroika*. Laws introducing further market mechanisms into the Czechoslovak economy had been passed just before 17 November and were scheduled to go into effect at the beginning of 1990.[118] Much of the initial support for a mixed economy seems to have grown out of this discourse on *prestavba*. As the debate on socialism intensified, Sweden was proposed as an alternate model—a step on the road to increasing support in 1990 for the adoption of radical free-market reforms.[119]

Humanness

Though all the aforementioned ideas were important, the central ideal of the revolution was suggested by the words *ľudskosť/lidskost* or *humanita*, which might be translated according to context as humanity, humaneness, or humanness. The desired new society was to be a society for people, not for parties, machines, systems, or bureaucracies. It was considered a form of violence to force human beings, with all their individual uniqueness, into such systems. Like its subject, *ľudskosť* is a concept that one intuitively appreciates but that cannot be precisely defined, and this indeterminacy was part of its appeal. The revolution is incomprehensible, or at least misunderstood, without appreciation of this concept. Humanness was the revolution's central ideal, to which all others were logically subordinate.

While nonviolence was the first revolutionary principle to be articulated—as a direct response to the events of 17 November—violence itself was condemned by reference to *humanita*. The violence of the massacre was denounced as "inhuman" (i.e., no human being should be capable of such a thing), and in the days following the attack students implored armed forces not to use violence by appealing to their "simple human honor."[120] The ideals of *humanita* and nonviolence were fre-

---

[116] Členovia JRD Svornosť, "Prehlásenie," Jaslovské Bohunice, 27 November 1989 (SNA: Archív VPN, fond. odd. I); *Štúdio Televíznych novín*, 24 November 1989.

[117] Studenti vysokých škol, "Dělníci, hutníci, havíři Ostravska!" (OL: Sbírka soudobé dokumentace, sign. 148–22).

[118] G. Hitzgerová, "Tržní mechanismus a co od ní očekáváme" (CB: sbírka dokumentace K1139); Michal Pullmann, *Konec experimentu: Přestavba a pád komunismu v Československu* (Prague: Scriptorium, 2011).

[119] "Švédský model," *Přetlak*, no. 18 (15 December 1989), p. 7.

[120] Studenti pražských a slovenských VŠ, "Výzva příslušníkům ozbrojených složek," Bratislava, 23 November 1989 (OL: Sbírka soudobé dokumentace, sign. 148–22). Versions of this flyer attributed only to Prague students can be found in PR and OV; a Slovak version, attributed to "Študenti slovenských a pražských VŠ," is preserved in BB.

quently invoked side by side, so close was their mental association. Provocation, for example, was condemned as being against the related principles of nonviolence and *humanita*, and for a journalist in Vranov nad Topľou, the whole revolution was "a return to universal human values," in opposition to violence.[121]

The association between *ľudskosť* and other ideals was also strong. Students declared that they wanted "to achieve the democratization of society exclusively by humane [*humánnymi*] means," and plural political parties were justified as a "natural" expression of human diversity.[122] Socialism, of course, was to be "socialism with a human face." This slogan captured the ideal of humanizing bureaucratic institutions—in Weberian terms, of finding a way out of the iron cage. Use of the metaphor was not limited to socialism, moreover. Soldiers in Most called for and established an association in support of "military service with a human face."[123] The revolution as a whole could be called "a revolution with a human face."

Humanita, of course, could mean many things in practice. For some, it meant a return to tradition and common sense. VPN Brezno saw the revolution as an opportunity to "return to tradition," and a journalist in Galanta, summing up all that had happened by 21 December, wrote, "We have restored to many words their time-honored human content."[124] Some applied *humanita* to their own social situation. "We believe," proclaimed electricians from a Stonava mine, "that the era of manipulation with human opinions is finally at an end and now workers will be able not just to work, but also to feel, to believe, and to think."[125] A disabled woman in Čadca wrote that "in truth, I've never especially felt the proclaimed concern for us. In the state apparatus I've always met with incomprehension when I came to ask for help. I believe that now everything will change, that even we invalids will find dignity in our new society."[126]

If the Gentle Revolution had an equivalent to the French slogan "liberty, equality, fraternity," it was "*humanita*, freedom, and democracy. And in the name of these noble ideals," wrote the newly reinstated pre-1969 editor of Topoľčany's district newspaper, "for the victory of which millions of the best sons and daughters of this planet have died, let us ever remain *people*."[127] The word *people* itself acquired a new significance; usages that in other contexts would seem banal now took on

---

[121] See, for example, "Občané Československa! Ostře odmítejte . . ." (JN: sbírka soudobé dokumentace, 1989–1991). L. Krivda, "K udalostiam," *Vranovské noviny*, 8 December 1989, p. 1.

[122] "My, študenti z koordinačného výboru . . . ," 28 November 1989 (BB: Zbierka písomností získaných od študentov Pedagogickej fakulty v Banskej Bystrici, 1989–1990).

[123] Alternativní sdružení pro vojnu s lidskou tváří, "Prohlášení," Most, 17 December 1989 (CB: Kronika města Českých Budějovic, box "Kronika—1989: Dokumentace A1-B48," oddíl A, folder 16 "Ostatní tiskoviny z mimořádných politických událostí").

[124] "Návrat k tradíciám," *Smer*, 22 December 1989, p. 3; Judita Púčeková, "Čas vianočný," *Víťazná cesta*, 21 December 1989, p. 1.

[125] Telegram from zaměstnanci Dolu 1. máj, závod 9. květen Stonava, úsek slaboproud, to OF Prague, 25 November 1989 (ÚSD: archiv KC OF, box 11, folder "Podpory—OF—stud. P-MP").

[126] Viera Markuláková, in "Verejná tribuna," *Kysuce*, 8 December 1989, p. 3.

[127] Anton Krumpar, "Čas nádejí a viery v človeka," *Dnešok*, 20 December 1989, p. 1 (emphasis added).

profundity. When the singer Marta Kubišová—who had been barred from performing since 1970—explained that she had endured the years of silence because "it was people that helped me [*pomohli mi lidé*]," she was invoking the most fundamental value of the collective effervescence.[128] Even those who remained inscribed within the rhetoric of *prestavba* while their more radical compatriots spoke of revolution identified the essence of what was happening as the elevation of humaneness. For a woman from Slovakia's Kysuce region, *prestavba* was "the renewal of interest in man, leading to the dignity of human life."[129] Collective farmers in Hříškov pledged themselves to "strive for the new centrality of the human and civic dignity of the person."[130] Striking students, for their part, hailed the revolution as a passage "from absurdity to humanity," and transportation department employees in Považská Bystrica called *ľudskosť* and *humanita* "the best idea of the century."[131]

A student poster archived in Banská Bystrica illustrates the shift that was perceived in the configuration of power in Czechoslovakia, concomitant with the centrality of *ľudskosť* in the revolutionary mind. In this poster, a little girl comes up behind a man pontificating at a podium (the universal graphic code for the functionaries of the old regime) and tells him, "Mama says to stop with this silliness immediately . . . are you listening?" The family—quintessentially human—was put above engineered power structures as being more authoritative.

Revolutionary Idealism

The ideals discussed above were principles that characterized the revolutionary community's ideal vision of itself. It was a clear vision, even if difficult to express in words, and citizens consciously endeavored to incarnate it—first in themselves and then in the surrounding human environment. The ideals of the revolution were none other than tenets of a new religion with a new sacred center: the mobilized community itself. As the previous chapter demonstrated, the events of 17 November sparked a reconfiguration of sacrality; in discovering solidarity with each other, Czechs and Slovaks experienced ontological transformation—transcendence. The ideals with which the new community identified sprang logically from the experience of coming together as a community: solidarity with the victims of violence resulted in a categorical rejection of violence, millions of individual decisions to act established the new community as self-organizing and democratic, and so on. This is not to say that these ideas had not existed before 17 November (obviously they had), but the experience of collective effervescence created a new logical framework

---

[128] "M. Kubišová: Pomohli mi lidé," *Svobodné slovo*, 23 November 1989, p. 5.

[129] Oľga Vavrová, "Vrátiť životu dôstojnosť," *Kysuce*, 22 December 1989, p. 10.

[130] "Dne 7.12. 1989 bylo při JZD Hříškov ustaveno OF . . ." (LN: fond 569, box 2).

[131] Koordinační stávkový výbor VŠ, "Občané! Ptáte se proč . . ." (KS: zbierka z Nežnej revolúcie, folder "Rôzne"); similar Czech versions can be found in OV and PV; various versions of a Slovak translation can be found in BB, KS, PP, PX, SV, and ZM. "Stanovisko pracovníkov Okresnej správy ciest v Považskej Bystrici ku dnešnému dianiu v našej vlasti," 1 December 1989 (SNA: Archív VPN, fond. odd. I), p. 2.

for the prioritization and interpretation of ideas. The intensity of the collective effervescence in Czechoslovakia, creating an "atmosphere" that people experienced
as transcendent, effectively sacralized the new sense of community and in turn the
ideas that characterized it. Reference to these ideals could legitimize or delegitimize
social institutions, whether old or new, because they were expressions of the new
community's conception of itself—that is, the sacred.

This understanding of the relationship between society and ideas can help us
make sense of several surprising aspects of 1989 in Czechoslovakia, including the
popular attachment to socialism. Gál may have been right that ordinary citizens
did not really "know" what socialism meant. Certainly many of the definitions
they gave in 1989 would not have satisfied a prescriptive sociologist. Pipe makers
in Neratovice wrote, "We are for socialism that will satisfy everyone's desires and
needs."[132] A laborer from Slovnaft who asked to speak on Bratislava's SNP Square
insisted that "workers understand the concept *socialism* as the well-being of the
people. They don't care about academic definitions."[133] If these statements are anything to go by, the word *socialism* was for many citizens simply a signifier of the
ideal society. Further research will be necessary to determine more precisely how
Czechoslovak citizens understood the term, but it would seem that the signifier itself was secondary; at stake was the signified—the ideal society. In the end, Czechs
and Slovaks would accept any social system, whether socialist, capitalist, or some
real or hypothetical blend, that could convincingly represent the ideal society they
desired. Indeed, the proponents of capitalism ultimately "sold" their program in the
early 1990s not by insisting on its economic superiority but by arguing that it would
ensure a beneficent transformation of human relations and the inauguration of the
ideal society that Czechoslovaks had envisioned in 1989.[134]

For a significant number of Czechoslovaks, "socialism" was a relic of an older
form of sacrality, which in 1989 had not yet lost its potency. The position of socialism
in Czech and Slovak minds in 1989 thus paralleled that of monarchy in French minds
in 1789. Dynamics the two revolutions set in motion arguably implied the dismantling
of both socialism and monarchy, respectively, but most Czechoslovak and French citizens were unable initially to draw this logical conclusion—to countenance the definitive dismissal of a representation of the social order with which they had so long
identified. The struggles over the legacy of socialism in the Czech and Slovak republics since 1990 (when the first controversial steps were taken to dismantle it) are thus
comparable in some ways to the ambivalent legacy of monarchy in France after 1792.

[132] Členové výrobního družstva Potrubáři Neratovice, "Podepsaní v příloze se plně stavíme . . . ,"
24 November 1989 (ÚSD: archiv KC OF, box 95).
[133] Peter Trnkal, Bratislava, 30 November 1989 (SNA: Archív VPN, fond. odd. I).
[134] See, for example, Jozef Kučerák in the transcript of VPN's third republican convention (Bratislava,
3 March 1990), pt. 2, p. 18 (SNA: Archív VPN, fond. odd. II); Marcel Strýko, interviewed in "Bratislavský
centralismus už poznáme," *Verejnosť*, 20 August 1990, p. 1; Iveta Vrbová, "Dva měsíce prázdnin: Rozhovor
s Ivanem Fišerou z KC OF a poslancem FS nejen o práci parlamentu," *Fórum* (Prague), 29 August 1990,
p. 12; and Václav Havel, quoted in "Privatizácia rozbije nomenklatury," *Verejnosť*, 10 September 1990, p. 2.

It is significant that the most sacred principle of the reconfigured symbolic system was initially the idea of humanity as such, rather than a more particular notion such as the nation or the working class. This is not to say that individuals advocating such deification did not exist, but their worldview did not immediately become dominant. Revolutionary Czechs and Slovaks were concerned not just for the future of their country but for the future of humanity as such, and they viewed their revolution as a microcosm or model of a transformation of consciousness sweeping the globe. "Each one of us is just one," wrote a woman in Levice,

> one little feather of an enormous bird. When these little feathers cooperate with each other, the bird can fly and gently touch the hearts of our brothers and sisters in America, in Australia, in Africa, in China, or in India—everywhere. And every little feather of this bird will cry: "Come with us!" and we will all do our best to meet the demands of a better and more beautiful future! Such a future, where all people of our planet will live together like one family in love and happiness.[135]

Students in Prague, after the end of their strikes, maintained and elaborated on this idea of world revolution:

> We will offer Europe and mainly ourselves a lifeline, which will evacuate all of us from the depths of the excrement of materialism back to nature, love, clean water, humility, respect for one's fellows, etc. And let us not think it is only we who need this lifeline. That is a mistake! All Europe needs it; the whole world needs it. In truth there now begins for us a second revolution, a revolution in ourselves, a revolution against ourselves, a revolution in which, if we win, we will gain ourselves and offer Europe again something new, something Czechoslovak.[136]

Naive though these convictions may appear in less excited times, they were nonetheless sincere, and cynicism holding that such grandiose aims were unrealistic was itself condemned in 1989 as being antihumanistic.[137] To avoid the destabilizing effects of cynicism and to assure the success of the revolutionary program, it was felt to be essential to maintain the collective effervescence, whereby people might mutually reinforce perception and keep the idea of humanity at the center of attention. "Let us remain united!" pleaded the citizens' initiatives in Považská Bystrica. "The

[135] Diana Febérová, "Pierko zjednotenia," *Fórum* (Levice), no. 3 (19 December 1989), p. 10.
[136] Miloš Rybáček, "Buďme svoji," *Informační bulletin celostátního koordinačního výboru vysokých škol,* no. 1 (23 January 1990), p. 2.
[137] "Naše stanovisko" (ÚSD: archiv KC OF, box 97).

conditions established by striking students are supported by the people. All of us!
Every movement in history was defeated once it suffered division. At stake are the
fates of all of us, who are *people*."[138]

The Originality of 1989

Jürgen Habermas dismisses 1989 for "its total lack of ideas that were either innovative or oriented toward the future," insisting that "the recent rectifying revolutions
took their methods and standards entirely from the familiar repertoire of the modern age."[139] Furet, similarly, writes that "with all the fuss and noise, not a single new
idea has come out of Eastern Europe in 1989."[140] Habermas and Furet proffered
these judgments, of course, without actually consulting much evidence. Now that
we have considered primary evidence of the life of ideas in Czechoslovakia in 1989,
what can we make of the pundits' assessments? Was there anything new or innovative about the ideals of November?

The thought of 1989 was of course informed by many ideas that had been around
for some time and can be considered part of Habermas's "familiar repertoire." The
French Declaration of the Rights of Man and the Citizen circulated in a reprint
with eighteenth-century graphics.[141] Students in Banská Bystrica quoted Goethe,
Lessing, and Hegel.[142] OF Cheb cited Rousseau, and OF Sokolov quoted Eduard
Bernstein.[143] A Slovak professor invoked the thought of the popes Pius XII and John
XXIII, and many of his countrymen found inspiration in 1848.[144] The ideas of John
Lennon and Abbie Hoffman further contributed to the mix. Not all the inspiration
was necessarily modern, however. Banská Bystrica students also quoted Cicero, and
biblical quotations were widespread across Czechoslovakia, with occasional Hussite
references in Bohemia.

An important intellectual tradition of the modern age that influenced thinking
in 1989 more than has been appreciated was, perhaps ironically, Marxism. Reform
Communist ideas that had flourished in Czechoslovakia in the 1960s were the inspiration for many citizens in 1989. For the vice principal of the *gymnázium* in

[138] VPN and OF Považská Bystrica, "Občianske iniciatívy v Považskej Bystrici informujú o nesplnených
požiadavkách študentov," 2 December 1989 (PX: súčasná dokumentácia, folder "Nežná revolúcia—1989")
(emphasis in original).
[139] Jürgen Habermas, "What Does Socialism Mean Today? The Rectifying Revolution and the Need for
New Thinking on the Left," *New Left Review,* no. 183 (September–October 1990): 5, 7.
[140] Quoted in Ralf Dahrendorf, *Reflections on the Revolution in Europe* (New York: Times Books, 1990),
p. 27.
[141] "Deklarace práv člověka a občana" (UH: sbírky UH, box 7, folder "Letáky a plakáty všeobecné"; CB:
sbírka dokumentace K1139).
[142] BB: Zbierka plagátov získaných od študentov Pedagogickej fakulty v Banskej Bystrici, 1989–1990.
[143] *Občanské fórum Cheb,* no. 10 (23 January 1990), p. 1; *Sokolovské infórum,* no. 17 (24 January 1990), p. 1.
[144] Juraj Gál, "Listy spoluobčanom" (BB: Zbierka písomností získaných od študentov Pedagogickej
fakulty v Banskej Bystrici, 1989–1990).

Čadca, what happened in November and December 1989 was "a renewal process, actually the continuation of that which began in 1968, a process of reconstruction [*prestavba*] and democratization."[145] According to a pensioner in Olomouc, "ordinary worker-Communists [in 1968] called for socialism with a human face, and thereby stood for practically all demands which are being proclaimed today."[146] A spokesman for Mikhail Gorbachev once quipped that the only difference between the Prague Spring and *perestroika* was "twenty years," and it should therefore not surprise us that many Czechs and Slovaks in 1989 drew as much inspiration from the contemporary Soviet example as they did from their own past. "We demand democracy and *přestavba* like that which is being implemented among our friends in the USSR under the leadership of Comrade Gorbachev," wrote a group of workers in Třebíč.[147] Soviet flags were flown among the Czechoslovak on Bratislava's SNP Square, and Ján Budaj described VPN activists as "ambassadors of glasnost."[148] The Marxist influence went deeper than these reformist models, however. Judging by the language of many contributors to the "conversation" of 1989, quite a few had internalized principles of Marxism and used them in criticizing the Communist regime and evaluating the likely evolution of the current situation. Students in Olomouc echoed the Marxist emphasis on "contradictions" within exploitative societies when they declared that their strike was "no longer against violence, but mainly against all contradictions in our state."[149] Economists in Bratislava's automotive works betrayed a lingering willingness to see the world in Marxist class terms when they declared that they were "for the realization of a pluralist system in socialism, in confidence that the working class will remain at the forefront of the progressive movement."[150] Even those critical of Marxist interpretive frameworks nonetheless drew inspiration from the Marxist intellectual tradition. According to Ivan Langer, a member of the student strike committee in Olomouc in 1989, he and his colleagues actually learned their revolutionary methods from courses on Marxism-Leninism:

> In this technology the Communists themselves paradoxically taught us. Even if one didn't want to, one read about strikes, about revolution, about partisans and the antifascist movement, about how struggles were organized. From

---

[145] Matúš Briestenský, in "Verejná tribúna," *Kysuce*, 8 December 1989, p. 1.

[146] Robert Březina, "Stávkovému výboru UP Olomouc," *Přetlak*, no. 8 (4 December 1989), p. 3.

[147] Letter from pracující OZ Uhelné sklady Třebíč to redakce *Rudého práva* (ÚSD: archiv KC OF, box 158).

[148] Martin Slivka, *Dni nádeje*, Slovenská televízia, 17 November 2004; "Veľvyslanci glasnosti," *Kysuce*, 8 December 1989, p. 2.

[149] Studenti Univerzity Palackého, Olomouc, "Stávka studentů pokračuje" (OL: Sbírka soudobé dokumentace, sign. 148–22).

[150] "Stanovisko pracovníkov ekonomického úseku," BAZ, Bratislava, 27 November 1989 (SNA: Archív VPN, fond. odd. I).

this it followed that we knew what and how. . . . We knew that there had to be some kind of structure based on free decision, which means elections, that a delegation of competencies was necessary; we had to know what all needed to be arranged. . . . Thus there emerged individual sections, each [member of the strike committee] was responsible for a certain section, and then we looked for something all-encompassing, which besides the people working in the sections would attract the broader mass. These then were the happenings.[151]

In a sense, Marxism was a museum of ideas that could ultimately be used for a purpose the Marxist regime did not intend; it preserved in popular awareness a detailed knowledge of the European revolutionary tradition that in the West had been forgotten. Years of painstaking research will be necessary to construct a full and accurate *Begriffsgeschichte* of popular thinking in the revolution of 1989, but it seems quite likely that, to a significant extent, it was Marxism that made it possible to "think" the revolution.

Czechs and Slovaks, however, did not just reiterate what they found in inherited traditions; they innovated. OF Semily adapted Rudolf Steiner's theory of *Dreigliederung* to create a program that, its authors claimed, would enable Czechoslovakia to complete the French Revolution.[152] Many citizens sought to improve on plans only partially implemented in 1968, modifying these plans in light of their experience.[153] As Pascal once observed, old ideas, arranged in a new order, make for a new discourse, and here we see that Habermas's and Furet's dismissal of 1989 is partly based on false expectations. Much of the originality of revolutions—whether in 1989 or otherwise—lies in their new combination of ideas and an attempt to apply them to contemporary, local circumstances. Czechs and Slovaks in 1989 could no more claim that their notions of freedom, democracy, and humanity were new in an absolute sense than could the French in 1789 of their ideas of liberty, equality, and fraternity. In both cases, however, they were experienced as innovative because there was a fresh opportunity to apply them in broad fields of political, social, and economic life where, to the revolutionary mind at least, they had hitherto been absent.

That said, the revolution of 1989 did introduce a number of novelties, at least with respect to the "repertoire" familiar to Habermas. The foremost of these was *ľudskosť*. Czechs and Slovaks in 1989 elevated humanness and human dignity above ideology; they insisted on never losing sight of human reality whatever rules,

---

[151] Ivan Langer, in Otáhal and Vaněk, *Sto studentských revolucí*, p. 521.

[152] OF Semily, "Memorandum Občanského fóra v Semilech," 4 December 1989 (ÚSD: archiv KC OF, nezpracovaná hromada č. 2).

[153] See, for example, "Programové prohlášení občanského fóra (OF) Přerovských strojíren," 7 December 1989 (ÚSD: archiv KC OF, nezpracovaná hromada č. 1), p. 1.

bureaucratic procedures, and other man-made systems might decree; they recognized that these systems can never fully encompass every human situation. They forswore placing human tools above human beings themselves, and in so doing, they chose to remain human rather than becoming machines themselves. Though the roots of this idea go back to Kant and before him to the Judeo-Christian tradition (whence it has ever and anon received new emphasis, as in the preaching of John Paul II), it found especially fertile soil in Czechoslovakia in the twentieth century. It was a central feature of Masaryk's philosophy of political culture and sprang up again with startling brilliance in the idea of "humane socialism" in 1968. Throughout the twentieth century, Czechs and Slovaks (at least certain of them) have led the struggle to humanize human institutions—regardless of the regime— and they did so again on a mass scale in 1989.[154] In no other modern revolution, however, has the idea of *humanita* been so elevated and consciously defended (with the exception, of course, of kindred revolutions in Poland and East Germany in the 1980s). The French in 1789 did not hesitate to attack venerable human practices and institutions in the name of "enlightenment" and "reason." The Russians in 1917 felt no qualms about using violence to refashion the human environment in accordance with ideology. From the religious revolutions of the fifteenth and sixteenth centuries to the revolutions that followed World War II, Europeans have always placed the sanctity of ideology above the sanctity of the human being. That in 1989 the dignity of the person was itself the logical foundation of revolutionary thought was a profound reversal.

The nonviolence of 1989 was a further novelty in the history of European revolutions. Though Czechs and Slovaks had engaged in nonviolent resistance to the Warsaw Pact invasion of 1968, it had not yet been a wholly principled nonviolence (for many, principled motivation in 1968 had still been mixed with the practical consideration that against the combined might of the Soviet Union and its allies there could be no hope of victory by force). The revolution of 1989, however, established nonviolence as a value that transcended practical considerations. To be sure, Czechs and Slovaks drew inspiration from Gandhi and the American tradition of civil disobedience, but as a mass phenomenon in modern European history, this principled insistence on nonviolence was new. Those initially brought to power in previous revolutions had also sought to minimize violence, as when Lafayette created the National Guard to maintain order amid the collapse of royal authority, but they had still counted on the use of violence to contain violence. The Gentle Revolution went further than any prior European revolution in that its central prohibition was against violence itself.

---

[154] For an anthropological perspective on the importance of *ľudskosť* in Slovak culture, see Jonathan Larson, *Critical Thinking in Slovakia after Socialism* (Rochester, N.Y.: University of Rochester Press, 2013).

This brings us to Patočka's theory of the solidarity of the shaken, which—though first articulated in the 1970s—was revealed afresh in 1989 possessing new relevance and power. One of the few dissident ideas actually to be discussed in November and December, Patočka's theory was widely invoked in flyers, bulletins, and speeches—and most memorably in Ivan Hoffman's song—as an explanation for the spontaneous coming together of Czechoslovak citizens in rejection of systemic violence.[155] Moreover, it decisively influenced the original conception of Civic Forum and Public against Violence as informal associations, not organizations. It did this by way of Charter 77, which Patočka had cofounded and on which Civic Forum was in many ways modeled, and through Václav Havel, who had developed Patočka's ideas in "The Power of the Powerless" and other writings and who was in many ways the founding father of Civic Forum.[156] The idea behind the informality of these associations was to keep them human, to allow them to evolve to suit human needs, rather than establishing yet another bureaucratic structure into which humans could fit only by deceit and contortion—that is, by metaphysical violence.

Finally, the Gentle Revolution articulated new ideas about representation and the culture of democratic politics. Whether or not they had read Arendt, Czechoslovak citizens agreed that "political freedom . . . means the right 'to be a participator in government,' or it means nothing."[157] Whereas American revolutionaries at the end of the eighteenth century had innovated by instituting checks and balances among branches of government, Czechs and Slovaks at the end of the twentieth century innovated by proposing checks and balances between government and people. Collectively, their demands for referenda, the power to recall deputies who had betrayed their trust, and other mechanisms for confronting lawmakers with public opinion amounted to a new model of democracy that was neither "liberal" nor "totalitarian" but sought to combine the virtues of representative and direct democracy while avoiding their defects. With this model and with their concern for representing modernized social estates, Czechs and Slovaks essentially sought to humanize democratic institutions and make them responsive, to ensure meaningful participation of the people in the government of their affairs. They turned their attention not just to the institutional side of the equation, moreover, but to the popular side as well, seeking to nurture a democratic political culture. In this concern, the revolutionaries of 1989 were united with those of 1789, but whereas the French had sought to create a democratic culture through rationalist means, Czechs

[155] For more on the discussion of dissident ideas in 1989, see Krapfl, "The Diffusion of 'Dissident' Political Theory," pp. 83–101.

[156] See Suk, *Labyrintem*, pp. 66–75.

[157] Hannah Arendt, *On Revolution*, rev. ed. (New York: Viking, 1965), p. 218.

and Slovaks—characteristically—adopted a more organic approach, emphasizing democratic practice rather than ideology. In this, too, their approach was novel.[158]

Ever since the French Revolution at the end of the eighteenth century, students of revolution have tended not to question the French revolutionary belief that a true revolution must involve profound newness, an attempt at radical departure from all preceding matrices of political and social organization. This despite the fact that since Tocqueville, at least, we have known how all these attempts are more or less constrained. It is surprising that Habermas and especially Furet (who did so much to demythologize the French Revolution) should remain, with their unquestioned reverence for absolute novelty, inscribed within the mythic structures of the French Revolution. Much of the perceived newness of French revolutionary ideas was just this—perception—and as Furet himself showed, the ideas had in many cases been around for some time. Much of the perception of newness in 1789 stemmed from the fact not that the ideas themselves were new but that they were applied in new combinations and in new contexts. We might similarly question Habermas's dismissal of 1989 for not being "future-oriented," asking what powers of clairvoyance allow anyone in the present to recognize what is future-oriented and what is not. If *ľudskost'* and nonviolence are not part of our future, can we really say that we have a future? In the end, late Communist Czechoslovakia was not so different from the rest of contemporary Western civilization that the problems to which revolutionaries turned their thought in 1989 are irrelevant elsewhere. The revolutions of 1989 can tell us perhaps as much about our present and future as the French Revolution did two centuries ago—if we are interested in knowing. For even if new ideas did not "come out" of Eastern Europe in 1989, they were there.

---

[158] Barbara Falk makes a similar point in *The Dilemmas of Dissidence in East-Central Europe* (Budapest: Central European University Press, 2003), pp. 313–64. Though dissident ideas other than Patočka's did not disseminate widely in Czechoslovakia before 1990, dissident practice had a profound influence on civic organization in 1989 by virtue of the fact that Civic Forum and Public against Violence were modeled on Charter 77. Krapfl, "The Diffusion of 'Dissident' Political Theory," pp. 83–101.

1. The "living altar" on Národní třída, 17 November 1989. Unknown author. Courtesy of the Masaryk University Archive, Brno (fond G39, box 42, folder 22).

2. Natural sciences students in Brno decide to go on strike, 20 November 1989. Photo by Jiří Dobrovolný. Courtesy of the Masaryk University Archive, Brno (fond G39, box 42, folder 12).

3. Reading flyers in Olomouc. Photo by Petr Zatloukal. Courtesy of Petr Zatloukal.

4. Part of the human chain in Brno to Petr Cibulka's prison, 26 November 1989. Photo by Jaroslav Luner. Courtesy of the Masaryk University Archive, Brno (fond G39, box 42, velká samostatná žlutá obálka).

5. The General Strike in Banská Bystrica, 27 November 1989. Photo by René Miko. Courtesy of the Slovak National Archive (Archív VPN, fond. odd. VI, fotografie, box 1, envelope "Generálny štrajk 27. 12. 1989").

6. A student from Brno addresses a civic forum in the south Moravian town of Ivančice, late November 1989. Unknown author. Courtesy of the Masaryk University Archive, Brno (fond G39, box 42, folder 11).

7. "A Fairy Tale for Children of the 1990s: The Communist Party and the Seven Dwarfs," Bratislava. Unknown author. Courtesy of the Historical Museum of the Slovak National Museum (box "Plagáty: 1989 a ďalej s číslom," poster no. 33675).

8. The Train of the Gentle Revolution leaves Bratislava, 6 December 1989. Photo by Zdeno Kajzr. Courtesy of the Slovak National Archive (Archív VPN, fond. odd. VI, fotografie, box 2, envelope "Zdeno Kajzr: november–december 1989").

9. The balloon happening at the Stalin/Lenin monument in Olomouc, 9 December 1989. Photo by Petr Zatloukal. Courtesy of Petr Zatloukal.

10. Daniel Brunovský's "Heart of Europe" overlooking the Danube, erected 10 December 1989. Photo by Daniel Brunovský. Courtesy of Daniel Brunovský.

11. Angelic students in Bratislava take up a collection for the victims of Romanian violence.
Photo by Martin Petrík. Courtesy of the Slovak National Archive (Archív VPN, fond. odd. VI, fotografie, box 1).

12. A shrine in Bratislava to the victims of 17 November, 17 December 1989.
Photo by Jana Šebestová. Courtesy of the Slovak National Archive (Archív VPN, fotografie, box 1, envelope "Než. rev.—atmosféra tých dní").

Chapter 4

The Boundaries of Community

"In unity is strength! We shall be victorious, because we have succeeded in uniting ourselves. It is something magnificent, this feeling of belonging to the nation. Nation? I'm not thinking now just of Czechs and Slovaks, but also of Hungarians, Germans, Ukrainians, Russians, of everyone who has proven capable of coming together for this noble goal: that we might breathe freely in a free and democratic country! This nation I mention here is one gigantic family, where we will find what we have hitherto dared only to dream of."[1]

Readers of the previous chapter may have wondered where national identity and self-determination fell among revolutionary ideals. The "velvet revolution" of 1989, after all, led directly or indirectly to the "velvet divorce" of 1992. Can we not find among "the ideals of November" at least a foreshadowing of what was to come?

The question must be placed in a broader context. To reiterate, the revolution of 1989 was first and foremost the genesis of transcendent solidarity. The emergence of a new sense of community was chronologically primary in the experiences of revolutionary protagonists, and initially terms such as *nation* and *people* were used to describe the community without thinking too carefully about their implications. Only once the movement to institutionalize this new sense of community was seriously under way were people forced to confront the question, who *exactly* are we? Answers to this question naturally implied boundaries between what the group under consideration was and was not, who was in and who was out. By virtue of reconstituting community, the revolution necessarily demanded a reconstitution of

[1] Diana Febérová, "Pierko zjednotenia," *Fórum* (Levice), no. 3 (19 December 1989), p. 10.

society—in which some would stand to gain and others to lose. Initially, of course, the main cleavage was between those who owed their positions in society directly to the Communist Party and those who argued that the Party should no longer play a leading role in society. Almost immediately, however, other cleavages began to manifest themselves, though they were generally not recognized as cleavages until much later. Even today the actors involved might deny that the movements they led and that contested the location of sacrality after 1989 were in any sense partisan departures from the unity of November 1989. As with many Czech and Slovak interpretations of the revolution, however, there is a tendency to extrapolate from local experience to global generalizations. It is only by setting the revolutionary experiences of different social groups side by side that the cleavages become apparent.

This chapter examines the evolution of thinking about identity and the boundaries of community in Czechoslovakia from the beginning of the revolution to the spring of 1990. It suggests that the road to adoption of nationalist sentiment by more than a fringe of the population led first through local patriotism, then through regionalism, with each new form of community identification a means of achieving the demands of the former. Urban rivalry is shown to have exacerbated conflicts over regional and national representation, with motives of empire trumping impulses toward federation. To illustrate how these processes worked, the chapter begins with an in-depth study of a little-known aspect of the revolution: the emergence and demise of Civic Forum in Slovakia. References to this example are then used to inform generalizations about the evolution of local, regional, and national senses of identity in Czechoslovakia as a whole.

The Short History of Civic Forum in Slovakia

Textbook accounts of the Gentle Revolution and the subsequent dissolution of Czechoslovakia relate that two separate citizens' initiatives emerged in 1989, channeling popular political engagement and orchestrating the democratic transition, and that one was Czech while the other was Slovak. This narrative matches what became the official position of the founders of these initiatives in Prague and Bratislava, but systematic examination of local initiative outside the capitals reveals a dramatically different story. While it is true enough that local activists in the Czech lands affiliated themselves with the association founded in Prague rather than that in Bratislava, it turns out that Slovaks were initially more likely to found chapters of the Prague initiative than they were to form branches of the Bratislava movement. This finding raises important questions about the nature of democracy, Czecho-Slovak relations, and possibilities for federation in revolutionary and post-Communist Czechoslovakia.

A handful of scholars have noted the existence of Civic Forum in some parts of Slovakia but have neither agreed on the details nor recognized its full extent.

Simon Smith notes that Civic Forum was founded prior to Public against Violence in Humenné and other towns of East Slovakia, while Jan Rychlík asserts that OF chapters were established in Košice and some parts of West Slovakia, and Jiří Suk writes that OF was founded prior to VPN in many parts of East and Central Slovakia. Rychlík suggests that Civic Forum's coordinating center in Prague abolished all Slovak OF chapters in late November or early December 1989, whereupon they were reorganized as branches of VPN, whereas Suk provides evidence that many OF chapters resisted incorporation into VPN into 1990.[2] The truth is that Civic Forum initially enjoyed a preeminent position in twenty-one of the thirty-eight districts into which Slovakia was divided in 1989, and it was present in at least seven others. At its height, in other words, OF was an important force across more than half of Slovakia's territory. Moreover, OF was dispersed across all three of Slovakia's administrative regions (East, Central, and West Slovakia), and even in Bratislava itself. While most Slovak Civic Fora did convert to VPN in late November and early December 1989, the process was not painless, and as Suk points out, many Slovak OFs struggled to maintain their original identity well into 1990.

As Carol Leff, Susan Mikula, and Abby Innes have observed, the institutionalization of separate Czech and Slovak party systems after 1989 was a factor in producing the political stalemate that led to the dissolution of the Czech and Slovak Federative Republic.[3] Though the Bratislava founders of VPN have repeatedly emphasized that their movement was conceived in solidarity with Prague and not as a kind of willful separation, the fact remains that the bifurcation of the civic movement along republican lines facilitated the emergence of separate party systems.[4] The extensive range of Civic Forum's appeal in Slovakia, however, suggests that this bifurcation was not inevitable. Indeed, many OF and VPN initiatives outside the Slovak capital established structures of local and regional cooperation—even federation—that might have provided generally applicable models. Given this starting

[2] Simon Smith, "Civic Forum and Public against Violence: Agents for Community Self-Determination? Experiences of Local Actors," in *Local Communities and Post-Communist Transformation: Czechoslovakia, the Czech Republic and Slovakia*, ed. Simon Smith (London: Routledge Curzon, 2003), pp. 49–51, 79–80; Jan Rychlík, "The Possibilities for Czech-Slovak Compromise, 1989–1992," in *Irreconcilable Differences? Explaining Czechoslovakia's Dissolution*, ed. Michael Kraus and Allison Stanger (Lanham, Md.: Rowman & Littlefield, 2000), p. 51; and "Průběh rozpadu Československa v letech 1989–92," in *Dělení Československa: Deset let poté . . .* , ed. Karel Vodička (Prague: Volvox Globator, 2003), pp. 270–71; Jiří Suk, *Labyrintem revoluce: Aktéři, zápletky a křížovatky jedné politické krize (od listopadu 1989 do června 1990)* (Prague: Prostor, 2003), p. 296.

[3] Carol Skalnik Leff, *The Czech and Slovak Republics: Nation versus State* (Boulder, Colo.: Westview, 1996), pp. 97–99; Leff and Susan B. Mikula, "Institutionalizing Party Systems in Multiethnic States: Integration and Ethnic Segmentation in Czechoslovakia, 1918–1992," *Slavic Review* 61, no. 2 (Summer 2002): 308–13; Abby Innes, *Czechoslovakia: The Short Goodbye* (New Haven, Conn.: Yale University Press, 2001), pp. 75–76.

[4] See, for example, Fedor Gál's account of VPN's origins in Ingrid Antalová, ed., *Verejnosť proti násiliu— Občianske fórum: Svedectvá* (Bratislava: Nadácia Milana Šimečku, 1999), p. 11.

point, the outcome of two democratic movements closely allied yet rigorously divided on national/republican lines is a problem to be solved. A close reading of the available archival evidence and contemporary local newspapers suggests that this outcome was the result of a struggle—not between Prague and Bratislava, as might be expected, but between Bratislava and other parts of Slovakia, in which the prize was the power to represent Slovakia.

FOUNDATION

Between the outset of revolution in Czechoslovakia on 17 November 1989 and the general strike ten days later, Civic Fora were founded in the workplaces and towns of at least twenty-eight of Slovakia's thirty-eight districts, including twenty-one district capitals.[5] Map 1 represents this initial dispersion.[6]

To understand how Slovak Civic Fora came into being, it is necessary to remember that OF and VPN were but two of many initiatives by which citizens responded to the events of 17 November. The first groups to organize, of course, were students and actors, who began full-time strikes on 18 November and appealed to citizens throughout the country to join them in a two-hour general strike nine days later. Between 19 and 21 November, strikes broke out in universities and theaters from Pilsen to Prešov, and the first workplace strike committees began to form. Thus, when news began to spread of the founding of OF and VPN in Prague and Bratislava on 19 November, it reached a country already in motion. OF and VPN, moreover, were by no means the only citizens' associations of their type to be founded. The Independent Hungarian Initiative (Független Magyar Kezdeményezés, or FMK) was founded in the southern Slovak town of Šaľa in the night from 18 to 19 November, and between 20 and 24 November such associations as the Liberec Initiative, the Moravian Civic Movement, and the Orava Initiative were all established, apparently without awareness of OF's or VPN's existence.[7] In towns throughout Czechoslovakia, moreover, concerned citizens began organizing as early as 19 November, even if they gave no names to their initiatives. In the

---

[5] The districts where OFs were founded in the district capital as well as workplaces and lesser towns (where such existed) were Banská Bystrica, Čadca, Humenné, Komárno, Košice, Levice, Liptovský Mikuláš, Lučenec, Nové Zámky, Poprad, Považská Bystrica, Prešov, Prievidza, Rožňava, Spišská Nová Ves, Trebišov, Trenčín, Vranov nad Topľou, Zvolen, Žiar nad Hronom, and Žilina. The districts where I have thus far found evidence of Civic Fora only in workplaces and/or lesser towns are Bratislava, Dolný Kubín, Galanta, Nitra, Topoľčany, Trnava, and Veľký Krtíš.

[6] Fluctuation between singular and plural forms of "Civic Forum" is meant not to jar the reader but to reflect the multiple valences of the term in revolutionary usage. It could refer both to individual, local groups (Civic Fora) as well as the statewide network of these groups (Civic Forum). In addition, *občianske fórum* could refer both to an informal activity (as an uncapitalized common noun) and to a semiformal association (as a capitalized proper noun). As will be shown, this versatility was part of Civic Forum's appeal.

[7] See "Komentář LI o shromáždění v Liberci," Liberec, 23 November 1989 (ÚSD: archiv KC OF, box 92); "Provolání Moravského občanského hnutí ze dne 20.11.1989," Brno, 20 November 1989 (UH: sbírky UH, box 7, folder "Letáky a plakáty všeobecné"); and "Verejnosť proti násiliu informuje," *Orava*, 13 December 1989, p. 2.

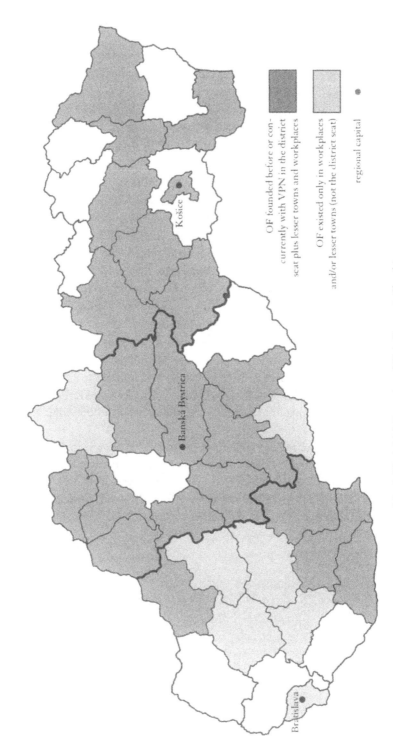

Map 1. The initial dispersion of Civic Forum in Slovakia

OF founded before or con-
currently with VPN in the district
seat plus lesser towns and workplaces

OF existed only in workplaces
and/or lesser towns (not the district seat)

● regional capital

Košice

Banská Bystrica

Bratislava

beginning, civic initiative was everywhere local and autonomous; this was genuinely spontaneous mobilization from below.

The story behind the founding of each local Civic Forum—as with each local group of VPN—was unique, but three broad patterns can be discerned. In the first, a small group came together and began engaging in revolutionary activity shortly after learning of the massacre and in conjunction with striking students and artists; they began calling themselves Civic Fora as early as 20 or 21 November in Košice and 23 November in Spišská Nová Ves. Later, on 26 and 27 November, they established themselves as citywide associations.[8] The Civic Fora in large towns like Banská Bystrica, Prešov, and probably Žilina were of this type.[9] In the second pattern, citizens demonstrating on a town square spontaneously identified themselves as a "civic forum" (that is, a group of citizens exchanging ideas about public matters), with a coordinating committee of "Civic Forum" (a semiformal association taking inspiration from the Prague initiative) coming into being later that evening or the next day. Thus an assembly of three hundred in Levice called itself a civic forum on 24 November, and a Civic Forum coordinating committee formally declared itself the next day.[10] The story in Poprad was similar.[11] In Rožňava, Civic Forum was established during a public meeting in the district House of Pioneers and Youth following the General Strike, with the assembled citizens electing spokesmen from their midst.[12] The final pattern was for the strike committees in a town to associate—during the General Strike or later that day—and collectively establish a municipal civic association. This was the case in Nové Zámky, where the association was called Civic Forum, and in Čadca, where the initiative (in the singular) was called "OF and VPN."[13]

What accounts for the wide dispersion of Civic Forum in Slovakia? We can generally reject the hypothesis that Slovaks established Civic Fora simply because they were unaware of VPN. Perhaps in Košice, where OF was first established in Slovakia, the founders had not yet heard of VPN, but in most places it seems clear that they had. The founding declarations of OF Lučenec, OF Prievidza, OF

[8] Ivan Dejmal and Vladislav Chlipala, quoted in Antalová, *Verejnosť proti násiliu—Občianske fórum*, pp. 14, 23; "Premeny v zrkadle týždňa," *Spišské hlasy*, 8 December 1989, p. 1.

[9] "Záverečné vyhlásenie," *Smer*, 28 November 1989, p. 2; "Slovu socializmus dajme konkrétny obsah," *Smer*, 29 November 1989, p. 4; "V centre Prešova," *Prešovské noviny*, 28 November 1989, p. 2; "Prvé kroky na ceste k dialógu," *Prešovské noviny*, 30 November 1989, p. 1; "Kronika uplynulých dní," *Cieľ*, 30 November 1989, p. 6.

[10] "Svedectvo týchto dní," *Fórum* (Levice), no. 1, p. 12; "Zhromaždenie Občianskeho fóra," *Pohronie*, 7 December 1989, p. 1.

[11] "V pondelok 27. novembra v okresnom sídle," *Podtatranské noviny*, 30 November 1989, p. 1; "Programové vyhlásenie" and "Vyhlásenie," *Podtatranské noviny*, 7 December 1989, pp. 1, 4.

[12] K. Bradovková, "Občianske fórum v Rožňave," *Zora Gemera*, 30 November 1989, p. 1.

[13] "Spoločne do ďalších dní," "V N. Zámkoch MKV," and "Umelci v našom meste," *Naše novosti*, 5 December 1989, pp. 1, 3; "Občania Kysúc," *Kysuce*, 1 December 1989, p. 4.

Rožňava, and OF Žilina all explicitly expressed agreement with the demands of VPN in Bratislava as well as OF in Prague.[14] After 24 November, when Slovak television broadcast a live debate wherein students and VPN spokesmen trounced Communist functionaries, it is difficult to imagine that anyone politically active in Slovakia could have been unaware of VPN. Most Slovak OFs, however, seem to have been founded after this date.[15] Despite their knowledge of VPN in Bratislava, they *chose* to identify themselves with Civic Forum.

A hypothesis commonly advanced by those aware of the existence of Civic Forum in Slovakia is that it was founded in places with stronger personal or historic ties to Prague than to Bratislava. This of course raises the question of why these ties were stronger, but there is evidence that in at least some instances a correlation did exist. At a Prague conference in 1998 about relations between OF and VPN, Peter Zajac (a former spokesman for VPN in Bratislava) speculated that activists in Košice must have founded OF because someone from Prague had gone there. A former OF Košice activist, Vladislav Chlipala, rebutted this hypothesis, pointing out that no one from Prague had appeared in Košice until 23 November, days after OF Košice had been founded. This was still before anyone from Bratislava appeared, however, and Chlipala himself observed that activists in Košice ardently sought visitors from Prague, whereas they felt no need to communicate with Bratislava. He further acknowledged that OF Košice founders had indeed learned about Civic Forum from acquaintances in Prague, albeit not face-to-face.[16] Former OF Humenné activists, in interviews conducted by Simon Smith, also recalled having more direct personal contact with Prague than with Bratislava.[17] It should be emphasized, however, that whatever contact there was with Prague, it was not necessarily with OF. The first revolutionary activist from Prague to visit Košice was a student, and OF Humenné activists report that they got their information from railway workers. For its part, the OF coordinating center (*koordinační centrum*, or KC) in Prague was oblivious to most grassroots activity in Slovakia (and even, to a surprising extent, in the Czech lands), such that by the end of November, the only Slovak Civic Fora of which it was evidently aware were Košice and Žilina.[18]

---

[14] "Dostali sme po uzávierke," *Ipeľ*, 28 November 1989, p. 2; "V N. Zámkoch MKV"; "Na aktuálnu tému s členom koordinačnej skupiny OF Ľubomírom Šaturom," *Prieboj*, 13 December 1989, p. 1; Bradovková, "Občianske fórum v Rožňave"; "Vyhlásenie Občianskeho fóra," *Cieľ*, 30 November 1989, p. 1.

[15] Eight OFs in district towns were definitely founded after the debate, five were definitely founded before; not enough information is yet available to date the foundings of the rest precisely.

[16] Antalová, *Verejnosť proti násiliu—Občianske fórum*, pp. 22–23.

[17] Smith, "Civic Forum," p. 49.

[18] Antalová, *Verejnosť proti násiliu—Občianske fórum*, pp. 14, 24–25; *Informační servis* (Prague), no. 10 (28 November 1989), p. 2. Other Slovak Civic Fora telephoned or sent letters or telegrams to the KC OF before the end of November, but it seems that their messages went unnoticed amid the hundreds of letters and telephone calls received daily at a time when mechanisms for processing them were still improvisational and chaotic, and when there were many other pressing matters to consider.

Even if founders of Civic Fora in Slovakia lacked personal connections with Prague, they were nonetheless likely to be better informed about developments in the Czechoslovak than in the Slovak capital. The regional newspapers in Central and East Slovakia and district newspapers everywhere initially provided far more information about demonstrations in Prague, the establishment of Civic Forum, and cadre shuffling in the Central Committee of the Czechoslovak Communist Party than they did about demonstrations in Bratislava, the establishment of Public against Violence, or reorganization within the Central Committee of the Slovak Communist Party. This naturally reflected the fact that mass media were tightly controlled by the Communist Party, which despite nominal federalization, remained highly centralized. To counter lacunae in the state-run media, of course, Czech and Slovak revolutionaries developed a vast samizdat literature of flyers and bulletins that reached the shop windows and bulletin boards of every town and perhaps most villages. In most of Slovakia, however, even this literature was strongly oriented toward Prague. As a result, Prague set the tone for much of the public debate in Slovakia, a fact that was reflected even in language. Activists across Slovakia struggled to find a proper translation of the Czech word *mluvčí* (spokesperson), and some of the flyers and posters that circulated in central and eastern Slovakia were written in a curious blend of Slovak and Czech.[19]

Perhaps the most important factor behind the relative dispersion of OF and VPN in Slovakia is the way the two initiatives were understood. In general, Civic Forum was understood to be relatively more open, Public against Violence relatively more restricted. The flyers that the coordinating centers of the two movements initially produced and that circulated across Slovakia prior to the General Strike supported such interpretations. In their very first declaration, for example, the founders of Civic Forum described their movement as one "open to all segments and strengths of the Czechoslovak public."[20] Subsequent proclamations issued by OF Prague and OF Brno between 22 and 25 November repeatedly encouraged citizens to establish their own Civic Fora in their workplaces and municipalities, without limiting this invitation to residents of Bohemia, Moravia, and Silesia. Rather, they emphasized that "anyone can join Civic Forum" and that it was "a movement of both our nations."[21] VPN's founding declaration, by contrast, allowed for the reading that it

[19] Examples can be found in BB: Zbierka plagátov získaných od študentov Pedagogickej fakulty v Banskej Bystrici, 1989–1990; KS: zbierka z Nežnej revolúcie, folder "Rôzne"; and SV: Zbierka plagátov, letákov a drobnej tlače, box 10. Similar examples of mixed language can be found in OL: Sbírka soudobé dokumentace, sign. 148–22.

[20] "Provolání. Na setkání v hledišti . . . ," 19 November 1989 (GA: súčasná dokumentácia, envelope "VPN Galanta. December 1989"; similar or identical copies are also preserved in BB). Reprinted in Milan Otáhal and Zdeněk Sládek, eds., *Deset pražských dnů (17.–27. listopadu 1989): Dokumentace* (Prague: Academia, 1990), pp. 47–48; and in Jiří Suk, ed., *Občanské fórum: Listopad-prosinec 1989*, vol. 2, *Dokumenty* (Brno: Doplněk, 1998), pp. 13–14.

[21] OF Prague, "Ku generálnemu štrajku," 22 November 1989 (PX: súčasná dokumentácia, folder "Nežná revolúcia—1989"; similar or identical versions are preserved in BB); OF Prague, "Provolání Občanského fóra,"

was a movement of only the "the cultural and academic public," and though it encouraged citizens to struggle "together with" VPN for dialogue and democracy,
it did not specifically invite people to join the association.[22] It is perhaps for this
reason that a group of Bratislava citizens decided in these early days to establish an
independent (and ephemeral) Bratislava Civic Forum as a more open counterpart
to VPN, whose spokesmen they nonetheless cheered. "We hold in deep esteem the
spokesmen and activists of VPN," they wrote, "whom we regard as genuine representatives of our city, deserving the trust of each one of us. . . . [However,] one of
our main goals (by which we differ from VPN) is the mobilization and enlisting
of *all* citizens."[23] VPN corrected for such misunderstandings in a proclamation of
22 November, which emphasized that the initiative was open to all citizens who rejected violence and added that VPN wanted to become "a society-wide movement,"
but it still said nothing about establishing branches outside Bratislava.[24] In stark
contrast with Civic Forum, it was not until 29 November that VPN disseminated
any statement explicitly addressing the possibility of autonomous branches outside
the Slovak capital.[25]

Judging by newspaper commentaries, citizens' letters to Public against Violence, and records of district national committees and civic associations, moreover,
it would seem that many in Slovakia initially thought VPN was part of OF. Several
OF Banská Bystrica documents, for example, suggest that people there thought
Public against Violence was just the peculiar name of Bratislava's Civic Forum,

23 November 1989 (PX: súčasná dokumentácia, folder "Nežná revolúcia—1989"; similar or identical versions
can be found in BB); OF Prague, "Prohlášení Občanského fóra k situaci 24. listopadu 1989 ve 23,30 hodin,"
24 November 1989 (BB: Materiály získané od hnutia Verejnosť proti násiliu v Banskej Bystrici, 1989, box
2); OF Brno, "Výzva k zakladaniu občianskych fór," 25 November 1989 (BB: Zbierka písomností získaných
od študentov Pedagogickej fakulty v Banskej Bystrici, 1989–1990; another copy is preserved in KS). The 22
and 23 November documents are reprinted in Otáhal and Sládek, *Deset pražských dnů*, pp. 247–48, 324–25;
those from 22, 23, and 24 November are reprinted in Suk, *Občanské fórum*, vol. 2, pp. 16, 19–20, 24–25.
[22] "Pobúření násilnými zákrokmi . . . ," Bratislava, 20 November 1989. Reprinted in Ľubomír Feldek, ed.,
Keď sme brali do rúk budúcnosť (Bratislava: Archa, 1990), p. 11; Ingrid Antalová, ed., *Verejnosť proti násiliu
1989–1991: Svedectvá a dokumenty* (Bratislava: Nadácia Milana Šimečku, 1998), p. 306; and Jozef Žatkuliak,
ed., *November 1989 a Slovensko: Chronológia a dokumenty (1985–1990)* (Bratislava: Nadácia Milana Šimečku
a Historický ústav SAV, 1999), p. 325. Archival copies are preserved in BB, PX, and ZM.
[23] "My, radoví obyvatelia mesta Bratislavy . . . ," 23 November 1989 (BB: Zbierka písomností získaných
od študentov Pedagogickej fakulty v Banskej Bystrici, 1989–1990) (emphasis added). Catholics probably
comprised the core group behind this initiative, judging by the founding declaration's praise for Cardinal František Tomášek of Prague and the Slovak Catholic dissident Ján Čarnogurský, as well as its stated
intention of mobilizing "believers and even nonbelievers." There is no trace of OF Bratislava beyond this
founding declaration, which suggests that its adherents probably joined VPN once they realized they could.
[24] "Občianska iniciatíva Verejnosť proti násiliu vznikla na pôde . . . ," Bratislava, 22 November 1989,
reprinted in Feldek, *Keď sme brali*, p. 23; Antalová, *Verejnosť proti násiliu 1989–1991*, p. 310; and Žatkuliak,
p. 337. Archival copies are preserved in BB and PX.
[25] They had, nonetheless, begun to form, though it seems that the diffusion of VPN generally lagged
behind that of Civic Forum.

and many of the letters received by VPN committees were actually addressed to
"OF."[26] Perhaps in order to gain popular recognition and support, the VPN coordinating committee (*koordinačný výbor*, or KV) in Bratislava indirectly fostered this
interpretation. On 26 November, for example, it published a statement expressing
full support for Civic Forum, noting that the actor Milan Kňažko was simultaneously a member of the KC OF as well as the KV VPN.[27] It was also significant
that the name *Civic Forum* could be used as a common as well as a proper noun
and could denote an action as well as an association or initiative. VPN Púchov,
for example, routinely organized public discussions that it called "civic fora," and
even as late as February 1990, in an album of sound recordings commemorating
the Gentle Revolution, the KV VPN spokesman Ladislav Snopko defined Public
against Violence as "Bratislava's civic forum."[28] As the cases of Poprad and Levice
show, it was a short and easy step from participating in a civic forum to formally
establishing a Civic Forum. The name *Public against Violence*, for its part, was
less versatile since it could not be an action and since it implied a specific program
(however laudable); *Civic Forum* sounded more open-ended. A comparison of the
mistakes that ordinary citizens occasionally made with the two names is revealing.
They were significantly less likely to get OF's name wrong, and when they did
they never erred with "Forum," but merely substituted "People's" (*Ľudové*) for
"Civic." In the cases where they got VPN's name wrong, if they did not address it
as "Civic Forum," they called it "Committee against Violence" or "Society against
Violence," replacing "public" with something more limited.[29] It would seem, then,
that *Civic Forum* initially resonated with popular mentalities slightly more readily
than *Public against Violence*.

The founders of VPN in Bratislava have frequently portrayed their association
as "an authentic Slovak manifestation" of the revolution of 1989.[30] This is certainly
true, but it would seem worth adding that civic associations founded in other parts
of Slovakia were at least as authentic as that which emerged in Bratislava, regardless
of what these groups called themselves—and regardless of whether they identified
more with Bratislava or with Prague. Everywhere the initial movement was spontaneous, and there is no evidence that the founders of Slovak Civic Fora were any

---

[26] BB: Materiály získané od hnutia Verejnosť proti násiliu v Banskej Bystrici, 1989, boxes 1–2; SNA:
Archív VPN, fond. odd. I.

[27] "Vyhlásenie občianskej iniciatívy Verejnosť proti násiliu zo dňa 26. novembra 1989, 13.00." Reprinted
in Feldek, p. 37; Antalová, *Verejnosť proti násiliu 1989–1991*, p. 311; and Žatkuliak, *November 1989 a Slovensko*, p. 359. Archival copies are preserved in BB, GA, KS, and PX.

[28] "VPN Púchov zvoláva občianske fórum" (PX: súčasná dokumentácia, folder "Nežná revolúcia—
1989"); VPN and Študentské hnutie, *Nežná revolúcia* (Bratislava: Opus, 1990), sound recording, side 1.

[29] ÚSD: archiv KC OF, boxes 91–98; SNA: Archív VPN, fond. odd. I. It should be noted that though
mistakes were more common with VPN's name than with Civic Forum's, they were still exceptional.

[30] See, for example, Martin Bútora and Zora Bútorová, "Neznesiteľná ľahkosť rozchodu," in Vodička,
Děleni Československa, p. 76.

more manipulated than founders of VPN branches, whether by Prague or by the secret police.[31]

PRAGUE AND BRATISLAVA DIVIDE THE WORLD BETWEEN THEMSELVES

Slovak OFs presented a problem for Bratislava. The VPN coordinating committee claimed to speak on behalf of the entire Slovak public and to represent the Slovak civic movement in negotiations with state and Party authorities at both the republican and federal levels. An independent association on Slovak territory, oriented toward Prague rather than Bratislava, implicitly questioned the legitimacy of the KV VPN's claim. The fact that Slovakia's other two regional capitals, Banská Bystrica and Košice, identified with OF (though there was an independent VPN in Košice) was particularly significant, since they could claim to be the mouthpieces of *their* entire regions. OF Banská Bystrica in fact officially declared that VPN was a phenomenon just of West Slovakia and that civic initiatives in Central Slovakia should align with OF.[32] Activists in Bratislava never fully realized how widespread Civic Forum was in Slovakia, but they knew about Košice.[33] Sometime between 21 and 25 November, Marcel Strýko and Erik Groch from OF Košice visited Bratislava and, according to Peter Zajac, said, "We've founded OF in Košice, why on earth have you established some kind of 'VPN' here?"[34] According to Vladislav Chlipala, Košice's self-confident divergence from the KV VPN's vision for Slovakia made Bratislava nervous.[35]

On 29 November, KV VPN and KC OF representatives met in Prague and agreed, in the context of a declaration on cooperation, to respect each other as the "sovereign" representative of the civic movements in each republic.[36] Prague thereby

---

[31] In fact, if there was manipulation, it seems more likely that the secret police encouraged the formation of VPN groups to compete with and destabilize existing OF groups. A letter from OF Zvolen to OF Prague, dated 27 November 1989, is suggestive in this regard. "We deem it necessary," wrote the forum's spokesman Dušan Kaštiel, "to draw your attention to the fact that 'information' is circulating in Slovakia to the effect that Civic Forum is an exclusively Czech affair and not statewide. Newly founded local initiatives of Public against Violence are officially standing in for OF; they are interpreted in this sense as the sole Slovak 'version' of Civic Forum. They distribute proclamations which often have very little to do with the renewal of political, economic, and social life in the sense of the demands and goals of Civic Forum. This causes disinformation, uncertainty, and speculation. It would be desirable [*bolo by potrebné*] to clear this question up with Bratislava—it seems indeed that an intentional, destructive campaign is taking place." (ÚSD: archiv KC OF, box 72.)

[32] "Slovu socializmus dajme konkrétny obsah."

[33] Peter Zajac, correspondence with author, 3 January 2010; Ján Budaj, interview by author, 25 August 2011.

[34] Quoted in Antalová, *Verejnosť proti násiliu—Občianske fórum*, p. 21.

[35] Ibid., pp. 22–23.

[36] "Spoločné komuniké OF a VPN," Prague, 29 November 1989 (PX: fond G1, box 4, folder 1). Reprinted in Suk, *Občanské fórum*, vol. 2, p. 39, and Žatkuliak, *November 1989 a Slovensko*, p. 381. See also Rychlík, "Průběh rozpadu," p. 271, and Jiří Suk, *Občanské fórum: Listopad—prosinec 1989*, vol. 1, *Události* (Brno: Doplněk, 1997), p. 91.

committed itself to a hands-off policy toward Civic Fora in Slovakia. Most Prague activists, of course, knew very little about life beyond the walls of their beautiful city and so had no basis for questioning VPN's claim to representativeness; the Praguers accepted at face value everything their colleagues in Bratislava told them about the situation in Slovakia. The same day, the KV VPN devoted new attention to initiatives outside Bratislava, issuing "A Word Today to Workers and Not Just Them," "A Proposal for the Work of Action Groups of VPN," and an explanation of "The Internal Organization of VPN."[37] In the first of these documents, the coordinating committee declared that "if hitherto branches of VPN have existed in the form of strike committees, it is desirable that they now come onto the platform of VPN as branches." Without actually acknowledging the existence of Civic Forum in Slovakia, this statement made it clear that groups in Slovakia that agreed with VPN's demands but had up to this point affiliated themselves with other revolutionary associations should refashion themselves as VPNs.

This placed Slovak OFs in an awkward position. They were called upon to risk confusing constituents who had already grown accustomed to using one name rather than another, and they were called upon to reorient themselves away from Prague and toward Bratislava. In other words, they were asked to undo much of what they had done. Some Slovak OFs responded to the challenge with more disgruntlement than others, but by June 1990, all had converted. We can again discern three patterns by which this occurred. The first was the mutation of a single OF into a single VPN in late November or early December 1989, in some cases with an intermediary stage where the association called itself "OF-VPN." The second was the coalescence of separate OF and VPN groupings in a given town or district, also in early December. The final pattern was close cooperation between OF and VPN groupings, which nonetheless remained separate into the new year.

The first pattern was the most common. In Liptovský Mikuláš, Nové Zámky, Prešov, Rožňava, and Spišská Nová Ves, the decision to change names and affiliation seems to have been reached fairly easily and relatively quickly. In Spišská Nová Ves the change occurred just a few hours after the citywide initiative had been announced, evidently because newer activists persuaded or outvoted the founding core of culture workers who had established the local movement.[38] (This, exceptionally, was on 27 November—before the official agreement between OF Prague and VPN

---

[37] "Slovo k dnešku robotníkom a nielen im," Bratislava, 29 November 1989 (PX: súčasná dokumentácia, folder "Nežná revolúcia—1989"; additional copies are preserved in BB, KS, and PP). "Návrh pre prácu akčných skupín VPN," Bratislava, 29 November 1989, in Žatkuliak, p. 380; archival copies are preserved in BB, KS, MI, PX, and ZM); "Vnútorná organizácia VPN," Bratislava, 29 November 1989 (KS: zbierka z Nežnej revolúcie, folder "Rôzne"; additional copies are preserved in BB, MI, PP, and PX). The latter two documents, incidentally, were nearly verbatim translations of OF Prague documents from the previous day, with "VPN" simply substituted for "OF" ("K práci občanských fór" and "Vnitřní organizace Občanského fóra," reprinted in Suk, *Občanské fórum*, vol. 2, pp. 35–38).

[38] "Premeny v zrkadle týždňa."

Bratislava.) The change in Nové Zámky seems to have been similarly unproblematic, occurring sometime between 29 November and 2 December, perhaps as the result of a visit by VPN representatives from Bratislava on 28 November.[39] Since OF Nové Zámky—uniquely—had expressed agreement with only Slovak students and what it called the "All-Slovakian Coordinating Committee" in the founding declaration of its municipal council, it would seem that it identified itself as Civic Forum initially only because it misunderstood the nature of the movement founded in Bratislava, toward which it was nonetheless oriented.[40] In Prešov the change, which occurred on 2 December, was evidently the subject of some discussion; the civic initiative there felt compelled to print an explanation in both the district newspaper and the bulletin of striking students at the local university. As explained in the bulletin,

> Directly following the shock of the brutal conduct of emergency units on Wenceslas Square [sic] there arose in both parts of our common state civic initiatives, mutually independent but agreeing on a common goal: Civic Forum and Public against Violence (VPN). In the short time that has passed from their founding, their program has at least partially crystallized for the immediate future and probably until the elections, which understandably will now be free. It is only natural that Prešov's Civic Forum, which spontaneously emerged perhaps a week after The Events, has now signed onto the program of Public against Violence in Bratislava. [This association] . . . is after all better able to consider the specificity of Slovakia—particularly regions more distant from the center, among which we must count ourselves.[41]

In Banská Bystrica, Čadca, and Humenné, activists tried for a time to maintain orientation toward both Prague and Bratislava by calling themselves "OF-VPN" or "the Civic Forum of the Public against Violence." Čadca, as we have seen, adopted this strategy from the beginning. In Banská Bystrica the switch from OF to OF-VPN probably took place on 30 November, but it lasted for only two days. On 2 December OF-VPN Banská Bystrica became VPN Banská Bystrica, and in the second issue of its bulletin (Fórum) it explained that

> in our democratizing movement there have thus far emerged two currents, that of Prague and that of Bratislava, which has been reflected in the very symbols of our movement and we have presented ourselves as the Civic

[39] "Umelci v našom meste."
[40] "V N. Zámkoch MKV."
[41] "Na vysvetlenie," *Prešovská zmena*, no. 2 (5 December 1989), p. 5. See also "Postoje sa nemenia," *Prešovské noviny*, 6 December 1989, p. 1.

Forum of the movement Public against Violence. Today our movement is crystallizing and taking on the form of the Bratislava movement, which demands a change of our name as well, so that henceforth we shall present ourselves and cooperate with Bratislava and Prague as the Civic Initiative Public against Violence Banská Bystrica.[42]

Whereas in the first pattern a single OF transformed itself into a single VPN, the second and third patterns were more complicated, with separate VPN groupings springing up independently of Civic Forum on the same territory. With the previously cited exception of OF Bratislava, it seems that the VPNs were always founded after the OFs, but in a few cases the order is unclear. As a rule the two civic associations cooperated with each other and ultimately merged. However, a salient difference can be seen in the extent to which the original Civic Fora resisted assimilation.

In Poprad, OF was established on 26 and 27 November, while VPN came into existence on 30 November. The institutionalization of the two movements came about under the auspices of socially disparate groups. Following the public assembly that called itself a "citizens' forum" on 26 November, the OF coordinating committee was created by a group of people who had organized civic resistance following the Warsaw Pact invasion of 1968.[43] The VPN coordinating committee, on the other hand, was established by representatives of strike committees.[44] The two groups immediately began cooperating, and by 1 December there were plans to create a common "emergency committee of civil disobedience," consisting of four OF representatives and four VPN representatives, together with an independent secretary (OF proposed a priest or lawyer).[45] On 5 December, however, the civic initiatives in Poprad "decided to accept the demand of the Slovak center and present themselves henceforth as the initiative Public against Violence."[46] In the Považská Bystrica district as well, separate OF and VPN groupings in the major towns and at the district level came into being independently of one another yet quickly established coordinating committees bearing both names. By 8 December, however, the allied initiatives had coalesced into single VPNs.[47]

[42] Fórum (Banská Bystrica), no. 2 (3 December 1989), p. 1.

[43] "Programové vyhlásenie."

[44] "Ovzdušie otvoreného dialógu" and "Minirozhovor s Pavlom Strážayom," Podtatranské noviny, 7 December 1989, pp. 1, 3.

[45] "Programové vyhlásenie."

[46] "Pod symbolom VPN," Podtatranské noviny, 14 December 1989, p. 4.

[47] VPN and OF Považská Bystrica, "Občianské iniciatívy v Považskej Bystrici informujú o nesplnených požiadavkách študentov," 2 December 1989 (PX: súčasná dokumentácia, folder "Nežná revolúcia—1989"); "Členovia občianskych aktivit 'Verejnosť proti násiliu' a 'Občianske fórum', ktorí pracujete v podniku Pov. Strojárne," Púchov (PX: súčasná dokumentácia, folder "Nežná revolúcia—1989"); "V znamení vecnosti, konštruktívnosti," Obzor, 14 December 1989, p. 1.

In the third pattern, separate OF and VPN groupings cooperated closely with one another and established common coordinating committees but remained distinct into 1990. In Žilina, for example, VPN was established by graphic artists with connections to Bratislava on 3 December—fully a week after OF Žilina had begun functioning.[48] By 5 December the two groups had agreed to create a common "coordinating committee of OF and VPN," and by 14 December this committee had expanded still further, to include the students of Žilina's Higher School of Transport and Communications.[49] In Komárno the situation was even more complicated. In that town there emerged not only OF, VPN, and FMK but also a "Free Forum" (Szabad Fórum, or SzF) as a Hungarian mutation of OF—all by 27 November.[50] On 1 December the chairman of the district national committee officially recognized as legitimate the demands of all these initiatives and promised to continue formal dialogue with them (it had already begun with OF and SzF).[51] By 16 December the four groups joined together to establish what they variously called "the coordinating committee of the Civic Forum Public against Violence," "the coordinating committee of the Civic Forum of the Public against Violence," and "the coordinating committee of Civic Forum and Public against Violence."[52] As in Žilina, this alliance continued into 1990, with the member initiatives remaining distinct. Košice, Prievidza, Trebišov, and Vranov nad Topľou also followed this pattern.

Often the transition from OF to VPN was accompanied by personnel changes, engendering some of the first acrimony that half a year later would paralyze VPN. This was most pronounced in those districts where OF and VPN groupings had sprung up independently and then agreed to merge. In Poprad, evidently, the original VPN activists defamed the newcomers from OF and ultimately excluded them from the common movement.[53] Even in districts like Levice and Rožňava, where apparently a single OF became a single VPN, it is remarkable how many names of coordinating committee members changed following the mutation. Not everywhere was the transition accompanied by hard feelings, though. In Považská Bystrica, where structures of cooperation had emerged while OF and VPN had still been separate, it seems that the founders of OF were fully welcomed into VPN as equal partners.

---

[48] "Verejný záujem povýšiť nad osobný," *Cieľ*, 7 December 1989, p. 3.

[49] "S podporou ľudu," *Cieľ*, 7 December 1989, p. 1.

[50] "Požiadavky Občianskeho fóra," "Občania vyjadrujú súhlas," and "November 27-én alakult meg...," *Dunaj*, 2 December 1989, pp. 3, 7; "Oprava," *Dunaj*, 9 December 1989, p. 2; "Z doterajšej činnosti VPN," *Dunaj*, 23 December 1989, p. 1; "A Nyilvánosság az Erőszak Ellen polgári kezdeményezés komáromi tevékenységéről," *Dunatáj*, 23 December 1989, p. 6.

[51] "Dialóg na pôde ONV" and "A demokrácia platformján," *Dunaj*, 9 December 1989, pp. 1, 5.

[52] "Z doterajšej činnosti VPN" and "A Nyilvánosság az Erőszak Ellen polgári kezdeményezés komáromi tevékenységéről"; "Zo zasadnutia občianskych iniciatív," *Dunaj*, 30 December 1989, p. 1; "Elfogadták a programnyilatkozatot," *Dunatáj*, 30 December 1989, p. 5.

[53] "Fórum občanov," *Podtatranské noviny*, 11 October 1990, p. 3.

In addition to personnel changes, the imposition of uniformity on the Slovak civic movement involved a rewriting of history, an erasure of fleeting but politically problematic memory. In December 1989, several VPN activists began using the past tense in ways that belied the original diversity of the Slovak civic movement, presenting Bratislava's vision of the way history *should* have unfolded as the correct narrative of the way it *did* unfold. Thus the KV VPN spokesman Miroslav Kusý, for example, responded to a question about Slovak Civic Fora by portraying their founding as a "misunderstanding," since "in Slovakia, the name *Public against Violence* was adopted."[54] What Bratislava had done, in other words, was what "Slovakia" had done, and any local initiative that defined itself independently was aberrant. Similarly, VPN spokesmen in Prešov explained that the local switch from OF to VPN had "occurred only because, as . . . the actor . . . Mikuláš Ľaš told us, the new name is particular to the renewal movement in Slovakia, while Civic Fora emerged and exist in the Czech towns of our homeland."[55] They might as well have said, "we did not do what we did," and "we surrender to another the authority to determine the meaning of our actions." There is no evidence of ill will or a premeditated plan to rewrite history, but the project was nonetheless successful, for few people today remember that OF was once as widespread as VPN in Slovakia, and no textbook mentions it.

RESISTANCE FROM BELOW

By the end of 1989 only six of the original twenty-one district-level fora still existed, all of them formally allied to local branches of VPN. Map 2 shows their distribution. More research will be necessary to ascertain how all these OF-VPNs ultimately assimilated completely into VPN, but it seems that by June 1990 the process was complete.

The process by which Bratislava finally "conquered" Slovakia did not go without resistance. On 5 January, Marcel Strýko from OF Košice and Vladimír Komár from OF Vranov appeared in Prague to seek support from Civic Forum's coordinating center. They informed their Prague colleagues of the spontaneous emergence of their initiatives prior to contact with VPN and of the continuance of OF in East and Central Slovakia. They explained that Slovak OFs wanted to orient themselves politically toward Prague without having to go through Bratislava, which they said was pretending to national authority. Strýko and Komár added that Bratislava was not consulting them, nor were they being invited to Bratislava to participate in decision making, and so they requested the right to participate in conventions of Civic Forum—at least as observers.[56]

---

[54] *Štúdio dialóg*, Slovenská televízia, 4 December 1989.

[55] "Postoje sa nemenia."

[56] "Zápis z Rady OF dne 5.1.1990 v 8.30 hod." (ÚSD: archiv KC OF, folder "Zápisy z rady OF (C)"), p. 1. See also Suk, *Labyrintem*, p. 296.

Map 2. Slovak districts where OF remained on 31 December 1989

• regional capital

Košice

Banská Bystrica

Bratislava

This was not the first time members of the Prague center had heard of the
continuing existence of Civic Forum in Slovakia. The ecological activist Josef
Vavroušek, who repeatedly demonstrated a much keener understanding of Slovakia than any of his colleagues in Prague, had drawn attention to the situation of
Slovak OFs on 28 and 30 December, asking whether it was correct that "we do not
acknowledge them." At the time, the lawyer Pavel Rychetský had raised doubts
about the internal strength of Public against Violence, concluding, "We don't need
VPN, but VPN needs us."[57] When Strýko and Komár presented their case in the
midst of this ongoing debate, they met with a mixed reaction. Zdeněk Rajniš, from
the KC OF's organizational committee, exclaimed that no one could be stopped
from joining this or that branch of what he claimed was essentially the same movement. "Even Czechs can join VPN," he said.[58] The consensus, however, was that the
Prague coordinating center ought not take any step that might harm VPN. It was
therefore decided to "recommend to VPN Bratislava that it invite representatives
of the regions to a convention." Prague further resolved to invite representatives of
Slovak OFs *and* VPNs to observe OF conventions and to encourage Bratislava to
give some economic resources to Košice. As a gesture of good will, the KC OF gave
Košice a photocopier.[59]

Strýko and Komár are not listed as having attended the OF convention that
took place in Prague the next day, but the issue of tensions between Bratislava and
other parts of Slovakia nonetheless came up. Šimon Pánek, the student delegate
to the convention, drew attention to conflict between students in Banská Bystrica,
Košice, Prešov, Zvolen, and Žilina on one hand and their colleagues in Bratislava
and Nitra on the other. He said the former agreed with students at Czech universities that a single student association should be institutionalized, while the latter
argued for two independent associations, one in each republic.[60] Josef Vavroušek
followed on this report to inform delegates of the results of the previous day's meeting with Strýko and Komár. "The situation in relations between OF and VPN is
not nearly so dramatic as among the students," he said.

In Central and East Slovakia there are strong Civic Fora which arose there
before information about the creation of VPN arrived. Now they call themselves OF+VPN. In Slovakia there is a certain internal conflict, because centers in Central and East Slovakia feel slighted by the KV VPN in Bratislava.

---

[57] "Zápis z jednání Rady KC OF dne 28.12. 1989," p. 2, and "Zápis z Rady OF dne 30.12.1989 v 8.30
hod.," p. 3, both in ÚSD: archiv KC OF, folder "Zápisy z rady OF (C)."

[58] "Zápis z Rady OF dne 5.1.1990 v 8.30 hod.," p. 1.

[59] Ibid., p. 1.

[60] "Zápis z druhého sněmu Koordinačního centra Občanského fóra konaného 6.1.1990" (ÚSD: archiv
KC OF, "OF—interní písemnosti: Sněmy OF," box 1, folder "Sněm KC OF 6.1.1990"), pp. 10–11.

This will soon be resolved, of course. The KC OF in Prague will keep these [Slovak] Fora informed, but it will respect territorial jurisdiction.[61]

As was often the case, this rosy prognosis turned out to be premature, and Vavroušek felt compelled once again to raise the question of Civic Fora in "northern Slovakia" at the next OF convention on 20 January. Though Strýko and Erik Groch from Košice were present (along with four VPN representatives from Banská Bystrica), the minutes do not record that they spoke up on the issue, and Petr Kučera from the KC OF's executive council evidently uttered the last word when he pointed to the "delicate situation" of VPN as a result of nationalism in Slovakia and said that OF must support VPN "as the most liberal element in Slovak political life."[62]

Thus it was that, by June 1990, Civic Forum disappeared from Slovakia. As it had been first, so Košice was apparently the last holdout. As Chlipala recalls, "It was still called OF until just before the elections, when we realized that it was a battle of political signs; thus VPN-OF went by the wayside, for we knew that people would vote for VPN and not OF. They couldn't."[63]

By way of a postscript, there was a short-lived attempt to resurrect something like Civic Forum in Poprad in October 1990. Following a summer characterized by the collapse of VPN's popularity across Slovakia and nasty squabbles within the leadership of VPN Poprad, three of the original founders of Civic Forum in the district reacted by creating anew a "Citizens' Forum."

Our goal will be mostly from ethical perspectives to evaluate pressing questions through print and other media. We will be critical, but we will also propose conceptually reasonable solutions. We want to be those capable of saying that the emperor is naked. The cause of democracy is sacred for us and we mean to fight for it by working together with movements and parties of the center. Those who have not profaned themselves by collaboration with the totalitarian regime and are interested in fulfilling the ideals of November, who are capable of arguing substantively and clearly formulating your ideas, join us![64]

Other than some exchanges in local newspapers, nothing significant came of this appeal.[65]

---

[61] Ibid., p. 11.

[62] "Zápis ze sněmu Koordinačního centra Občanského fóra ze dne 20. ledna 1990" (ÚSD: archiv KC OF, "OF—interní písemnosti: Sněmy OF," box 1, folder "Sněmy OF 20.1.1990"), pp. 1, 6.

[63] Quoted in Antalová, *Verejnosť proti násiliu—Občianske fórum*, p. 22.

[64] "Fórum občanov."

[65] Blažej Herman, interview by author, Tatranská Kotlina, 7 August 2011, tape recording.

The Quest for Empire

Could things have turned out differently? The evidence suggests they could have. VPN was founded after a meeting of several hundred artists, environmentalists, and others in Bratislava's Umelecká beseda on 19 November 1989. At the meeting, which lasted from five to six o'clock in the afternoon, a coordinating committee was elected, which met later that evening in the apartment of Ján Langoš. Between 8:30 and 9:00 p.m., this committee chose for the initiative the name *Public against Violence*. By the time the whole group met again at noon the next day, however, its members had heard about the creation of Civic Forum in Prague and stormily discussed whether or not to change their name accordingly. They decided to stick with *Public against Violence* on the grounds that news of the emergence of VPN had already been disseminated by telephone across Slovakia and that a change of name at this stage would unnecessarily confuse the public.[66] As has been demonstrated, however, the news of VPN's founding had not spread quite as widely by this time as those who argued for maintenance of the name evidently thought, nor was Bratislava quite the model for the rest of Slovakia that denizens of the Danubian metropole assumed it was. By later forcing Slovak Civic Fora to change *their* names, VPN Bratislava may have confused even more people than if it had changed its name at the beginning. We cannot help but wonder if the "dual power" situation caused by the simultaneous existence of OF and VPN in Slovakia did not provide a model for the later emergence of rival VPNs in Slovak towns and workplaces—a phenomenon that seems to have been much more common in Slovakia than in the Czech lands and that contributed to a significant decline in VPN's popularity by the June 1990 elections.

A second juncture where history might have followed a different course was when the KV VPN and the KC OF agreed not to combine their movements on 29 November. As the examples of numerous OF-VPNs in Slovakia demonstrate, an integrated symbiosis was possible even without rejecting the name Public against Violence. Had such a union occurred, the question of internal federation would surely have come up, just as it did within the originally unified student movement, but it might have resulted in a functional and democratic federalization that could have served as a model for other realms of political life. The question of internal democracy plagued both VPN and OF from late December onward, with district-level activists arguing ever more vociferously that the districts were the natural building blocks of the movements and that collectively they should elect central decision-making bodies. The Prague and Bratislava coordinating committees, well into 1990, argued against democratization, claiming that they were sufficiently representative of the movements as wholes to speak in their names. Had OF and VPN united, the issue would probably have come to a head much sooner than it

[66] Rudolf Sikora, quoted in Antalová, *Verejnost' proti násiliu 1989–1991*, pp. 33–34.

did in the separate movements, since Bratislava would in no case have accepted virtual representation by Prague. It is possible that the negotiating positions of the districts would have been stronger in such a scenario (particularly if peripheral Czech and Slovak regions had made common cause), forcing democratization at an earlier stage and a federalization of the movement on the basis of districts or regions rather than republics. Such an arrangement did in fact emerge in East Slovakia, where by the end of December a regional coordinating committee had been established with two representatives from each district, including representatives of both OF and VPN.[67] In a formal statewide union of the two movements, regions like East Slovakia might have been harder to ignore, possibly providing the impetus for a more democratic federalization than either Prague or Bratislava desired. This is not to say the Czecho-Slovak federation would necessarily have survived if OF and VPN had formally united; what was necessary for the federation to survive was a federalist mind-set, which such a union might have incarnated—but which in fact was generally missing.

Instead, the operative dynamic was not federalism, but empire. Each city desired to speak in the name of as large a territory as possible. Prague claimed to represent all of Czechoslovakia, Bratislava all of Slovakia. Banská Bystrica claimed to represent all of Central Slovakia, while Brno claimed to represent not just the South Moravian region but all of Moravia and Silesia. Initiatives in district capitals frequently claimed to speak not just for their town but for the entire district. There were exceptions, of course. East Slovakia, as just mentioned, established a federal structure from the beginning, and the towns of the Považská Bystrica district worked out a similar arrangement for district-level coordination early and amicably. The principle of domination was more widespread, however, causing no end of rancor and strife within the ostensibly democratic movements. A pattern of 1848 in the Habsburg Empire was repeated at a smaller scale—with midlevel powers protesting the domination of higher-level powers, only to have lower-level powers appeal to the higher entities in protest of midlevel domination. Thus Olomouc and Opava appealed to Prague against the pretensions of Brno. Považská Bystrica appealed to Bratislava against the pretensions of Banská Bystrica. Ružomberok appealed to Banská Bystrica against the pretensions of Liptovský Mikuláš. And Košice appealed to Prague against the pretensions of Bratislava. In the end, towns like Brno and Banská Bystrica lost out (OF Brno never saw the institutionalization of all-Moravian structures, while VPN Banská Bystrica found itself stripped of regional authority in the summer of 1990). Bratislava won. In a very real political sense, we can speak of the period from November 1989 to June 1990 as the time when Bratislava conquered Slovakia.

---

[67] "Zápis z Rady OF dne 5.1.1990 v 8.30 hod.," p. 1.

A Constitutional Moment

The collective effervescence following 17 November ushered in a constitutional moment. The history of Civic Forum in Slovakia provides us with several examples of this phenomenon, beginning with the founding of autonomous civic initiatives in localities across Slovakia and continuing with efforts to establish structures of coordination among the initiatives, with contrary impulses toward institutionalization coming from below and from above. Efforts to constitute civic associations, however, were just the tip of the iceberg. Beginning at the end of November and continuing into the 1990s (and arguably until EU accession in 2004), citizens of Czechoslovakia sought to constitute or reconstitute every organization or institution in their collective social life, from chess clubs and youth associations to economic enterprises, churches, local administrative organs, legislatures, and the state as such. All these manifold efforts stemmed from a single imperative: the irresistible desire to represent the new sense of community that had come into being after 17 November in concrete and durable human institutions.

The example of Slovak civic initiatives illustrates how the constitutional momentum ended up coming from two different directions, which ultimately worked at cross-purposes. First was the momentum that came "from below," which we can identify as democratic. We have seen this dynamic in action in Komárno, Poprad, Považská Bystrica, and Žilina, where independent civic initiatives, spontaneously emerging as the coordinated efforts of concerned citizens, agreed among themselves to establish structures of cooperation. We have seen it in a more advanced stage in East Slovakia, where structures of cooperation emerged not just at the municipal or district level but across an entire region. In all these examples, the citizens or groups of citizens agreeing to establish structures of coordination naturally settled on arrangements that were federative in form. The coordinating committee in Žilina federated three independent groups, OF-VPN in Komárno was really a federation of four independent groups, and the coordinating committee for East Slovakia was a federation of district-level coordinating committees. Federalism, then, was the natural partner of democratic self-organization. Constitutional efforts from below also resulted in forms of social organization that were incredibly diverse. None of the coordinating committees that OF, VPN, and other revolutionary groups spontaneously established in Slovakia were identical in structure because in every case the groups in question devised structures creatively to suit their particular needs.

In opposition to constitutional impulses from below were constitutional impulses "from above." If we identified the former as democratic, the salient feature of the latter was centralism. OF Banská Bystrica desired that all civic initiatives in Central Slovakia conform to its central vision, while VPN Bratislava insisted that all initiatives in Slovakia reconfigure themselves in accordance with the model that *it* provided. While democratic self-organization tended to produce a colorful array of diverse structures suiting the needs of the citizens and groups that created them, these structures defied general systematization. For those who aspired to coordinate social life from a central location, or who needed to negotiate with central authorities in the name of a larger social unit, this lack of system was frustrating. For them, standardization was a paramount concern, as it would facilitate centralized representation.

Though the notions "from below" and "from above" are convenient, it is necessary to recognize that, in the beginning, all revolutionary initiative was "from below." The primordial impulse everywhere was democratic—spontaneously reaching out to other citizens in reaction to the earthquake of 17 November. Even Prague and Bratislava were, in the very beginning, just two localities among others. Centralizing impulses emerged later, if only by a matter of hours or days, and they emerged at least in part from the local interests of groups in cities that identified themselves as central places. To some extent we can see this as a mirroring of the structures of the old regime, since the initiative in Prague took upon itself the role of negotiating with federal power holders, the movement in Bratislava with republican organs, the association in Banská Bystrica with regional administration, and so on. There was, however, a more fundamental, cultural process at work—a chain of imitation going back to the Habsburg Empire, wherein cities aped Vienna and vied with one another over the perks that came from representing imperial authority as the capital of a province, the seat of a district, and so forth. The notion that some communities had a natural right to administer others—without the consent of those others—had not yet given way before the advance of democracy. For this reason, the revolution of 1989, much like that of 1789, set in motion a maelstrom of urban rivalry that worked at cross-purposes with democracy.[68]

The revolution caused this storm precisely because it opened up a constitutional moment in which all social structures were subject to reconsideration. In this, the Gentle Revolution was like all other genuine revolutions—the essential feature of which is a return to a foundational state of society. In every case, collective effervescence produces a redefinition of a community's sense of itself as a community (what Durkheim calls the sacred), and this must find representation in the institutions of that community. In every case, moreover, democratic impulses to institutionalize from below come into conflict with centralist efforts to systematize from above. In France, the delegates to the Estates General who constituted themselves as the National Assembly declared it their task to write a constitution for the kingdom.

---

[68] Ted Margadant, *Urban Rivalries in the French Revolution* (Princeton, N.J.: Princeton University Press, 1992).

They frequently had to revise their work, however (e.g., on the night of 4 August), to keep up with the reconstitution that was spontaneously happening on the ground. In Russia, since the Provisional Government could not claim democratic legitimacy in the way the French assembly could, it scheduled elections for a constitutional convention. By the time the elections had taken place and the Constituent Assembly met, however, it was too late—the real reconstitution had already occurred. In Czechoslovakia, though there were popular calls for a constitutional convention beginning in November and Civic Forum even disseminated a draft constitution for public discussion in December, it was agreed at the federal roundtable that the Federal Assembly, rather than a specially elected body, would write a new constitution, and eventually this was postponed until after the elections of June.[69] This did not stop popular efforts to reconstitute society from below, however. We will discuss in chapter 5 how citizens sought to reconstitute their workplaces and organs of local government. Now let us focus on the reconstitution of political community as such at local, regional, and "national" levels.

LOCAL PATRIOTISM

Before there was ethnic nationalism, there was local patriotism. With a few singular exceptions, Czechs and Slovaks did not talk about achieving greater national glory or sovereignty when they assembled in 1989; they did, however, talk about restoring the glory—or sovereignty—of their localities. This is understandable, because the community everyone could see on the squares—the community of which participants in manifestations felt most directly a part—was their local community. As a VPN journalist in Bánovce nad Bebravou wrote, "In the changed conditions of life in our country we can express the healthy side of local patriotism."[70]

In January 1990, before any discussion of inserting a hyphen between "Česko" and "Slovensko" began, revolutionary activists were concerned with restoring the glory of their hometowns. This was particularly visible in discussions about monuments and names. Civic Forum in Pilsen's railway station worked to remove a Gottwald statue from the station's courtyard and install a more appropriate monument of local significance.[71] The civic initiatives in Komárno wanted to restore statues of one of Czechoslovakia's founders, M. R. Štefánik, as well as of a locally significant Austro-Hungarian general.[72] They also began the process of reclaiming a fortress and chateau—local architectural treasures—for civilian use after the

---

[69] See, for example, "Prohlášení Občanského fóra v Bystřici nad Pernštejnem," 30 November 1989 (ÚSD: archiv KC OF, nezpracovaná hromada č. 4). "Zákonodární iniciativa Občanského fóra: Návrh nové ústavy," *Svobodné slovo*, 7 December 1989 (flyer versions available in LN and in Slovak translation in KS).

[70] F. Ďuriš, "Udrží si mesto svoju tvár?" *Hosť do domu*, no. 3 (24 January 1990), p. 1.

[71] M. Sojka, "Pomník poctivé práce," *Plzeňský student*, no. 1 (8 January 1990), p. 3.

[72] Koordinačný výbor VPN v Komárne, "Informácia pre našich čitateľov" *Reflex*, 8 February 1990, p. 2.

departure of Soviet troops.[73] Contributors to the VPN newspaper in Trnava emphasized the need to care for the graves of "renowned Trnavans."[74] Similar examples
could be given from perhaps every town in the country. Many municipalities also
saw the revolution as an opportunity to change their names. Gottwaldov—which
reclaimed its pre-1948 name, Zlín, on 15 December 1989—was the most famous
example, but name changes of this sort continued at least until 1992.[75]

Long before there was any serious talk of Slovak or Czech independence, municipalities across Czechoslovakia sought to secede from one another left and right.
Many communities that had been incorporated into larger towns under the old
regime took the opportunity to declare their independence. The Civic Forum of
a recently annexed part of Brno declared at the beginning of 1990 that the existing structure of regional, district, and municipal national committees was "utterly
unsuitable." Instead of having a national committee for all of Brno's second district,
with responsibility for one hundred thousand people, they wanted a committee for
their quarter, Bystrc, serving just the thirty-five thousand people who lived there.[76]
In cooperation with civic initiatives elsewhere in Brno, the residents of Bystrc acquired self-government in November 1990 as part of a complete municipal reorganization. Residents of Dobroměřice began considering secession from the town
of Louny in March of 1990, and ultimately plebiscites were held in the district on
multiple questions of municipal independence.[77] In the Trutnov district, ten new
municipalities officially came into existence on 1 September 1990—and this was
not viewed as the end of the process.[78] While demands for secession were most common, there were also calls for reunion of previously sundered administrative divisions. Over 95 percent of the inhabitants of thirteen villages in the district of Vranov
nad Topľou signed a petition to be reincorporated into the district of Prešov, whence
they had been removed some twenty years previously. "Former functionaries decided this instead of the people," they said, and foreshadowing a line of reasoning
that would soon become common, they added, "To the region of Šariš [a former
Hungarian county, the seat of which had been Prešov] we decidedly belong *ethnically*."[79] Such reconceptualization of community boundaries continued throughout

[73] Okresný koordinačný výbor VPN, "Národná pamiatka alebo kasáreň?!" *Reflex*, 11 January 1990, p. 1.
[74] "Kto bol Franko Veselovský?" *Trnavská verejnosť*, 12 January 1990, p. 1.
[75] See, for example, "Ha Ön Bátorkeszi polgár" (KN: zbierka plagátov, folder "Bátorove Kosihy").
[76] *Zpravodaj brněnského OF*, no. 10 (14 January 1990), p. 2.
[77] *Hlas*, 2 March 1990, p. 1; 19 October 1990, p. 2.
[78] TU: fond "KC OF Trutnov," folder "Volby—městský národní výbor"; "Seznam obcí okresu Trutnov—stav k 1. září 1990" (TU: fond "KC OF Trutnov," box 1, folder "Výsledky voleb: různé").
[79] Pavol Bašista, Milan Bašista, and Ján Sabol, "Medzianky chcú naspäť do prešovského okresu," *Premeny*, no. 2 (12 January 1990), p. 6 (emphasis added). It should be noted that this invocation of ethnicity had
nothing to do with distinctions between Slovaks and Magyars, as the population in question was almost
exclusively Slovak. At stake were "ethnic" distinctions *among* Slovaks.

the 1990s. Eventually this phenomenon came to be seen as a microcosm of the dissolution of the ČSFR—a perceptive interpretation as long as one recognizes that the micro came before the macro.[80]

Consistent with revolutionary understandings of democracy and valuation of self-organization, there was widespread demand for greater local control of affairs, requiring devolution of power from district, regional, or even republican levels.[81] Citizens in Brezno, for example, complained that the city's urban planning was coordinated by people who lived elsewhere, resulting, they argued, in badly situated housing and plans to build a school with only half the necessary classrooms.[82] Following the local elections of November 1990, Poprad's new city council adopted bylaws declaring that citizens were sovereign and cities both sovereign and independent.[83]

Beyond desires for greater local sovereignty, Czechoslovak citizens evinced strong desires to augment the standing of their localities with respect to others, or within a regional or even wider framework. Proposals to establish a local university were particularly common, being voiced in Opava (where it indeed came to pass) as well as in Cheb, Louny, and Michalovce (where it did not).[84] In Komárno, a night watchman donated twelve thousand crowns to VPN and FMK for the purpose of establishing a new, Hungarian-language university in the town.[85] A contributor to the VPN newspaper in Nitra observed that the first bishopric to be established in what became Czechoslovakia had been established in their city (one hundred years before there was a bishop in Prague) and lamented that the modern Slovak archdiocese was based in Trnava, not Nitra.[86] Still another contributor argued that Nitra was the "natural center" of the West Slovakian administrative region and deserved at least as much as Žilina and Prešov to have a professional orchestra and secondary music school. The author observed that Nitrans had been fighting for these things for years and encouraged them to seize the opportunity the revolution provided.[87] Towns did not strive to distinguish themselves only in positive ways; from January at least through March 1990, people reveled in the magnitude of the Communist disaster, and towns vied with each other to be the

---

[80] "Stanovisko okresné a městské rady OH Trutnov k referendu o osamostatnění Poříčí" (TU: fond "KC OF Trutnov," box 3, folder "Zde je náš domov: regionální program").

[81] See, for example, "Návrh volebního programu Občanského fóra Lánov" (TU: fond "KC OF Trutnov," box 3, folder "Zde je náš domov: regionální program").

[82] Emil Caban, "Z dialógu o výstavbe," *Breznianska verejnost'*, no. 1 (late January or early February 1990), p. 2.

[83] "Organizačný poriadok mestského zastupiteľstva mesta Poprad" (PP: súčasná dokumentácia, box "Voľby '91, '92: Letáky, pozvánky, pohľadnice," folder "Súčasná dokumentácia 1991"), p. 13.

[84] Jiří Urbanec, "Do Opavy vysokou školu!" *Nové Opavsko*, 22 December 1989, p. 3; Lounská občanská koalice, "Volební program pro komunální volby 1990" (LN: fond 569, box 2); Rado Varga, "Aby sme neľutovali . . . ," *Premeny*, no. 6 (9 February 1990), p. 6.

[85] "Prvý skutočne odvážny a nezávislý, veľkorysý sponzor," *Reflex*, 11 January 1990, p. 2.

[86] Laco Zrubec, "Prečo nie v Nitre?" *Nitrianska verejnost'*, 12 January 1990, p. 1.

[87] Štefan Madari, "Orchester v Nitre," *Nitrianska verejnost'*, 12 January 1990, p. 3.

worst at something (and hence most deserving of public funds to remedy the situation).[88] In Bohemia there were also complaints as late as October 1990 that Prague gobbled up supplies, causing shortages in the surrounding areas.[89] Everywhere, smaller towns resented bigger ones, insisting that "the large towns of our homeland are not the whole republic."[90]

REGIONALISM

How do we get from this local patriotism, prevalent in December 1989 and early 1990, to the nationalism that erupted amid the hyphen debate and ultimately contributed to the demise of the Czech and Slovak Federative Republic? With a few exceptions, the road leads through regionalism. As early as November 1989 we can discern citizens reaching out from their localities to organize themselves regionally, and in every case this led to the articulation of political demands relevant to the region in question. This regionalism took widely different forms in different places, however; in some regions—particularly those around the capitals—it even took the form of antiregionalism.

We have already seen how civic initiatives in East Slovakia spontaneously organized themselves along regional lines. Moravians, too, found it natural in the revolutionary months of 1989 and early 1990 to act in concert with one another. Moravian workers announcing their intention to participate in the General Strike were more likely to send their proclamations to students in Brno or Olomouc than all the way to Prague, and frequently they even credited student demands as being those of Brno or Olomouc students rather than the work of brains in the capital. By 5 December, striking students in Brno, Gottwaldov, Olomouc, and Ostrava had established a coordinating committee of Moravian university students parallel to similar groups created in Prague and Bratislava.[91] Whether or not members of the Prague coordinating committee had any objection to this arrangement, they found it practical; by delegating responsibility to Brno and Olomouc for distributing and collecting information in the eastern half of the Czech Republic, they reduced their own workload substantially.[92] It remains to be determined when Civic Fora in Moravia began to act concertedly; at the latest they did so on 4 January, when a regional conference of district-level representatives was held in Olomouc.[93]

[88] See, for example, *Hlas*, 30 March 1990, p. 2.

[89] *Hlas*, 12 October 1990, p. 2.

[90] Antonín Zachoval (OF Černá Hora), "Bez pomoci občanů to nepůjde," *Nový život* (Blansko), 25 April 1990, p. 4.

[91] See Koordinační stávkový výbor moravských vysokých škol, "Podmínky pro ukončení stávky vysokých škol," Brno, 5 December 1989 (UH: sbírky UH, box 7, folder "Letáky a plakáty všeobecné").

[92] Prague students frequently telexed news updates to Brno for further distribution throughout Moravia and asked students in Olomouc or Brno to solicit the opinion of other Moravian universities on the texts of proposed declarations.

[93] *Zpravodaj brněnského OF*, no. 7 (5 January 1990), p. 1.

Even beyond these revolutionary circles, in the context of revisiting the principles of associational life that practically every club and society underwent in early 1990, many Moravians found some regional network desirable. A meeting of Moravian musicians on 7 January, for example, discussed three variants of association; they rejected two that would have involved connections with Prague and "unambiguously" decided to create their own organization.[94]

The spontaneity of this organization along regional lines—at a time when all organization had to emerge from below—suggests that widespread calls for restoration of Moravia's territorial integrity were what their protagonists initially claimed them to be: a translation of the revolutionary rejection of decision making "about us without us" into terms regionally relevant. The spontaneous organization shows that communication networks within Moravia were denser than they were between Moravia and other parts of Czechoslovakia and that regional identity was not the artificial construct that Praguers later claimed it to be. Just as Civic Forum in Prešov decided to realign itself with VPN because Bratislava was closer and hence more likely to defend regional interests, so Moravians in late December and early January began demanding institutional guarantees that decisions about Moravia would be made with Moravian input rather than by Praguers alone. Thus, at Civic Forum's first convention on 23 December 1989, the Brno delegates Petr Cibulka and Jaroslav Šabata objected to the fact that although Moravians comprised roughly half the Czech population, they had disproportionately low representation at the convention and practically no representation in Civic Forum's coordinating center—which in negotiations with federal and republic powers was making decisions that affected the whole country.[95] (In contrast, the KC OF *did* consult with VPN Bratislava, on Slovak interests, before taking any important stance in federal negotiations.) By the end of December Moravian citizens—who noted that all the Czech members of the new federal government were Praguers—began demanding a refederalization of Czechoslovakia to make Moravia a constituent republic alongside Slovakia and Bohemia.[96] At the same time, Moravian students proposed dividing student movement monies in a tripartite fashion among Bohemia, Moravia, and Slovakia according to population.[97] Later they insisted on a separate Moravian chamber in the student parliament, just like the one the Slovaks had negotiated.[98] By early January the Moravian question was being discussed from Šumperk in the north to Břeclav in

[94] *Zpravodaj brněnského OF*, no. 8 (8 January 1990), p. 2.

[95] "Zápis ze sněmu Občanského fóra 23. 12. 1989" (ÚSD: archiv KC OF, "OF—interní písemnosti: Sněmy OF," box 1, folder "Sněmy OF 23.12.1989"), pp. 2, 6–7.

[96] Jan Opálka, "Charta 12/1989," Olomouc, 29 December 1989, reprinted in *Přetlak*, no. 32 (18–19 January 1990), p. 3.

[97] "Zápis ze schůze KSV 30.12.1989" (MU: fond G38, box "Koordinační stávkový výbor brněnských VŠ," folder "Schůze KSV: 27.11.89–12.3.90").

[98] Stávkový výbor FF UJEP, "Zásadní připomínka FF UJEP k návrhu ústavy Studentské stavovské unie," Brno, 11 January 1990 (MU: fond G38, box "Koordinační stávkový výbor brněnských VŠ," folder "Schůze KSV: 27.11.89–12.3.90").

the south, with citizens in a number of public assemblies adopting resolutions supporting the restoration of Moravian administrative integrity.[99] Throughout these debates, the demands were all couched in terms of the revolutionary understanding of democracy. As one student in Brno remarked,

> We regard it as self-evident that Slovaks should decide about matters pertaining to Slovakia, but at the same time it seems senseless to us that only Prague should decide about what happens here [in the Czech lands]. . . . No, I am not an anarchist, but let us realize that every system, whether intentionally or not, suppresses freedom—especially a system which becomes enmeshed in complex bureaucratic relationships. And it is especially sad when at the summit of this pyramid stand people who can in no case be considered a representative sample and most of whom are representatives of Prague and only one or two stand in for "the countryside."[100]

The principle here was the same as that which OF Prešov had used to justify its conversion to VPN: that citizens living in a given region should be able to decide in concert on affairs pertinent to that region. As yet it had nothing to do with nationalism.

Regional coordination and regionalist sentiment emerged in Czech Silesia as well during the first weeks of the revolution, but the size and geography of the territory—as well as rivalry between its two chief municipalities—severely limited their scope. Under Habsburg rule, the small slice of Silesia remaining attached to the Bohemian crown after 1742 had been a distinct province with Opava as its capital. Because of its small size and the fact that Moravian enclaves existed within Silesian territory, Czech Silesia was attached for administrative purposes to Moravia in the First Republic, forming the self-governing province of Moravia-Silesia. When Moravians in 1989 began calling for a restoration of this province, Silesians protested that this would in practice mean that Moravians, with their much greater numbers, would decide on Silesian affairs. Most Silesian regionalists therefore opposed altering the Communist-era, unitary system of territorial administration in the Czech lands, opting for strictly cultural expression of Silesian identity instead. One of the chief forms that this was to take was a new Silesian University, which citizens of Opava proposed to locate in their town. The much larger city of Ostrava, straddling historically Silesian and Moravian territory, argued that it had better infrastructure to support a university and proposed that the Silesian University have campuses in both municipalities. In the end, the two municipalities could not agree, and two separate universities were founded.

[99] See, for example, Josef Zelenka, "Z Občanského fóra Boskovice," *Nový život* (Blansko), 31 January 1990, p. 2; and *Zpravodaj brněnského OF*, 8 January 1990, p. 1.
[100] Tomáš Kubíček, "Praga caput regni," *Reff: Revue filozofické fakulty*, no. 1 (5 March 1990), pp. 15–16.

East Slovakia was similar in many ways to Moravia and Silesia. Geographically the region is distinct from the rest of Slovakia; its waters flow into the Tisa River, not the Danube, and technological advances have not yet annulled the natural effect of this topography on communication networks (though Slovakia's second and third largest cities lie in the east, to this day no freeway connects them with the west). As in Moravia, students and civic associations in East Slovakia naturally organized themselves on a regional basis. Because East Slovakia had no history as a self-governing province, however, political demands initially just took the form of alliance with Prague in opposition to Bratislava—a position structurally similar to that of Silesia. By November 1990, however, easterners would graduate to proposing a quadripartite federation (map 3), arguing that it was the only way to prevent Bratislava-centrism from simply replacing Pragocentrism in Slovakia.[101]

Nationalism

In Bohemia and "Danubian" Slovakia, regionalist sentiment took on overtones of antiregionalist nationalism. In Bohemia it was not very pronounced before the hyphen debate, but in light of what came later, certain linguistic formulations of December and January are telling. During the presidential election campaign, the Prague artist Joska Skalnik argued that Havel would make the best president because "with him morality will return to Czech society and politics [not to Czechoslovak society and politics]."[102] A Civic Forum activist in České Budějovice rejoiced in an "awakening national consciousness of Czech [not Czechoslovak] statehood."[103] A contributor to Domažlice's Civic Forum bulletin argued that the success of the Velvet Revolution depended on a renaissance of "our Czech thought, philosophy, and politics."[104] In all these contexts, the word Czechoslovak would arguably have been more appropriate, but it was not what sprang first to many Bohemian minds. Moravians, for their part, were less likely to make this slip. Here it was significant that the Czech word for an inhabitant of Bohemia is also the word for someone ethnically Czech. Language, therefore, forced Moravians to make a distinction between regional and ethnic identity that in Bohemian usage could be blurred.

In Slovakia, though some isolated individuals appeared in Bratislava's November assemblies bearing nationalist placards, popular accentuation of Slovak identity in these early days was generally patriotic rather than nationalist. Even the Matica slovenská, a cultural foundation that had been established in the nineteenth cen-

---

[101] Dionýz Milly and Jaroslav Tomko, "Východ sa hlási o slovo," Košice, 22 November 1990, in Premeny, vol. 2, no. 50 (14 December 1990), p. 6; Martin Hybler, "Federace na Hanou," Respekt, 15 April 1991, p. 2.

[102] Suk, Labyrintem, p. 206.

[103] Mojmír Prokop, "Vážení přátelé . . . ," Informační servis (České Budějovice), no. 18 (18 January 1990), p. 2.

[104] Z. Vyšohlid, "Křižovatky myšlení a . . . ," Domažlické inForum, no. 4 (19 January 1990), p. 2.

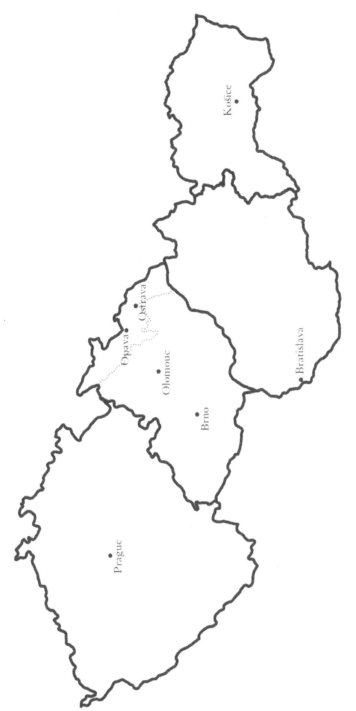

Map 3. Eastern Slovaks' proposal for a quadripartite federation

tury to oppose magyarization and that was renewed in early December 1989, gave primacy initially to a regional rather than ethnic basis of community, issuing statements that welcomed even ethnic Hungarians into its ranks.[105] In this it was similar to regionally based cultural foundations in the Czech lands, the Matice moravská and Matice slezská, which were also renewed at this time. By mid-December, however, decidedly nationalist rhetoric began appearing in north-central Slovakia, in an arch stretching roughly from Topoľčany through Martin to Ružomberok and including the Orava region. The first domestic proposal to end the common Czecho-Slovak state seems to have been made in Dolný Kubín on 12 December.[106] In January, Matica slovenská groups in this region exchanged the organization's initially inclusive attitude toward Slovakia's Hungarians for a chauvinistic one, demanding, for example, "that all children in the southern parts of Slovakia study in Slovak schools in Slovak and that they be taught by Slovak teachers," and railing against "incrimination of the Slovak nation by representatives of citizens of Hungarian nationality." They also demanded a return to the Czechoslovak Socialist Republic's "original" name: "the Czecho-Slovak Republic."[107] Since the Matica's national headquarters were in Martin, the nationalist perspective from this locality soon became the official line of the foundation as a whole.

Though 12 December was evidently the first time any "domestic" Slovaks publicly demanded the dissolution of the federation, it was not the first time the proposal had been made. Slovak émigrés who had prospered in Jozef Tiso's clerical fascist state but had gone into exile after World War II began in October 1989 to smuggle in and circulate flyers protesting the "Czech occupation" of their country and demanding Slovak independence.[108] Immediately after 17 November they intensified their efforts. Representatives of a Slovak community in Australia, for example, wrote to Slovakia's prime minister on 20 November demanding an end to the federation and warning of a Prague-engineered genocide of Slovaks.[109] An émigré from Stuttgart wrote to VPN and what he called the "All-Slovakian Association of Students" on 16 December, proposing a sequence of strikes to achieve Slovak

[105] "Spomienkový," *Prešovské noviny*, 14 December 1989, p. 3.

[106] "Odsúdili nečestné konanie skompromitovaných," *Orava*, 20 December 1989, p. 3.

[107] "Prehlásenie miestneho odboru MS v Bánovciach nad Bebr. dňa 20. januára 1990," *Hosť do domu*, no. 3 (24 January 1990), p. 3. On the problematic nature of historical claims regarding Czecholovakia's "original" name, see Milan Šútovec, *Semióza ako politikum alebo "Pomlčková vojna": Niektoré historické, politické a iné súvislosti jedného sporu, ktorý bol na začiatku zániku česko-slovenského štátu* (Bratislava: Kalligram, 1999), pp. 183–95.

[108] Národná Rada za Oslobodenie Slovenska so sídlom v Mníchove, Frakcia pôsobiaca na území Slovenska, "Vyhlásenie Frakcie NRzOS pôsobiacej na domácom území k 71. výročiu ČSR," 28 October 1989 (PX: súčasná dokumentácia, folder "Nežná revolúcia—1989").

[109] Letter from J. K. and J. S., Strawberry Hills, N.S.W., to Ivan Knotek, Bratislava, 20 November 1989 (SNA: Archív VPN, fond. odd. I).

independence by 10 January.[110] Initially these foreign crackpots hoped to ride VPN's coattails, but the horrified KV VPN ignored them, forcing the émigrés to look for another vehicle. During the height of the revolution in December, émigrés went about Bratislava stamping student posters with the Slovak heraldic emblem and writing in criticisms on posters that praised Masaryk or affirmed Czecho-Slovak unity. Students replied by correcting grammatical errors in the graffiti, writing in that the authors should learn Slovak.[111] Following this rejection in Bratislava, the émigrés took refuge among sympathizers in the more nationalist heartland discussed above until the outbreak of the "hyphen war"gave them a new opportunity to curry favor in the capital.

Despite these early intimations of ethnic nationalism in Bohemia and Danubian Slovakia, most Czechs and Slovaks in 1989 and at the beginning of 1990 understood community primarily in civic, not ethnic terms. Thus, although Czechoslovakia consisted of two ethnically defined nations and several nationalities, the word *nation* was initially used almost exclusively in the singular. Residents of a South Bohemian village, declaring their resolve to participate in the General Strike symbolically while continuing to work, explained, "We devote our work during these two hours to the nation."[112] Posters appearing in Louny and Prague asked, "Communists, to whom will you give your vote??? The Central Committee or your nation?"[113] A poster in Bratislava demanded "for the whole nation democracy without qualifying adjectives."[114] While it is possible that the authors of these texts had specifically Czech or Slovak nations in mind, the context makes it clear that that was not the point; the term referred primarily to the assembled populace—the revolutionary community. There are, moreover, many examples from late 1989 and early 1990 where singular use of the word *nation* clearly denoted a single Czecho-Slovak community. In the Slovak television debate of 24 November, the student Miloš Lauko observed that the number of participants in manifestations on Wenceslas Square far exceeded the number of students in Prague, concluding that what had started as a student movement was now a movement "of the entire nation."[115] The Brno literary critic Ivo Osolsobě, addressing an audience in Nitra on the semiotics of the revolution, spoke of "our people [*náš lid*]," clearly including both Czechs and Slovaks within the singular noun.[116] In Košice, people

---

[110] Letter from F. M. (SNA: Archív VPN, fond. odd. I).

[111] See, for example: HM: Zbierka plagátov, box "Plagáty: 1989 a ďalej s číslom," nos. 33598 and 33647; and box "Malé plagáty r. 1989 + voľby—1. demokratické," nos. 33609 and 33626.

[112] "My občané Vimperka se připojujeme . . . ," 24 November 1989 (ÚSD: archiv KC OF, box 47).

[113] LN: fond 569, box 2, unlabeled folder; private collection of Kevin McDermott, Sheffield, England.

[114] SNA: Archív VPN, fond. odd. I.

[115] *Štúdio Televíznych novín*, 24 November 1989.

[116] Quoted in "Vážení priatelia!" *Nitrianska verejnost'*, 19 January 1990, p. 1.

continued to speak of a single Czechoslovak nation at least as late as June 1990.[117] Even OF and VPN leaders in Prague and Bratislava originally spoke of a single nation and began using the plural only on 22 November (after an emissary from VPN Bratislava had made Prague aware of VPN's existence). After this date, moreover, they still frequently slipped back to the singular noun. When Václav Havel spoke in the Slovak National Theater on 29 November, he recalled the role of theaters in awakening the Czech nation in the nineteenth century and concluded that a new national awakening was occurring; presumably, given the place where he was speaking, this contemporary "nation" was not Czech but Czechoslovak.[118] In mid-January, in an interview with the Bratislava student bulletin Zmena, Milan Kňažko spoke again of a single "Czechoslovak nation."[119] Though there were contexts when both these prominent individuals used nation in its plural, ethnic sense, they were equally likely to employ the word in its singular, civic sense. Havel once even mixed both meanings (speaking of a Czechoslovak nation and separate Czech and Slovak nations) in the same speech.[120] For most Czechs and Slovaks, then, the word nation initially signified both a civic and an ethnic community, but we may deduce that the former bond was experienced as more salient.

Impulses that would favor the ethnic understanding of nationhood—and ultimately supplant singular use of the word nation with the plural—can first be discerned in the context of VPN Bratislava's desire to speak on behalf of the entire Slovak public and to maintain independence vis-à-vis OF in Prague. Peter Zajac from the KV VPN visited the KC OF in Prague late in the evening on 21 November, recording an impromptu speech from a flustered Václav Havel about replacing "federalized totalitarianism" with "a democratic federation."[121] The speech was played in Bratislava the next day, and KC OF spokespersons began trying to pluralize their usage of the word nation.[122] On 25 November, VPN and the student coordinating committee in Bratislava issued a joint list of twelve demands, the first of which was "to create out of the Slovak National Council a genuine parliament of the Slovak nation, in which all segments of our society will have representation." The declaration further called for "a thoroughly democratic federation of Czechs and Slovaks and legal arrangements guaranteeing the rights and standing of nationalities according to the principle of full and real equality."[123] Between the

[117] O. R. Halaga, "Porozumením k stabilite," Akcia, no. 9 (15 June 1990), p. 3.

[118] Verejné fórum, Slovenská televízia, 29 November 1999.

[119] "Herec alebo politik?" Zmena, no. 18 (January 1990), p. 4.

[120] Václav Havel, speech on Czechoslovak Television, 16 December 1989, reprinted in Suk, Občanské fórum, vol. 2, pp. 243–46.

[121] Havel's speech is reprinted in Feldek, Keď sme brali, p. 21.

[122] "Zásadně nesouhlasíme se způsobem . . . ," in Suk, Občanské fórum, vol. 2, pp. 16–17. For Zajac's account of his visit, see his Sen o krajine (Bratislava: Kalligram, 1996), pp. 9–11.

[123] "Programové vyhlásenie občianskej iniciatívy Verejnosť proti násiliu a Koordinačného výboru slovenských vysokoškolákov," Bratislava, 25 November 1989, reprinted in Feldek, Keď sme brali, p. 35;

idea of a "Slovak nation," clearly understood ethnically, and the idea of a civic nation, according to which "all segments of society [including national minorities] will have representation," tension is obvious. It is perhaps worth noting that just three days before this the students had issued a proclamation appealing to soldiers in the Czechoslovak People's Army not to act against their (singular) nation.[124] It is also worth noting that, aside from the north-central region discussed above, Slovaks outside Bratislava and a few adjacent districts did not at this time give such prominence to the national question (if, indeed, they mentioned it at all). That the attention given the national question in Bratislava was so unrepresentative, together with the fact that those who raised it vacillated between civic and ethnic meanings of the word *nation*, supports the interpretation that Bratislavans introduced the question in order to augment the power not so much of their nation but of their city.

The presidential campaign of December 1989 further underscores the disparity in thinking about the nation between the civic movements in the capitals and most of the rest of the Czechoslovak public. Historians of the revolution have reproduced an error of prominent activists in the KV VPN and especially the KC OF, who from their rather sheltered positions assumed that Dubček was more deeply popular in Slovakia than in the Czech lands, such that if they backed Havel for president instead of Dubček, it would be taken as an affront to the Slovak nation.[125] The view from the capitals was myopic, and Dubček's candidacy was not initially a national issue, since he was popular among Czechs as well as Slovaks. In surveys conducted before 10 December in Prague and Brno, Dubček by a wide margin topped the list of personages that citizens there would choose as head of state.[126] Even when public opinion shifted to support for Havel, there is evidence that it may have shifted just as dramatically in Slovakia as in the Czech lands. An early December survey conducted by the Civic Forum of Bratislava's Institute of Philosophy and Sociology showed that while Dubček enjoyed more favor than Havel among blue-collar workers in Slovakia, among white-collar workers the rankings were reversed.[127] Given this virtually identical starting point, it would not be surprising

identical, similar, and markedly divergent versions (with a thirteenth point) can be found in BB, KS, PP, PX, and ZM.

[124] Koordinační výbor študentského hnutia, "Výzva k robotníkom a roľníkom!" Bratislava, 22 November 1989, reprinted in Feldek, *Keď sme brali*, p. 18.

[125] Recording of conversation between VPN and OF representatives in Prague, 6 December 1989, quoted in Suk, *Občanské fórum*, vol. 2, p. 97. See also Suk, *Labyrintem*, p. 200.

[126] Ladislav Zajíček, "Výsledky průzkumu veřejného mínění z 22.11.1989," Prague (JN: Sbírka soudobé dokumentace, 1989–1991); Ladislav Zajíček, "Výsledky průzkumu veřejného mínění z 24.11.1989," Prague (ÚSD: archiv KC OF, box 34); Ladislav Zajíček, "Výsledky průzkumu veřejného mínění ze soboty 25.11.1989," Prague (ÚSD: archiv KC OF, box 152); "Vyhodnocení studentské ankety," *Pravda vydĕsí*, no. 3 (1 December 1989), pp. 5–7; "Chceme znát váš názor!" 8 December 1989 (ÚSD: archiv KC OF, box 35, envelope "Anketa 8.12."); Suk, *Labyrintem*, p. 200.

[127] OF Ústavu filozofie a sociológie SAV, "Vážení spoluobčania, všetci cítime . . . ," 1st ed., 30 November 1989 (BB: Materiály získané od hnutia Verejnosť proti násiliu v Banskej Bystrici, 1989, boxes 1–2) and 2nd

to find that the student campaign to mobilize support for Havel's candidacy was just as successful in Slovakia as in the Czech lands. By misreading the situation, the KV VPN played into the hands of rival political forces in Slovakia who sought to nationalize Dubček for their own profit.[128] It also led the KC OF to subtly foster Czech nationalism in order to rally support for Havel. Havel's 16 December speech, for example, essentially reduced Dubček's value to his Slovakness.[129] All the evidence from late December and early January, however, suggests that Havel was at that time equally as popular in Slovakia as in the Czech lands; even the Slovak Communist daily, *Pravda*, which had supported Dubček, switched at the beginning of January to adulation of Havel in harmony with sentiments being expressed throughout the country.[130]

Why did Bratislava couch its demands in national rather than regional terms? Either definition of community could have been used to argue for devolution of power. At least three factors were involved. First was the overpowering institutional legacy of the federalization that had been accomplished in 1968 according to the Soviet model. This arrangement had sanctified the ethnic national principle as the justification for federalization, giving Czechs and Slovaks separate "national councils" as ostensibly representative lawmaking bodies in each republic. Though the civic sense also had its institutional incarnation in the national committees at every level of local government (reflecting mentalities during the reunification of Czechoslovakia at the end of the Second World War), any talk of devolving institutional power to *Slovakia*, as opposed to some other type of region, necessarily had to engage with the ethnic conception of nationhood. A second, related factor was the existence of regions in Slovakia—especially East Slovakia—where people did not unreservedly recognize Bratislava as their capital. Visiting Košice in March, Ján Budaj opened a speech by noting, "In the past I've felt that Bratislava is not everywhere naturally accepted as the capital city," implying that things were now different.[131] A number of easterners rewarded him a few months later by proposing that the Slovak capital be moved from Bratislava to the more central (and in their view, prettier) town of Martin.[132] A hypothetical accentuation of regional identity on Bratislava's part might have invited serious challenges to its rule over all of Slovakia; the idea of a unitary Slovak nation made Bratislava's hegemonic claims less assailable. Finally, VPN's partnership with FMK was significant. The

ed., 5 December 1989 (BB: Materiály získané od hnutia Verejnosť proti násiliu v Banskej Bystrici, 1989, box 2 [also available in BV]); Jozef Košta et al., "Prvá diagnóza nežnej revolúcie," *Verejnosť*, 19 December 1989, p. 8.

[128] The Slovak National Front began playing the national card on 12 December. Suk, *Labyrintem*, p. 178.
[129] Havel, speech of 16 December 1989.
[130] *Pravda* (Bratislava), 2 January 1990, pp. 1–2.
[131] "Ideály v ľudoch zostali," *Večer*, 5 March 1990, p. 1.
[132] Pavol Lóška, "Spor o hlavné mesto?" *Akcia*, no. 9 (15 June 1990), p. 5.

arrangement reached between leaders of VPN and FMK (all of whom lived in Bratislava) was that FMK would be allied with VPN, not part of it. Since FMK had defined itself from the beginning as an ethnic association of Slovakia's Hungarians, it was but the logical corollary for VPN to be an ethnic association of Slovakia's Slovaks.[133]

Nonetheless, throughout December and for most of January, expressions of Czechoslovak identity remained much more the norm in Slovakia than any emphasis on an exclusively Slovak community. This is particularly evident with regard to a symbol of political community that was frequently discussed during this period: Tomáš Garrigue Masaryk. Best characterized as a product of Austro-Hungarian multiculturalism (son of a Slovak father and German-Austrian mother, born in Moravia), Masaryk had been part of a triumvirate including the Czech Eduard Beneš and the Slovak Milan Rastislav Štefánik that had spearheaded negotiations with the Great Powers to create Czechoslovakia after World War I. Masaryk had been maligned as a Pragocentrist under Tiso's regime and condemned as bourgeois during the Communist period, but the revolution witnessed a revival of popular reverence for him. Despite having advocated the idea of a single Czechoslovak nation, Masaryk was initially just as popular in Slovakia as Štefánik. A group of citizens in Nitra argued against plans to move a Masaryk statue from a warehouse to the municipal gallery, insisting that the statue should be placed outdoors, perhaps on the grounds of the Topoľčany chateau (which Masaryk had often visited), where it could have a more salutary effect on public morals.[134] Citizens in Martin founded a Club of the Friends of Masaryk and Štefánik in order to propagate their ideas.[135] (That this example comes from a town otherwise associated with chauvinistic nationalism should be taken as further evidence of how strong Czechoslovak identity was throughout Slovakia.) In December, Bratislava students painted an enormous poster praising Masaryk, Štefánik, and Beneš (which émigré nationalists defaced).[136] In mid-December, the bulletin *Zmena* also published an article highly favorable to Masaryk (though the editors qualified their praise a month later in response to critical letters from readers in north-central Slovakia).[137]

The hyphen debate marked a turning point. It began on 23 January, when President Havel introduced a motion in the Federal Assembly to adopt a new state

---

[133] Czechs living in Slovakia, for their part, joined VPN (or one of the Civic Fora that were later subsumed within VPN), while Slovaks living in the Czech lands joined OF. As far as they were concerned, the distinction between the two movements was purely geographic.

[134] R. Schmuck (VPN PKO Nitra), "Chceme meniť veci k lepšiemu," *Nitrianska verejnosť*, 19 January 1990, p. 4.

[135] *Martinská verejnosť*, 10 January 1990, p. 2.

[136] HM: box "Plagáty: 1989 a ďalej s číslom," poster no. 33647.

[137] Róbert Letz, "Gottwald nebol prvý," *Zmena*, no. 15 (19 December 1989), p. 7; "Polemika k článku o T. G. Masarykovi: Čierna škvrna na humanistickom štíte," *Zmena*, no. 18 (15 January 1990), p. 10.

emblem and to strike the word *Socialist* from the official name of both the federal state and the two republics. Havel's gesture came on the heels of Pithart's antirevolutionary speech and in the context of mounting public confusion; the change of state symbols was intended to rally public unity.[138] There is evidence that it might have done so. Citizens from Chrudim to Košice had called in December for the restoration of a crown on the Czech lion in the state emblem—in place of the red star the Communists had substituted.[139] In Nitra, VPN in the Park of Culture and Rest had called for the removal of the word *Socialist* from the country's name "because that word has been discredited by the uncultured politics of the Communist Party not just in the 1960s, but mainly in the last years of 'real socialism.' We are for returning to our country its original name, that is, the Czechoslovak Republic."[140] The response of the Federal Assembly to Havel's proposal, however, was explosively divisive. A number of Slovak Communist delegates, aware of a certain level of support back home for the insertion of a hyphen in the state's name, took the opportunity to divert attention from their party affiliation (and potentially to attract voters) by countering Havel's motion. There followed nearly three months of agonized debate over orthographic technicalities that riveted public attention on the national question (and away from the question of socialism, which had hitherto been a much more prominent topic of debate). Meetings of the Federal Assembly were televised, and citizens from Louny to Košice sent letters to Prague and participated in demonstrations on behalf of particular name proposals. Bohemians rejected the hyphen in part because it had been used once before—between the Munich crisis and Hitler's occupation of rump Bohemia and Moravia in 1939—and they disliked the association.[141] Slovaks welcomed the hyphen as a way of emphasizing to the outside world that they were not Czechs, as well as to symbolize equality within the federation.[142] (Moravians, for their part, jokingly proposed calling the whole country Moravia, after the medieval Great Moravian Empire, which had arguably been Czechs' and Slovaks' first common state.) The Federal Assembly eventually adopted two separate names (a different one to be used in each republic) on 29 March, but popular demonstrations forced reconsideration on 19 April.[143] The final compromise, "Czech and Slovak Federative Republic," was an elegant one, but the cost had been high.

In Slovakia, the hyphen debate gave a new lease on life to the previously marginal nationalists, who found that it was not necessary to have a large number of

---

[138] Petr Pithart, quoted in Irena Suková, ed., *Proměny politického systému v Československu na přelomu let 1989/1990* (Prague: Nadace Heinricha Bölla, 1995).

[139] "Prohlášení zaměstnanců KOLI Chrudim," 12 December 1989 (ÚSD: box 11, folder "Různé"); KS: zbierka z Nežnej revolúcie, folder "Plagáty. Rôzne."

[140] Schmuck, "Chceme menit'."

[141] Letter from B. R. to Alexander Dubček, Louny, 21 March 1990 (LN: fond 633, box 1).

[142] Robert Sedláček, *Tenkrát 2: Šance pro Slovensko*, Česká televize, 5 January 2000.

[143] Suk, *Labyrintem*, p. 355.

supporters in order to rivet media attention at demonstrations. Steadily they gained support among Bratislava students, who over the course of February and March transformed *Zmena* into a nationalist tabloid. The émigré-led separatist National Council for the Liberation of Slovakia held a meeting on 4 April in the dormitory of Bratislava's Technical University, suggesting that the council by this time had student sympathizers.[144] Even though the majority of Slovaks remained in favor of the common state (as they continued to be until the very end), the hyphen debate stimulated a significant extension of radical nationalist discourse.[145]

Czech nationalism also took a more radical turn. One group of Bohemians established a Club for the Defense of the Czech Nation, claiming that Slovaks were betraying Czechs once more, just as they supposedly had in 1938. As a result they called from their side for the dissolution of the federation.[146] Additional research will be necessary to determine how widespread these ideas were, but certainly the intensity of Czech attachment to the federation diminished in the course of the hyphen debate.[147] It is also interesting that, during and after the debate, Civic Forum activists in some Bohemian districts began reaching out to populations of ethnic Czechs in Russia and Romania. OF Benešov was concerned that Russian Czechs be allowed to immigrate to Czechoslovakia.[148] OF Trutnov sent food aid to Czech villages in the Banat, established a Czech library there, and brought Czech children from Romania to visit "Czechoslovakia" (but really just Bohemia) in June.[149] "Help our countrymen," they appealed, "who are thirsting for Czech culture."[150] Nationalism was clothed as humanitarian aid.

Needless to say, Czech nationalism was stronger in Bohemia than in Moravia. In the eastern province, however, a Moravian nationalist movement emerged in the spring of 1990. The reaction to Moravian regionalism in Prague was incomprehension mixed with horror. Beginning in December 1989 and continuing through the spring of 1990, OF leaders in Prague consistently responded to the problem by asking, why now?, by insisting that consideration of the constitutional status of regions must await the resolution of questions concerning "all of Czechoslovakia,"

---

[144] "Míting Národnej rady . . ." (SNA: Archív VPN, fond. odd. II).

[145] Surveys attesting to Czech and Slovak support for continued federation are reproduced in Viera Hlavová and Jozef Žatkuliak, eds., *Novembrová revolúcia a česko-slovenský rozchod: Od česko-slovenskej federácie k samostatnej demokratickej slovenskej štátnosti: Výber dokumentov a prejavov (november 1989–december 1992)* (Bratislava: Literárne informačné centrum, 2002).

[146] K. Vitek, "Všem českým občanům! Slováci opět rozdělují . . . ," Prague, 7 March 1990 (PX: súčasná dokumentácia, folder "Nežná revolúcia—1989," subfolder "Materiály. Strana zelených").

[147] For a discussion of how Czechs sometimes define themselves in opposition to Slovaks, see Ladislav Holý, *The Little Czech and the Great Czech Nation* (Cambridge: Cambridge University Press, 1996).

[148] "Zpráva o sněmu OF Benešov dne 13.12.1990" (BN: soudobá dokumentace, box "Volby 1990, 1992").

[149] "Žádost o poskytnutí finančného příspěvku" and "Zájezd dětí a mládeže z rumunského Ravenska do ČSFR" (TU: fond "KC OF Trutnov," box 1, folder "Rumunsko").

[150] "Pomozte krajanům, kteří jsou žízniví po české kultuře" (TU: fond "KC OF Trutnov," box 1, folder "Rumunsko").

and by promising that a committee of "experts" would take up the Moravian question after the parliamentary elections.[151] Praguers argued against institutionalizing Moravian structures by claiming that Moravians were ethnically Czechs, thus lacking the rationale Slovaks had for a separate place in the federation. This Stalinist line of argument succeeded in dividing opinion in Moravia, leading even Šabata to agree that a tripartite federation would not be justified, though he still envisioned some kind of institutional structure for Moravia.[152] Others, accepting the major premise on which the Prague syllogism was based, began asserting that Moravians were indeed ethnically distinct from Czechs, ultimately persuading 40 percent of Moravians to identify their nationality as "Moravian" in the 1991 census.[153] While initial support for reconstituting Moravia as a political entity—couched entirely in the language of democracy—had been widespread across the region, the new argumentation based on notions of Moravian ethnic or national distinctiveness was largely confined to Brno and adjacent areas of southern Moravia. This difference can be explained by seeing the emergence of nationalist rhetoric as the result of an urban rivalry between Prague and Brno, where Brno activists invoked nationalism in order to strengthen their bargaining position vis-à-vis Prague. By this time, however, a different urban rivalry had further weakened the movement's original unity: this was the question of which city, Brno or Olomouc, should be the capital of a politically coherent Moravia. Praguers first raised the question in February and used it as an additional reason for postponing serious debate on Moravia's future, saying Brno and Olomouc would need to come to an agreement on this first. In a speech in Olomouc in May 1990, Václav Havel spoke of the town as one "which for long years has walked in the shadow of Ostrava and Brno and lacked the statutes it deserved."[154] This can be read as an attack on the Moravian movement, stoking divisions within Moravia. Thus it was that, although Moravian regionalism was initially widespread and parties demanding Moravian political integrity ultimately won 31 percent of the Moravian vote in the June 1990 elections (with the largest vote getter, Civic Forum, still being officially open to Moravian proposals), Moravian nationalism remained largely confined to Brno and adjacent regions.[155] Still, it was only when regionalist demands were blocked that proponents began adding nationalist rhetoric to arguments that originally invoked only the revolutionary emphases on democracy and self-organization.

[151] Libor Prudký, quoted in "Zápis z Rady—12.3.90 v 16 hod.—pondělí" (ÚSD: folder "Zápisy z rady OF (C)"), p. 1; "Setkání zástupců OF krajských a okresních měst Čech a Moravy dne 16.12.1989 v Praze" (ÚSD: archiv KC OF), p. 3.

[152] Zpravodaj brněnského OF, 5 January 1990, p. 1.

[153] "V kuloárech parlamentu sa hovorí otvorene," Verejnosť, 20 July 1990, p. 1; Petr Daněk, "Moravian and Silesian Nationalities: A New Phenomenon in the Ethnic Map of the Czech Lands?" GeoJournal 30, no. 3 (1993): 251.

[154] "Čestný doktorát," Občanský deník, 29 May 1990, p. 2.

[155] Daněk, pp. 251–52.

Questions of community boundaries, identity, and structure were the inevitable consequence of the renewed sense of community that swept Czechoslovakia after 17 November. They were essentially questions of how to institutionalize this sense, or as Lynn Hunt puts it, to invest sacrality in a particular location, or "sacred center."[156] From this perspective it becomes noteworthy that the discourse of nationhood invoked increasingly religious allusions as the 1990s wore on. In May 1990, for example, a "pilgrimage" of "the entire nation" was organized to the Slovak village of Bradlo, site of Štefánik's grave.[157] It became the occasion of what Mona Ozouf calls "antagonistic festivals," with some attending as advocates of a Czecho-Slovak civic nation, and others protesting in the name of a distinctly Slovak ethnic nation.[158] Later, Slovak nationalist meetings typically began with a religious ceremony or reference; many gatherings commenced with masses.[159] What was essentially happening was a contest over the localization of sacrality, whether it resided in one nation or two, and whether it should be represented in Prague or Bratislava (or possibly Brno).[160]

Within the debate on how to institutionalize revolutionary ideas of community, cities and towns vied with one another for the power that would come with the right to represent the community. This urban rivalry was a key factor in dividing the originally united Czechoslovak community into smaller ones. This is not to say that other factors, such as the different classes of intellectuals Gil Eyal analyzes, did not play a part, but this part was played on particular urban stages.[161] Especially in central Europe, where geographic mobility remains exceptional, individuals separated by class differences may nonetheless share certain outlooks by virtue of the place from which they are looking.

The hyphen debate polarized the contest, causing many ordinary Czechs and Slovaks who had previously been indifferent to the national question to adopt a nationalist stance. The timing of this shift is significant. It came at a time when the force of popular mobilization was beginning to encounter stiffening resistance from previously cowed local officials of the old regime and in the wake of Petr Pithart's dramatic speech dissuading citizens from revolutionary enthusiasm. This

[156] Lynn Hunt, *Politics, Culture, and Class in the French Revolution* (Berkeley: University of California Press, 1984), p. 87.

[157] HM: Zbierka plagátov, box "Malé plagáty r. 1989 + voľby—1. demokratické," poster no. 33738.

[158] Mona Ozouf, *Festivals and the French Revolution*, trans. Alan Sheridan (Cambridge, Mass.: Harvard University Press, 1988).

[159] See, for example, "Slovenská národná jednota Vás pozýva na celonárodné oslavy 52. výročia . . ." and "73. výročie Pittsburskej dohody" (SNA: Archív VPN, fond. odd. II).

[160] In negotiations about the federation VPN once proposed that the federal capital be moved to Brno, so that Prague and Bratislava elites would share the travel burden, but Praguers dismissed the notion out of hand. Karen Henderson, *Slovakia: The Escape from Invisibility* (London: Routledge, 2002), p. 33; and Juraj Mihalík, *Spomienky na zlyhania* (Bratislava: Príroda, 1993), p. 51.

[161] Gil Eyal, *The Origins of Postcommunist Elites: From Prague Spring to the Breakup of Czechoslovakia* (Minneapolis: University of Minnesota Press, 2003).

enthusiasm could not so easily be dismissed, however, and it may be that the hyphen debate became so volatile because it gave citizens something they could act upon when other efforts were being frustrated. The question of the state's name thus had the rallying effect Havel had intended, though not in the way he intended. It is significant, moreover, that the national question superseded the question of socialism, which, judging from the popular discourse of 1989, one might have expected to be more controversial.

Chapter 5

Power in the Streets

"Power, even according to their Marxist theories, comes from below. And now that power has genuinely emerged from below, from those who were most defenseless: from students and young people. And 'They,' they're still around somewhere, still sitting in their chairs, but they no longer have power! Power has come among the people and it is awesome."[1]

In the afternoon of 27 November, shortly after the General Strike, the district committee of the Communist Party in the north Bohemian town of Louny held a crisis meeting. Its members easily reached consensus that they had lost the initiative. "We're at least five days behind everything against which we're competing," lamented one of the comrades.[2] Another said, "In all seriousness, we lost the first week," concluding that the Party's tactic of forbidding workers from striking had only made matters worse.[3] "I think we can all agree," sighed one secretary, "that the situation is very serious even here in our district, despite the fact that just fourteen days ago we considered it stable."[4] Committee members complained of a lack of direction from Party structures above, and defection of Party members below. "Until this morning the *aparát* was very good, but now this afternoon some are beginning to doubt and have had enough."[5] Committee members wrung their hands that the

---

[1] Jaroslav Hutka, 2 December 1989, quoted in "Jaroslav Hutka v Olomouci," *Přetlak*, no. 9 (5 December 1989), p. 4.

[2] Miloslav Valenta, quoted in "Zápis mimořádné schůze POV KSČ v Lounech 27.11.1989" (LN: fond "OV KSČ Louny"), p. 6.

[3] František Ritter, quoted ibid., p. 4.

[4] Jan Boček, quoted ibid., p. 6.

[5] Josef Nágl, quoted ibid., p. 7.

district's workers had gotten hold of the video from 17 November. Most of all, they worried about how many people had shown up on the town square during the General Strike and how many would gather again for a manifestation at 4:00 p.m., where a municipal Civic Forum was likely to be established. "It's evident that we're going to have to engage in dialogue," said the leading secretary, "in order to break up the groups that have formed. . . . I want to go to the square and have a look; who will go with me?"[6] Committee members squabbled over who should go, no one showing enthusiasm, but eventually it was decided to send the leading secretary and three others, who would try to get people off the square by proposing indoor meetings between the district committee and representatives of the crowd.[7] None of the delegation succeeded in speaking on the square, however.[8] After they came back to report this, the committee meekly resolved to try again at the square in subsequent days. "There's nothing for it," said one secretary, "we'll have to go with our skin to the market."[9]

Though Czechoslovakia's written constitution still gave the Communist Party a leading role in society, it was clear after the General Strike that the Party had lost power. If it was to attempt to regain power—or in the words of one Louny Communist, "to save what can be saved"—it would have to go to the square.[10] Power was in the streets, and the square was the seat of authority. Not only the Party realized this; after the General Strike, the people realized it, too.

The Hungarian political theorist and former roundtable participant János Kis, generalizing from his own experience, identifies the process that commenced in Czechoslovakia and elsewhere in central Europe in 1989 as "regime change" or "coordinated transition" rather than revolution, because although the legal system changed significantly, every change was technically made by the political institution constitutionally endowed with the prerogative of making the change. Legal continuity was preserved.[11] This pedantic focus on form, however, misses the substantive shift that occurred in the realm of power. If Czechoslovakia's Communist parliament voted to remove from the constitution the clause about the Party's leading role, if it voted to make Havel president, if it voted ultimately to reconstruct itself on a more democratic basis, it did not do so because its members had suddenly embraced democratic principles; it did so because it was afraid of the new power that had arisen as a result of the successful constitution of a community independent

---

[6] Alexandr Hnízdiuch, quoted ibid., p. 2.

[7] Ibid., p. 3.

[8] Ibid., p. 6.

[9] Boček, p. 8.

[10] Ritter, p. 4.

[11] János Kis, "Between Reform and Revolution: Three Hypotheses about the Nature of the Regime Change," in *Lawful Revolution in Hungary, 1989–94*, edited by Béla Király (Boulder, Colo.: Social Science Monographs, 1995): 33–59 (esp. p. 42); and "Between Reform and Revolution," *East European Politics and Societies* 12, no. 2 (Spring 1998): 300–383 (esp. p. 323).

of the Party. If Civic Forum (with VPN's approval) allowed all these changes to take the form of legal continuity, it was not because it had to do so. Indeed, other alternatives were considered. In December 1989, Civic Forum's executive council considered asking the Czech and Slovak national councils—rather than the Federal Assembly, as required by the constitution—to elect Havel president.[12] In January, Civic Forum's republican convention considered dissolving parliament altogether and creating a directory to rule until free elections could be held.[13] In both instances, however, Civic Forum *chose* to maintain legal continuity. Since the fact of legal continuity depended on the choice of those who had power to choose, this power would seem to have been the more critical factor.

Civic Forum had this power in December and January because it defined itself as "the representative of the square," and because "the square" explicitly approved this definition in loud, vocal acclamation as well as in thousands upon thousands of signatures to letters and proclamations attesting to the legitimacy of this representation.[14] The square, then, was the seat of real power, and as we have seen in chapter 1 and as Jiří Suk demonstrates amply, the square made this clear several times in November and December when it compelled Civic Forum to press demands more radical than its leaders otherwise countenanced. As the site where the revolutionary community most vividly manifested itself, the square embodied the sacred center of the new society, and so it was from the square that legitimacy proceeded. The square thus had the power to determine how it was represented; in other words, it was the seat not only of power but of authority. It would not last, of course. As early as 25 November, Timothy Garton Ash "trembled" at the ease with which skillful speakers could sway the crowd, and by January's end citizens were once again complaining—with justification—that important decisions were being made "about them without them."[15] Though OF and VPN leaders in Prague and Bratislava could sometimes sway the square in certain directions, however, they could not always do so, and they certainly lacked the capacity to direct citizens facing decisions at local levels. Instead, they explicitly encouraged citizens to act on their own initiative, and citizens did so. For roughly two months, power was in the streets.

Revolutionary citizens took to heart the students' injunction to "think globally, act locally" by seeking to implement "the ideals of November" in their workplaces

---

[12] Jiří Suk, *Labyrintem revoluce: Aktéři, zápletky a křížovatky jedné politické krize (od listopadu 1989 do června 1990)* (Prague: Prostor, 2003), p. 220.

[13] "Zápis ze sněmu Koordinačního centra Občanského fóra dne 20. ledna 1990" (ÚSD: archív KC OF, "OF—interní písemnosti: Sněmy OF," box 1, folder "Sněmy OF 20.1.1990"), p. 4.

[14] "Zápis z jednání rady Občanského fóra ze dne 13.12.89," Rada KC OF, 13 December 1989 (ÚSD: archív KC OF, folder "Zápisy z rady OF (C)"), p. 2.

[15] Timothy Garton Ash, *We the People: The Revolution of '89 Witnessed in Warsaw, Budapest, Berlin & Prague* (London: Granta, 1990), p. 100.

and local communities.[16] Though on 29 November the constitution was amended to abolish the Communist Party's leading role, the Party continued to dominate political, social, and economic life at most levels. Citizens consequently set about removing compromised functionaries from positions of authority in their factories, schools, national committees, or whatever lay close at hand. They took it upon themselves, in other words, to ensure that the constitution was enforced. They did not claim legislative power, perhaps, but they claimed judicial and executive power.

Citizens did not need to claim legislative power because the existing laws of the Czechoslovak Socialist Republic technically provided them with an array of methods by which they could democratically effect sweeping changes. In the past, however, the extralegal methods of the Party had rendered these procedures impotent. Charles University law students led the movement to rectify this situation by disseminating flyers on how to dismiss workplace directors legally, how to create independent unions, and how to recall deputies to lawmaking and administrative bodies. These flyers were constantly reprinted and expanded from November through mid-January and were among the most widely distributed of all revolutionary texts. While people were concerned to effect changes legally, however, this was primarily because they were concerned to effect them nonviolently; the former was seen as a means to the latter.[17]

A new government, a new president, even a new parliament were not enough to transform Czechoslovakia. Hundreds of thousands of people had to effect concrete changes on the ground—in their workplaces and places of residence. We cannot understand the revolution, therefore, unless we look at local activity during the critical months when popular initiative went largely unfettered. The purpose of this chapter is to shed light on this hitherto neglected aspect of the revolution.

The People on the Offensive

The programmatic declaration of the district OF-VPN coordinating committee in Komárno from early January 1990 provides as good a place as any to begin.

1. Thoroughly realize the repeal of article 4 of the constitution, about the leading role of the Communist Party, in the social life of the district without unnecessary delay.

---

[16] Studenti FF UJEP, "Myslete globálně a jednejte lokálně," Brno (MU: fond G39, box 2, A50; varying versions are available in OL, SM, and SV).

[17] The revolutionary understanding of legality is tellingly summarized in a remark by students of Charles University's Law Faculty: "Law is also a form of social consensus regarding certain forms of behavior. As long there is social consensus (agreement), one can never speak of the violation of valid law." ("Pracovně právní důsledky případného přerušení práce," Prague, 25 November 1989 [BB: Materiály získané od hnutia Verejnosť proti násiliu v Banskej Bystrici, 1989, box 1; identical or similar versions can be found in BN, DÚ, OL, PR, PV, and UH].)

2. Abolish basic organizations of the Communist Party in enterprises, facto-ries, organizations, and cooperatives and exclude Party functionaries from economic administration.

3. Create, by means of democratic elections, new representations of working men and women in unions at all levels.

4. Create additional action groups of VPN in workplaces of all types in the district. We demand that leading workers of state power respect the deci-sion of the federal government of the Czechoslovak Socialist Republic in accepting action committees as equal partners in negotiations at all levels of administration. Action groups of VPN are a means of citizens' self-defense and a check on state power.

5. Thoroughly implement the replacement of all compromised functionar-ies at all levels of national committees and organizations of the National Front. We demand that the vacated offices be occupied, prior to free elec-tions, with honest people possessing the necessary organizational and ex-pert qualifications.

6. We demand that all deputies representing the citizens of our district, at all levels, meet with their voters and inform them of their work to this time and of their stance toward the process of renewal in our country.

7. We call on action committees of OF-VPN in the district to express with their signatures no confidence in the vice chairman of the Slovak National Council Ing. Kazimir Nagy, whom we recognize as a person compro-mised and therefore unfit to advocate the interests of the Slovak nation and national minorities at any level of state power or administration.

8. We declare confidence in the government of the Slovak Socialist Republic and the federal government of national understanding. We declare our deep confidence in the president of the republic. . . .

11. The coordinating committee of OF-VPN in the district of Komárno will adopt standpoints toward newly emerging parties based on analysis of their programmatic declarations. From the beginning we will take the initiative of impartial review [kontrola], to ensure that compromised peo-ple in new clothes do not rise to prominence in these parties.

12. Civic Forum will continue to resolve the district's problems in unity and mutual cooperation with all civic initiatives active in the district.[18]

A few things are worth noting about this declaration. First, OF-VPN is under-stood to be a genuine expression of the people, such that OF-VPN action commit-tees can legitimately represent them in monitoring and checking state power and acting generally as a public watchdog. Second, the continued existence of many

[18] "Programnyilatkozat" and "Programové vyhlásenie okresného koordinačného výboru občianskych iniciatív VPN Komárno," *Reflex*, 5 January 1990, pp. 1, 4.

structures and institutions from the Communist era goes unquestioned: national committees, the National Front, and a formally majoritarian electoral system. Third, belief is implied in both the power and meaningfulness of people's ability to declare confidence or no confidence in holders of leadership positions, whether the declaration is made directly or through OF-VPN action committees. It was just as important to declare explicit confidence in the president and Slovak government as to declare no confidence in compromised functionaries; it was assumed that no leader could legitimately hold office without the ongoing and expressed confidence of the people. Finally, OF-VPN did not regard itself as the only legitimate civic association capable of playing a public role between the people and institutionalized power; it explicitly recognized the existence of others and pledged to cooperate with them. With the partial exception of this final point, which reflected the exceptionally diverse constellation of civic initiatives that emerged during the revolution in Komárno, the assumptions underlying the Komárno OF-VPN programmatic declaration were typical of civic initiative pronouncements throughout Czechoslovakia.

Let us leave for the moment the question of how OF, VPN, and other civic initiatives viewed their role in society; at present, our focus is on how mobilized citizens sought to reconstitute society directly, at the local level, without waiting for intervention from above or the free elections tentatively scheduled for May (and eventually postponed to June). The Komárno declaration was again typical in identifying four areas where the people, either directly or through the civic associations, should take immediate action: (1) replacing compromised workplace directors, (2) democratizing unions, (3) reconstructing the executive councils and administrative organs of national committees and National Front organizations, and (4) insisting that deputies to representative assemblies, from the most local national committee to the Federal Assembly, meet personally with their voters to justify their records—and replacing those who failed to pass muster. This was, essentially, a vision of democracy where government should always accurately represent the will of the governed regardless of when regular elections are scheduled. To accomplish this vision, all that was legally necessary was to observe procedures that the Communists themselves had put on the books but applied in practice only when they had served the Party's interests. Initially, proponents of this vision met with great success in transforming the social order; increasingly, however, resistance mounted and grew more effective on the part of both the old guard and revolutionary protagonists who worried about where this kind of democracy might lead. To understand what was at stake in this conflict, it is best to begin by mapping the initial achievements of popular power.

DEMOCRATIZING WORKPLACE ADMINISTRATION

As the *spiritus movens* of the revolution, striking university students were among the first to seek thoroughgoing restructuring of their workplaces, and they achieved the most extensive and lasting changes. University students achieved representation in university government, changes in policies, and personnel changes on faculties. A few days after the constitution was amended to remove the Party's leading role, the Czech ministry of education proposed that the law on universities be changed to allow for student participation in their administration.[19] The ministry proposed that this change not take effect until the following academic year, but students were not this patient. In Pardubice, for example, "by the end of 1989 an academic senate was elected in which students from each year were represented, chosen in direct elections. Furthermore, each department was represented, as were the cafeteria and employees. The senate was elected for one year."[20] In Košice, Olomouc, and at several universities elsewhere, the ratio of students to faculty established in the senates was one to one.[21] Students also secured changes in policies, including a ban on required lecture attendance, an end to the requirement that male students submit themselves to weekly military training, and the abolition of required courses in Marxism-Leninism. Pedagogical collectives, constituting themselves as Civic Fora or Academic Fora, supported the students and frequently added their own demands, such as the abolition of cadre and defense departments within university administration.[22] The extent of this support varied widely, however: in Olomouc, for example, it was strong; in Prešov it was weak.[23] Nonetheless, by January 1990 the place of students in universities was completely different from what it had been before November. As a journalist in Košice noted, "[To decide] about them without them is no longer possible [*o nich bez nich sa už nedá*]."[24]

Student demands were not limited to representation and policy changes. They also sought staffing changes, including the dismissal of faculty members who had "obtained their titles and positions by 'political engagement' and membership in the Communist Party, regardless of their talents and skills."[25] Students began by voting confidence or lack thereof in individual teachers, taking care to ensure that only those who had studied under the individual concerned took part in the voting, and then pressured university administrators to take appropriate action.[26] Those dismissed were not necessarily left unemployed. At the medical faculty in Martin, for example, after students voted no confidence in four professors, they were

[19] "Návrh akčního programu ministerstva školství, mládeže a tělovýchovy ČSR," *Přetlak*, no. 10 (6 December 1989), p. 3.

[20] "Akademický senát VŠCHT Pardubice," *Studentský list*, no. 21 (11 January 1990), p. 2.

[21] "Študujú, organizujú, nadväzujú kontakty," *Večer*, 23 February 1990, p. 2; "Volby," *Přetlak*, no. 21 (18 December 1989), pp. 5–6.

[22] See, for example, OF Univerzity Palackého, "Otevřený dopis rektorovi UP," Olomouc, 4 December 1989, reprinted in *Přetlak*, no. 9 (5 December 1989), p. 6.

[23] Jožo Gomolčák, "Problémová fakulta," *Premeny*, no. 3 (19 January 1990), p. 2.

[24] "Študujú, organizujú, nadväzujú kontakty."

[25] "Stávka nekonč," *Přetlak*, mimořádné čslo (1989), p. 1.

[26] Daniela Pomajdíková, "Strašidelný zámok??," *Premeny*, no. 4 (26 January 1990), p. 1.

accordingly relieved of teaching duties but given jobs in the university hospital.[27] At the same time that students sought to get some teachers removed, they endorsed the reinstatement of qualified academics who had been fired as part of the normalization following 1968. To be sure, those who had been expelled organized on their own; in Nitra, for example, academic victims of normalization gathered on 16 December to express their willingness and will to return to former posts and to coordinate their efforts. The students and Sixty-eighters were natural allies, however, and found each other early in the revolution. Under pressure from both groups, as well as sympathetic members of existing pedagogical collectives, universities offered reinstatement to all who desired it.[28]

Much more complicated efforts to subject administration to the democratic will of the administered took place in factories, on collective farms, and in other workplaces. In late November, Prague law students issued guidelines on how to dismiss workplace directors who had lost the trust of employees. Section 29 of the law on state enterprises gave employees the right to remove directors from their positions by casting secret ballots in an assembly of that enterprise's workers. Such an assembly was required if one-third of an enterprise's workforce called for it, and voting was to be by simple majority.[29] Subsequent flyers confirmed that the same procedures could work in other types of enterprises and that on collective farms, members of the collective could recall not only their director but all members of the farm's administration.[30]

Komárno again provides us with a typical example of how this procedure worked. Employees of Interhotel Európa received instructions from the Slovak ministry of commerce "on how elections, or rather voting of confidence, should take place, in order that it be democratic." An assembly was accordingly held on 23 January with 87 of the hotel's 109 employees present. Voting proceeded by secret ballot, and by a ratio of 58 to 29, the employees expressed no confidence in their director. The ministry of commerce, under which the hotel fell, accordingly terminated the director's appointment and called a search for a new one.[31]

In most cases it seems that voting proceeded in an orderly fashion comparable to that in Komárno's Hotel Európa. There was much discussion about proper reasons for voting no confidence, and it was generally agreed—at least in public—that it should be for genuine incompetence or failure to maintain humane working

[27] Oľga Foglarová, "Študentské 'násilie': Majú z nás strach?," *Zmena*, no. 18 (January 1990), p. 13.

[28] E. Turi Nagyová, "Nádej na návrat po 20 rokoch," *Nitrianska verejnosť*, 19 January 1990, p. 2.

[29] Studenti PF UK, "Jak odvolat ředitele podniku," Prague, 30 November 1989 (BB: Zbierka písomností získaných od študentov Pedagogickej fakulty v Banskej Bystrici, 1989–1990; identical or variant versions are available in DÚ, KS, MU, OL, PR, PV, PX, TA, and ZM). See also "Ako postupovať pri výmene skompromitovaných vedúcich pracovníkov," *Reflex*, 18 January 1990, p. 3.

[30] Studenti PF UK, "Práva členské schůze JZD," Prague (TA: sbírka soudobé dokumentace, sign. CI8f, folder "Studentské hnutí: Prohlášení a výzvy studentů").

[31] "Kam kráčaš Európa?" *Reflex*, 2 February 1990, p. 3.

TABLE 1.
Changes in workplace administration

Is there a new leadership in your organization?	Czech (*n* = 171)	Czech (%)	Slovak (*n* = 50)	Slovak (%)	Total (*n* = 221)	Total (%)
Yes, the director and a majority of managers	12	7.0	5	10.0	17	7.7
Yes, the director and a minority of managers	13	7.6	3	6.0	16	7.2
Yes, only the director	9	5.3	0	0.0	9	4.1
Only some managers; the director remains	45	26.3	8	16.0	53	24.0
Neither the director nor any managers, and this is good	7	4.1	2	4.0	9	4.1
Neither the director nor any managers, and this should change	68	39.8	29	58.0	97	43.9
The director's chair is vacant	17	9.9	3	6.0	20	9.0

Source: Prepared by the author from original questionnaires in "Anketa OF a VPN pro čs. podniky a organizace," March 1990 (ÚSD: archiv KC OF, boxes 34–35).

conditions for employees rather than for strictly enforcing discipline. Naturally, though, debates over motives frequently erupted in cases where directors sought to challenge a negative vote. It should be emphasized that votes of confidence were not uncommon. For the most part, moreover, employees made a point of firing their directors in a dignified fashion, widely invoking the legal provision that they did not have to give reasons for their decisions in order to avoid airing dirty laundry. In some cases, however, negative votes were accompanied by symbolic forms of retribution. In Nitra, for example, after workers in a puppet theater voted no confidence in their director, finance officer, and administrative officer, one employee created a puppet tableau of the event and displayed it in the window of a neighboring shop.[32]

The extent to which workplace administration changed in late 1989 and early 1990 varied widely according to type of workplace. Positions very much in the local public spotlight, such as elementary and secondary school directors, were widely re-staffed. That this was exceptional, however, is revealed by an OF-VPN survey from March 1990 which showed that by that time only 19 percent of workplace directors had been replaced. Staffing changes had occurred among the lower-level management in an additional 24 percent of all enterprises, but in 44 percent no changes had occurred—to the dissatisfaction of OF or VPN activists in those enterprises. (In 4 percent no changes had occurred because the workforce had voted full confidence in the existing leadership; in the remaining cases, the director's chair was vacant.) Table 1 summarizes this data.

[32] *Nitrianska verejnost',* 12 January 1990, p. 3.

DEMOCRATIZING UNIONS

The next point in the Komárno program (but actually undertaken earlier and more widely) was the democratization of unions. Before the revolution there had been a single union for all working people in Czechoslovakia: the Revolutionary Union Movement (ROH). Naturally, elections to union organs were from candidate lists approved by the Communist Party and usually did not involve a choice among candidates. Since both union and management policy were tied to the Party, a common complaint to emerge in 1989 was that unions did not really represent workers' interests.

As they had done with regard to workplace management, Prague law students issued guidelines affirming the right of ROH members to recall at any time a local committee that had lost its members' confidence, and outlining the procedures for electing a new committee. The procedure was similar to that for recalling workplace directors: a local ROH committee was obliged to call a meeting of the local membership whenever at least half the membership requested it; should the committee refuse, members had the right to organize the meeting on their own. At such a meeting, employees were to discuss whether existing committee members were satisfactorily advocating the interests of the group; should the general opinion be negative, the votes of a simple majority of those present would suffice to recall a committee member or to dissolve the entire committee. The assembly would then be free to elect new committee members.[33]

The first free elections to union committees were held shortly after 17 November, and they became common after the General Strike.[34] Indeed, the position of local union committees on employees' participation in the General Strike was often the crucial factor employees considered in deciding whether to keep or reconstitute these committees. Resistance was common, as were attempts to falsify election results, such that four variants quickly emerged by which workers were represented within their workplaces. In the first, there was a single union committee, either preserved or reconstituted, in harmony with workers' desires and entrusted with coordination of strike readiness. In the second, an affirmed or reconstituted committee coexisted with a newly elected strike committee, with a division of labor between them; in some cases, there was overlapping membership. The third variant was for a union committee antagonistic to the revolution to continue, either through manipulation of elections or genuine failure to achieve the necessary number of votes to reconstitute the committee, and a separate strike committee to come into

[33] "ZV ROH nejsou funkční" (PV: sbírka soudobé dokumentace, box "Občanské fórum: Plakáty a různé," folder "Materiály již neaktuální").
[34] The archives of the Civic Forum coordinating center in Prague and the coordinating committee of Public against Violence in Bratislava are full of reports from workplace collectives on these elections and the resistance they faced.

existence claiming to be the legitimate representation of workers' interests. Finally, it happened in some cases that a backward-looking, unreconstructed union committee continued as the sole body claiming to represent workers' interests in a given enterprise. (There was further complexity in that strike committees often doubled as or overlapped with workplace branches of OF and VPN, but that need not concern us here.) While a statistical analysis that would reveal the relative frequency of these variants remains to be performed, the third was at the time perceived to be most common.[35]

Immediately after the General Strike two federations of strike committees were established: the Association of Strike Committees, originally with its coordinating center in Prague's Institute for Economic Forecasting, and the Forum of Coordinating Committees, based in Bratislava. Unfortunately, no study yet exists on the history of these two very important organizations, and their origins remain mysterious. They had in any case come into existence by 30 November, when the Association of Strike Committees issued a flyer entitled "What is to be done?"[36] It identified three goals for strike committees in the wake of the General Strike: (1) to ensure the fulfillment of the strike's demands, (2) to defend workers against any persecution that might follow from their participation in the strike, and (3) to see to the creation of a union organization that would enjoy the full confidence of working men and women—something that the existing ROH decidedly was not. It called on strike committees to encourage workers to express no confidence in the ROH, especially its central structures, and to support the dissolution of the ROH and creation of a new union movement based on professional associations.

Power holders in the ROH refused to yield to the strike committees without a fight. In many organizations elections had to be held twice because "the first was organized according to the resolutions and election procedure of the ÚRO [Central Workers' Organization], which dictated the composition [zloženie] and undemocratic manner of elections."[37] There was particular unclarity in Ostrava around elections to workshop and factory committees of the union there. An OF meeting of transit workers on 16 January revealed that many employees did not even know when the elections were taking place.[38] Students supported the strike committees by identifying them as workers' sole legitimate representatives.[39] The Government of National Understanding, as well, supported the strike committees by recognizing on 4 January both the Association of Strike Committees and the central ROH

[35] Sdružení stávkových výborů, "Co máme dělat?," 30 November 1989, in Přetlak, no. 11 (7 December 1989), p. 6; the same or similar versions are available in BB, DÚ, JN, KS, OL, OV, and PV.
[36] Ibid.
[37] Jozef Szitkey, "Odbory pracujú naďalej," Trnavská verejnosť, 12 January 1990, p. 2.
[38] "Je jasno . . . ," Hlasatel, no. 2 (17 January 1990), p. 2.
[39] "Výzva k založení nových odborů," Přetlak, no. 13 (10 December 1989), p. 8.

committee, for the time being, as its legally required union partners.[40] Two days later, the Association of Strike Committees and the Forum of Coordinating Committees held a joint conference in Brno. Delegates from strike committees across Czechoslovakia voted no confidence in the ROH central committee and declared that the Association and Forum de facto represented the unions.[41] They voted to establish a coordinating center with equal representation of the Czech Association of Strike Committees and the Slovak Forum of Coordinating Committees, plus representatives of the country's twenty most important enterprises, to serve temporarily as the highest union organ in Czechoslovakia.[42] It was to serve only until conventions of workers, organized into professional associations, elected delegates to a grand convention of all associations, which would be empowered to establish more permanent representation at the republican and federal levels. Local and district-level meetings of union members later adopted resolutions confirming that the Brno conference represented their wishes.[43]

The renewal of the union movement generated considerable discussion at the grass roots. In keeping with the revolutionary emphasis on self-organization, it was widely agreed that unions should be built from below, and the Association's plan to reorganize the unions on the basis of professional associations merely made a program out of a phenomenon that was already occurring spontaneously.[44] Many basic organizations, particularly in education and culture, sought independence from union structures where they were represented by people from other professions.[45] Reflecting the concern with local affairs that was exceptionally strong at the beginning of 1990, some proposed to leave all dues in the basic organizations.[46] In keeping with the revolutionary antagonism toward bureaucracy, teachers in Louny suggested eliminating the union's programs for recreation, loans, and other member services so that it could better focus on advocating workers' interests. Employers, they believed, should take care of services.[47]

By all accounts, the reformation of unions was one of the revolution's greatest success stories. According to the OF-VPN survey cited earlier, union organizations in 76 percent of all workplaces were completely reconstructed by March 1990, and in a further 19 percent they were partially reconstructed. Table 2 presents a more detailed breakdown of this data.

---

[40] Igor Pleskot, "Současná situace a úkoly československého odborového hnutí," *Zpravodaj stávkových výborů*, no. 3 (16 January 1990), p. 2.

[41] *Zpravodaj brněnského OF*, no. 8 (8 January 1990), p. 1.

[42] "O nezávislých odboroch," *Večer*, 8 January 1990, p. 1.

[43] "Co nového v odborovém hnutí," *Občanské fórum Cheb*, no. 11 (1 February 1990) p. 4.

[44] At the same time that the Association came into existence, groups of professionals like teachers and telecommunications workers began establishing their own Fora.

[45] Szitkey, "Odbory pracujú naďalej."

[46] "Zprávy," *Věstník Občanského fóra pedagogů a Učitelského fóra okresu Louny*, no. 2 (January 1990), p. 2.

[47] J. Hašek, "Slovo o odborech," ibid., p. 3.

TABLE 2.
Degrees of union reconstruction

Are there in your organization democratically elected independent union organs?	Czech (n = 167)	Czech (%)	Slovak (n = 50)	Slovak (%)	Total (n = 217)	Total (%)
Yes, in the entire structure	134	80.2	30	60.0	164	75.6
Yes, but only in part of the structure	27	16.2	15	30.0	42	19.4
Not yet	6	3.6	5	10.0	11	5.1

Source: Prepared by the author from original questionnaires in "Anketa OF a VPN pro čs. podniky a organizace," March 1990 (ÚSD: archiv KC OF, boxes 34–35).

RECONSTRUCTING LOCAL ADMINISTRATION

Shortly after the Federal Assembly formally abolished the Party's leading role, citizens pressed to make the change real in municipal and district administration. Usually they did this through the medium of local Civic Fora or branches of Public against Violence, but sometimes students and churches were also involved. Civic initiatives began presenting citizens' demands to local authorities in early December, usually demanding that the executive council be reconstructed to give a majority of seats to non-Communists and calling for the replacement of "compromised" functionaries (i.e., the heads of departments responsible for education, transportation, etc.) with more qualified individuals.

To understand how the revolution transformed local administration in Czechoslovakia, it is necessary to understand the logical but distinctive system of geographically defined national committees upon which this administration was based. In general, village and town national committees (miestne/místní národné/í výbory, or MNV, and mestské/městské národné/í výbory, or MsNV/MěNV) stood at the lowest level and answered to district national committees (okresné/í národné/í výbory, or ONV). These in turn answered to ten regional national committees (krajské/krájské národné/í výbory, or KNV), which answered directly to the interior ministers in each republic. (In larger cities there were also national committees for the various urban quarters.) Every national committee consisted of a plenum, an executive council, and a series of departments. The plenum was ostensibly elected by voters in geographic constituencies and generally consisted of fifty to sixty members in districts and towns, with villages having fewer. The plenum elected from its midst an executive council, which consisted of anywhere from five to fifteen members. While plenums might meet only four times per year, councils were supposed to meet at least fortnightly and were responsible for day-to-day administration. National committee departments were sometimes but not necessarily chaired by members of the plenum; they answered to the executive council for administration of their particular sphere—education, health care, construction, transportation, agriculture, culture, etc.

In keeping with the revolutionary emphasis on nonviolence, miners in Ostrava declared that compromised functionaries should simply feel the pressure of public opinion and leave of their own accord.[48] To a surprising extent, many did. The Topoľčany district is a good example. Public against Violence in Topoľčany met with representatives of the district national committee during the first week of December, and at an extraordinary meeting on 7 December, the executive council experienced something of the spirit of 4 August 1789. After changing the name of the district newspaper from *This Socialist Day* to *This Day*, firing the chief editor, and restoring the pre-1969 editor to his position, the council agreed that a plenary session should be held the following week to elect a council with a nonpartisan majority and to replace a number of committee heads. The chairman, Tibor Masaryk, thereupon resigned from the council and invited his colleagues to do the same at the plenum. In turn, council members then stated their positions. The minutes read as follows:

Ivan Antala—sees the need for an objective resolution of the executive council's composition and therefore resigns.

Ján Ďurčo—said that he had always tried to do the maximum for the development of our entire society, the entire district and his electoral district. He thinks that he would be violating his honor if he resigned because he never in any way harmed the interests of working men and women, and therefore he does not resign.

Marián Rýdzi—in order to permit the recomposition of the council, resigns.

Pavol Peťovský—seconds the words of Dr. Antala and resigns.

Gabriela Krajčírová—said that she is the oldest member of the council. She tried to support what was best with respect to the whole society. It was not always possible to comply with demands raised in her electoral district. If the other members of the council resign, she will also do so.

Stanislav Krošlák—said he was willing to resign in the interest of resolving the new composition of the council.

Ján Podmanický—said that for his entire period in office he had tried to perform his duties as deputy and as vice chairman of the ONV for the benefit of the citizens of the Topoľčany district. He understands the present events in society such that it is his duty to appear before all deputies of the ONV and he recommends that the entire executive council appear before the plenum with the proposal to resign as a unit. He resigns his membership in the council.

[48] "Hlasy horníků při setkání zástupců stávkových výborů OKR v sobotu 2. 12. na DOLE HLUBINA," *Přetlak*, no. 10 (6 December 1989), p. 6.

Daniela Kahúnová—seconds the words of Vice Chairman Podmanický and
added that she will resign in favor of someone else at any time.
Milan Koterec—joins the other members of the executive council. If the entire council resigns, then he will resign.[49]

On 15 December, meeting before the plenum, the council confirmed its decision to
resign as a whole. Masaryk asked the one who had refused to resign, as well as two
who had been missing, if they would agree to this gesture, and they did. They also
agreed unanimously to recommend that the plenum recall the chairs of six departments.[50] The plenum accepted the council's resignation, recalled the chairs of five
departments, and abolished the cadre department altogether.[51]

The pace of changes in municipal national committees tended to lag behind that
of changes in district committees, and the Topoľčany district was no exception. At
a plenary meeting of the MsNV in Bánovce nad Bebravou on 19 December, a VPN
representative presented that association's demand that the entire council resign and
that all functionaries resign by the end of the month.[52] (He also proposed resched-
uling the meeting from 9:00 a.m. to 4:00 p.m. so that more of the public could attend, but this motion failed.) The chairman then gave his obligatory speech, where
among other things he said,

> In consequence of current changes in political life but also the justified de-
> mands of our citizens, especially in connection with the modification of the
> state constitution of the ČSSR, that is with the elimination of the KSČ's lead-
> ing role, cadre changes will take place at this plenary session in accordance
> with the state law on national committees. At issue are changes in the MsNV
> executive council and its supplementation by nonmembers of the party. These
> fundamental changes stem from the revolutionary transformations in our
> society.[53]

The secretary thereupon announced the council's resignation, and a new council
composition was proposed, featuring five non-Party members to four Commu-

[49] "Zápisnica zo 17. mimoriadnej schôdze rady ONV v Topoľčanoch, ktorá sa konala dňa 7. decembra
1989" (TO: fond "ONV Topoľčany"), pp. 245, 247–49. See also "Zmeny v našich novinách," Dnešok, 12
December 1989, p. 1.
[50] "Zápisnica z 18. riadnej schôdze rady ONV v Topoľčanoch, ktorá sa konala dňa 15. decembra 1989"
(TO: fond "ONV Topoľčany"), pp. 251–54.
[51] "Prvé kádrové zmeny na ONV," Dnešok, 20 December 1989, p. 1.
[52] "Zápisnica z 19. riadneho plenárneho zasadnutia MsNV konaného dňa 19.12.1989" (TO: fond "MsNV
Bánovce n/B"), pp. 2–3.
[53] Pavol Peťovský, speech delivered at the plenary session of the municipal national committee in Bánovce
nad Bebravou, 19 December 1989, p. 2, attached to "Zápisnica z 19. riadneho plenárneho zasadnutia MsNV
konaného dňa 19.12.1989" (TO: fond "MsNV Bánovce n/B").

nists. All proposed members were elected by open voting, with the aforementioned secretary as the new, interim chair.[54] At an extraordinary meeting of the MsNV council in Topoľčany on 21 December, with VPN representatives in attendance, the chairman asked each council member to declare whether he would continue on the council. Two council members resigned, and three more said they would consider it. This was far more than VPN had requested: namely, that two members it trusted from the plenum be put on the council. In the course of the meeting, however, VPN ratcheted up its demands and proposed that a majority of the council be non-Party members.[55] Six days later, the council accordingly recommended that the plenum—scheduled for later that day—recall seven people from the thirteen-member council, and it suggested replacements.[56] The district's third major town, Partizánske, was the odd one out. No VPN representatives took part in MsNV meetings there until 30 January, and no significant reconstruction took place either.[57]

More research will be necessary to determine where and when, across Czechoslovakia, the executive committees of the various national committees were reconstituted and to what extent. Mapping such data at the regional and especially the district level would—together with related sociogeographic data—help answer the important question of where the revolution was more or less radical. This, obviously, is a question that must be answered before we can begin to ask *why* it was more radical in some places than others. Currently, in the absence of any study on the geography of the revolution (outside Prague), there is a mistaken perception that varieties of popular engagement and even the course of local change were everywhere more or less the same.[58] The example of the Topoľčany district, however, shows that significant differences existed.

Democratizing Representative Assemblies

Even before issuing instructions for dismissing workplace directors, law students in Prague composed guidelines for recalling deputies to the Federal Assembly, national councils, and national committees at all levels.[59] These flyers were similarly

[54] "Zápisnica z 19. riadneho plenárneho zasadnutia MsNV konaného dňa 19.12.1989," p. 5.

[55] "Zápisnica zo 17. mimoriadnej schôdzky rady MsNV v Topoľčanoch, ktorá sa konala dňa 21. decembra 1989" (TO: fond "MsNV Topoľčany"), pp. 3–4.

[56] "Zápisnica z 18. mimoriadnej schôdzky rady MsNV v Topoľčanoch, ktorá sa konala dňa 27. decembra 1989" (TO: fond "MsNV Topoľčany"), p. 1.

[57] "Zápisnica z 2. riadnej schôdze rady MsNV v Partizánskom, konanej dňa 30.1.1990" (TO: fond "MsNV Partizánske").

[58] One study on the geography of the revolution *in* Prague exists, but it limits itself to November and December 1989. Michael Kukral, *Prague 1989: Theater of Revolution* (Boulder, Colo.: East European Monographs, 1997).

[59] Studenti PF UK, "Možnosti odvolání poslanců nejvyšších zastupitelských sborů," Prague, 25 November 1989, reprinted in *Přetlak*, no. 11 (7 December 1989), p. 2; the same or similar versions can be found in BB, CB, KS, MI, MU, OL, OP, PR, PV, PX, SV, ÚSD, and ZM. See also Pravnická fakulta UJEP, "Chcete

widely distributed. By law, deputies could at any time be recalled by their voters; all that was necessary was for the National Front organization that had nominated them to call a public meeting in the district they represented and for a simple majority of those present at the meeting to vote for the deputies' removal from office. The only problem was that it was sometimes difficult to ascertain what districts deputies represented and which grouping within the National Front had theoretically nominated them. In routine violation of the electoral law, the central or regional committees of the Communist Party had generally decided who deputies would be, seeing to it that some district was found for them and that some National Front grouping could be associated with their names.[60] Frequently, of course, this meant that deputies "represented" districts where they did not actually live and were "nominated" by National Front organizations like the Czech Women's League or the Revolutionary Union Movement without anyone from these organizations being aware of the fact.

The first petitions to recall deputies from the Federal Assembly and the Czech and Slovak national councils began circulating immediately after the student guidelines were released, and signing them sometimes figured among General Strike activities. The students highlighted certain deputies as most urgently requiring dismissal, including Vasil Biľak. Citizens in Prešov, which Biľak ostensibly represented, voted no confidence in the man in early December, and the district committee of the Communist Party (which had nominated Biľak) sent him a letter apprising him of this fact.[61] Biľak accordingly resigned. Petitions to recall national committee deputies began to appear shortly after those to dismiss legislators. In Vranov nad Topľou, for example, VPN organized a petition drive to recall the ONV chairman in the electoral district he theoretically represented. A majority of voters expressed no confidence in him, and on 1 January he resigned.[62]

A significant number of deputies resigned before formal recall procedures were even put in motion; popular pressure was enough. In Bánovce, a tableau about MsNV deputies in a department store window caused the national committee chairman to complain about "a debasement of the office of deputy," which had "nothing to do with democracy" but which was nonetheless on deputies' minds at the plenary meeting held on 19 December.[63] Early in this meeting, a VPN representative demanded that discredited deputies resign, with by-elections to be held to

---

odvolat své poslance?," Brno, 11 December 1989 (PV: sbírka soudobé dokumentace, box "Občanské fórum: Plakáty a různé," folder "Přebytky od archívu").

[60] Dušan Dvořák, "K jednání s OV NF v Olomouci," *Přetlak*, no. 11 (7 December 1989), p. 2; "Poslanci okresu ve Federálním shromáždění," *Přetlak*, no. 11 (7 December 1989), p. 3.

[61] "V. Biľak sa vzdal funkcie poslanca," *Pravda* (Bratislava), 20 December 1989, p. 3.

[62] "Oznamy," *Premeny*, no. 1 (5 January 1990), p. 8.

[63] Pavol Peťovský, quoted in "Zápisnica z 19. riadneho plenárneho zasadnutia MsNV konaného dňa 19.12.1989," p. 7.

replace them.[64] In response, five deputies (of fifty-eight present and sixty-five total) announced their resignations. Three cited reasons of health and one a change of residence, but one justified his action on the grounds that he had not been elected democratically and had not managed to ensure connectedness between the citizens of his electoral district and the MsNV.[65] OF and VPN in Bánovce later agreed to nominate seven candidates to fill the five empty seats.[66] A public assembly was held to acquaint voters from the affected districts with their candidates on 2 January, with elections planned for 22 January.[67] An extraordinary, public plenary session was scheduled for the following day to swear in the new deputies—who were then immediately supposed to take up membership in the executive council or to head national committee departments.[68] As it happened, though, the by-elections never took place. The Slovak National Council decided in mid-January that national committee plenums could co-opt new deputies into their ranks by means of a simple public vote. Consequently, when Bánovce's MsNV plenum met on 23 January, it was not to swear in new deputies elected by voters, as planned; rather, it was to vote whether or not to co-opt as deputies the candidates that VPN, in cooperation with some newly emerging parties, had nominated. (By this time, incidentally, the number of vacant seats had risen from five to fourteen.)[69] Though this new procedure paradoxically sidestepped democracy in order to achieve a more representative assembly (and there were complaints about it), the municipal VPN did what it could to stamp the co-optation with democratic legitimacy: namely, it chose its candidates on the basis of a straw poll held at a public meeting on 21 January.[70] When the plenum met, it voted to accept all the candidates that VPN and its partners proposed.[71]

Resistance from Above

At the statewide conference of strike committees in Brno on 6 January, Igor Pleskot from the Association of Strike Committees cautioned that "the first phase of the

[64] "Zápisnica z 19. riadneho plenárneho zasadnutia MsNV konaného dňa 19.12.1989," p. 2.

[65] Ibid., pp. 3–4.

[66] "Zápisnica z mimoriadnej schôdzky RADY MsNV, konanej dňa 21. decembra 1989" (TO: fond "MsNV Bánovce n/B"), pp. 1–2.

[67] "Zápisnica z mimoriadnej schôdzky RADY Mestského NV v Bánovciach nad Bebravou, konanej dňa 27. decembra 1989" (TO: fond "MsNV Bánovce n/B"), p. 2; "Zhromaždenie občanov" and "Voľba poslancov," Hosť do domu, no. 1 (15 January 1990), p. 1.

[68] "Mimoriadne plenárne zasadnutie," Hosť do domu, no. 1 (15 January 1990), p. 1.

[69] "Snaha o rovnováhu síl v mestských organoch," Hosť do domu, no. 3 (24 January 1990), p. 3; E. Bartíková, "Otvorene demokraticky," Hosť do domu, no. 5 (8 February 1990), p. 1.

[70] Jozef Sroka, "Poslanci pod verejnú kontrolu," Ozveny Tatier, 16 February 1990, p. 1; "Z nedeľného mítingu občanov mesta," Hosť do domu, no. 3 (24 January 1990), p. 3.

[71] "Snaha o rovnováhu síl v mestských organoch" and "Otvorene demokraticky." Co-optation to national committees took place slightly later in the Czech Republic, but the process was similar; for an example, see Edvard Lachman, "Z činnosti OF ve Kdyni," and Tomáš Svoboda, "Představitelé OF nemohou být samozvanci," Domažlické inForum, no. 6 (2 February 1990), pp. 2–3.

so-called Velvet Revolution" was over. The next period, he said, would be characterized by remnants of old power structures beginning to consolidate and prepare for
long-term struggle.[72] The editor of the VPN newspaper in Nové Zámky expressed
similar thoughts a fortnight later:

> Unfortunately, there are still some who have not understood the times, who
> continue with old practices; the "brotherhood" still lives, and the people is
> dangerously indignant. We must add that this indignation is justified, for
> how can a compromised functionary, in whom the people has expressed no
> confidence, continue to live it up in a leading position?

The editor cited three examples from letters the VPN coordinating committee had
received. The first was a vice chairman of the ONV who had resigned his seat on the
executive council on 31 December after a vote of no confidence in his constituency.
He did not give up his seat in the plenum, however, and on 2 January he returned
to his former workplace (an elementary school) and reclaimed his old directorship
there—expelling the person who had been occupying that office. Teachers did not
want him, and over five hundred citizens of the affected municipality signed a petition backing the teachers up. "Does he understand at all, or will the national committee in the end respect the will of the people?" The second example was another
ONV vice chairman, who had resigned from the plenum after a vote of no confidence but who was now acting as director of the ONV's department of local economy. The last was the recently deposed ONV chairman, who had tried to reclaim
his former position as chairman of the collective farm in Dubník. When the collective farmers there decisively rejected him, he endeavored to become chairman of the
collective farm in Tvrdošovce. Considering these examples of discredited functionaries seeking to reestablish themselves in positions of power, the editor asked,

> Do we want to return to where we were? I think not. . . . All those who think
> so are greatly mistaken. The people does not sleep; it is alert and vigilant.
> This is confirmed by many letters coming to the district coordinating com-
> mittee of VPN in Nové Zámky. . . . The people has awoken, is no longer
> afraid, and openly speaks and will speak to those who have represented not
> the will of the people, but only the desires of an individual, the materialistic
> wishes of an "almighty" district, town, enterprise, factory, institution, etc.[73]

---

[72] "Současná situace a úkoly československého odborového hnutí," *Zpravodaj stávkových výborů*, no. 3
(16 January 1990), p. 2. Pleskot had been an industrial sociologist before being fired in 1969 for his political activities the previous year; since 1970 he had worked as an analyst for construction and office machine
enterprises.

[73] Margita Bogdanová and OKV VPN Nové Zámky, "Kde sa zašili?" *Slobodný občan*, 25 January
1990, p. 2.

It is perhaps worth emphasizing that no one sought to punish the functionaries in question. There were no serious efforts even to prevent them from doing the type of work for which they were trained (as had happened after 1968). People simply did not want these individuals to remain in leadership positions. Consequently, when "the will of the people" was flaunted, citizens at this stage of the revolution were willing to dig in their heels.

One of the most dramatic examples of popular resistance to functionaries' tenacity took place on the collective farm in the south Slovakian village of Pribeta:

Everything began on December 28, when in Pribeta's collective farm a VPN action group was founded. About 25 people signed on. At the same time, a Document was drawn up: "Declaration of no confidence in compromised members of the collective farm's economic leadership." From the Document: democracy in the cooperative is not working; instead there is only Potemkin democracy. Demand that the entire membership (probably 610 people) might exercise its right to vote on the declaration of confidence or no confidence.

From this day, every day, the most agile members of the action committee met. And Pribeta's little Gentle Revolution began: every day more assembled: on the second day 40, the next days 55, 75, 100, 120 (numbers are approximate). Their entire activity was in these days directed primarily at overcoming fear among collective farm members. Yes, people were AFRAID to sign the Document. A great victory of the Gentle Revolution: most people overcame their fear and more than half of all collective farm members—334!—signed.

January 3: in the morning a 22-member collective farm delegation, of which half are members of the local VPN, comes to the collective farm chairman JUDr. František Nagy. The chairman receives them in his office. The delegation demands his immediate resignation with reference to the presented Document. And the card game begins:

(Ceaușescu-style) COUNTER! The chairman refuses to acknowledge the delegation's demand; he is willing to resign only before the assembled membership.

(Successful) RECOUNTER! The collective farm tom-toms work reliably. Within fifteen minutes the entire membership currently at work (more than 300 people) stands before the main entrance to the office building.

(Rather awkward) SUBCOUNTER! The chairman, seeing the situation, "surreptitiously" gets lost and leaves the battlefield through the back door. He would have gotten into his business Lada if two vigilant VPN members had not placed themselves in front of it. The chairman fights further and continues on foot. Direction: as far as possible from his office. About 200 meters farther his pilgrimage to the unknown ingloriously ends, because the "alarm" has in the meantime spread even to the village and arriving people, like an octopus, surround the chairman and nonviolently engulf him. . . . The (ex-)

chairman humbly returns to the office building, takes out some paper and reads from it to the membership present his immediate resignation. He does not turn the paper over to anyone, however, but puts it away (?). Still in the presence of the ex-chairman the collective decision is announced to hold an extraordinary membership meeting tomorrow, January 4, at 6:00 p.m. Thereafter the satisfied membership disperses to its places of work.

January 4, 6:00 p.m.: The table reserved for the resigned chairman was left to yawn with emptiness. The membership wondered, however, at something completely different (INTER-MEZZO): present was namely the ex-chairman's son (also a lawyer, an employee of Priemka Komárno). He was called to leave immediately (at least ten times) with the explanation that the meeting was not open to the public but was only for members of the collective farm. He decided to leave the room only when microphones were planted against him.

After this little episode the 492-member assembly unanimously (!) accepted the resignation of the incumbent chairman. Immediately thereafter it was motioned that a new chairman be elected. The assembly approved the motion and unanimously elected to the office (and thus expressed complete confidence in) Ing. Juraj Benyó, with the caveat that the election be valid only until the annual collective farm membership meeting.[74]

Sometimes not only did directors refuse to vacate their offices after failing to pass muster with their workers, but the national committees (to which most organizations in the planned economy reported) declined to dismiss them. Museum workers in Cheb, for example, voted no confidence in their director on 10 January (the vote was twenty-one to seven with three abstentions). The director himself notified the ONV of the demand that he be dismissed and his position advertised but added that he was determined to remain in his post. The head of the ONV's culture department demanded to know the reasons for the no-confidence vote. Since the law did not require that any reasons be given, workers denied the head's request and insisted that their vote was itself sufficient reason. They explained that "airing dirty laundry would not help anyone."[75] The case ultimately came to the ONV executive council, which dismissed the director and announced an open competition for his position on 31 January.[76]

Sometimes it was neither directors nor national committees that resisted no-confidence votes but employees whom the ousted director had favored. To cite one

[74] Ivan Scholtz, "Prehratý mariáš pribetského predsedu JRD," *Reflex*, 11 January 1990, p. 2.

[75] Pavel Šebesta, "Zkuste to také, není to lehké!" *Občanské fórum Cheb*, no. 9 (16 January 1990), p. 3.

[76] "Stanovisko OF v Chebském muzeu k situaci v muzeu," 16 January 1990 (CH: fond 1063, SB46, box 1, folder 7, subfolder "Prohlášení, stanoviska chebského OF"); "Ad: Zkuste to také, není to lehké," *Občanské fórum Cheb*, no. 11 (1 February 1990), p. 4.

instance, employees of Czechoslovak Bus Lines (ČSAD) in East Slovakia elected a new director on 23 January. The election was clear, but "this new kind of democracy did not please a small, elite group of long-distance drivers. They felt that their positions were threatened and so decided to nullify the results. . . . They got into their trucks and blocked off the exits to all traffic seeking to leave the depot. They demanded the annulment of the elections and the departure of VPN from the enterprise." Only when these drivers found that VPN would not budge and was supported by the signatures of eight hundred employees (a clear majority) did they give up.[77]

When dogged insistence failed, citizens turned to the form of protest that had seemingly proven so effective in November: the strike. Frequently the threat of a strike was enough. Employees of the dental section of the District Institute of National Health in Prešov, for instance, voted no confidence in their director on 13 December. The section's VPN committee transmitted the decision to the clinic's director, who declined to act on it. It was only when dental employees threatened to strike that the clinic director finally dismissed the director of the dental section, on 16 January. A new director, with the section's expressed confidence, was appointed the same day.[78]

The next step, of course, was actually to go on strike. In the East Slovakian town of Kežmarok, *gymnázium* students took this step on 11 January. The faculty had decided to hold an internal election for the school directorship rather than opening an external search, and the students—disliking all nominated candidates—insisted that election proceedings be halted until structures were established whereby students would be able to contribute to the decision-making process. When the teaching staff refused, the students went on strike. VPN Košice sent an ambassador to try to mediate, but all he achieved was the existing school director's agreement to resign. In the end, the strike was successful. On 15 January the students presented the faculty with three concrete proposals for a common decision-making structure modeled on that being established in universities and offered to switch from striking to "strike readiness" if the demands were accepted. The teachers agreed.[79]

These are just a few examples of local struggles that seemed to grow ever-more dramatic as the first weeks of 1990 went by. Students in Prague wrote on 23 January that "what at first glance may seem like the calm after a fight is really the preparation of further attacks."[80] Their colleagues in Prešov's Pedagogical Faculty, who were at "heightened strike readiness" because teachers were resisting their demand

[77] Karel Fröhlich, "Lekcia do volieb," *Premeny*, no. 4 (26 January 1990), p. 4.
[78] Ján Macko, "Odvolanie z funkcie primára," *Premeny*, no. 4 (26 January 1990), p. 4.
[79] "Kežmarskí gymnazisti v štrajku," *Premeny*, no. 3 (19 January 1990), p. 1.
[80] Tomáš Kroutílek, "Kolegové," *Informační bulletin celostátního koordinačního výboru vysokých škol*, no. 1 (23 January 1990), p. 1.

"to improve the quality of the faculty" through personnel searches open to outsiders, explained that their actions were necessary for "the bringing of our revolution to a victorious conclusion." Practically quoting Stalin, they added that "it continues in ever more challenging forms."[81] Editors of the VPN/FMK newspaper in Komárno, responding to functionaries who questioned the civic associations' authority to press for the enforcement of no-confidence votes, wrote,

> Gentlemen, or rather comrades, let us not forget that there is a REVOLU-TION going on here. It may be the most gentle of all in the world, but still. Revolution, as even Marxists know, is a rapid, qualitative change in the development of society. A change that must remove without trace the old social order—in our case the dictatorial system of government by one party, outdated laws and regulations—in other words, everything that stands in the revolution's way![82]

Throughout Czechoslovakia, citizens struggled in December and January to reconstitute society at the local level in accordance with their revolutionary understanding of democracy. They also took pains to do so in keeping with the revolutionary commitment to nonviolence. Though declarations of confidence and no confidence were the order of the day, citizens sought no more than to exercise their legal rights, and for the most part the methods they used to do so were measured to minimize confrontation. Nonetheless, the intensification of conflict—however nonviolent—presaged the shaking of revolutionary certitude that had proceeded from the founding difference of 17 November.

Shaken Certitude

Not all of January's collective action pitted revolutionary protagonists against old-regime diehards unwilling to obey the law. In some cases, the actions of particular groups were at cross-purposes with the legitimate interests of others. In Bratislava, for example, garbage collectors complained at the beginning of January that they had nowhere to empty their trash. Rather than choosing a problem-solving strategy that might have attracted fellow citizens to their cause, they dramatically parked their full, odorous trucks on SNP Square with signs addressing the town hall.[83] In Ostrava, conservatory students launched an occupation strike on 22 January to

[81] Gomolčák, "Problémová fakulta."
[82] "Kto sme, odkiaľ prichádzame, kam sa poberáme? Úvahy o ľudoch občianskych iniciatív," *Reflex*, 18 January 1990, p. 3.
[83] "Páni z radnice, kde budete sypať?," *Zmena*, no. 17 (January 1990), p. 5.

protest "inadequate conditions for study" and to demand the assignment of "appropriate school buildings." If their demands were not met by 31 January, they threatened, they would go on a hunger strike.[84] In both these cases, particular groups essentially insisted that municipal or regional authorities give priority to their claims over those of other groups in the community. For onlookers in the community, the worthiness of these forms of collective action was ambiguous.

If these concrete examples of the dubious extension of revolutionary activity led some to begin asking whether something was not amiss, unsubstantiated cases were even more destabilizing. The student bulletin *Zmena* reported in early January that people in an "unnamed village" in southern Slovakia wanted to hang a collective farm agronomist and that the VPN chairman in an unidentified Bratislava enterprise had been physically attacked.[85] It also reported a rumor that a meeting of the district Communist Party committee in Humenné had broken down into a fight that left five hospitalized, but unlike the other rumors the editors reported, this one they checked and found to be false.[86] The OF bulletin in České Budějovice reported on 15 January that "capable and decent people are being recalled from leadership positions, or nominated for recall, because they demanded work from their charges and did not cultivate an *ad captandum* policy. Those who managed to turn their coats quickly, however, remain."[87] It was a sensational report, but no details were provided to substantiate it. The VPN bulletin in Martin observed that

> rumors have recently circulated that VPN groups in some enterprises are organizing strikes in order to force the resignation of leading workers. Consequently we invited representatives of VPN action committees from the concerned enterprises to a meeting on 10 January. After explaining the individual cases we asked participants for written statements about the situations in their enterprises. We determined that none of the alarming reports reflect the truth.[88]

In short, rumor was rife in January of 1990. The ubiquity of alarmist rumors led many to fear that the revolution was getting out of control, and even skeptical readers of the abysmal journalism that characterized this period were left wondering what was really true. While rumors sometimes reflected and reinforced romantic perceptions of an ongoing battle between the forces of good and evil, more often

---

[84] *Informační bulletin celostátního koordinačního výboru vysokých škol*, no. 1 (23 January 1990), p. 4.

[85] "Kuchta, ktorá syčí," *Zmena*, no. 17 (January 1990), p. 2.

[86] "Kmásali sa za vlasy funkcionári OV KSS v Humennom?" ibid.

[87] Jana Vondráčková, "Jsem lékařka . . . ," *Informační servis* (České Budějovice), no. 17 (15 January 1990), p. 2.

[88] *Martinská verejnosť*, no. 2 (15 January 1990), p. 1.

they simply shook the certitude and clarity that revolutionary protagonists had enjoyed in December.

There was a similarity between the rumors of January and secret police provocations of November and December, leading some to suggest that the Communists were behind it all. After several of OF's bulletin boards in Cheb were torn down and walls plastered with anonymous flyers, one Civic Forum activist argued that "fossilized Stalinists" must have done it. Another insisted that the monthly bulletin of the district Communist Party was full of disinformation and that it broke the law because it did not list the name of its editor or any contact information.[89] Civic associations in many towns ascertained that wiretapping was continuing in January, but they encountered evasion when they pressed telecommunications officials for details about where and how it was done.[90] Some began to voice fears of a Communist resurgence. "There is still a danger that our revolution might be reversed into some sort of consolidation," Bratislava students warned. "Let us be careful: by imprudence we might contribute to another tragedy, another epoch of darkness for our nation."[91]

Dissension and distrust spread even within the civic associations. Some worried that OF and VPN were being infiltrated by people who did not have the interests of the community at heart. "Unfortunately it is true," wrote a student in Pardubice, "that in many so-called Civic Fora people are worming their way to the forefront who cry as loudly today as they did little in the past. Thus it comes to such senseless activities as the removal of capable managers who 'discredited themselves' by uncompromisingly demanding discipline during working hours."[92] A scientist in East Slovakia, who had been dismissed from his post as supervisor of a computing center (allegedly because the enterprise director wanted to give the post to a minion with only a secondary education), complained that the spokesman for VPN in the enterprise did not stand up for him—adding that before 17 November this spokesman had been an active member of the Communist Party.[93] Sometimes struggles broke out within local civic associations. In Prešov, 217 transit workers disagreed with their VPN action committee's decision to express confidence in an MsNV vice chairman. The committee had done so, evidently, because of the vice chairman's cooperativeness at a roundtable meeting. The workers, however, pointed out that this vice chairman had condemned the students after 17 November and with threats of violence had sought to dissuade transit workers from participating in the

[89] J. Koupal st., "Všem poctivým komunistům," and "Podnět okresní prokuratuře," *Občanské fórum Cheb*, no. 12 (8 February 1990), p. 2.

[90] See, for example, László Finta, "Odpočúvanie telefónov, cenzúra, archívy!" *Reflex*, 18 January 1990, p. 3, and "Odpočúvanie, cenzúra, archívy," *Reflex*, 2 February 1990, p. 3.

[91] "Kuchta, ktorá syčí."

[92] "Kam kráčíš demokracie?" *Studentský list*, no. 21 (11 January 1990), p. 2.

[93] Marko Ondík, "Požiadavky doby—áno, či nie," *Premeny*, no. 2 (12 January 1990), p. 6.

General Strike. They demanded that he and the entire MsNV council be recalled and proposed another candidate for the vice chairmanship. They also demanded that the four VPN action committee members who had expressed confidence in the vice chairman resign from the committee.[94]

In the context of this mounting uncertainty, many civic association activists appealed for moderation. "I think," wrote an OF activist in Louny, "that at this moment the difference between *we*, *you*, and *they* should disappear. Only *we* and *now*."[95] An activist in České Budějovice urged, "Let us leave these contemptible Communists, in whom the desire for power, standing, and career has not yet died. Let them liquidate each other. Let us not taint the name of our 'gentle revolution'!"[96] A Pilsen man wrote,

> We've already tried twice to part with Stalinism and its variants; let's make this new attempt definitive. . . . Let us not seek new scapegoats and new fetishes of chauvinism. Let us not stone false prophets, but neither let us listen to their rehashed promises and blandishments. With truth, love, perseverance, and deliberation let us do what is necessary to end our velvet revolution velvetly.[97]

The most significant and memorable of these admonitions was the speech that OF's chief spokesman, Petr Pithart, delivered on federal television on 19 January. Because of its centrality in subsequent debate, it is worth quoting at length:

Dear friends,
    Always we turn to you when we feel that in our land something is happening which should not. I personally have doubts about whether that which is playing out in our land should properly be called a revolution. I am a little afraid of that word. Rather than revolution I would say that we are simply liberating ourselves from conditions that were indecent and unreasonable. We are liberating ourselves not only from violence, which did not always have to take the form of imprisonment and persecution; it was unbridled domination of people with the help of fear, corruption, and the almighty state party.
    We have rid society of the fear of one-party government, of Communists, but I am afraid that we may now have to rid people of the fear of ourselves. In short, the activity of Civic Fora should not in any way resemble

---

[94] "Nesúhlasíme s vyslovením dôvery," ibid., p. 7.

[95] Jaroslav Čása, "O co jde?," *Zpravodaj Galerie B. Rejta a OF Louny*, no. 1 (11 January 1990), p. 2.

[96] Jitka Střelečková, "Úvahy o komunistech a našem vztahu k nim," *Informační servis* (České Budějovice), no. 17 (15 January 1990), p. 5.

[97] J. Klepetář, "Stop stalinským metodám!," *Plzeňský student*, no. 2 (15 January 1990), p. 3.

the rampages of National Front action committees after February 1948. I don't know whether I'm hearing the grass grow but it seems to me that more and more often can be heard the voices of people saying: it's the same, just in light blue. Certainly, these voices are exaggerating, perhaps they arise from untypical cases, but in any case it is a warning that we cannot ignore.

Yes, all compromised Communists—but also all those without party affiliation who are like them—must depart from all positions of responsibility. All dilettantes, who kept their high places thanks only to a party card or the favor of the powerful, must also go. But how to do this decently, reasonably, and at the same time not naively? How not to overwhelm the day-to-day functioning of enterprises, schools, hospitals, and national committees? Quackish methods of resolving personnel problems will rebound not only against us, Civic Fora, but against the whole society. I therefore urgently appeal to OFs in workplaces and localities to eschew all pseudorevolutionary methods.

I know of an OF that extorted the right to cosign with the enterprise director all economic contracts; I know of Civic Fora that are taking up the management of purely operational problems. Our friends from VPN also confirm that they are encountering similar extremes. Civic Fora may exert pressure, even strong pressure for change, but only as citizens, under no circumstances like a party which issues ultimatums, which takes down the directors of factories or hospitals only because they're Communists.

Is every Communist really an immoral person and is every Civic Forum activist an idealist beyond reproach?

Let us reason soberly. The Communist Party, which had 1,700,000 members, could not be only a party of Stalin's and Brezhnev's posthumous children, unscrupulous consolidators and cynical mafiosi, or incompetent people whom the Party offered an extraordinary chance for an unjustified career. In the Communist Party were people who had other reasons for their membership. Sometimes it was a desire to stand out, to make oneself useful, for others it was a certain consciousness of responsibility toward their work collective, toward their enterprise, town, and sometimes even in their manner to society. Did they participate in evil with their membership? Were they insufficiently brave? Who has the right to judge just because he was not a Party member? Who has the right to judge according to the principles of collective guilt?

Sometimes it occurs to us that provocateurs may be standing behind ill-judged purges. If only that were the whole truth. I am afraid that within the ranks of OF there are sincere but unreasonable zealots, but that there are also careerists who have sensed their opportunity. And there are even people who were active in the old structures and who today act in the same manner among us.

We do not have in the coordinating center of the Civic Forum of Bohemia and Moravia secretaries who might come to a district or workplace and set things in order there. We can't do it and we don't even want to do it. We are not a party that gives orders and establishes order—as used to be said—among the cadres. We are a movement of democratically engaged nonpartisans. We can only persuade, refer to good and bad examples. With your help we would like exemplarily to put to shame those who in the name of OF are drawing all power to themselves and behaving as KSČ secretaries behaved for forty years. Let Civic Fora in localities and workplaces gradually—I emphasize gradually—force out those who were buttresses of the old order, but above all let them decide on a method how new people will henceforth be found for the leadership of enterprises and institutions. Open competitions [konkursní řízení] would seem to be a very apposite method. Even before these, let union organizations revive themselves in workplaces, let them act where necessary to modify workers' councils. Let them, however, eschew the role of almighty judges who— without there even being rules of the game—decide which side will score a goal and when.

What threatens otherwise? The disintegration of enterprises, a decline in production; there threatens the faltering of the functioning of institutions which we need in our everyday lives.

I ask you, I demand of you—let us finish as soon as possible the dismantling of everything old, and let us begin to build. To build a state, an independent civil society, a prospering economy, simply a civilized European society capable of cultured self-government.

The situation, when two or more Civic Fora exist in a workplace and each tries to distinguish itself by greater radicalness, is a situation that puts us in an uncommonly awkward light. To be sure, there are Fora that have fallen under the control of reclothed adherents of the old totalitarianism and we can't leave them in peace. But even here let us act like citizens and under no circumstances like old apparatchiks. Let us convoke meetings for everyone, let us organize assemblies, perhaps even demonstrations in the yards of factories or towns, but let us have before us citizens, in no case just the "company" OF. I am afraid that these days all sorts of persons can appropriate this.

Let us act reasonably and decently, without demagogy, but at the same time energetically and in no case naively. Our enemies, however, do not these days have any better opportunity to score points than to take advantage of our mistakes, our haste, our eccentricity, the transparent motives of those who see in OF primarily an opportunity to get ahead.

In all this no one is going to help you. No people from Prague or from Brno or Bratislava will put your affairs in order; you alone must do this.

Today we can fear only one thing: that we unconsciously adopt the methods of those against whom we all stood forth.

Civic Forum is not here to settle accounts with Communists. It is here that we may finish with Communist practices.

If you want, continue to call what is happening a revolution. It is in the end a matter of taste. That which we do, however, let us do decently—decently and reasonably. In the elections we will succeed not by means of what influence or power we build up but above all by means of how we achieve that influence or power. The means will decide; the manner in which we act will decide.

We are a forum, that is, the square. Behind it must stand people, many people, who believe us and are not afraid of us, and who will not try to get ahead of us.

We are a forum of citizens, so let us act like citizens, not like apparatchiks, cadres, or secret police agents.

Maybe I am hearing the grass grow. If something like this is growing, however, it is not grass, it is a weed—an aggressive weed. It is unfortunately a strain of something that has overgrown this land, the strain of totalitarianism.

And we must defend ourselves against totalitarianism—that which stands in opposition to us as well as that which—I do not like to say it—might grow out of us.[98]

Pithart's comedic speech seems generally to have met with a positive reaction, but it also seems that people generally interpreted it according to their own still-romantic proclivities. The editor of the student bulletin in Olomouc wrote that the speech had grieved him. "Suddenly I see wolves, some even with an OF button on their lapel, pointing their fingers and crying 'How can he be in that function when . . . (he was in the Party, he disagreed with the strike, he was against Havel, etc.).' It reminds me too much of witch hunts." "In any case," the student continued, "it is necessary to point out violence and chicanery, not to let it in peace. . . . Write to us about everything that might injure our velvet revolution, that goes against the ideals from which it rose."[99] Developments in Cheb illustrated where this new impulse to finger-pointing could lead. On a page in the district OF bulletin headed by a quotation from Rousseau's *Social Contract*, one activist wrote,

We are witnesses of how the demeanor and some practices of so-called spokesmen, representatives, or members of various basically democratic initiatives

[98] "Projev P. Pitharta v čs. tevizi [sic]," *InForum*, no. 11 (23 January 1990), pp. 1–3. For the Slovak translation, see "Je to revolúcia?," *Telefax VPN*, no. 1 (2 March 1990), pp. 1–3.
[99] Milan Hanuš, "Motto: '. . .jsi zodpovědný za svou růži. . .'," *Přetlak*, no. 33 (25–26 January 1990), p. 3.

are reminiscent of the—to put it mildly—"cabinet politics" of the former black marketers of the totalitarian regime. There is a real danger that under democratic slogans and the emblem of a strike committee or Civic Forum such persons will hide as do not have clean hands or hearts, whose personal ambitions are their main motivations.

The activist concluded that "it is necessary to place every so-called spokesman under popular control . . . so that we don't end up in the near future with tricolored secretaries instead of red ones."[100] A number of OF spokespersons were dismissed in these days.[101] A former spokesman of Civic Forum in one of Cheb's larger enterprises accused the remaining spokespersons of being condescending toward laborers, claiming that many of the latter were thinking of leaving OF as a result. "I think," he wrote, "that the statement 'I hear the grass growing' is symptomatic. It seems, moreover, that in the grass are a lot of weeds."[102]

There is no evidence that Pithart's speech achieved its intended effect. Votes of confidence and no confidence continued with just as much intensity as before, and indeed Pithart's injunction that people themselves must put their affairs in order could be used to justify them. The spokesman for Civic Forum in one of Cheb's trade schools drew attention to the "artificial survival of certain leading workers," asserting that "more than one workplace remains a state within a state and has its own monarchy." Practically quoting Pithart, he continued that "none of us can expect that order will be created for us by itself, or that someone 'from above' will help us. We must act on our own." In particular, he suggested that the director of his school (who had been against the General Strike) should go.[103] Pithart's speech also seems to have destabilized local Civic Fora, both by stimulating finger-pointing within the ranks and by giving ammunition to potential "victims" of civic initiative. "Just as not long ago Jakeš's quip about a post in a fence circulated widely, so these days Pithart's announcement that he hears the grass growing is popular. All 'oppressed Communists' have taken it up and are making out of Civic Forum a forum of criminals, careerists, mafiosi, conjuncturalists, etc."[104] If anything, then, it seems that Pithart's speech exacerbated the situation he had sought to defuse. His gesture was symptomatic, however, of mounting confusion within Czechoslovak society.

---

[100] "I v Chebu je slyšet trávu růst," *Občanské fórum Cheb*, no. 10 (23 January 1990), p. 1.

[101] See, for example, "Ředitel má důvěru," *Občanské fórum Cheb*, no. 10 (23 January 1990), p. 2; Koordinační výbor OF Eska Cheb, "Ad. Bývalý mluvčí OF Esky dementuje," *Občanské fórum Cheb*, no. 14 (22 February 1990), p. 2; and "Z jednání sněmu OF v Chebu 26. února 1990," *Občanské fórum Cheb*, no. 15 (1 March 1990), p. 2.

[102] Jiří Šubrt, "Bývalý mluvčí OF Esky dementuje," *Občanské fórum Cheb*, no. 13 (15 February 1990), p. 4.

[103] Jan Wolf, "A přece jenom zpomalený film," *Občanské fórum Cheb*, no. 10 (23 January 1990), p. 2.

[104] Pavel Šebesta, "Nejsme jako oni," *Občanské fórum Cheb*, no. 11 (1 February 1990), p. 1.

The unity of November was eroding, and with it the clarity of meaning-generating difference.

Anti-Communism had not actually been common in Czechoslovak discourse prior to Pithart's speech, but it became so afterward. Unlike Leninist parties in neighboring countries, the Communist Party of Czechoslovakia refused to disband or rename itself, and a series of mysterious bomb scares in late January and early February reinforced fears of a Communist putsch.[105] Brno students in February intercepted a circular from the Communist Party central committee urging members to join Civic Forum in order to destabilize it, and apparatchiks could still be heard rallying supporters around the slogan "to save what can be saved."[106] No putsch, but significant reversals did begin to occur in connection with co-optation to representative assemblies in February and March. In Levice, for example, Communist deputies to the municipal and district national committees went back on roundtable agreements to support a number of VPN candidates into office.[107] More dramatically, the Communist chairman of the Slovak National Council, Rudolf Schuster, backed out of an agreement to surrender his office to the VPN spokesman Ján Budaj. Schuster was supported in this instance by a crowd of nationalist demonstrators (among whom many secret police agents were later recognized from photographs) who broke into the National Council building accusing Budaj (incorrectly) of being a Magyar and insisting that any "Slovak" was better, even a Communist (despite the fact that Schuster was of German-Magyar parentage).[108] This event made citizens throughout the country fear that if something were not done soon, Communists would roll back all the achievements of the revolution.[109] Students responded by placing themselves in strike readiness.[110]

Dismay at such reversals, and fear that the Communist Party might use its wealth and continuing control over much of the press to influence the upcoming elections to its advantage, led to one of the last great mass actions of the revolution. Coincidentally on the same day as the upset in the Slovak National Council, Civic

---

[105] Jožo Gomolčák "PRAVDA (Peter) očl kole," *Premeny*, no. 4 (26 January 1990), p. 2; Šebesta, "Nejsme jako oni"; Jozef Sroka, "Na sneme VPN," *Ozveny Tatier*, 3 February 1990, p. 2; Jano Lašák, "To sú študenti Otec biskup!" *Premeny*, no. 5 (2 February 1990), p. 2; "Na radnici opět bomba," *Profórum*, no. 5 (9 February 1990), p. 2.

[106] "Ľudia, bdejte!" *Premeny*, no. 8 (23 February 1990), p. 1 and "I KSČ se představuje," *Občanské fórum Cheb*, no. 15 (1 March 1990), p. 4; "Výstupenie člena výboru VPN," 8 February 1990, *Fórum* (Levice), no. 4 (March 1990), p. 2.

[107] "Už niekoľkokrát . . ." and "Komunisti zase nedodržali slovo," *Fórum* (Levice), no. 4 (March 1990), pp. 1, 4.

[108] Milan Šútovec, *Semióza ako politikum alebo "Pomlčková vojna": Niektoré historické, politické a iné súvislosti jedného sporu, ktorý bol na začiatku zániku česko-slovenského štátu* (Bratislava: Kalligram, 1999).

[109] "Lze žít s KSČ?" [March 1990] (TU: fond "KC OF Trutnov," box 2, folder "Různé").

[110] Transcript of VPN's third republican convention, Bratislava, 3 March 1990 (SNA: Archív VPN, fond. odd. II), pt. 2, p. 26.

Forum in Prague's massive ČKD machine works issued a call for a general strike to take place in April if the Communist Party did not voluntarily surrender its property to the state beforehand or the Federal Assembly did not pass a law nationalizing this property. As we will see in the next chapter, local branches of OF and VPN had already compelled the Party to surrender some of its most important real estate, but much remained under Party control. Though non-Communist deputies in the Federal Assembly responded positively to the ČKD appeal, Communists rejected it. As a result, approximately 1,400 enterprises and organizations joined the symbolic ten-minute strike on 11 April. The Federal Assembly reacted by formally ending the Party's right to use state property as its own and by calling on all parties and political movements to submit an inventory of their assets, but a robust response to ČKD's appeal would have to wait for the new parliament to be elected in June.[111]

As the elections approached, the Communist Party increasingly came to symbolize the dangers facing Czechoslovakia, providing a pole of certainty (even if negative) in uncertain times. The explosion of a bomb on Prague's Old Town Square the week before the elections, resulting in a number of injuries, reinforced this mild hysteria.[112] Fears that Communists would win the elections did not come to pass, but the battle lines were drawn, and the new "Government of National Sacrifice," led by Civic Forum and Public against Violence, would be charged with securing a definitive victory.

---

[111] Suk, *Labyrintem*, pp. 386–89.
[112] "Včera popoludní v Prahe," Bratislava, 3 June 1990 (SNA: Archív VPN, fond. odd. II).

Chapter 6

The Will of the People

"Civic Forum is a space for the renewal of genuinely civic attitudes and life. . . . The reason for the activity of local Civic Fora is the voluntary activation of civic conduct and action in political and everyday life. . . . In the course of broad, democratic discussion, local Civic Fora should pin down and clarify citizens' opinions. . . . Local Civic Fora may concern themselves with the resolution of local problems that existing social structures are not satisfactorily managing. Local Civic Fora should support all citizens, wherever in contact with existing undemocratic structures human rights in the broadest sense are violated. Local Civic Fora are thus a means of citizens' self-defense."[1]

We have glimpsed already how spokespersons for Civic Forum and Public against Violence understood these associations' role in revolutionary society. OF-VPN in Komárno declared that it was "a means of citizens' self-defense and a check on state power." VPN in Nové Zámky identified itself with "the will of the people." Petr Pithart emphasized that Civic Forum represented the square, the seat of popular authority. From the beginning, the civic associations identified themselves as the voice of the public, expressing its demands and able to take action to ensure their

---

[1] "Vnitřní organizace Občanského fóra," Prague, 28 November 1989, in Milan Otáhal and Zdeněk Sládek, eds., *Deset pražských dnů (17.–27. listopad 1989): Dokumentace* (Prague: Academia, 1990), p. 553, and in Jiří Suk, ed., *Občanské fórum: Listopad-prosinec 1989*, vol. 2, *Dokumenty* (Brno: Doplněk, 1998), pp. 35–36.; identical or similar versions can be found in BB, BE, CK, DÚ, HIA, KS, OL, OV, PR, and PV; Slovak translations can be found in KS and ZM. "Vnútorna organizácia VPN" (Bratislava, 29 November 1989) was essentially the same document, with "VPN" merely substituted for "OF" (BB, KS, MI, PP, PX, and SNA).

fulfillment.[2] During the week prior to the General Strike, Václav Havel declared that one of Civic Forum's primary activities was "to unify all raised demands in a common list," and an OF proclamation added that another was "to ensure the dialogue of the public with the powers that be."[3] In the guidelines it issued to VPN branches, the coordinating committee in Bratislava defined Public against Violence as "a civic initiative that seeks to uncover, identify, and analyze diverse problems, suggest necessary solutions to them, and insist on their resolution."[4] In short, OF and VPN saw themselves as representations of the people and instruments through which the will of the people could be realized.

There has been a tendency in literature on the revolution, emphasizing the highest levels of elite politics, to limit the importance of OF and VPN to the federal and republican roundtable negotiations and the elections of June 1990, and to characterize the associations as umbrella organizations sheltering nascent political parties. They were, however, much more than this. As a forum where the nonpartisan majority could actively and effectively participate in politics, the civic associations were a rarely seen political phenomenon.[5] They were, essentially, the councils that Hannah Arendt identifies as "the lost treasure" of the revolutionary tradition.

> Both Jefferson's plan and the French *sociétés révolutionnaires* anticipated with an utmost weird precision those councils, *soviets* and *Räte*, which were to make their appearance in every genuine revolution throughout the nineteenth and twentieth centuries. Each time they appeared, they sprang up as the spontaneous organs of the people, not only outside of all revolutionary parties but entirely unexpected by them and their leaders. Like Jefferson's proposals, they were utterly neglected by statesmen, historians, political theorists, and, most importantly, by the revolutionary tradition itself. . . . They failed to understand to what an extent the council system confronted them with an entirely new form of government, with a new public space for freedom which was constituted and organized during the course of the revolution itself.[6]

---

[2] "Provolání. Na setkání v hledišti . . . ," Prague, 19 November 1989, in Suk, *Občanské fórum*, vol. 2, p. 13; identical or similar versions can also be found in BB, DÚ, GA, HIA, JN, OV, PR, PV, and TU.

[3] Václav Havel's speech on Wenceslas Square, 22 November 1989, in Suk, *Občanské fórum*, vol. 2, pp. 17–18. "Provolání Občanského fóra," Prague, 23 November 1989, reprinted in Otáhal and Sládek, *Deset pražských dnů*, p. 324, and Suk, *Občanské fórum*, vol. 2, p. 19.

[4] "Návrh Verejnosti proti násiliu pre prácu akčných skupín VPN," Bratislava, 29 November 1989, reprinted in Jozef Žatkuliak, ed., *November 1989 a Slovensko: Chronológia a dokumenty (1985–1990)* (Bratislava: Nádacia Milana Šimečku a Historický ústav, 1999), p. 380.

[5] According to the Institute for Public Opinion Research in Prague, 47% of the Czechoslovak population had signed on with OF or VPN by 12 December 1989. Considering that citizens continued to join the associations until March 1990, it is highly probable that a majority of Czechoslovak citizens sooner or later participated in the movements. According to a December survey, moreover, 78% of all citizens "connected their hopes for the future" with OF or VPN. *Přetlak*, no. 21 (18 December 1989), p. 2.

[6] Hannah Arendt, *On Revolution*, rev. ed. (New York: Viking, 1965), p. 249.

Citizens active in OF and VPN understood these associations in much the same way that Arendt described the councils, as places where "men act together in concert" and spaces "where freedom can appear."[7]

How did OF and VPN seek to identify, channel, and implement the will of the people? Why did they ultimately fail? The central theme of this chapter is how local activists in the civic associations sought to distill and implement the popular will and the conflicts to which this commitment led them. Local activists were crucial to the development of a post-Communist political culture in Czechoslovakia. This political culture was no mere import from the West; rather, it was forged in the particular circumstances of the revolution itself. Even after the Government of National Understanding had been established, Havel had been elected president, and the student strikes had ended, a popular power independent of state institutions remained: the square was still the sacred center of society and claimed authority to oversee all that was done in its name. Insofar as Civic Forum and Public against Violence could legitimately claim to represent the square, they were the means by which citizens sought to exercise this authority. Naturally, to understand how a new political culture was established, it is necessary to look at the local level, where activists came into direct daily contact with ordinary citizens—where, indeed, ordinary citizens became activists. This chapter thus complements Jiří Suk's exhaustive study of Civic Forum's coordinating center in Prague. Suk notes how conflict between district-level activists and the coordinating center led ultimately to the demise of Civic Forum, but he assumes that, in their struggle with Prague, local activists were primarily motivated by desire for positions.[8] The argument presented here is that, at least through the spring of 1990, most local activists were motivated rather by a sincere and at times naive desire to channel and realize "the will of the people." It was frustration of this desire that stimulated center-periphery conflict in both OF and VPN, and led simultaneously to the withdrawal of many of the original activists from political engagement and the search of those who remained for more effective, institutional means of getting things done.

We begin by taking a brief look at who the local activists were, sketching their social profile in terms of occupation, age, and gender. We then examine how local activists tried specifically to mediate the popular will in the spring of 1990. Finally, we consider the origins and intensification of center-periphery conflict over representation that culminated in the dissolution of the civic movements, the rise of partisan successors, and the breakup of Czechoslovakia.

---

[7] Hannah Arendt, *Between Past and Future: Six Exercises in Political Thought* (New York: Viking, 1961), p. 4.

[8] Jiří Suk, *Labyrintem revoluce: Aktéři, zápletky a křížovatky jedné politické krize (od listopadu 1989 do června 1990)* (Prague: Prostor, 2003), p. 386.

Spokespersons and Culture Brokers

Who were the local spokespersons of the civic movements? We can reconstruct a partial social profile of these men and women by examining surviving registration data (insofar as it is accessible). District and national coordinating committees of both OF and VPN attempted to register local branches in workplaces and municipalities (as well as among certain interest groups) in December 1989 and January 1990. The process was chaotic, with a variety of registration forms in use that asked for different kinds of information; many groups, moreover, wrote their own letters and provided what data they thought important rather than using any form. Nonetheless, sufficient evidence is available to make generalizations about the gender, occupations, and with especial caution the ages of OF and VPN spokespersons. The evidence is most complete for Civic Forum, with data about thousands of local branches throughout Bohemia, Moravia, and Silesia (there is some data about Civic Fora in Slovakia, but it has been omitted for this analysis). No comparable body of data for VPN is yet accessible at the national level (if it still exists), but we do have complete information about VPN branches in one Slovak district—Považská Bystrica. Located in what was then the Central Slovakian administrative region along the Moravian border, it was a relatively typical district, with no substantial ethnic minorities and no large cities. It is obviously not possible to make generalizations about VPN as a whole on the basis of evidence from just one district, but the typicality of the district means that the evidence can at least orient us.

The typical OF spokesperson was male and was a skilled manual laborer, with some scope for independence in his work. Only 14 percent of OF spokespersons were women. In identifying their profession, spokespersons indicated every possible occupation from agronomists to zoologists. If we limit ourselves to geographically defined Civic Fora, where occupation was not itself a precondition for engagement (as it naturally was in workplace OFs), we find that the largest group of spokespersons identified themselves as "laborers" (12.0%), followed by "engineers" (9.6%), "teachers" (9.0%), "pensioners" (7.0%), "drivers" (3.6%), and "managers" (*vedoucí*) of various kinds (3.4%). Figure 2 shows the relative percentages of the most common professions spokespersons listed (over 1%).[9]

By grouping professions together into a few general categories based on the level and kind of education their members customarily had, we can achieve a clearer picture of the social profile of Civic Forum spokespersons. Figure 3 illustrates how such a conceptualization might look. Since most laborers at the end of the 1980s were skilled, all "laborers" otherwise not specified in the lists are for this analysis

---

[9] This analysis is based on a random sample of 676 OF spokespersons from Bohemia, Moravia, and Silesia who listed their occupation in the registration lists preserved in the KC OF archive at the Institute for Contemporary History in Prague.

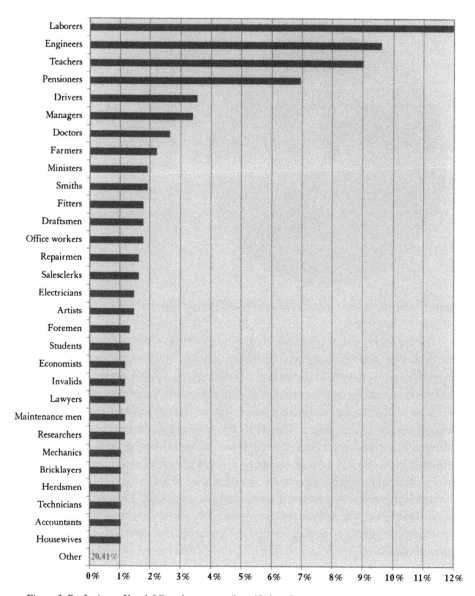

Figure 2. Professions of local OF spokespersons (by self-identification)

considered skilled, even though the actual number was probably lower.[10] (If, on the other hand, we assumed that all unspecified laborers were unskilled, the ratio of skilled to unskilled manual laborers would be almost one to one, although the combined number of skilled manual and nonmanual workers would still exceed the number of unskilled.)

[10] A reason that skilled laborers may have been inclined to list their profession simply as "laborer" was that revolutionary discourse, if anything, heightened the sense of honor that socialism had attached to the title.

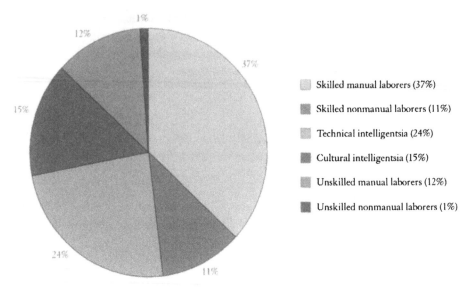

Figure 3. Professions of local OF spokespersons (by educational category)

While it is possible to question the assignment of some professions to the "skilled" or "unskilled laborers" category, the division between the university-educated intelligentsia and workers with secondary or lower education, as between the technical and cultural intelligentsia, is relatively straightforward. In any case it is clear that while men and women whose occupations did not require higher education were a majority in local Civic Forum leadership, the intelligentsia was more prominent in this leadership than would be expected if the social profile of spokespersons exactly mirrored the educational and occupational breakdown of society as a whole.[11] It is also clear that though the cultural intelligentsia played a significant role in the coordinating center of the movement in Prague, it was not dominant at the local level. Data about the professional background of district-level spokespersons were evidently not collected centrally (or if they were, they have been lost or are today in private hands), but records of the district coordinating centers in Cheb, Louny, and Trutnov indicate that the intelligentsia was more prominent there than at more basic levels. Socially, then, the districts occupied a middle ground between local fora and the coordinating center in Prague, where manual laborers (whether skilled or unskilled) were rare. These social differences—particularly between cultural intellectuals in the centers and technocrats in the districts—would provide an experiential background to the political cleavages that would develop over the course of 1990.

[11] In 1989, only 6% of the Czechoslovak population had university educations. Miloš Zeman, "Fakta o současné situaci v ČSSR" (HIA: Czech Subject Collection: box 8, folder "Czechoslovakia. 1989 Revolution. Fliers & Bulletins"); various versions of this common flyer can also be found in BB, DO, KS, OL, OV, PP, PR, PV, PX, and SV; Slovak translations are preserved in BB, KS, PX, and SV.

The typical VPN spokesperson in the Považská Bystrica district was also male and—if we again assume that all "laborers" were skilled—was also a skilled laborer. (If, however, we assumed that all unspecified "laborers" were unskilled, the total number of unskilled workers among spokespersons would exceed that of their skilled counterparts.) Figure 4 depicts the relative distribution of types of occupations among spokespersons in the district, following the pattern of Figure 3.[12] The combined total of the cultural and technical intelligentsia (43%) harmonizes with the 39 percent in Civic Forum, and it is clear that in both cases technicians dominated. The percentage of women among VPN activists in Považská Bystrica was significantly higher than in the Czech lands as a whole: 21 percent. Again, it is impossible to say whether this was representative of Slovakia as a whole, but it is noteworthy that gender issues were unusually prominent in public discourse in Považská Bystrica in 1989.[13] Finally, registration data from Považská Bystrica include age information that is absent from the Civic Forum evidence. The average age of a VPN spokesperson in the district was thirty-eight; the oldest was sixty-eight and the youngest sixteen. Two-thirds were between the ages of twenty-nine and forty-nine.

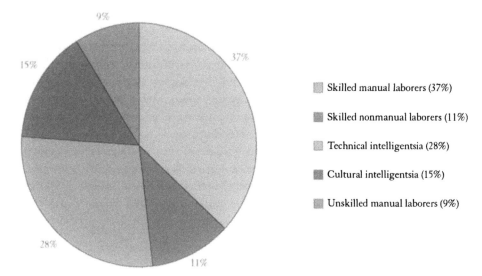

Skilled manual laborers (37%)

Skilled nonmanual laborers (11%)

Technical intelligentsia (28%)

Cultural intelligentsia (15%)

Unskilled manual laborers (9%)

Figure 4. Professions of VPN spokespersons in the Považská Bystrica district (by educational category)

[12] Data about VPN spokespersons in the Považská Bystrica district, of whom 116 listed their occupation and 199 listed their age, are located in PX: fond G1, box 4.

[13] See, for example, "Programové vyhlásenie fóra žien podporujúcich koordinačný výbor Verejnosť proti násiliu" (PX: fond G1, box 1, folder "KDS 1989"); Dagmar Ondrášiková, "Zoberme veci žien do vlastných ženských rúk," Obzor, 21 December 1989, p. 3; and "Výzva občiankam," Obzor, 11 January 1990, p. 2.

Can we characterize the civic association spokespersons as "culture brokers," to borrow Lynn Hunt's term?[14] Insofar as the social position of these men and women is concerned, it is impossible to provide a conclusive answer without further information. A defining feature of Hunt's political class was that its members occupied the interstices of social networks, maintaining ties between their locality and the outside world or coming from marginal social backgrounds. The 39 to 43 percent of OF and VPN spokespersons with university educations certainly fit this bill, as did less highly educated spokespersons with occupations like those of managers and drivers. The extent to which other individuals occupied social interstices, however, cannot be determined on the basis of occupational data alone. The notion of "culture brokers" is nonetheless useful for understanding what these men and women actually did as spokespersons. They were responsible for mediating between their local groups on one hand and workplace managers, national committees, and other branches of the civic associations on the other. It was these men and women who composed the letters expressing their group's opinions, they who negotiated with institutional representatives on behalf of their groups, and they who reported to their groups on the results of these negotiations. Their position as local political activists was very much at the interstices of social networks even if their personal backgrounds were not.

It should be emphasized that Civic Forum and Public against Violence were not the only important associations of the revolutionary period. Others included the Association of Strike Committees, the Forum of Coordinating Committees, Christian Democratic clubs (in Slovakia), and the various student associations. Though in the beginning they all usually worked together, tensions sometimes arose between them, as when the Civic Forum of education workers allegedly presented as its own the Association of Strike Committees' initiative to transform a hastily conceived union convention into a preparatory conference for an altogether new union organization.[15] From November 1989 to at least the late spring of 1990, however, OF and VPN were the largest and most trusted of the civic associations.[16] They were also, initially, the most powerful ones, and as nonpartisan "means of citizens' self-defense" they were an extraordinary historical incarnation that merits further investigation.

Mediating the Popular Will

An early OF document stated that "one of the most important tasks of Civic Fora at present is to inform fellow citizens, collect their demands and present these to

---

[14] Lynn Hunt, *Politics, Culture, and Class in the French Revolution* (Berkeley: University of California Press, 1984), pp. 180–212.

[15] *Zpravodaj stávkových výborů*, no. 2 (4 January 1990), p. 9.

[16] "Čo hovorí verejná mienka?" (SNA: Archív VPN, fond. odd. II).

local and central organs."[17] During the first few months of 1990, local OF and VPN activists took seriously their role as interpreters and defenders of the public will. This led them, first of all, to take pains to determine public opinion and identify popular demands, and then to seek ever more effective means of translating these demands into action. Efforts of local VPNs and OFs through much of 1990 centered on mediating between citizens and government or enterprise organs to solve concrete problems.

To inform citizens and collect their demands, the quintessential medium remained in 1990 the public assembly, variously called a civic forum (by both OF and VPN) or *míting/k*.[18] When it invited citizens to a January *mítink* on Brno's main square, that city's Civic Forum promised that "there on the spot concrete problems of the city of Brno will be solved."[19] Public assemblies in Louny were still debating and adopting resolutions in March 1990, with participants bold enough to demand that they be broadcast nationwide.[20] In the bylaws it adopted in the summer of 1990, OF Louny officially made open public assemblies the basic unit of its structure.[21]

Many local OF and VPN branches took even more active approaches to identifying "the will of the people."[22] Civic Forum in Pilsen's Škoda works established a commission to make recommendations about the enterprise's future and "confront the opinions of the workers with those of the economic leadership." To do so it solicited "as many opinions as possible from the widest range of workers," and by 11 January it had collected some 120 written contributions adding up to over a thousand pages.[23] OF in Louny and VPN in Považská Bystrica set up boxes in frequented locations about their towns where citizens could drop slips of paper with opinions and recommendations. The Teachers' Forum in Topoľčany (associated with VPN) reported that "each school has its elected activists, who collect demands and suggestions and transmit them to higher, competent places for their resolution."[24]

[17] "K práci občanských fór," Prague, 28 November 1989 (OV: "Revoluce 1989: Materiály 1989–1990"); reprinted in Suk, *Občanské forum*, vol. 2, pp. 37–38. VPN translated this document and inserted its name to produce "Návrh pre prácu akčných skupín VPN," Bratislava, 29 November 1989 (available in slightly divergent versions in HIA, KS, MI, PX, and ZM).

[18] Though the word had been current in the later years of Habsburg rule and in the First Republic, it had fallen into disuse under Communism.

[19] *Zpravodaj brněnského OF*, no. 10 (14 January 1990), p. 1.

[20] "Na veřejném shromáždění . . . ," 13 March 1990 (LN: fond 633, box 1, subfolder "Měsíc březen 1990").

[21] "Návrh struktury OF v okrese Louny" (LN: fond 633, box 1, subfolder "Měsíc srpen 1990").

[22] This formulation, incidentally (with *people* as a singular noun), appeared first in a Civic Forum statement from 20 November 1989. "Občanské fórum není politická strana . . . ," Prague, 20 November 1989, in *Informační servis* (Prague), no. 2 (21 November 1989), p. 1; reprinted in Suk, *Občanské forum*, vol. 2, p. 14.

[23] Přemysl Odehnal, quoted in M. Kupilík, "Na aktuální téma," *Plzeňský student*, no. 2 (15 January 1990), p. 3.

[24] V. Jakabová, "Učiteľské fórum," *Hosť do domu*, no. 1 (15 January 1990), p. 1.

The level of citizens' trust in the students and civic associations as their representatives is revealed by the volume of letters citizens addressed to them. Editors of the Bratislava student bulletin *Zmena* reported receiving over four hundred letters in January. Typically, they read and endeavored to answer all of them. "We can't after all fail to take seriously the confidence of people who place their hopes in us."[25] By February the editors admitted that they were falling behind, and asked correspondents to limit their letters to a maximum of three pages.[26] Regardless of volume, local civic associations encouraged citizens to send them letters. VPN in Martin, for example, appealed "to all citizens, that they write their reservations or bad experiences with the work of the ONV and MsNV. We also welcome the opposite experiences. We ask for honest and concrete information. This will be offered to VPN, the ONV, and the MsNV."[27] If the KV VPN in Považská Bystrica and the KC OF in Louny are any indication, district-level activists in the civic associations responded to and tried to act upon every letter they received. VPN Považská Bystrica even tried to act on anonymous letters—obviously a mistake, but indicative of how seriously it took its role (OF Louny, by contrast, adopted an explicit policy of ignoring anonyms).[28] Most of the concerns citizens raised in these letters were quite mundane, such as noise problems with neighbors or difficulty finding housing, but activists nonetheless took pains to contact officials or interested parties with power to solve the problems and followed up to make sure they were resolved.

Students and local civic association activists also tried to use their bulletins or newspapers as a means of soliciting public opinion. "We want our paper to become an open platform," wrote the editors of Pilsen's student bulletin.[29] OF Kutná Hora defined its bulletin as "a space for the written expression of the friends of the velvet revolution."[30] Spokespersons for VPN in Trenčín told readers of their bulletin that it was a means of "entering into DIALOGUE with you. For this we need you not only as readers, but as partners/contributors."[31] "Therefore," added the editors of the VPN newspaper in Prievidza, "we impatiently await your contributions regarding every problem of our life today."[32] While the loftier aims of the bulletins were never quite fulfilled, they did in the beginning publish an extraordinary variety of submissions from the public and often allowed space for the side-by-side articulation of divergent opinions within the civic movements.

---

[25] Jana Bogárová, "Niekoľko viet o listoch," *Zmena*, no. 21 (February 1990), p. 5.

[26] "Píšete Zmene," *Zmena*, no. 23 (February 1990), p. 8.

[27] *Martinská verejnosť*, no. 3 (19 January 1990), p. 2.

[28] "OF Louny informuje," *Zpravodaj Galerie B. Rejta a OF Louny*, no. 2 (18 January 1990), p. 1.

[29] *Plzeňský student*, no. 1 (8 January 1990), p. 1.

[30] "Co chceme," *Fórum* (Kutná Hora), no. 0 (13 January 1990), p. 1.

[31] "Zverejnite svoj názor," *Trenčianska verejnosť*, no. 1 (11 January 1990), p. 4.

[32] "Vážení občania okresu Prievidza," *Hornonitrianska verejnosť*, 8 February 1990, p. 1. See similar calls for public input in *Ozveny Tatier*, 5 January 1990, p. 5; *Reflex* (Komárno), 5 January 1990, p. 3.

Upon ascertaining the popular will, the logical next step was to seek to implement it. This commitment led OF and VPN activists to pursue a wide variety of aims in the winter and spring of 1990, but their methods remained remarkably consistent. We have considered in the previous chapter how OF and VPN spokespersons negotiated with local national committees for the reconstruction of the executive committees, departments, and plenums in charge of local administration. The civic initiatives also negotiated with these bodies for the enactment of particular policies. Beyond the structures of local administration, OF and VPN negotiated with the still powerful Communist Party for transfer of its property to public control, took steps to demilitarize their localities, mediated conflicts between workers and management, and generally facilitated the development of civil society.

One of the main concerns of local civic initiatives in December and January was to secure the existence of free and independent local media. Most important, this meant extracting district newspapers from Communist Party control. Beginning immediately after the General Strike, spokespersons for OF and VPN in district towns (together with striking students in university seats) began lobbying the district national committees to declare themselves the sole publishers of the district newspapers (sometimes together with the National Front) and thereby exclude the district committees of the Communist Party. Most district national committees agreed to make the change during the first two weeks of December, but Gottwaldov pioneered the movement at the end of November, and some districts did not see any change until the third week of December (in Šumperk, where the People's Militia had trained to attack demonstrators in Prague, the change did not take place until January). Map 4 represents the temporal-geographic distribution of this trend. After the newspapers were freed from direct control by the Communist Party, some changed their style of reporting radically and even allowed OF, VPN, or students to edit pages. In other districts, citizens complained that the style of reporting remained unchanged.[33] This mirrored the situation at the national level, where *Práce*, a Czech daily published by the Revolutionary Union Movement, refused to give space to the Association of Strike Committees, and where *Zemědělské noviny*, a daily catering to collective farmers, stonewalled Civic Forum's repeated appeals for the inclusion of independent perspectives.[34] KV VPN activists estimated in March that the Communist Party still held de facto power over a majority of the press because the Party was allotted more paper than any other publisher, and financially it could afford to print more.[35] They had in mind particularly the situation at the

[33] See, for example, Zdeno Horváth, "Premaľovaná firma," *Premeny*, no. 2 (12 January 1990), p. 2.

[34] *Zpravodaj stávkových výborů*, no. 3 (16 January 1990), p. 3; "Zápis z Rady KC OF dne 16.1. 1990—pondělí 9.00 hod.," p. 3, and "Zápis z Rady ze dne 22.1.1990 9.00 hod.," p. 1 (ÚSD: archív KC OF, folder "Zápisy z rady OF (C)").

[35] "Zápisnica KC VPN dňa 20.3.90" (SNA: Archív VPN, fond. odd. II). See also the KV VPN communiqués from 1 and 4 February 1990 (SNA: Archív VPN, fond. odd. II), and Stanislav Glasa, "O tri mesiace tri kroky späť," *Zmena*, no. 24 (February 1990), p. 11.

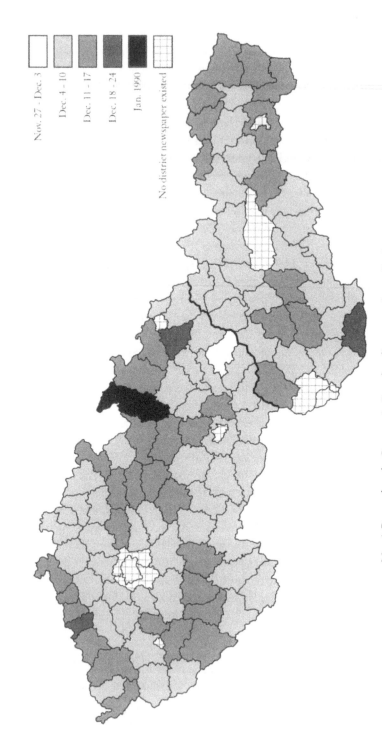

	Nov. 27 - Dec. 3
	Dec. 4 - 10
	Dec. 11 - 17
	Dec. 18 - 24
	Jan. 1990
	No district newspaper existed

Map 4. Dates when the Communist Party lost direct control over district newspapers

national level, but if they had turned their attention to the districts, they might have added that many editors were still in place who had obtained their positions only through proven ideological subservience to the Party. In the problematic districts, therefore, OF and VPN spokespersons negotiated with the national committees for the dismissal of newspaper editors, meeting with mixed success. In Nitra, VPN convinced the ONV chairman on 4 January to reemploy the editor who had been fired in the post-1968 purges, but he was hired only as an assistant editor; the normalization-era chief editor remained.[36] The coordinating center of Civic Forum in Louny similarly demanded the resignation of its district newspaper's chief editor on 3 January, insisting that the national committee launch an open search to fill the position "with a professional and experienced journalist." "This standpoint reflects the opinion of citizens expressed this evening at a public assembly," OF declared.[37] The ONV executive council declined the request, however, and citizens had to wait until the council was reconstructed in the following month.[38]

In Slovakia, VPN and FMK frequently responded to the absence of independent local newspapers by establishing their own. VPN Nitra set the precedent on 9 December; the coordinating centers in Bratislava followed a week later when VPN launched *Verejnost'* (*The Public*) and FMK introduced *Nap* (*Day*)—full-fledged newspapers claiming republic-wide relevance that initially appeared twice weekly and became dailies in May 1990.[39] Eight additional district- or municipal-level branches of VPN and FMK began publishing their own local newspapers in January 1990.[40] There was no counterpart to this development in the Czech lands. While the OF coordinating center in Prague established a weekly at the end of January and a daily in May 1990, no local Civic Fora took the initiative to publish their own newspapers. Of the revolutionary associations in the Czech lands, only students did so (first in Prague and Brno and later in Pilsen).[41]

[36] "Rokovali sme s . . ." *Nitrianska verejnost'*, 12 January 1990, p. 2.

[37] "OF Louny informuje," *Zpravodaj Galerie B. Rejta a OF Louny*, no. 2 (18 January 1990), p. 1.

[38] The position was advertised on 16 March, at which time the old chief editor was demoted to assistant chief editor. After he quit the job in April, he was replaced by another member of the editorial staff, who in June became the new chief editor. *Hlas*, 16 March 1990, pp. 7–8; 4 May 1990, p. 4; 29 June 1990, p. 4.

[39] On the founding of the Nitra newspaper, see Zuzana Maďarová, "Ženy Novembra: Analýza rozhovorov s aktérkami nežnej revolúcie," in *Politiky a političky: Aspekty politickej subjektivity žien*, ed. Jana Cviková (Bratislava: Aspekt, 2011), pp. 31–33.

[40] The districts were Komárno, Nitra, Nové Zámky, Poprad, Prievidza, and Trnava; the municipalities were Malacky, Pezinok, and Piešťany. In the summer of 1990, VPN Košice joined the group by transforming its bulletin into a newspaper.

[41] A study in 2004 determined that civil society was stronger in Slovakia than in the Czech lands. Pavol Frič claims that this is explained by the resistance Slovaks were compelled to mount in opposition to Vladimír Mečiar between 1992 and 1998, but if the disparity in the tendency of civic associations to found newspapers in 1990 is an indicator, it may be that Slovak tendencies toward a stronger civil society actually preceded Mečiar's ascendancy. Pavol Frič, "The Place of History in the Sociology of Social Movements in Central Europe" (presentation at the conference "The Weight of History and the Games of Interpretations: Societies of Central Europe in the Twentieth Century," Budapest, 11 September 2004.)

Citizens were concerned about many aspects of local administration besides local newspapers, and civic association spokespersons took these matters in hand as well. As Civic Forum in Františkovy Lázně maintained, "all national committee activity" should be under the public control of citizens.[42] Some of the people's first concerns were symbolic, such as changes to the names of streets, squares, and in some cases municipalities. OF and VPN usually invited nominations for new names and then organized surveys to determine majority opinion. Uses of public space were another common concern, for both symbolic and practical reasons. In Nitra, where the Communist administration was in the process of remodeling a central square, VPN convinced the MsNV chairman to halt the erection of a leaning concrete pylon intended as an architectural embellishment but which most townspeople thought ugly.[43] In Podhrad u Chebu, Civic Forum prevented the parceling up of a soccer field and persuaded planners about to fell a number of riverside trees to consider alternatives.[44] Mundane as these achievements might seem, they were real victories in a context where public opinion on such matters had routinely been ignored. Perhaps more weightily, the civic associations monitored assignments of real estate falling under national committee administration. OF in Františkovy Lázně oversaw the distribution of apartments to ensure that functionaries and their families got no advantage.[45] In Nitra, VPN achieved the restructuring of the committee responsible for allocating buildings so that it would include representatives of VPN (speaking for the public) as well as representatives of the organizations with a potential stake in the buildings in question. In accordance with popular demands, it also saw to it that health care was given priority.[46] In addition, the civic associations took steps to civilize Public Security forces (not renamed "police" until July 1991) and to dismantle the apparatus of repression.[47]

One of the civic associations' most successful endeavors between December 1989 and April 1990 was the effort in perhaps every district to compel the Communist Party to surrender its buildings to national committee administration, and to oversee the subsequent assignment of this real estate. The first obstacle was, obviously, getting the Party to relinquish its property. In some cases Party officials agreed gracefully, but in others their recalcitrance was protracted. In Louny, for example, the Party offered to rent out its property but not surrender it. Civic Forum therefore called a demonstration in January where citizens created a human chain around the district Party headquarters (aka "the Coconut") and demanded

[42] "OF ve Fr. Láznich nezaháli," *Občanské fórum Cheb*, no. 9 (16 January 1990), p. 4.

[43] "Rokovali sme s . . . ," *Nitrianska verejnosť*, 19 January 1990, p. 2.

[44] "Občanské fórum Podhrad," *Občanské fórum Cheb*, no. 9 (16 January 1990), p. 4.

[45] "OF ve Fr. Láznich nezaháli."

[46] "Rokovali sme s . . . ."

[47] VPN Nitra, for example, met with the district public security authority on January 16; OF Domažlice did so on January 17 and again on February 2. "Rokovali sme s . . ."; "OF informuje," *Domažlické inForum*, no. 4 (19 January 1990), p. 4.

its surrender to public hands.[48] Sooner or later all district Party committees gave in. The next question was who should be able to use the buildings in the Party's stead. Universally, public opinion held that the buildings should go to institutions offering community services, but it was sometimes difficult to determine which of the many claimants—usually schools, hospitals, and cultural organizations but sometimes also the national committees—had most need of the space and could put it to best use. As they had done with renaming, so many OF and VPN branches solicited proposals from the public on how to use Communist buildings and then conducted surveys to determine which variants were most popular. Citizens of Louny put forth a wide array of possible uses, ranging from a nonsmoking coffeehouse in part of the building to a "house of democracy" where all political parties and movements could have their offices. One citizen proposed a library for previously prohibited literature, in which "we could learn from domestic and foreign authors how to think freely, about democracy, about human, civil, and other rights, and so forth." "In any case" wrote another, "it should serve the public and not just be fitted with offices, as is our custom here."[49] Since architectural information about the buildings' interiors and construction was not necessarily public, it was often difficult to judge which organizations could best use them. VPN Poprad accordingly had to compel the district Party committee to open its building to public viewing for five days in early January.[50] In Louny, it seems that Civic Forum managed to achieve general agreement on use of the building, but in other places, like Cheb, there was acrimonious conflict among rival claimants.[51] In the end, most buildings were given to schools or hospitals whose own buildings were overcrowded and in need of repair.

Antimilitarism was a prominent popular sentiment in 1990. First and foremost, citizens demanded the withdrawal of Soviet troops stationed on Czechoslovak territory, and here again, the civic initiatives played a key mediating role. In Trutnov, for example, it was not the national committee but Civic Forum that took the initiative in negotiating troop withdrawal ahead of schedule.[52] Characteristically, OF spokespersons organized negotiations around the stakeholder principle, with all groups to be affected by the withdrawal invited.[53] They also made sure that buildings the

[48] "Zápis o konání 'živého řetězu' kolem budovy OV KSČ Louny (16. ledna 1990)" (LN: fond 633, box 1, folder 3, subfolder "Měsíc leden 1990").
[49] LN: fond 633, box 2, folder "Dopisy občanů k budově OV KSČ"; "Palác pro všechny slušné lidi—využití budovy OV KSČ," Zpravodaj Galerie B. Rejta a OF Louny, no. 1 (11 January 1990), p. 2.
[50] "Na žiadosť VPN," Ozveny Tatier, 5 January 1990, p. 2.
[51] Občanské fórum Cheb, no. 12 (8 February 1990), p. 1.
[52] "Zápis z prohlídky prostor užívaných sovětskými vojsky dočasně umístěných na území ČSSR, v posádce Trutnov, výcvikový prostor Volanov," 1 February 1990 (TU: fond "KC OF Trutnov," folder "Odchod sovětských vojsk"). Soviet troops began leaving Czechoslovakia on 26 February. "Sovieti odchádzajú," Večer, 27 February 1990, p. 1.
[53] "Záznam z jednání na sovětské posádce v Trutnově dne 31. ledna 1990 ohledně úpravy prostor užívaných sovětskými vojsky dočasně umístěnými na území ČSSR" (TU: fond "KC OF Trutnov," folder "Odchod sovětských vojsk").

Soviets vacated would not go to the Czechoslovak army but would become wholly civilian. Demilitarization efforts were not directed only against Soviet troops, however. In Brno, spontaneous popular protests spurred Civic Forum to negotiate the closing of a Czechoslovak military airport, which citizens complained made too much noise. This development prompted Civic Fora in České Budějovice and the northern Bohemian town of Postoloprty to parallel undertakings.[54]

The activities of local OF and VPN activists were manifold in these early days. At the beginning of January, after President Havel amnestied over 23,000 of Czechoslovakia's approximately 31,000 prisoners, OF and VPN spokespersons organized emergency efforts to find shelter, clothing, and jobs for the amnestied.[55] Later, spokespersons helped mediate conflicts between workers and management. OF Trutnov, for instance, took action to support the effort of employees in the District House of Pioneers and Youth to dismiss their director, who they said was lacking in "moral and character traits."[56] OF and VPN also worked to facilitate the overall development of civil society. Many local branches sponsored cultural events, established free legal clinics, and helped political parties and associations get themselves established. VPN in Bánovce nad Bebravou, for example, gave the local Green Party and Christian Democratic club space in its building and its bulletin.[57]

In their efforts to ensure the implementation of popular will, OF and VPN consistently adopted moderate methods. They did not have to do so. When Civic Forum in Louny summoned citizens to demonstrate against the Party's unwillingness to surrender its building, spokesmen had to intervene after some of the nine thousand participants decided not just to encircle the structure with a human chain but to occupy the entrance (where they shouted and whistled at those inside).[58] VPN in Bánovce repeatedly had to tell citizens,

> We are not an executive power. . . . We are glad that people consider members of the coordinating committee to be their spokespersons in negotiations

[54] *Informační servis* (České Budějovice), no. 18 (18 January 1990), p. 3; *Zpravodaj Galerie B. Rejta a OF Louny*, no. 2 (18 January 1990), p. 1.

[55] "První krok Václava Havla v úřadu – rozsáhlá amnestie," Česká televize, 1 January 2010; "Děkujeme," *Občanské fórum Cheb*, no. 10 (23 January 1990), p. 1; "OF oznamuje," *Domažlické inForum*, no. 5 (25 January 1990), p. 3; J. Musil, "Sněm OF 1.2.1990 v JBC" and "Setkání zástupců církví," *Profórum*, no. 5 (9 February 1990), pp. 5–6. Havel's decision was not uncontroversial; reports of rising crime began to circulate immediately afterward, and a large number of those released from prisons were soon back. Eduard Malý, "Jak dál?" *Sokolovské infórum*, no. 17 (24 January 1990), p. 3.

[56] Letter from Zdeněk Šmíd (KV OF Trutnov) to Jaroslav Hartl (ONV), 19 April 1990 (TU: fond "KC OF Trutnov," box 1, folder "OF města: MěstNV v Trutnově").

[57] "Strana zelených" and "Prvé kroky," *Host' do domu*, no. 1 (January 1990), pp. 1–2.

[58] "Zápis o konání 'živého řetězu'." This was, incidentally, just three days after a similar crowd had stormed the Stasi headquarters in Berlin.

with other organizations, that they seek advocates against the incorrect approach of superior organs. However, we are not an organization and we do not have the right to dictate laws or our standpoints to others. We can only advance your complaints to the appropriate organs and then monitor their resolution.[59]

It would seem, then, that if civic association spokespersons had chosen to use extra-legal or even violent methods of achieving their aims, they would have had some popular support in doing so. Instead they consistently chose a graduated approach: first negotiation, and should that fail, the exertion of popular pressure through nonviolent demonstrations and publicity campaigns. This was obviously in keeping with the commitment to nonviolence that had lain at the heart of revolutionary mobilization from the beginning. In December the waves of popular revolutionary enthusiasm had seemed all-powerful, but as they began in early 1990 to crash against institutional resistance, citizens increasingly began to question the wisdom of thoroughgoing nonviolence and the commitment to strict legality that nonviolence supposedly required. A Trutnov woman, for example, wrote to the town's Civic Forum with the opinion that "in many cases we're really too 'velvety.' It's nice, but even though I'm not a Christian I've read the Bible and there the idea is also propagated 'to turn the other cheek.' And how did Christ end? On a cross!"[60] Such arguments did not persuade district-level OF and VPN spokespersons to alter their methods, but mounting popular frustration did encourage them to seek help from the state.

Districts against Centers

Between December and March, Civic Forum and Public against Violence placed many of their own people or allies at the head of prominent ministries in both federal and republican governments. During the same period they also saw many of their supporters co-opted into the Federal Assembly and national councils, according to ratios agreed upon at federal and republican roundtables. Local OF and VPN spokespersons believed that this should give the civic associations in their national valence powerful influence on the formation of government policy and the passage of legislation. To exert this influence, however, local activists would have to go through the coordinating centers in Prague and Bratislava.

As initially conceived, OF and VPN were explicitly *not* organizations. In one of its first statements, the KC OF in Prague declared, "Civic Forum is not a political

[59] "Nie sme výkonný orgán," *Host' do domu*, no. 3 (24 January 1990), p. 1.
[60] Letter from R. V. to OF Trutnov, 13 March 1990 (TU: fond "KC OF Trutnov," box 2, folder "Různé").

party, nor is it any kind of organization accepting members. It is an utterly open society of all those who feel responsible for the positive resolution of an insufferable political situation."[61] Though it may not have considered itself an organization, however, Civic Forum naturally *had* an organization, and on 28 November it spelled out what that was:

(a) ... Civic Forum will not create a complicated hierarchy, but only a horizontal network with all local civic fora, affiliated with a single coordinating center.

(b) The coordinating center is only an informational and organizational center; in no sense is it a directive center. Its task is to collect and further distribute information from local OFs and to inform about accomplished and planned activities. All local civic fora work in their local frameworks entirely independently.

(c) The coordinating center represents Civic Forum in negotiations with central state and international institutions, and this above all on the basis of suggestions and recommendations of local OFs.[62]

Public against Violence adopted this formulation verbatim (substituting VPN for OF) in a statement of *its* internal organization the following day.[63] This initial insistence on being associations, not organizations, testifies to OF's and VPN's anarchic character, as originally conceived and established. It also reflected the important fact that each Civic Forum or Public against Violence grouping—from the capitals to the smallest village—started out as a local endeavor of citizens in a given locale. Local OFs and VPNs (both workplace and geographic) sometimes sent "ambassadors" to Prague and Bratislava in November and December to exchange concerns, and they sent in the requested "suggestions and recommendations," but there was no mechanism for local associations to define the positions that the coordinating centers took "in negotiations with central state institutions."

The idea for a convention where central and provincial activists could meet one another was first raised in a KC OF statement made during the General Strike.[64] Civic Forum did not organize its first republic-wide convention until 23 December, however, and VPN did not do so until 27 January.[65] Prague and Bratislava had very differing conceptions of how these conventions should look and what their purpose

---

[61] "Občanské fórum není politická strana . . . ," *Informační servis* (Prague) no. 2 (21 November 1989), p. 1; reprinted in Suk, *Občanské forum*, vol. 2, p. 14.

[62] "Vnitřní organizace Občanského fóra."

[63] "Vnútorná organizácia VPN."

[64] "Stanovisko OF ke dni 27. listopadu 1989," Prague, 27 November 1989, reprinted in Suk, *Občanské forum*, vol. 2, p. 33.

[65] They had, however, held informational meetings with provincial activists on 16 and 9 December, respectively.

should be. While the KC OF had in mind nothing more than a consultative chat among a handful of activists, the KV VPN imagined a massive democratic meeting where every branch in Slovakia would have the opportunity to contribute to discussion. In the event, ninety-two activists and invited guests showed up for the OF convention—but without there having been any system put in place to determine who should attend. Nearly two-thirds of the participants were actually Praguers; only twenty-three appeared from other parts of Bohemia and just twelve from Moravia and Silesia. The debate was mostly about proposed bylaws for the movement and the structure of the coordinating center. Moravians in particular argued that a more representative system should be established whereby activists from different parts of the country might share equitably in the formation of Civic Forum policy toward the state. A vote was held on their proposal, but given who the majority of voters were, it is not surprising that it failed.[66] If the first OF convention suffered from what might be called a democratic deficit, the first VPN convention illustrated the opposite extreme. Originally the KV VPN invited every basic VPN group in Slovakia to elect one delegate to send to Bratislava and proposed that everyone be allowed two minutes to speak.[67] When it became apparent that thousands of groups were planning to accept the invitation, far exceeding the capacity of the building that had been reserved, let alone the time allotted for discussion, the coordinating committee rather awkwardly announced that the principles of selection would have to be changed. In the new system, district coordinating committees were entrusted with the task of choosing twenty to twenty-five delegates to represent each district.[68] Even with this revised mechanism, roughly a thousand people crowded into the ROH convention hall in Bratislava on 27 January. While representation was clearly fairer here than it had been at Civic Forum's first convention, the numbers obviously made it impossible for much consequential discussion to take place within the framework of a one-day meeting. Ján Budaj later admitted to having no experience organizing such an assembly.[69] The bylaws were approved except for the question of whether Communists should be allowed in VPN coordinating committees; the question evidently unleashed such violent emotions that it was postponed to the next convention—which organizers made sure was smaller.[70]

In subsequent months, district-level activists in the civic associations made increasingly vociferous demands for democratic representation within the movements. Even though VPN conventions had a more straightforwardly democratic structure, the executive councils of the coordinating centers—which were

---

[66] "Zápis ze sněmu Občanského fóra 23. 12. 1989" (ÚSD: archiv KC OF, "OF—interní písemnosti: Sněmy OF," box 1, folder "Sněmy OF 23.12.1989"), pp. 2, 6–7.

[67] "Prvý snem VPN," *Verejnost*, 9 January 1990, p. 1; "Kto na snem," *Verejnost*, 12 January 1990, p. 1.

[68] "Snem VPN," *Verejnost*, 23 January 1990, p. 1.

[69] "Nultý snem VPN," *Reflex*, 2 February 1990, p. 4.

[70] Ibid.; "Druhý pracovný celoslovenský snem VPN," *Verejnost*, 13 February 1990, p. 1.

responsible for day-to-day decision making and policy formation vis-à-vis central authorities—still consisted primarily of the original founders and associates they had brought on board. They were also, for the most part, residents of the capitals. While in 1989 provincial activists seem universally to have accepted the coordinating centers as at least provisionally representative (the only tension being between OF and VPN adherents in Slovakia), local spokespersons came increasingly to feel in the new year that opinions of the central executive councils were not the opinions of the movements as wholes. The result was a long, drawn-out battle to make council membership elective and open to representatives from the districts. Delegates from district-level Civic Fora achieved this dramatically at the fourth republican convention on 3 February. After the executive council proposed that conventions be held *less* frequently, delegates from the districts stormily rejected this idea and put forward their own motion that they be represented on the council. A majority of those present voted for the motion, but according to the bylaws it failed because the convention lacked a quorum. It turned out that those missing were members of the Prague coordinating center, who evidently thought the convention a waste of their time. Undaunted, district delegates successfully insisted that the bylaws be disregarded, and they obtained the right to have nine representatives on the twenty-five-member council.[71] Needless to say, this would not be the end of the story. Delegates to VPN's second republican convention on 10 February created a "Slovak VPN Council" to be the association's operative decision-making body between conventions. It included district representatives from the start—but still not enough of them to satisfy provincial activists. The impracticality of meeting on a daily or even weekly basis, moreover, meant that day-to-day decision making still had to take place in the Bratislava coordinating committee (renamed "coordinating center" in March). As a result, in April a district convention in Považská Bystrica adopted the following resolution, which expressed the general feeling outside Bratislava:

> We demand that the KC VPN in Bratislava clarify the manner of its emergence and reveal its composition by name, and also that the VPN bylaws clearly define the manner by which this organ is created and its competence. . . . We demand that cadre questions of the Slovak VPN Council be fundamentally resolved at the next republican convention of VPN. We disagree with the meager representation of districts in that organ.[72]

To some extent the dispute relaxed during the election campaign between April and June 1990, partly because energies were diverted elsewhere but mostly because polls were showing declining support for the civic associations, motivating activists

---

[71] Suk, *Labyrintem*, pp. 305–6.
[72] "Zápis napísaný dňa 21.4.1990 z okresného snemu VPN v Pov. Bystrici" (PX: fond G1, box 7, folder 4).

to downplay differences in an effort to restore public confidence. The electoral process nonetheless occasioned further conflict between centers and peripheries over the formation of common policy. District activists had been angered in January when the coordinating centers had agreed on an electoral law with roundtable partners without consulting district-level activists, let alone the general public. There was abundant evidence that public opinion had supported a majoritarian or mixed electoral system, but the coordinating committees had agreed to the system of proportional representation favored by the political parties sitting with OF and VPN at the federal roundtable. To many, this deal had smacked of the "cabinet politics" and "about us without us" decision-making style that had mobilized citizens against the Communist regime in November.[73] District activists were further infuriated when they received the candidate lists the centers had devised. Though representation was to be proportional, seats were still to be allocated geographically, with each of Czechoslovakia's ten regions (plus the capitals) receiving a certain number of them. Many activists were therefore surprised to discover that many of the most electable seats in each region were given to Praguers and Bratislavans with little or no connection to the regions they would theoretically represent. Several districts complained that their own nominees had been rejected or positioned so low on the lists that they could not be elected.[74] Prague and Bratislava responded that, to win the elections, it was best to put forth well-known personages. Many district activists, however, found this disturbingly close to the Communist practice of deciding behind closed doors who would be "elected" and then finding districts for them to "represent"—a practice that citizens in November and December had loudly condemned.

The elections themselves, despite OF and VPN victories, gave grassroots activists new reasons to criticize the coordinating centers. In Slovakia, just after the polling booths closed, members of the KC VPN went on television to announce that their top candidate to the Slovak National Council, Ján Budaj, had not passed lustration and was therefore withdrawing his candidacy. Budaj denied having collaborated with the secret police and no evidence was ever produced against him, but the scandal nonetheless left many VPN supporters confused and concerned that the coordinating center, by waiting until the elections were over to make the announcement, had manipulated voters—dishonestly taking advantage of Budaj's popularity.[75] Following the creation of new federal and republican governments, district

[73] Suk, *Labyrintem*, pp. 268–77.

[74] See, for example, LN: fond 633, box 1, folder 3, subfolder "Měsíc květen 1990"; OKV VPN Považská Bystrica, "Prehlásenie," 22 June 1990 (SNA: Archív VPN, fond. odd. II); "Návrh usnesení sněmu OF konaného v Praze dne 30.6.1990" (ÚSD: archiv KC OF, "OF—interní písemnosti: Sněmy OF," box 1, folder "Sněmy OF 30.6.1990," subfolder "Sněm 30.6.90").

[75] The most thorough account of this affair is in Vladimír Ondruš, *Atentát na nežnú revolúciu* (Bratislava: Ikar, 2009). It seems beyond doubt that Slovakia's preelection interior minister, Vladimír Mečiar, had a hand in framing Budaj.

spokespersons expressed frustration with ministers elected on OF and VPN tickets who refused to vacate their parliamentary seats in favor of candidates who had been lower on the lists. "In the election campaign we promised that those who became ministers would give up their seats," one district OF spokesperson complained, recommending that "those ministers who refuse to surrender their mandates should go on television and explain why." Typically, the KC OF's new chief spokesman, Ivan Fišera, trivialized the problem, saying that the holding of multiple offices was normal in other democratic countries.[76] A number of activists left the movements as a result of these affairs, some of them signing a "New Few Sentences" petition that alluded ironically to a dissident petition of the previous year. It suggested that nothing had really changed since 1989—that OF and VPN had merely replaced the KSČ as undemocratic hegemons, with "totalitarian" leaderships that engaged in "cabinet politics."[77]

After the Federal Assembly and national councils went on vacation, the civic associations' rank and file complained with mounting bitterness that politicians who had emerged from OF and VPN—as well as the associations' leaders—were not doing enough to realize the will of the people. OF Hradec Králové warned against passivity in the face of Communist apparatchiks, who had perhaps lost political power but were now consolidating economic power in the workplaces, persecuting Civic Forum activists and "ruining the successes of the November revolution."[78] OF Chrudim complained that the investigation of 17 November had halted, that former officials who had abused their power had not been brought to justice, and that no one had presented a scenario for economic reform; the Chrudimites warned that "confusion, hopelessness, and disgust are spreading among those who believed in the ideals of the November revolution."[79] VPN Trnava demanded that politicians and central VPN leaders "bring the revolution to its conclusion" by resolving the issue of Communist property and allowing VPN to return to the workplaces, where

[76] "Zápis ze Sněmu Občanského fóra ze dne 21. července 1990" (ÚSD: archiv KC OF, "OF—interní písemnosti: Sněmy OF," box 1, folder "Sněmy OF 21.7.1990"), p. 3. Jan Urban, who had been the KC OF's chief spokesman after Pithart's elevation to the office of Czech premier in February, had resigned immediately following the elections. See also "Uznesenie zo zasadnutia zástupcov VPN z 8 okresov SSK zo dňa 15.6.90" (SNA: Archív VPN, fond. odd. II).

[77] Ladislav Nešpor, "Niekoľko viet 1990," Prague, 29 June 1990, in Premeny, vol. 2, no. 39 (28 September 1990), p. 1; Daša Havlová, "Několik poznámek k Novým několika větám," InForum, no. 35 (14 August 1990), p. 1. The original petition, "A Few Sentences" of June 1989, had been the first citizens' petition critical of the Communist regime to break the divide between dissident groups and the rest of the population; even though most citizens did not get a chance to read the text until November 1989, it circulated widely enough (in part thanks to the ridiculous style of Miloš Jakeš's public condemnation) that forty thousand citizens signed it before 17 November (Charter 77, by contrast, garnered only about two thousand signatures over a dozen years). "Několik vět," Lidové noviny, vol. 2, no. 7–8 (June 1989), p. 2 (flyer versions are available in BB, BE, HIA, JN, KO, KS, OL, OV, PV, PX, ZL, and ZM); Michal Pullmann, Konec experimentu: Přestavba a pád komunismu v Československu (Prague: Scriptorium, 2011), p. 206.

[78] Okresní sněm OF v Hradci Králové, "Výzva," 17 July 1990 (CH: fond 1063, SB46, box 1, folder 8).

[79] Okresní sněm OF Chrudim, "Nikdo nic neví?," Respekt, 8 August 1990, p. 3. Also in CH.

it might aid workers in their fight against the *nomenklatura*.[80] VPN Topoľčany and VPN Prievidza pointed out that many of the "open competitions" in workplaces had been run so as to exclude candidates who had not been part of the *nomen-klatura*; they called for the mass dismissal of workplace directors and new, better-executed searches to solve the problem.[81] In the absence of a satisfactory response, some district spokespersons took matters into their own hands. To get a sense of the situation, OF Hodonín made a list of all enterprises in the district still managed by *nomenklatura* members.[82] The Teachers' Forum in Nitra, affiliated with VPN, per-suaded the ONV to dismiss all school directors and restaff the positions in searches that would be open to the old directors but supervised jointly by the ONV and the Teachers' Forum.[83] The central responses to these provincial initiatives was sharply negative. Petr Pithart, who had been reappointed Czech premier following the June elections, publicly compared OF Hodonín's initiative to the Holocaust.[84] The West Slovakian KNV overturned the Nitra ONV's decision, and when the issue was brought to the attention of the KC VPN, it supported the KNV rather than VPN Nitra.[85] The coordinating centers did try to exert pressure on the governments by establishing a "Kollegium" (OF) and "Ministerial Club" (VPN) where they might meet regularly with ministers and parliamentary leaders who had emerged from the civic associations, but since these initiatives depended on the goodwill of the politicians invited to attend, their success was limited. The civic initiatives had no power to enforce discipline.

By mid-August, grassroots activists had begun proclaiming the need for "a sec-ond revolution" to overcome the obstacles that had seemingly brought the first to a halt.[86] President Havel explicitly supported this notion in his greetings to Civic Forum's republican convention on 18 August, and he gave the idea statewide cur-rency when he addressed the public three days later on the anniversary of the 1968 Warsaw Pact invasion.[87] "The twenty years we lost have had tragic consequences," he declared, enumerating the many problems about which citizens were currently complaining. "These facts confirm again and again that our revolution is not over. On the contrary, the main part must still begin." Havel urged citizens to intensify pressure on their parliaments and governments to pass good laws and make bold

---

[80] "Zápisnica zo zasadnutia Rady Slovenska VPN (3. VIII. 90)" (SNA: Archív VPN, fond. odd. II).

[81] "Vyhlásenie okresného koordinačného výboru VPN v Topoľčanoch," *Verejnost*, 15 August 1990, p. 2; "Vyhlásenie OKV VPN v Prievidzi," *Verejnost*, 17 August 1990, p. 2.

[82] "Zápis ze Sněmu OF dne 18.8.1990" (ÚSD: archiv KC OF, "OF—interní písemnosti: Sněmy OF," box 2, folder "Sněmy OF: 18.8.1990"), pp. 5–6.

[83] "Nový školský rok s novými riaditeľmi," *Nitrianska verejnost*, 26 July 1990, p. 1.

[84] Milena Šindelářová, "Nepoučitelný premiér," *Respekt*, 1 August 1990, p. 2.

[85] Sandra Švardová, Yva Hollá, and Daniela Gáliková, "Jan Amos nepomôže," *Verejnost*, 4 September 1990, p. 1; "Vyhlásenie KC VPN k súčasnej situácii na pracoviskách," *Verejnost*, 3 August 1990, p. 2.

[86] "Z jednání sněmu OF," Cheb, 13 August 1990 (CH: fond 1063, SB46, box 1, folder 9).

[87] Petr Kučera, "Období druhé revoluce," *InForum*, no. 36 (21 August 1990), pp. 4–5.

decisions and to use all legal and political means at their disposal to remove local survivals of the old regime.[88] Havel's speech met with an overwhelmingly positive public response and inspired the Federal Assembly presidium—which had the power to decree "legal measures" during parliamentary recesses—to at last address the *nomenklatura* problem by enlarging the category of managers and directors who could be replaced on orders from the pertinent ministry. Some commentators, however, noted ironically that Havel merely advocated the same kind of local initiative that central OF and VPN leaders had themselves dampened earlier in the year.[89] Indeed, when Pithart later vetoed OF involvement in the process whereby ministries determined which managers to replace, leaving recommendations up to national committee departments and unions that were not always fully reconstructed, Civic Forum activists pointed to Pithart's January speech as one of the causes of "today's *via dolorosa* with Communist cadres."[90] At the republican convention OF held in October, a number of district spokespersons proclaimed that Pithart no longer represented the association and demanded his resignation.[91]

The Second Revolution

When district representatives converged on Prague for the October convention, they were on the warpath. Though they did not succeed in recalling Pithart, they did effect a dramatic reconfiguration of power within their movement. At the September convention they had agreed to create the position of Civic Forum chairman, and in October they decisively rejected the executive council's nominee for the office, the Charter 77 signatory Martin Palouš, in favor of the federal finance minister Václav Klaus.[92] Klaus, who had been regarded as a dark horse just a week previously, had recently unveiled his economic reform proposals to the reconvened Federal Assembly, and though he himself never made the claim, many of his supporters enthusiastically predicted that his plan to privatize most state-run enterprises would finally break the power of the *nomenklatura*.[93] Klaus was also esteemed in the districts for his technical competence, decisiveness, and willingness to engage with provincial activists as equals (the fact that Klaus shared the technical background of most local

[88] "Projev prezidenta V. Havla na Václavském náměstí v Praze," *Lidové noviny*, 22 August 1990, pp. 1, 4; for the Slovak translation, see "Prejav prezidenta ČSFR Václava Havla," *Verejnosť*, 22 August 1990, p. 3.

[89] Martin Weiss, "První fáze, druhá fáze," *Respekt*, 29 August 1990, p. 2.

[90] Jan Vávra, "Co přinesl Sněm," *Fórum*, 19 September 1990, p. 2.

[91] Beata Berníková, "Znovu kolem premiéra," *Fórum*, 17 October 1990, p. 2.

[92] Klaus received nearly 70% of the valid votes (115 of 167). "Sněm OF," *InForum*, no. 44 (17 October 1990), p. 1.

[93] Jan Vávra, "Kolik je kandidátů na předsedu OF?" *Fórum*, 10 October 1990, p. 2; "Privatizácia rozbije nomenklatúry," *Verejnosť*, 10 September 1990, p. 2; KC OF Trutnov, "Návrh základní politické linie Občanského fóra pro období září-prosinec 1990," 16 September 1990 (TU: fond "KC OF Trutnov," box 4, folder "OF 1990–1991").

spokespersons was doubtless important in this regard). In his acceptance speech, Klaus promised to transform Civic Forum from an indistinct entity to one with a clear face. "The dominant opinion regarding the identity and future of our OF must be the opinion of participants in our convention," he said, "as an expression of the representation of voters, not administrators." As for his own role with respect to this "dominant opinion," Klaus proclaimed that "in today's situation I would like to be . . . the symbol of a program that has not yet been written."[94] In form, then, Klaus's program was populist, even if he himself would "symbolize" the content.

Klaus promptly undertook a thorough housecleaning of the coordinating center, demarcating the competencies of the executive council and Kollegium, defining the functions of bureaucrats in the KC and limiting their number, abolishing committees whose existence no longer seemed justified, and transforming OF's daily newspaper from a relatively independent publication to one that would more effectively reflect OF's "political line."[95] At the end of October Klaus took the more controversial step of declaring that Civic Forum no longer recognized two internal groupings, the Left Alternative and Obroda (Renewal, a club of Dubčekite '68ers), as part of the association.[96] When members of the executive council objected that OF's bylaws did not give Klaus authority to take such a step, he retorted that any discussion of his competencies was "irrelevant." "The convention voted for a fundamental change in OF's managing organs," he said, adding that participants in *mítinky* across the country had convinced him that he had a mandate to change the structure of Civic Forum.[97]

Tensions within Public against Violence had not grown as acute over the summer as they had in Civic Forum, in part because the Slovak premier, Vladimír Mečiar, made every effort to seem like a tribune of the people (quite unlike his Czech counterpart) and in part because the chairman of VPN's Slovak Council, Ján Budaj, was known to speak up for district activists in their disputes with the coordinating center.[98] Consequently, whereas delegates to OF's September convention created the office of a chairman they could elect, delegates to VPN's September convention expressed dismay that their chairman had decided to step down. After a long, simmering feud with individuals in the KC VPN, Budaj had accepted the argument that his scandal-ridden past might harm VPN's chances in the November elections, but district activists at the convention tried to get him to reconsider. Fedor Gál, the chairman of the coordinating center, threatened to resign if this happened, whereupon Budaj announced that, for the sake of peace, he really would

[94] Quoted in "Václav Klaus: Jakou roli bude hrát?," *InForum*, no. 44 (17 October 1990), p. 8.

[95] "Zápis z Rady 16.10.1990," *InForum*, no. 45 (25 October 1990), p. 1.

[96] Jan Vávra, "Pravidla hry," *Fórum*, 7 November 1990, p. 2.

[97] "Zápis z Rady OF 30. 10. 1990" (ÚSD: archiv KC OF, folder "Zápisy z rady OF (C)").

[98] Although Budaj had withdrawn his candidacy for political office in June, he had remained active in the movement.

step down. Delegates also expressed frustration that the agenda for the one-day meeting gave them only two hours for discussion—and this only about bylaws and the upcoming elections. "The second stage of the November revolution should be taking place," exclaimed a Nitra delegate, who successfully moved to replace a half-hour break with a discussion of politics. Thirty minutes, however, proved long enough just for a brief exchange of experiences. Finally, delegates complained about proposed changes to the bylaws. They allowed for regular conventions to take place only once per year, placed provincial activists at a disadvantage in elections to the Slovak Council, and reserved to the council the power to elect its chairman. The convention ultimately adopted the bylaws, but the result was a council on which only seven of the twenty-five members were not from Bratislava and the election of Fedor Gál—Budaj's rival—as chairman.[99] Afterward, many delegates complained that the convention had been "manipulated."[100]

Tensions exploded the following month.[101] The spark was evidently the KC VPN's rejection of a language law proposed by the Matica slovenská in favor of a more moderate version made with input from FMK, resulting in major nationalist demonstrations as parliament met to consider the proposals in early October.[102] In reaction to what they saw as disharmony between the center's policies and the will of the people—and with no prospect of a regular convention where they might express their grievances—delegates from thirty-two of Slovakia's thirty-eight districts gathered on their own initiative in Trnava on 20 October. They drafted a statement calling for reconstruction of VPN's central organs "so that districts and regions might have a share in the formation and realization of VPN's political program" and suggested that it was an insufficiency of internal democracy and failure to engage the public as a partner that had caused VPN's decline in popularity.[103] Though Juraj Flamik, the new chairman of VPN's coordinating committee, condemned the initiative as a "putsch," its participants called for dialogue to solve the problem, and the coordinating committee indicated its responsiveness by printing both

[99] "Program republikového snemu konaného dňa 8.9.1990," "Snem—začiatok," "Volebný poriadok republikového snemu VPN," "Kandidátka na voľbu členov SR VPN," and "Otvorenie snemu" (SNA: Archív VPN, fond. odd. II); Peter Duhan and Michal Galát, "Bez odvahy na zmeny stratíme aj Šancu pre Slovensko," and Duhan, "Inštitucionalizovať vzťahy víťazných hnutí," Verejnosť, 10 September 1990, pp. 2, 4; Jozef Ruttkay, "Zo šera fráz," Verejnosť, 11 September 1990, p. 1.

[100] Petr Bartoš, "Sněm VPN: Decentralizace nebo akceschopnost," Fórum, 12 September 1990, p. 2; "Zasadnutie rozšírenej Rady Slovenska VPN, 13. 10. 1990" (SNA: Archív VPN, fond. odd. II).

[101] The metaphor is taken from Ľuboš Kríž, "Vybuchla v Trnave bomba?" Verejnosť, 22 October 1990, pp. 1, 3.

[102] KV VPN Bratislava III, "Závery z pracovného rokovania zástupcov okresných a mestských rád a koordinačných výborov VPN. . . . Konkretizácia pripomienok ku kvalite politickej práce Rady VPN Slovenska a KC VPN" (SNA: Archív VPN, fond. odd. II).

[103] "Závery z pracovného rokovania zástupcov okresných a mestských rád a koordinačných výborov VPN, zvolaného na základe podnetov z jednotlivých regiónov Slovenska," Telefax VPN, no. 24 (24 October 1990), p. 3.

the Trnava declaration and Flamik's rejoinder in its newsletter.[104] It is significant, though, that participants in the Trnava Initiative felt compelled to adopt extralegal means to press for satisfaction of their demands. Just as district-level Civic Forum activists had disregarded bylaws in order to achieve representation on the OF executive council, so their colleagues in VPN, six months later and in a tenser situation, also resorted to "revolutionary" methods. These were, in essence, revolts within the revolution—with the aim of capturing the state.

Not everyone in the districts followed the rebels. Some (including many of the most altruistic) withdrew from politics altogether over the course of 1990. Others launched initiatives of their own. Karel Hronec, for example, had been a member of Trutnov's municipal OF council at the beginning of 1990, but by autumn he had withdrawn. He nonetheless campaigned in the local elections of November as an independent candidate. He also appealed to citizens to participate in a civic demonstration on the town's main square on 17 November, "the first anniversary of the victory of the democratic revolution, which has already lost its effectiveness." In the event, he mobilized support for the students' "stolen revolution" proclamation and the New Few Sentences of 1990.[105]

Some provincial activists saw the local elections of November 1990 as the culmination of the revolution. Others, noting how much less publicity the campaign was receiving in comparison with the republican and federal elections of June, spoke of the "little elections" of November.[106] The election campaign demonstrates that activists for the most part remained committed to the idea of acting as conduits for the popular will. In many places, the civic associations drafted their platforms for the communal elections not behind closed doors but on the basis of surveys and meetings in which the general public was invited to participate.[107] OF Louny, for example, asked the general populace who its candidates should be, and OF Tanvald formulated both its election platform and its candidate list in response to public surveys.[108]

After the elections, in which OF and VPN performed poorly by their June standards and in which Communists regained control of many municipalities, the conflicts within the civic initiatives led them to division. Civic Forum held a working meeting of district and coordinating center representatives in Olomouc on 8 and 9 December. The main question on the agenda was the postelection trajectory

[104] "Ministerský klub, konaný dňa 19. 10. 1990" (SNA: Archív VPN, fond. odd. II); Juraj Flamik, "Stanovisko k stretnutiu v Trnave," *Telefax VPN*, no. 24 (24 October 1990), p. 3.

[105] TU: fond "KC OF Trutnov," box 1, folder "Kandidáti do obecních voleb."

[106] "Zápis z jednání politických stran na okresní úrovni, konaného dne 14.11.1990" (TU: fond "KC OF Trutnov," box 5).

[107] See, for example, "Poklady pro volební program za obvod Horní Staré Město (HSM)," 8 October 1990 (TU: fond "KC OF Trutnov," box 3, folder "Zde je náš domov: regionální program").

[108] "Vyhodnocené ankety OF v Lounech" (LN: fond 633, box 1, subfolder "Měsíc září 1990"); OF Tanvald, "OF Tanvald představuje kandidáty volební program" (JN: sbírka soudobé dokumentace, 1989–1991, folder "Revoluce 1989—dokumentace," subfolder "Reakce KSČ na listopadové události r. 1989").

of the association, and a majority voted to transform it into a political party.[109] Though Klaus gave a speech endorsing this proposal and arguing that it must result in a "right-wing" party, we should not assume that supporters of the transformation were motivated primarily by ideological principles.[110] Fedor Gál, who observed the meeting as a guest from VPN, concluded, "I sat there the whole day, I know these people intimately, but I don't know the platform of this party. I know only that these people feel they need to found a party."[111] Klaus even emphasized that the party should not be bound to an ideology, that it should not have clear outlines the way West European parties did; the main thing was for it to have a structure, full-time functionaries, and the ability to enforce discipline on its politicians.[112] The next OF convention, in January 1991, took up the Olomouc recommendations and voted accordingly to transform OF into a party, with specifics to be decided the following month. In the meantime opponents of the party principle rallied support for the preservation of Civic Forum's existing, nonpartisan, associational structure. The result was a divorce between the two groups at the February convention, where it was agreed to dissolve Civic Forum and divide its assets equally between the two successors: the Civic Democratic Party (ODS), constituted as Klaus had outlined it in Olomouc, and the Civic Movement, led by dissenters from the majority opinion who sought to preserve a nonpartisan associational framework.

The split of VPN was more protracted. At a conference in Bratislava on 9 February 1991, representatives of district councils informed the Slovak Council that recent district conventions had supported the idea that VPN should not follow in OF's footsteps, that VPN should instead remain a nonpartisan movement at least until the 1992 elections. The representatives added, however, that the conventions wanted changes in the Slovak Council, such that district representatives would be able to participate directly in its work and decisions.[113] These two desires came into conflict at an extraordinary convention called on the districts' initiative (but in accordance with the bylaws) for 23–24 February in Topoľčany. There, veterans of the Trnava Initiative proposed a change in the bylaws that would enable the convention to elect the Slovak Council chair directly, in a fashion they hoped would give them the kind of control over the coordinating center that their Civic Forum colleagues had gained in October.[114] Though it is likely that a majority of

[109] "Většinový návrh usnesení sekce pro organizační strukturu," *InForum*, no. 52 (13 December 1990), p. 8.
[110] Václav Klaus, "Projev Václava Klause," *InForum*, no. 52 (13 December 1990), pp. 1–3.
[111] Quoted in "Odznelo na brífingu KC VPN dňa 12.12.1990," *Telefax VPN*, no. 29 (21 December 1990), p. 7.
[112] Klaus, pp. 1–2.
[113] "Konferencia VPN," *Telefax VPN*, no. 3 (11 February 1991), p. 1.
[114] Milan Žitný, "Budúcnosť VPN," *Respekt*, 14 January 1991, p. 3; Žitný, "Boj o moc na sneme VPN," *Respekt*, 4 March 1991, pp. 2–3.

the district representation voted for the motion, this contingent was not a majority of the entire body of voting participants at the convention, since these included members of the executive council, VPN deputies in the Federal Assembly and the Slovak National Council, and other "personages" selected by the executive council.[115] In reaction to the motion's failure, Trnava Initiative spokespersons announced the following week the creation of "VPN—For a Democratic Slovakia" (VPN-ZDS), which they claimed represented "the original platform" of VPN. They emphasized that it was not their intention to split the movement but rather "to return to it its face and preserve its identity," and they called on all VPN supporters to "establish clubs of the original platform of Public against Violence."[116] Vladimír Mečiar (who would have become VPN's chairman if the Topoľčany motion had passed) and Milan Kňažko (now Slovakia's minister for international affairs) supported the new movement, and just as Klaus had spent the summer visiting Civic Forum activists in Czech districts, so Mečiar and Kňažko devoted the rest of March and April to traveling around Slovak districts, establishing preparatory committees.[117] A genuinely popular movement was once more set in motion.

VPN in Košice had received letters in the fall of 1990 criticizing the movement for not organizing enough meetings anymore. "The ruling gentlemen have not cultivated the feedback which is a check on power," one citizen wrote; "VPN has in general forgotten that it arose from the streets and squares."[118] Though VPN's Bratislava leaders had believed—like their colleagues in Prague—that the time of mass meetings was over, large segments of the Slovak population evidently did not agree. More than anything, it was VPN-ZDS's insistence on engaging the people that soon made the movement the most popular political formation in Slovakia. In keeping with the intentions district representatives had expressed at the beginning of February, VPN-ZDS chose to remain a nonpartisan civic movement, though increasingly the leader it chose (Vladimír Mečiar) stamped it with his own personality. Amid much acrimony between leaders of the old and new VPNs (each considering the other the new one), a second extraordinary convention was arranged to take place in Košice on 27 April. There it was agreed, as with OF, to divide assets equally between the two successor movements: ZDS and a rump VPN.

---

[115] "Stanovy politického hnutia Verejnosť proti násiliu," *Verejnosť*, 10 September 1990, p. 5; prezenčná listina topoľčanského snemu (SNA: Archív VPN, fond. odd. II).

[116] "Vyhlásenie zástupcov Trnavskej iniciatívy VPN," Bratislava, 5 March 1991, and "Vyhlásenie zástupcov OR VPN pri konštituovaní pôvodnej platformy VPN zo dňa 5.3.1991 v Bratislave," both in *Smena*, 6 March 1991, p. 3.

[117] Peter Schutz, "Test inteligencie," *Košická akcia*, no. 8 (8–23 April 1991), p. 2. Though Budaj had been on the ZDS preparatory committee and was even responsible for its name, he decided in the end not to join the movement. "Chcú isť tam, kde boli v Novembri. . . . ," *Smena*, 6 March 1991, p. 4; "Sú ľudia, ktorí skončili aj horšie," *Domino fórum*, 17–23 June 1999, p. 5.

[118] Quoted in Peter Schutz, "Opijeme sa rožkom demagógie?" *Akcia*, no. 22 (5–11 November 1990), p. 3.

(ZDS subsequently renamed itself "The Movement for a Democratic Slovakia," i.e., HZDS.)

Even if not everyone joined Klaus's supporters in hailing his election to the OF chairmanship as "the second revolution," they were forced to recognize it as a turning point.[119] Together with the "putsch" that was the Trnava Initiative, it marked the beginning of a new phase in the development of post-Communist political culture—a movement away from attempts at what might be called consensus politics (or "nonpolitical politics," as some identified it at the time) toward the populist partisan politics that would characterize the 1990s.[120] The nationalist and neoliberal ideologies according to which HZDS and ODS would later seek to refashion the Slovak and Czech republics were still only in formation in 1990–91, but the demise of the transcendent unity of 1989 and the attendant rise of uncertainty had already created a need for the meaning that ideology could impose.[121] Accordingly, supporters of the "second revolution" justified their actions by bewailing that the first had tragically been "stolen" or left "unfinished," or that it had "ended in a stalemate."[122] The founding of ODS and ZDS provided hope to local spokespersons and erstwhile supporters of the civic movements that transcendence might still be possible, and it was thus with a great deal of romantic enthusiasm that they established preparatory committees. As ODS founders in the East Bohemian town of Dvůr Králové exclaimed, "We must immediately mobilize our forces and finish the revolution everywhere where its lack of follow-through allowed the preservation or renewal of old structures!"[123] In Košice, ZDS organizers announced simply, "We're marching on!"[124] Just as the romance of 1989 had generated representations of students as knights and Havel as a saint, so participants in the new romance of the 1990s would perceive Klaus as their knight in shining armor and portray Mečiar in the company of religious figures.[125] This time, however, it was not a romance in which all citizens of Czechoslovakia could share, nor were they invited to do so.

[119] Bohumil Pečinka, "Skutečná revoluce," *Studentské listy*, vol. 1, no. 20 (November 1990), p. 2.

[120] Jan Vávra, "Začátek nové kapitoly," *Fórum*, 17 October 1990, p. 2.

[121] For details of HZDS and ODS ideologies, see Kieran Williams, "National Myths in the New Czech Liberalism," in *Myths and Nationhood*, ed. Geoffrey Hosking and George Schöpflin (London: Hurst & Co., 1997), pp. 132–40; Tim Haughton, "HZDS: The Ideology, Organisation and Support Base of Slovakia's Most Successful Party," *Europe-Asia Studies* 53, no. 5 (July 2001): 745–69; Seán Hanley, *The New Right in the New Europe: Czech Transformation and Right-Wing Politics, 1989–2006* (London: Routledge, 2008).

[122] Iveta Vrbová and Jiří Doležal, "17. listo-PAT," *Fórum*, 14 November 1990, pp. 6–7.

[123] "Informační list Občanské demokratické strany ve Dvoře Králové nad Labem," [late February or early March 1991] (TU: box 4, folder "OF 1990–1991").

[124] *Košická akcia*, no. 11 (20 May–3 June 1991), p. 1.

[125] For examples of this new romantic rhetoric, see Václav Klaus, *Nemám rád katastrofické scénáře* (Ostrava: Sagit, 1991), and Igor Chaun's four-part agitprop documentary, *Léčba Klausem* (Klaus Therapy), from the spring of 1991. Chaun, a student strike committee member in 1989, later became a leader of the "Thank you, now leave" movement against Klaus and other prominent politicians in 1999.

From the founding of Civic Forum and Public against Violence in 1989 to their breakup in 1991, district-level activists remained for the most part committed to the idea of mediating "the will of the people." Their quarrel with the coordinating centers was motivated not by the desire for positions simply for the sake of having positions but by the desire to see more effectively to the implementation of popular will. The rebellions of the peripheries against the centers should be seen as the continuation of a revolutionary mentality that favored as direct a democracy as possible. The Trnava Initiative, for example, identified VPN-ZDS as a movement "true to the ideals of 17 November 1989."[126] What Klaus called "the magic date of 17 November" was still powerful, and even though he argued for the need to move on from it, most of those who supported him—like most of those who joined HZDS—did so for reasons that ultimately reached back to 17 November.[127] As a sacred reference point, the revolutionary beginning could still serve as the fertile foundation for new—and large—sociocognitive structures.

In the successors to the citizens' movements, however, we can see a number of ironies. At the republican convention that the rump VPN held in Poprad in October 1991 (where it was decided to transform that association into a party) the former head of the coordinating center's regional committee, Jozef Kučerák, sardonically dismissed those activists who had thought the revolution would empower citizens' initiatives.[128] It was an ironic thing for someone in his historical position to say, of course, but it was even more ironic that ODS and HZDS initially drew much of their support from local activists who wanted to do just this. Though these two political formations, which decisively won the 1992 elections, would later do much to hinder democracy in Czechoslovakia and its successor states, their grassroots founders originally intended them to be means of more effectively realizing the will of the people.[129] It is therefore ironic that once they gained control of state power, they found it difficult to tolerate independent institutions or associations of "citizens' self-defense" that might function as a "control on state power." After August 1992, when ODS and HZDS leaders agreed to split Czechoslovakia despite polls showing that most Czechs and Slovaks wanted to preserve the common state, Klaus and Mečiar rejected a petition signed by two and a half million of the country's fifteen

---

[126] "Vyhlásenie zástupcov Trnavskej iniciatívy VPN," Bratislava, 5 March 1991, in *Smena*, 6 March 1991, p. 3.

[127] "Projev Václava Klause."

[128] Jozef Kučerák, speech at the republican convention of VPN, Poprad, 19 October 1991 (PP: súčasná dokumentácia, box "Súčasná dokumentácia: Voľby '91, '92: Letáky, pozvánky, pohľadnice," folder "Súčasná dokumentácia 1991").

[129] On the dubiously democratic practices of ODS and HZDS following the breakup of Czechoslovakia, see Carol Skalnik Leff, *The Czech and Slovak Republics: Nation versus State* (Boulder, Colo.: Westview, 1996); Abby Innes, *Czechoslovakia: The Short Goodbye* (New Haven, Conn.: Yale University Press, 2001); and Karen Henderson, *Slovakia: The Escape from Invisibility* (London: Routledge, 2002).

million citizens demanding a referendum on the question.[130] The elections, Klaus said, had been a referendum, even though at the time both ODS and HZDS had promised to maintain the federation. There was a certain democratic logic to this position—after June 1992, ODS and HZDS could claim to have won the elections, such that they clearly represented the will of the people, which it would be undemocratic to resist. The ironic thing was that this was no longer the same conception of democracy that Czechoslovak citizens had by and large espoused in 1989—a blend of representative and direct democracy which sought to ensure that inaccuracies in political representation could be corrected as they came to light. It was now a version of representative democracy where the only space for popular involvement was in infrequent elections. The greatest irony of all was that ODS and HZDS—movements arising from the sincere desire of grassroots activists to empower the popular will—ultimately agreed to the dissolution of the ČSFR against the will of a majority of both the Czech and Slovak peoples.

---

[130] Innes, *Czechoslovakia*, p. 211; Michael Kraus and Allison Stanger, "Lessons from the Breakup of Czechoslovakia," in *Irreconcilable Differences? Explaining Czechoslovakia's Dissolution*, edited by Michael Kraus and Allison Stanger (Lanham, Md.: Rowman & Littlefield, 2000), p. 302.

Conclusion

The theme of this book has been the cultural history of the Gentle Revolution, focusing on the experiences of ordinary citizens rather than political elites. The book has argued that the revolution was, most essentially, the genesis of a new sense of community. The experience of coming together in response to the sacrificial dynamics of 17 November was profoundly moving, establishing the perceived new community itself as a transcendent referent—the center of a new symbolic system. This experience generated a new relationship to meaningfulness itself, a new framework for determining meaning that was reflected in a shift from ironic to mythic and romantic modes of perception and rhetoric. The happenings, manifestations, and samizdat publications that characterized the transcendent atmosphere of November and December were thus instruments of the rapid expansion of a new symbolic system, producing rituals, moral codes, and myths that became the hallmarks of a distinct revolutionary culture.

In the course of this collective effervescence, an explosion of discourse occurred in a newly reconstituted public sphere, where the ideals of a new society were articulated. The core ideals with which the revolutionary community identified included nonviolence, self-organization, democracy, fairness, and above all humanness. In the beginning, the collective expression of these ideals exhibited a remarkable coherence; the only ideal that was widely but not universally embraced was that of "socialism." Though these ideas and others all predated the revolution, the revolution transformed the social context for their discussion and interpretation, with the result that this particular combination of ideas was selected as essential to the new community's self-definition, while other ideas, familiar from earlier revolutions in European history, were rejected. The chosen ideas were combined and refined in fresh and creative ways, forming a system of values that was both experientially and positively new.

The revolution ushered in a constitutional moment, when citizens sought to incarnate their collective ideals in social, political, and economic institutions. It was here that conflict, rather than mere disagreement, began to emerge within the revolutionary community, as the tidal wave of democratic practice that the revolution had unleashed crashed against the rocks of elite resistance. The related questions of when to "end" the revolution and who should represent the community in positions of power pitted elites (both old and new) against the revolutionary populace, a cleavage starkly visible in the contrast between the increasingly comedic rhetoric of elites and unflaggingly romantic popular rhetoric. Less publicly, the conflict manifested itself in the behind-the-scenes machinations that swept Havel into the presidential office and the closed-door negotiations that institutionalized an electoral system most of the population did not want. This was the beginning of the exclusion of the *demos* from what had begun as a genuinely democratic revolution.

The cleavage over support for socialism escalated into conflict shortly thereafter, as workers throughout Czechoslovakia began democratizing state enterprises in accordance with their understandings of socialism and democracy, only to meet with increasing resistance from power holders within the enterprises. This culminated in the second half of January with disconcerting appeals from central OF and VPN spokesmen to end the "cadre war" and, at the same time, to end the revolution. It was no coincidence that the "hyphen war" broke out just a few days later, with the national question supplanting the question of socialism at the center of public attention. Both questions were essentially constitutional questions about the nature and boundaries of a community that was in the process of institutionalizing itself afresh.

The impasse resulting from these unexpected conflicts, which continued into the summer and fall of 1990, led to increasing support for radical measures to break the impasse and *decide* the questions. Rhetorically, this growing openness to radicalism was reflected in tragic narratives of the revolution's history, which posited that the revolution had gone off course and which sought to identify the mistakes in order to remedy them. Such narratives went hand in hand with new ideologies—nationalist, neoliberal, and so forth—which purported to explain the errors of the recent past and spell out appropriate solutions. These new ideologies, moreover, were metaphysically violent. They did not call for armed conflict or terror to achieve their aims, but they nonetheless increasingly advocated the forceful exclusion of individuals and groups who represented a danger to the pure social system they envisioned, even at the risk of violating explicit or implicit rules. Ironically, the measures taken—from the purging of Civic Forum to the sacrifice of the federation—entailed a weakening of the kind of democracy that the revolution had sought to empower and an exclusion of the people from the meaningful participation in their government to which they had aspired in 1989.

Insofar as this sequence of developments is concerned, what happened in Czechoslovakia was not unique in the history of revolutions. As historians of the eighteenth-century French and twentieth-century Russian revolutions have demonstrated, the revolutionary break is always followed by an explosion of popular democratic enthusiasm, but once new elites have been chosen as representatives of popular power, they always promulgate policies that restrict it.[1] Theorists of revolution from Trotsky to Goldstone have noted that revolutions generally begin with a euphoric break concomitant with the collapse of old regime authority, that initially moderates rise to power who seek to compromise with agents or structures of the old regime, and that moderates are then supplanted by radicals who implement partisan policies in the name of the people, the nation, or the working class, until a reaction produces at least a partial return to moderation.[2] In Czechoslovakia, we can see this pattern repeated with the romantic, heroic period of November and December leading to the moderate Government of National Understanding and the still moderate Government of National Sacrifice following the June 1990 elections. The "sacrifice," however, proved inefficacious, ultimately allowing the accession to power of the more radical and partisan formations, ODS and HZDS, which were then relatively free to implement their policies in the name of "the nation" until the electoral reactions of 1998 restored a greater degree of pluralism, if still not exactly the democracy that had been envisioned in 1989.

While similarities in the temporal patterns of revolutions have been widely noted, an investigation of the cultural history of revolutions allows us to identify the deeper, semiotic processes that produce this pattern. Revolutions, in general, would seem to be reconfigurations of sacrality, re-creating the symbolic systems that are cultures on the basis of a new and transcendent experience of communion. The force of this experience can find expression only in mythic or romantic rhetoric— hence the universally heroic narratives of a revolutionary break. The emphasis on communion in these early days fosters tolerance, which allows for formation of such moderate and inclusive governments as the constitutional monarchy that governed France until 1792 and the Provisional Government that held nominal power in

---

[1] See, for example, Orlando Figes and Boris Kolonitskii, *Interpreting the Russian Revolution: The Language and Symbols of 1917* (New Haven, Conn.: Yale University Press, 1999); Lynn Hunt, *Politics, Culture, and Class in the French Revolution* (Berkeley: University of California Press, 1984); Mona Ozouf, *Festivals and the French Revolution*, trans. Alan Sheridan (Cambridge, Mass.: Harvard University Press, 1988); and Mark Steinberg, *Voices of Revolution, 1917* (New Haven, Conn.: Yale University Press, 2001).

[2] Leon Trotsky, *The Permanent Revolution, and Results and Prospects* (New York: Merit Publishers, 1969); Jack Goldstone, "The Comparative and Historical Study of Revolutions," in *Revolutions: Theoretical, Comparative, and Historical Studies*, 3rd ed., ed. Jack Goldstone (Belmont, Calif.: Wadsworth, 2008), pp. 2–4.

Russia for most of 1917. The inability or unwillingness of these formations to appreciate the urgency of the constitutional moment, however—reflected in their promulgation of comedic narratives of a completed revolution despite popular momentum to continue it—opens space for radicals. The radicals reject the moderates' conciliatory policies, advocating more exclusivist programs to raise the fortunes of a more narrowly defined but nonetheless sacred "people," "class," or "nation" at the expense of "aristocrats," "*burzhoii,*" "Leftists," "federalists," or others who had "betrayed" the revolution, threatening it with tragic failure to achieve its original, transcendent ideals. Once they acquire sufficient popular support to seize power, nothing any longer keeps the radicals from implementing their programs, but the essentially reductionist nature of the thinking behind these programs inevitably disillusions many of their erstwhile supporters, who increasingly find their vision of democracy thwarted by the impersonal mechanisms the radicals set in motion. Eventually, this leads to a reaction, as well as to a greater or lesser popular ambivalence about the revolutionary process in general.[3]

Even though the *demos* emerged at the end of the Czechoslovak revolution less powerful than it was at the beginning, it would be too much to say that it was defeated or that the revolution "committed suicide." The symbolic system that the revolution had generated remained, as did the sacred center of this system—the people itself. Thus it is that the revolution still serves as a transcendent reference point against which all subsequent social and political phenomena are judged. The new regimes in Czechoslovakia's successor states are considered legitimate (rather than merely tolerated) only insofar as they refer back to the revolutionary, founding moment, when the entire "nation" assembled and collectively articulated its highest values and its expectations for future development.[4] The source of political legitimacy in the Czech and Slovak republics lies not in their written constitutions (which were in any case never submitted to popular vote) but in the memory of the collective effervescence of 1989. Thus it is that the memory of 1989 remains heavily politicized, for ultimately it remains a source of power. Today, narratives of the revolution's history are inescapably myths of legitimacy, connecting present-day institutions back to the sacred founding moment.

Anniversary commemorations every 17 November—a state holiday in both successor states—provide stark illustration of this phenomenon, from the "Thank you, now leave" initiative that former student strikers of 1989 launched in 1999 (calling on prominent Czech politicians to resign), to the "Inventory of Democracy" that matriculated Czech students conducted between the nineteenth and twentieth anniversaries, to the Slovak "Gorilla" protests against systemic politi-

[3] See, for example, François Gendron, *The Gilded Youth of Thermidor* (Montreal: McGill-Queen's University Press, 1993).
[4] The former student strike committee member Jiří Křečan articulated this image at a fifteenth-anniversary roundtable at Palacký University in Olomouc.

cal corruption that took place on 17 November 2012. The fifteenth-anniversary commemorations were relatively quiet in comparison, but perhaps for this very reason can be instructive. In Prague, disagreement over the proper way to commemorate 17 November 1989 led to a clash that dramatically mirrored the events of that date. The mayor, Pavel Bém, decreed that the anniversary should not be celebrated "just by wreath laying" and arranged for a concert to take place in the middle of Národní třída, on the spot where the "massacre" had occurred fifteen years previously. For those who still wished to light candles and place wreaths at the memorial under the arches, Bém made sure that even they were required to celebrate "Národní differently": next to the memorial he had a flashing blue police light installed, along with life-size posters of riot police and a banner with the letters VB (for *Veřejná bezpečnost*, the Communist-era "public security" forces). Meanwhile, however, students from several Czech universities planned a march to follow the route of their predecessors fifteen years previously, beginning at Albertov and continuing along Národní to Wenceslas Square, in protest against "apathy to the end of time" (an allusion to the Communist-era slogan "with the Soviet Union to the end of time").

Evening twilight was passing and the concert had already started as the student procession turned the corner from the embankment onto Národní. Participants wearing tricolor pins carried candles, Chinese lanterns, and numerous placards identifying their schools ("Ostrava University," "medical faculty," etc.) or their political positions ("Klaus minions belong in trash cans," "Don't talk to Communists," "Let us not be apathetic," etc.). At the head of the procession they bore flags and a banner with the motive of their march: "1939—We do not forget—1989." Though the majority of the marchers were students, there were many middle-aged and elderly persons among them. Aleš Brichta and his band were performing as the procession arrived at the concert site, crying, "Now we're here!" Though the crowd around the bandstand was not more than perhaps a dozen persons deep, the bandstand itself was so large that, together with the crowd, it effectively blocked the students' path. The rock music continued but was soon drowned out by students booing, whistling, and shouting, "Let us pass!" This aural conflict continued for several minutes before Bém himself appeared on the bandstand, proclaiming his interpretation of the revolution's history as complete, its goals fully realized, and telling the students they were misguided. The speech met with loud boos and cries of "fúúúj!"

While Bém was speaking, sirens sounded from behind the procession, and those who looked back saw that three or four police cars were following the marchers up the street, pressing them forward. "We have empty hands!" cried one of the students, half in jest, half in confused dismay. It certainly seemed that an impasse had been reached not without parallels to that of fifteen years previously. Once again, a student procession found its path to Wenceslas Square blocked. This time, of course, it was not armed riot police in the service of a violently repressive regime that blocked the way; rather, it was the mayor's bread-and-circus attempt to create "Národní differently." Different methods, but perhaps the same ends? The police, inexplicably pressing the crowd forward, provided a disturbing reminder of continuity.

The booing stopped when one of the students was allowed onto the platform. He gave a short speech, the point of which was "there is no one to vote for" and which earned widespread applause. Thereafter Bém again took the floor, this time encouraging the concertgoers to yield a path to the students. "Let us show them that we are a liberal and free state," he said. A student on the corner of Národní and Spalená—where with police assistance a way was now being made—led the procession from the concert with the cry "Students march on!"

When the neatly regrouped marchers at last entered Wenceslas Square from Vodičkova, they proceeded to the statue of Saint Wenceslas (enclosed for the occasion in scaffolding and tarp), while several broke off from the crowd to light candles at the memorial to Jan Palach and Jan Zajíc (students who immolated themselves in 1969 to protest their compatriots' apathy). From a small, improvised platform and with the help of a weak microphone, several speakers addressed the assembly, including the 1989 student Šimon Pánek and the former dissidents Jiřina Šiklová and Tomáš Halík, as well as two of the student organizers of the event. One of these, Jan Hron, began by noting that he and most people present had been small children in 1989 and so knew about what had happened then only through narration (*vyprávění*). Nonetheless, he claimed that "the legacy of 17 November is alive and relevant to the present," and he lamented the demise of the ideals of 1989—particularly the fact that few people were willing to do things for the public good. He echoed Šiklová's claim that Czechs were living through a "new normalization" and rebuked people who thought that democracy privileged a focus on private well-being.[5] Hron's colleague then voiced his opinion that the most important slogan of the day was "there is no one to vote for" and argued against simply blaming the Communists or seeing the continuing existence of the Communist Party as the root problem. The root problem, he said, was that the other parties presented no real alternative. The meeting ended with Jaroslav Hutka leading the crowd in two of his songs, followed by the national anthem and an unplanned moment of silence.[6]

---

[5] Šiklová has developed this view in "Everyday Democracy in the Czech Republic: Disappointments or New Morals in a Time of Neo-Normalization," in *The Contemporary Moral Fabric in Contemporary Societies*, ed. Grażyna Skąpska and Annamaria Orla-Bukowska (Leiden: Brill, 2003), pp. 93–101. See also Václav Bělohradský et al., *Kritika depolitizovaného rozumu: Úvahy (nejen) o nové normalizaci* (Všeň: Grimmus, 2010).

[6] This narrative has been pieced together from evidence presented in "Národní 'jinak'," *Samopal revue*, no. 12, http://www.hutka.cz/new/html/sam12c.htm; Tereza Nejedlá and Filip Fuxa, "Praha si připomněla patnácté výročí 17. listopadu demonstracemi," *I-Forum*, http://ktv.mff.cuni.cz/IFORUM-1488.html; Tomáš Pánek, "Národní jinak," *O Životě*, 22 November 2004, http://ozivote.cz/clanky/2004/11/22/narodni-

Though this incident was clearly telling, hardly any mention of it appeared in the mainstream Czech media the next day. Though the leading dailies devoted pages upon pages to empty and repetitive statements about the revolution by prominent political figures like Klaus, Havel, and the various party chairmen, coverage of nonelite reflections on the meaning of contemporary history was limited to a few short and superficial paragraphs. As was usual at the time, Slovak media provided markedly wider coverage, reporting at length on student appropriation of 17 November for protests against government proposals to introduce university tuition fees; publishing or broadcasting interviews and debates on the meaning of 1989 with former revolutionary activists, even if they had never held political posts; and even devoting attention to recollections and commemorative activities outside the capital.

At one of these roundtables, a colorful tetralogue emerged. Ján Budaj, one of VPN's most popular spokesmen in 1989, emphasized that

> today we can be self-confident citizens of Slovakia and at the same time be in the European Union because we remember that here we acquired democracy by common exertion, that it was not some kind of agreement that a few Communists transferred power to some other group and people passively learned that the regime had changed. Here the citizen actively participated and he *lends* legitimacy to politicians. . . . Let us never be ashamed that we lived that experience of freedom with emotion, let us not be ashamed of the ideals we had then, because without ideals no society can have values on which it can stand.

Anton Popovič, one of the most prominent student activists in 1989, lamented "a certain retreat from the substance and ideals of November, that [new elites] began trading with the Communist Party in a kind of pragmatic fashion. . . . From my perspective we took a detour. . . . People dispersed from the squares, the euphoria faded away and pragmatists led us to the situation we're in today."

> What is for me most important about 1989 is that I had one basic illusion— not an ideal, an illusion—that when the opponents of the regime would come to parliaments and governments they would take from their drawers projects, laws, and norms—that they simply had it somehow coordinated. I study music . . . and music has taught me that when things do not fall together from every side, then it simply doesn't sound, the miracle of music doesn't come about. . . . So for me it is essentially a question of an expert approach, how to

jinak; "15 let poté: Studenti proti lhostejnosti," http://strada.ff.cuni.cz/listopad/tisk/tisk_zprava.doc; Vlasta Remišová, "Studenti na Václaváku," *O Živote*, 19 November 2004, http://ozivote.cz/clanky/2004/11/19/stu denti-na-vaclavskym-vaclavaku/; and the author's eyewitness experience.

look from the perspective of humanity's most up-to-date knowledge, i.e. not with models from 1950 or 1930, with technologies that long, long ago basically became part of the past. It's just that political elites have absolutely no interest, and equally no knowledge, of what the present offers, in 2004. For me it is actually a slow, mass raid on a blind alley—for it is not a question just of Slovakia, it is a model that we can now see in many countries at many levels. The manner according to which foreign affairs are resolved, what kind of communications there are, how ethnic conflicts are resolved—these are all outdated methods that will never bring us what we seek, and that is harmony.

Ján Čarnogurský, a former minister in the Government of National Understanding and founder of Slovakia's Christian Democratic Movement, countered that Popovič lived in "an artificial world of intellectuals, artists, literary critics, and so forth, who, let us say, sat in coffeehouses or somewhere in libraries and imagined what the best society would be like, but the real world is such that then there was, well, even though the majority wanted change, clear will for some kind of throwing out of Communists was not there." Čarnogurský added that "Slovakia isn't so bad," citing as an example the recently introduced flat tax and how it was making Slovakia the wonder of Europe. Into this dispute Zuzana Mistríková, another of the most prominent students of 1989, interjected something of a synthetic perspective. Addressing Popovič, she pointed out that "if those ideals [of November] were that this society should be democratic and have genuinely secret, direct, and such elections as we took to be the foundation of democracy, then this has come to pass, and the result of these elections is that that man [Ševc, a Communist] is sitting in parliament. I don't understand it either." Continuing after an interruption, she added,

> We had some basic ideals formulated, all of which have more or less been fulfilled; it's just that their concrete form and content do not always wholly match what each of us on the Square imagined. But I'm afraid that if what we can call the institutional instruments have been created—we have democracy, we influence affairs directly with our decisions—then it would seem that the fulfillment of our ideals is up to each one of us, even though I understand that not all of us know how to directly influence things that upset us in society, but we probably cannot find another way. . . . The fact is that the social regime is built the way it is built, and another way of influencing it, with the instruments that were created in November, does not exist.[7]

The fifteenth-anniversary commemorations in Prague and Bratislava illustrate once again the variety of modes according to which unfolding history can be nar-

[7] *Regionálne noviny*, Slovenská televízia, 17 November 2004.

rated and the political import of each alternative. Ján Budaj demonstrated that it is still possible to articulate a romantic interpretation of 1989, though to do so requires that one focus squarely on 1989 itself. (Indeed, when Budaj later in the debate was asked to consider the political situation of 2004 in relation to 1989, he adopted a position close to Popovič's, though he still insisted that the revolution had been "successful," even if he did not think "that we should be satisfied.") Popovič and participants in the student march in Prague expressed essentially tragic interpretations of the revolution, holding up the bright "ideals of November" and asking why the situation in 2004 did not correspond. Bém and Čarnogurský provided comedic narratives of their countries' development since 1989, essentially arguing—with greater or lesser flamboyance—that all's well that ends well. Mistríková, finally, offered an ironic (though definitely not satirical) understanding of the same history, recognizing the failure to make reality "harmonize" with the ideal, but suggesting that "like a child who is told three times he will burn himself, but nonetheless tries on his own, so we somehow had to follow this course."[8]

All these interpreters of the revolution, both in Prague and Bratislava, were socially successful "winners of the transition" and active participants in the public sphere, if not in politics narrowly defined. It is perhaps significant, however, that the proponents of comedic interpretations were all active or retired politicians, whereas none of the narrators of tragedy had ever held political office for more than a few months. The sharpest conflict, moreover, was precisely between the comedic and tragic viewpoints. In Prague the conflict was quite vivid, recalling even the conflict that had taken place on the same site fifteen years previously; in Bratislava it was more amicable, but it is worth noting that Čarnogurský and Popovič were the only ones not to use the familiar second person with each other. Comedic narration, as we have seen, tends to support a relatively conservative approach to political engagement, insisting on acceptance of existing mechanisms and structures. Tragedy, by contrast, hopes for the radical transcendence of these same mechanisms and structures to attain others more likely to bring "harmony." Disputes over the proper way to remember 1989 are thus simultaneously disputes over power—not necessarily over *who* should occupy positions of power, but how power should be constituted.

In a struggle over the nature of power where divergent interpretations of contemporary history are important weapons, it is inevitable that conflict over the way to remember should involve conscious or unconscious attempts to determine *what* is remembered. One of the most remarkable findings of the research underlying this book has been the selectiveness of memory—and forgetting—among Czechs

---

[8] Ibid. According to Frye, "irony with little satire is the non-heroic residue of tragedy, centering on the theme of a puzzling defeat." Northrop Frye, *The Anatomy of Criticism: Four Essays* (Princeton, N.J.: Princeton University Press, 1957), p. 224.

and Slovaks since 1989. From forgetfulness of the original extent of Civic Forum in Slovakia to silence on the question of revolutionary upheaval at the local level, public memory in Czechoslovakia's successor states has been characterized by a striking impoverishment. In both countries there has been a tendency to reduce the history of the revolution to the history of elite negotiations in the capitals, with popular engagement counting for little more than window dressing. This pattern of memory and forgetting naturally tends to facilitate both comedic and satirical interpretations of the revolution. It reinforces comedic emplotments by assigning meaningful public roles only to recognized elite actors, and it resonates with satirical emplotments by reinforcing the idea that there was no revolution—understood as a popular movement from below that acts consequentially to transform the social and political system in accordance with popular ideals. Needless to say, these are the interpretations most conducive to those who wield power in the Czech and Slovak republics today, with comedy championed by elites like Klaus and Bém, who came to power as a result of the revolution, and satire preferred by former members of the Communist Party like Slovakia's Róbert Fico, who once claimed not to have noticed any fundamental change in 1989.[9] It would be too much to claim that the post-1989 power elite has itself determined the memory of 1989, but the tendency of the media to give preferential coverage to elite interpretations has undoubtedly channeled public discussion down narrow paths of the elites' choosing.

The power of political elites to determine truth is constrained, however, and nothing shows this better than the fact that in contemporary debates on the nature of power and the constitution of society, the revolution of 1989 remains a central referent which even those who at the time noticed nothing "fundamental" cannot ignore. The interest of power holders in particular narratives of the revolution results from the fact that particular narratives reinforce perception of particular relationships between themselves and the sacred moment of foundation. The various interpretations of 1989 essentially serve as legitimizing—or delegitimizing—myths. Of the mythoi underpinning interpretive frameworks, only satire (militant irony) challenges the sacred to which legitimacy refers, and though satire is now common in Czech and Slovak discourse about 1989, the anniversary commemorations demonstrate that the revolution remains meaningful for a significant portion of Czech and Slovak citizens. Indeed, even Fico—after becoming Slovakia's prime minister—was forced to acknowledge "the November Gentle Revolution" as the moment when "we began to build the Slovak Republic as a state governed by the rule of law."[10]

Though the gravest threat to democratic political culture lies with satirical interpretations of the revolution, since these tend to promote political apathy, the most virulent conflict remains that between proponents of the comedic and tragic

---

[9] "When I look back, I do not find that any fundamental change occurred in my life in 1989." Quoted in *Domino fórum* (Bratislava), no. 50 (2000).

[10] Quoted in "Vláda si podľa Fica ctí výročie pohybu k demokratizácii," *Sme*, 16 November 2007.

interpretations. The struggle here is essentially a struggle over the nature of de-mocracy—a struggle that recurs in the aftermath of every democratic revolution. In her study of revolutionary France, Lynn Hunt observed that "democracy was never efficient; it was usually unpredictable and always potentially dangerous. As a consequence, the modernizers, those who valued rationalization and standard-ization *above all else*, flocked to the Napoleonic banner instead. It was possible to be modern without believing in democratic republicanism."[11] There is of course no counterpart to Napoleon in the Czech and Slovak republics today, but the es-sential conflict between the deontological imperative of democracy and pragmatic concerns to achieve results efficiently has nonetheless characterized the revolution of 1989 and its aftermath, as it characterizes all polities where political legitimacy derives from a sacred referent that is "the people." We have encountered this tension in the way Havel's initial presidency was engineered, in the reluctance of elites in the capitals to involve provincial colleagues in decision making, and finally in the breakup of the Czech and Slovak Federative Republic against the wishes of the majority of its citizens. Had we continued the story into the mid-1990s and beyond, we would have discovered many more examples.

Václav Bartuška, a journalism student at Charles University in 1989 and a mem-ber of the parliamentary commission investigating the crimes of 17 November, wrote in his memoir that "from my own experience I now know that in times of struggle for democracy there is no time for democracy."[12] Bartuška was not the first to express this thought; it has been known for centuries. We can, however, ask, If in revolution there is no time for democracy, when is there?

---

[11] Hunt, *Politics, Culture, and Class*, p. 211 (emphasis in original).
[12] Václav Bartuška, *Polojasno: Pátrání po vinících 17. listopadu 1989* (Prague: Ex libris, 1990), p. 6.

Chronology

1989	*November 17*	The Prague "massacre."
	November 18	Beginning of student and theater strikes. Founding of the Independent Hungarian Initiative (FMK).
	November 19	Founding of Public against Violence (VPN) and Civic Forum (OF).
	November 26	First official negotiations between Prime Minister Adamec and Civic Forum.
	November 27	General Strike.
	Late November	District and municipal roundtables begin meeting.
	December 3	The "15:5" government.
	Early December	Beginning of workplace democratization.
	December 7	Adamec resigns. Vice Premier Čalfa replaces him.
	December 8	First meeting of "decisive political forces" at the federal level.
	December 10	President Husák swears in the "Government of National Understanding," then resigns. Theater strikes end. Presidential candidates declare themselves.
	December 28	Alexander Dubček co-opted into the Federal Assembly and made chairman.
	December 29	The Federal Assembly elects Havel president.

1990	*January 1*	President Havel amnesties most prisoners.
	January 3	End of student strikes.
	January 19	Petr Pithart's speech against "revolutionary methods."
	January 23	Beginning of the "Hyphen War."
	February 6	Pithart (OF) becomes prime minister of the Czech Republic.
	February 26	Soviet troops begin withdrawing from Czechoslovakia.
	March 1	Slovak nationalists invade the National Council building in Bratislava, preventing the election of Ján Budaj (VPN) as chairman of the Slovak National Council.
	April 11	General strike for nationalization of Communist Party property.
	April 20	The Czechoslovak Socialist Republic is renamed the Czech and Slovak Federative Republic.
	June 8–9	Federal and republican elections.
	June 27	The "Government of National Sacrifice" is formed by a coalition of OF, VPN, and Slovak Christian Democrats. Čalfa (now VPN) reappointed federal prime minister. Vladimír Mečiar (VPN) named prime minister of the Slovak Republic.
	June 28	Pithart reappointed prime minister of the Czech Republic.
	July 5	The Federal Assembly reelects Havel president, then joins the Czech and Slovak national councils in a two-month recess.
	October 13	Václav Klaus elected chairman of Civic Forum.
	October 20	Trnava Initiative criticizes VPN leadership.
	October 25	The Slovak National Council rejects the Matica slovenská's proposed language law and passes the governing coalition's more moderate version.
	November 17	Antagonistic commemorations of the first anniversary.
	November 23–24	District and municipal elections result in partial Communist resurgence.
	December 8–9	An OF "working meeting" in Olomouc votes to transform the association into a party.
1991	*January 26*	Beginning of small privatization.
	February 23	Civic Forum splits into Civic Democratic Party (ODS) and Civic Movement.
	March 5	Founding of VPN-For a Democratic Slovakia (VPN-ZDS).
	April 23	The presidium of the Slovak National Council dismisses Mečiar from his post as Slovak premier, replacing him with the Christian Democrat Ján Čarnogurský.

April 27	The Movement for a Democratic Slovakia (HZDS) breaks away from VPN.
November 1	Launching of large privatization.
1992 *June 5–6*	ODS and HZDS emerge as victors in federal and republican elections.
June 24	Mečiar again named Slovak premier.
July 2	Klaus becomes Czech premier; a marginal politician (Jan Strásky, ODS) is named federal prime minister.
July 23	At a meeting in Bratislava, Klaus and Mečiar agree to split Czechoslovakia.
August 5	Klaus and Mečiar definitively reject a petition, signed by more than 2.5 million of Czechoslovakia's 15 million citizens, demanding a referendum on the federation's future.
December 31	The Czech and Slovak Federative Republic dissolves at midnight.

Bibliography

Archives

Archiv Masarykovy univerzity, Brno
    Fond G38 "Koordinačný stávkový výbor brněnských vysokých škol"
    Fond G39 "Stávkový výbor Filozofické fakulty UJEP (1989–1990)"
Archiv města Ostravy, Ostrava
    Sbírka soudobé dokumentace
Divadelní ústav, Prague
    Sbírka "Pražský podzim '89"
Fórum Intézet, Šamorín
    A Magyar Polgári Párt (Független Magyar Kezdeményezés) irattár (1989–98)
Historické múzeum Slovenského národného múzea, Bratislava
    Zbierka plagátov
Hoover Institution Archives, Stanford, California
    Czech Subject Collection
    Slovak Subject Collection
Slovenský národný archív, Bratislava
    Archív VPN
Státní okresní archiv Benešov
    Sbírka soudobé dokumentace
Státní okresní archiv Beroun
    Fond "ONV Beroun"
    Fond "OV KSČ Beroun"
    Sbírka soudobé dokumentace

Státní okresní archiv Brno-venkov, Rajhrad
  Sbírka soudobé dokumentace, sign. F-8.04
Státní okresní archiv Břeclav, Mikulov
  Fond "ONV Břeclav"
  Sbírka fotografie
Státní okresní archiv Cheb
  Fond 1063, SB46 "Občanské fórum"
Státní okresní archiv České Budějovice
  Kronika města Českých Budějovic
  Sbírka dokumentace K1139
Státní okresní archiv Český Krumlov
  Sbírka dokumentace
Státní okresní archiv Domažlice, Horšovský Týn
  Sbírka soudobé dokumentace
Státní okresní archiv Jablonec nad Nisou
  Fond "MěNV Jablonec nad Nisou"
  Sbírka soudobé dokumentace, 1989–1991
Státní okresní archiv Kolín
  Sbírka 1989
Státní okresní archiv Kutná Hora
  Sbírka dokumentace
Státní okresní archiv Louny
  Fond 569 "Sbírka dokumentů k 17. 11. 1989—30. 11. 1990 v Lounech"
  Fond 633 "OF Louny, 1989–1991"
  Fond "OV KSČ Louny"
Státní okresní archiv Olomouc
  Sbírka soudobé dokumentace, sign. 148–22: "Studentský stávkový výbor Olomouc,
    1989–1990B."
Státní okresní archiv Opava
  Sbírka dokumentačních materiálů—rok 1989
Státní okresní archiv Pardubice
  Fond "Občanské fórum Pardubice"
Státní okresní archiv Prostějov
  Sbírka soudobé dokumentace
Státní okresní archiv Přerov
  Inv. č. 355 "Dokumentace k listopadovým událostem roku 1989"
Státní okresní archiv Semily
  Fond "OF Semily"
Státník okresní archiv Šumperk
  Fond "Občanské fórum Šumperk"
Státní okresní archiv Tábor
  Sbírka soudobé dokumentace, sign. CI8f: Drobné tisky
Státní okresní archiv Trutnov
  Fond "Koordinační centrum OF Trutnov"
Státní okresní archiv Uherské Hradiště
  Sbírky UH

Státní okresní archiv Zlín
  Fond "Divadlo pracujících"
  Sbírka plakátů
Štátny archív v Banskej Bystrici, pobočka Banská Bystrica
  Fond "ONV Banská Bystrica"
  Materiály získané od hnutia Verejnosť proti násiliu v Banskej Bystrici, 1989
  Predvolebné materiály politických strán a hnutí k voľbám r. 1990
  Zbierka písomností získaných od študentov Pedagogickej fakulty v Banskej Bystrici, 1989–1990
  Zbierka plagátov vyvesených v Banskej Bystrici v dňoch od 23.11. 1989 do 27.12. 1989
  Zbierka plagátov získaných od študentov Pedagogickej fakulty v Banskej Bystrici, 1989–1990
Štátny archív v Banskej Bystrici, pobočka Veľký Krtíš
  Fond "MsNV Veľký Krtíš"
  Fond "ONV Veľký Krtíš"
  Zbierka fotografie
  Zbierka plagátov a letákov
Štátny archív v Bratislave, pobočka Šaľa
  Súčasná dokumentácia
Štátny archív v Bratislave, pobočka Trenčín
  Súčasná dokumentácia
Štátny archív v Bytči, pobočka Považská Bystrica
  Fond G1 "VPN Pov. Bystrica"
  Súčasná dokumentácia
Štátny archív v Košiciach, pobočka Košice
  Fond "ONV Košice-vidiek"
  Zbierka z Nežnej revolúcie
Štátny archív v Košiciach, pobočka Michalovce
  Fond "MsNV Michalovce"
  Fond "MsNV Sobrance"
  Fond "ONV Michalovce"
Štátny archív v Levoči, pobočka Poprad, Spišská Sobota
  Súčasná dokumentácia
Štátny archív v Nitre, pobočka Komárno
  Fond "MNV Vojnice"
  Fond "MsNV Komárno"
  Fond "ONV Komárno"
  Zbierka plagátov
Štátny archív v Nitre, pobočka Levice
  Fond "MsNV Levice"
  Fond "ONV Levice"
  Súdobá dokumentácia
Štátny archív v Nitre, pobočka Topoľčany
  Fond "MsNV Bánovce nad Bebravou"
  Fond "MsNV Partizánske"
  Fond "MsNV Topoľčany"
  Fond "ONV Topoľčany"

Štátny archív v Prešove, pobočka Svidník
    Zbierka plagátov, letákov a drobnej tlače
Ústav pro soudobé dějiny, Prague
    Archiv KC OF
Zemplínske múzeum, Michalovce
    Zbierka plagátov a letákov

Bulletins

Akcia (Košice)
Bleskový bulletin (Prague)
Bojler (Prague)
Breznianska verejnosť (Brezno)
Bulvár (Prague)
Coproto (Prague)
Domažlické inForum
Ekonóm (Bratislava)
EM '89 (Prague)
Fámyzdat (Prague)
Fórum (Banská Bystrica)
Fórum (Kutná Hora)
Fórum (Levice)
Fórum (Prievidza)
Hajcman (Ostrava)
Hlasatel (Ostrava)
Hlava '89 (Prague)
Hosť do domu (Bánovce nad Bebravou)
I-Fórum (Košice)
Informační bulletin Občanského fóra Cheb, which mutated to *Občanské fórum Cheb*
Informační bulletin celostátního koordinačního výboru vysokých škol (Prague)
Informační leták (Most)
Informační servis (Prague)
Informační servis OF okresu Beroun
Informační zpravodaj OF (Horšovský Týn)
Informačný spravodaj Pedagogickej fakulty v Banskej Bystrici
Informátor (Ostrava)
InForum (Prague)
Jediné přání (České Budějovice)
Kalamář (České Budějovice)
Kassai Polgári Fórum híradója (Košice)
Kontakt (Louny)
Královédvorské fórum (Dvůr Králové nad Labem)
Krkonošský len (Trutnov)

Kroměřížské fórum
Lánské noviny (Lány)
Létající ryba (Prague)
Martinská verejnosť
Moravský jih (Břeclav)
Mostfórum (Most)
Náš hlas (Liberec)
Nezávislí (Prague)
Nezávislost (Uherské Hradiště)
Nos (Chomutov)
Novomestská verejnosť (Nové Mesto nad Váhom)
Nový život (Banská Bystrica)
Občanské fórum Litoměřice
Občasník studentů Filosofické fakulty (Prague)
Oběžník (Prague)
Ohajská verejnosť (Dolný Ohaj)
Olomoucký zpravodaj
Piešťanska verejnosť
Plzeňský student
Poslední zvonění (Brno)
Post-fórum (Postoloprty)
Pravda vyděsí (Brno)
Prešovská zmena, which mutated to *Premeny*
Profórum (Jablonec nad Nisou)
Proto (Prague)
Přetlak (Olomouc)
Psáno brkem (Louny)
Púchovská verejnosť
Rakofórum (Rakovník)
Reff: Revue filozofické fakulty (Brno)
Romano lav (Prague)
Růžové právo (Prague)
Sami o sobě (Havířov)
Servis O. F. v Českých Budějovicích, which mutated to *Informační servis*
Situace '89 (Prague)
Slovo (Košice)
Slovo za VPN (Hubová)
Sokolovské infórum (Sokolov)
Správa (Poprad)
Spravodaj Kresťanskodemokratických klubov
Spravodaj Občianskeho fóra Košice
Spravodaj študentov PF UPJŠ (Košice)
Spravodajca (Topoľčany)
Spravodajca (Vranov nad Topľou)

Stávkové noviny (Brno)
Studentské mlýny (Brno)
Studentský list (Pardubice)
Szabad Kapacitás (Bratislava)
Šanca pre Gemer (Rimavská Sobota)
Štiavnická verejnosť (Banská Štiavnica)
Šudák (Ostrava)
Študentský slobodník (Košice)
Telefax VPN
Trenčianska verejnosť
Úfórum (Ústí nad Orlicí)
Verejnosť informuje verejnosť (Partizánske)
Veřejné mínění (Brno)
Věstník Občanského fóra pedagogů a Učitelského fóra okresu Louny
Voknoviny (Prague)
Vysokoškolský zpravodaj (Liberec)
Zmena (Bratislava)
Zpráva (Brno)
Zpravodaj (Trutnov)
Zpravodaj brněnského Občanského fóra
Zpravodaj členům KSČ a občanům okresu Šumperk
Zpravodaj Galerie B. Rejta a OF Louny, which mutated to *Zpravodaj OF Louny*
Zpravodaj krajského informačního centra Občanského fóra v Plzni
Zpravodaj MSS (Prague)
Zpravodaj Občanského fóra OkSS Zlín
Zpravodaj Občanského fóra v Prostějově
Zpravodaj OF CHZ (Litvínov)
Zpravodaj stávkového výboru PdF UJEP
Zpravodaj stávkových výborů
Zvon (Spišská Nová Ves)

Newspapers

Akcia (Košice), which mutated to *Košická akcia*
Budovatel (Beroun)
Budovatel (Chrudim)
Cesta Vysočiny (Havlíčkův Brod)
Cieľ (Žilina)
Csalloköz (Dunajská streda)
Českolipský nástup
Domino fórum (Bratislava)
Dukla (Svidník)
Dunaj (Komárno), the Hungarian version of which mutated to *Dunatáj*

Echo (Bratislava)

Echo Záhoria (Malacky)

Fórum (Prague)

Garamvölgye (Levice)

Gemerské zvesti (Rimavská Sobota)

Haladás (Veľký Krtíš)

Hlas (Louny)

Hlas Rokycanska

Hornonitrianska verejnosť (Prievidza)

Hraničář (Cheb)

Hraničář (Prachatice)

Ipeľ (Lučenec)

Jiskra (Benešov)

Jiskra (Český Krumlov)

Jiskra (Děčín)

Jiskra (Jihlava)

Jiskra (Třebič)

Jiskra Orlicka (Ústí nad Orlicí)

Jiskra Rychnovska (Rychnov nad Kněžnou)

Kladenská záře

Krkonošská pravda (Trutnov)

Kroměřížská jiskra

Kultúrny život (Bratislava)

Kupředu (Kolín)

Kysuce (Čadca)

Lidové noviny (Prague)

Liptov (Liptovský Mikuláš)

Ľubovnianske noviny (Stará Ľubovňa)

Moravské noviny (Brno)

Nap (Bratislava)

Nástup (Chomutov)

Nástup (Pelhřimov)

Náš život (Vyškov)

Naše novosti (Nové Zámky)

Naše pravda (Gottwaldov/Zlín)

Naše slovo (Šumperk), which mutated to *Moravský sever*

Necenzurované noviny (Brno)

New York Times

Nitrianska verejnosť

Nitriansky hlas

Nové Domažlicko, which mutated to *Domažlicko*

Nové Hradecko (Hradec Králové)

Nové Klatovsko

Nové Mělnicko

Nové Opavsko, which mutated to *Naše Opavsko*

Nové Přerovsko

Nové Příbramsko

Nové Svitavsko

Nové Valašsko (Vsetín)

Noviny Jablonecka (Jablonec nad Nisou)

Nový čas (Náchod)

Nový život (Blansko)

Nový život (České Budějovice)

Nový život (Plzeň-jih)

Nymbursko

Občanský deník (Prague)

Obzor (Považská Bystrica)

Orava (Dolný Kubín)

Ozveny Tatier (Poprad)

Ozvěny-Echo (Frýdek-Místek)

Palcát (Tábor)

Pezinská verejnosť

Piešťanská verejnosť

Poddukelské noviny (Bardejov)

Podtatranské noviny (Poprad)

Podvihorlatské noviny (Humenné)

Pohronie (Levice)

Pokrok (Veľký Krtíš)

Pravda (Bratislava)

Prešovské noviny

Prieboj (Prievidza)

Proud (Litoměřice)

Předvoj (Jičín)

Reflex (Komárno)

Respekt (Prague)

Rovnost (Brno)

Rozkvět (Nový Jíčin)

Roztocké noviny (Roztoky u Prahy)

Rozvoj (Most)

Rozvoj (Plzeň-sever)

Rozvoj (Rakovník)

Rozvoj (Semily)

Sever (Ústí nad Labem)

Slobodný občan (Nové Zámky)

Slovácká jiskra (Uherské Hradiště)

Slovácko (Hodonín)

Slovo Zemplína (Trebišov)

Sme (Bratislava)

Smena (Bratislava)

Smer (Banská Bystrica)

Směr (Brno-venkov)

Směr (Teplice)

Socialistický dnešok (Topoľčany), which mutated to *Dnešok*

Sokolovská jiskra

Spišské hlasy (Spišská Nová Ves)

Stráž lidu (Olomouc)

Stráž lidu (Prostějov)

Stráž míru (Karlovy Vary)

Studentské listy (Prague)

Svobodné slovo (Prague)

Szabad Polgár (Nové Zámky)

Štít (Jindřichův Hradec)

Tachovská jiskra (Tachov)

Trenčianske noviny

Trnavská verejnosť

Trnavský hlas

Úder (Kutná Hora)

Večer (Košice)

Verejnosť (Bratislava)

Víťazná cesta (Galanta)

Vpred (Zvolen)

Vpřed (Bruntál)

Vpřed (Liberec)

Vranovské noviny (Vranov nad Topľou)

Vysočina (Žďár nad Sázavou)

Záhorák (Senica)

Zář (Pardubice)

Zář Mladoboleslavska

Zempléni szó (Trebišov)

Zemplínske noviny (Michalovce)

Zítřek (Písek)

Znojemsko (Znojmo)

Zora Gemera (Rožňava)

Zora Východu (Košice)

Zprávy Karvinska

Žiara socializmu (Žiar nad Hronom)

Žitný ostrov (Dunajská streda)

Audiovisual Material

Dni nádeje. Directed by Martin Slivka. Slovenská televízia, 2004.

Jak šly dějiny. Directed by Aleš V. Poledne. Česká televize, 2004.

"*Kde jsi byl, když hřmělo?*" Directed by Jaroslav Bouma. Česká televize, 1999.

Labyrintem revoluce. Directed by Petr Jančárek in cooperation with Jiří Suk. Česká televize, 2006.

Langer, Ivan and Zdeněk Zukal. *Happening.* Olomouc: Univerzita Palackého, 1990. Video recording.

Léčba Klausem. Directed by Igor Chaun. Československá televize, 1991.

Regionálny denník. Slovenská televízia, 17 November 2004.

Štúdio dialóg. Slovenská televízia, 4 December 1989.

Štúdio Televíznych novín. Slovenská televízia, 24 November 1989.

Študenti a November '89. Directed by Martin Slivka. Slovenská televízia, 2001.

Televízny klub mladých. Slovenská televízia, 8 December 1989.

Tenkrát 2: Šance pro Slovensko. Directed by Robert Sedláček. Česká televize, 2000.

Verejné fórum. Slovenská televízia, 1999.

Verejnosť proti násiliu and Študentské hnutie. *Nežná revolúcia.* Bratislava: Opus, 1990. Sound recording.

Books and Articles

Adamson, Kevin, and Sergiu Florean. "Discourse and Power: The FSN and the Mythologisation of the Romanian Revolution." In *The 1989 Revolutions in Central and Eastern Europe: From Communism to Pluralism*, edited by Kevin McDermott and Matthew Stibbe, 172–91. Manchester, U.K.: Manchester University Press, 2013.

Anderson, Benedict. *Imagined Communities: Reflections on the Origins and Spread of Nationalism.* London: Verso, 1983.

Antalová, Ingrid, ed. *Verejnosť proti násiliu 1989–1991: Svedectvá a dokumenty.* Bratislava: Nadácia Milana Šimečku, 1998.

——, ed. *Verejnosť proti násiliu—Občianske fórum: Svedectvá.* Bratislava: Nadácia Milana Šimečku, 1999.

Arendt, Hannah. *Between Past and Future: Six Exercises in Political Thought.* New York: Viking, 1961.

——. *On Revolution.* Rev. ed. New York: Viking, 1965.

Bartuška, Václav. *Polojasno: Pátrání po vinících 17. listopadu 1989.* Prague: Ex libris, 1990.

Bělohradský, Václav, Pavel Barša, Michael Hauser, Václav Magid, Petr Schnur, Ondřej Slačálek, Tereza Stöckelová, Martin Škabraha, and Mirek Vodrážka. *Kritika depolitizovaného rozumu: Úvahy (nejen) o nové normalizaci.* Všeň: Grimmus, 2010.

Ben-David, Joseph, and Terry Nichols Clark, eds. *Culture and Its Creators: Essays in Honor of Edward Shils.* Chicago: University of Chicago Press, 1977.

Benda, Marek, Martin Benda, Pavel Dobrovský, Martin Klíma, Roman Kříž, Monika Pajerová, and Šimon Pánek. *Studenti psali revoluce.* Prague: Univerzum, 1990.

Beneš, Bohuslav, and Václav Hrníčko. *Nápisy v ulicích.* Brno: Masarykova univerzita, 1993.

Blažek, Filip. *Plakáty Sametové revoluce: Příběh plakátů z listopadu a prosince 1989.* Prague: XYZ, 2009.

Blažek, Jiří, and Tomáš Kostelecký. "Geografická analýza výsledků parlamentních voleb v roce 1990." *Sborník geografické společnosti* 96, no. 1 (1991): 1–14.

Bombík, Svetoslav. *Bližšie k Európe: Štúdie a články.* Bratislava: Slovenská nadácia pre európske štúdie, 1995.

Boštík, Martin. *Sametová revoluce v Litomyšli: Příspěvek k politickým dějinám okresu Svitavy v letech 1989–1991.* Litomyšl: Regionální muzeum v Litomyšli, 2009.

Bradley, John. *Czechoslovakia's Velvet Revolution: A Political Analysis.* Boulder, Colo.: East European Monographs, 1992.

Brook, Daniel. *Modern Revolution: Social Change and Cultural Continuity in Czechoslovakia and China.* Lanham, Md.: University Press of America, 2005.

Bunčák, Ján, Valentína Harmadyová, and Zuzana Kusá. *Politická zmena v spoločenskej rozprave.* Bratislava: Veda, 1996.

Burián, Michal. "Prognostici v takzvané Sametové revoluci." *Soudobé dějiny* 4, no. 3–4 (1997): 492–509.

Castle, Marjorie. *Triggering Communism's Collapse: Perceptions and Power in Poland's Transition.* Lanham, Md.: Rowman & Littlefield, 2003.

Cigánek, František, et al. *Kronika demokratického parlamentu 1989–1992.* Prague: Cesty, 1992.

Cviková, Jana, ed. *Politiky a političky: Aspekty politickej subjektvity žien.* Bratislava: Aspekt, 2011.

Cysarová, Jarmila. "Čas prelomu: Garáž OF ČST: 21. listopadu 1989–11. ledna 1990." *Soudobé dějiny* 6, no. 2–3 (1999): 297–307.

Čarnogurský, Ján. *Cestami KDH.* Prešov: Vydavateľstvo Michala Vaška, 2007.

———. *Videné od Dunaja.* Bratislava: Kalligram, 1997.

Čermáková, Barbora, Zbyněk Černý, Pit Fiedler, and Dietrich Kelterer, eds. *Občanská odvaha vstupuje do politiky, 1989/90: Občanské fórum v Chebu, Nové Fórum v Plavně.* Prague: Ústav pro soudobé dějiny, 2009.

Dahrendorf, Ralf. *Reflections on the Revolution in Europe.* New York: Times Books, 1990.

Dale, Gareth. *The East German Revolution of 1989.* Manchester, U.K.: Manchester University Press, 2006.

Daněk, Petr. "Moravian and Silesian Nationalities: A New Phenomenon in the Ethnic Map of the Czech Lands?" *GeoJournal* 30, no. 3 (1993): 249–254.

Dennis, Mike. *The Stasi: Myth and Reality.* Harlow, U.K.: Pearson/Longman, 2003.

Derrida, Jacques. *The Gift of Death.* Translated by David Wills. Chicago: University of Chicago Press, 1995.

Dienstbier, Jiří. *Od snění k realitě: Vzpomínky z let 1989–1999.* Prague: Lidové noviny, 1999.

Douglas, Mary. *How Institutions Think.* Syracuse, N.Y.: Syracuse University Press, 1986.

———. *Implicit Meanings: Essays in Anthropology.* London: Routledge & Paul, 1975.

———. *Purity and Danger: An Analysis of Concepts of Pollution and Taboo.* New York: Praeger, 1966.

Durkheim, Émile. *The Elementary Forms of the Religious Life.* Translated by Joseph Ward Swain. New York: Macmillan, 1915.

———. *Sociology and Philosophy.* Translated by D. F. Pocock. Glencoe, Ill.: Free Press, 1953.

Durman, Karel. "Některé negativní mezinárodní faktory ovlivňující demokratickou revoluci 1989–1990." *Soudobé dějiny* 6, no. 2–3 (1999): 308–20.

Ekiert, Grzegorz, and Jan Kubik. "Contentious Politics in New Democracies: East Germany, Hungary, Poland, and Slovakia, 1989–93." *World Politics* 50, no. 4 (1998): 547–81.

Elster, Jon, ed. *The Roundtable Talks and the Breakdown of Communism.* Chicago: University of Chicago Press, 1996.

Eyal, Gil. *The Origins of Postcommunist Elites: From Prague Spring to the Breakup of Czechoslovakia.* Minneapolis: University of Minnesota Press, 2003.

Falk, Barbara. *The Dilemmas of Dissidence in East-Central Europe.* Budapest: Central European University Press, 2003.

Feldek, Ľubomír, ed. *Keď sme brali do rúk budúcnosť.* Bratislava: Archa, 1990.

Figes, Orlando, and Boris Kolonitskii. *Interpreting the Russian Revolution: The Language and Symbols of 1917.* New Haven, Conn.: Yale University Press, 1999.

Frye, Northrop. *The Anatomy of Criticism: Four Essays.* Princeton, N.J.: Princeton University Press, 1957.

Furet, François. *Interpreting the French Revolution.* Translated by Elborg Forster. Cambridge: Cambridge University Press, 1981.

Gál, Fedor. *Z prvej ruky.* Bratislava: Archa, 1991.

Gál, Fedor, and Peter Zajac. *1+1.* Bratislava: Petrus, 2004.

Garton Ash, Timothy. *History of the Present: Essays, Sketches, and Dispatches from Europe in the 1990s.* New York: Random House, 1999.

——. *We the People: The Revolution of '89 Witnessed in Warsaw, Budapest, Berlin & Prague.* London: Granta, 1990.

Geertz, Clifford. *The Interpretation of Cultures.* New York: Basic Books, 1973.

Gendron, François. *The Gilded Youth of Thermidor.* Montreal: McGill-Queen's University Press, 1993.

Girard, René. *Violence and the Sacred.* Translated by Patrick Gregory. Baltimore: Johns Hopkins University Press, 1977.

Girard, René, Guy Lefort, and Jean-Michel Oughourlian. *Things Hidden since the Foundation of the World.* Translated by Stephen Bann and Michael Metteer. Stanford, Calif.: Stanford University Press, 1987.

Gjuričová, Adéla, and Michal Kopeček, eds. *Kapitoly z české politiky po r. 1989.* Prague: Paseka, 2008.

Gjuričová, Adéla, Michal Kopeček, Petr Roubal, Jiří Suk, and Tomáš Zahradníček. *Rozděleni minulostí: Vytváření politických identit v České republice po roce 1989.* Prague: Knihovna Václava Havla, 2011.

Glenn, John K. *Framing Democracy: Civil Society and Civic Movements in Eastern Europe.* Stanford, Calif.: Stanford University Press, 2001.

Goldstone, Jack. *Revolutions: Theoretical, Comparative, and Historical Studies.* 3rd ed. Belmont, Calif.: Wadsworth, 2008.

Grabowski, Tomek. "The Party That Never Was: The Rise and Fall of the Solidarity Citizens' Committees in Poland." *East European Politics and Societies* 10, no. 2 (Spring 1996): 214–54.

Gross, Jan T. *Polish Society under German Occupation: The Generalgouvernement, 1939–1944.* Princeton, N.J.: Princeton University Press, 1979.

——. *Revolution from Abroad: The Soviet Conquest of Poland's Western Ukraine and Western Belorussia.* Rev. ed. Princeton, N.J.: Princeton University Press, 2002.

Habermas, Jürgen. "What Does Socialism Mean Today? The Rectifying Revolution and the Need for New Thinking on the Left." *New Left Review,* no. 183 (September–October 1990): 3–21.

Halada, Jan, and Mirko Ryvola. *Něžná revoluce v pražských ulicích.* Prague: Lidové nakladatelství, 1990.

Hanley, Seán. *The New Right in the New Europe: Czech Transformation and Right-Wing Politics, 1989–2006.* London: Routledge, 2008.

Hanzel, Vladimír, ed. *Zrychlený tep dějin: Reálné drama o deseti jednáních.* Prague: OK Centrum, 1991.

Haughton, Tim. "HZDS: The Ideology, Organisation and Support Base of Slovakia's Most Successful Party." *Europe-Asia Studies* 53, no. 5 (July 2001): 745–69.

Havel, Václav. *Open Letters: Selected Writings, 1965–1990.* Edited by Paul Wilson. New York: Vintage Books, 1992.

———. *Summer Meditations.* Translated by Paul Wilson. New York: Knopf, 1992.

———. *To the Castle and Back.* Translated by Paul Wilson. New York: Knopf, 2007.

Henderson, Karen. *Slovakia: The Escape from Invisibility.* London: Routledge, 2002.

Hlavová, Viera, and Jozef Žatkuliak, eds. *Novembrová revolúcia a česko-slovenský rozchod: Od česko-slovenskej federácie k samostatnej demokratickej slovenskej štátnosti: Výber dokumentov a prejavov (november 1989–december 1992).* Bratislava: Literárne informačné centrum, 2002.

Hlušíčková, Růžena, and Milan Otáhal, eds. *Čas Demokratické iniciativy, 1987–1990: Sborník dokumentů.* Prague: Nadace Demokratické iniciativy pro kulturu a politiku, 1993.

Holmes, Leslie. *The End of Communist Power: Anti-Corruption Campaigns and Legitimation Crisis.* New York: Oxford University Press, 1993.

Holubec, Petr, ed. *Kronika sametové revoluce.* Prague: ČTK, 1990.

Holý, Ladislav. *The Little Czech and the Great Czech Nation: National Identity and the Post-Communist Social Transformation.* Cambridge: Cambridge University Press, 1996.

Horáček, Michal. *Jak pukaly ledy.* Prague: Ex libris, 1990.

Hořec, Jaromír, and Ivan Hanousek, eds. *Občanské fóry: Pražský podzim 1989.* Prague: Odeon, 1990.

Hosking, Geoffrey, and George Schöpflin, eds. *Myths and Nationhood.* New York: Routledge, 1997.

Hunt, Lynn. *Politics, Culture, and Class in the French Revolution.* Berkeley: University of California Press, 1984.

———. "The Sacred and the French Revolution." In *Durkheimian Sociology: Cultural Studies,* edited by Jeffrey Alexander, 25–43. Cambridge: Cambridge University Press, 1992.

Husák, Petr. *Budování kapitalismu v Čechách: Rozhovory s Tomášem Ježkem.* Prague: Volvox Globator, 1997.

———. *Česká cesta ke svobodě: Revoluce či co?* Prague: Vovlox Globator, 1999.

Innes, Abby. *Czechoslovakia: The Short Goodbye.* New Haven, Conn.: Yale University Press, 2001.

Isaac, Jeffrey. "The Strange Silence of Political Theory." *Political Theory* 23, no. 4 (November 1995): 636–52.

Jenne, Erin. *Ethnic Bargaining: The Paradox of Minority Empowerment.* Ithaca, N.Y.: Cornell University Press, 2007.

Jeseň nádeje, alebo História pisaná v uliciach. Košice: Východoslovenské vydavateľstvo, 1990.

Ježek, Tomáš. *Zrození ze zkumavky: Svědectví o české privatizaci, 1990–1997.* Prague: Prostor, 2007.

Jičinský, Zdeněk. *Československý parlament v polistopadovém období: Federální shromáždění mezi 17. listopadem 1989 a 8. červnem 1990.* Prague: Nadas-AFGH, 1993.

Johnson, Lonnie. *Central Europe: Enemies, Neighbors, Friends.* 2nd ed. New York: Oxford University Press, 2002.

Jowitt, Kenneth. *New World Disorder: The Leninist Extinction.* Berkeley: University of California Press, 1992.

Judt, Tony. *Postwar: A History of Europe since 1945.* New York: Penguin, 2005.

Karklins, Rasma, and Roger Petersen. "Decision Calculus of Protesters and Regimes: Eastern Europe 1989." *Journal of Politics* 55, no. 3 (August 1993): 588–614.

Kavan, Jan, and Libor Konvička. "Youth Movements and the Velvet Revolution." *Communist and Post-Communist Studies* 27, no. 2 (1994): 160–76.

Keane, John. *Václav Havel: A Political Tragedy in Six Acts.* New York: Basic Books, 2000.

Kenney, Padraic. *A Carnival of Revolution: Central Europe 1989.* Princeton, N.J.: Princeton University Press, 2002.

Kipke, Rudiger, and Karel Vodička, eds. *Rozloučení s Československem: Příčiny a důsledky česko-slovenského rozchodu.* Prague: Český spisovatel, 1993.

Kis, János. "Between Reform and Revolution." *East European Politics and Societies* 12, no. 2 (Spring 1998): 300–383.

———. "Between Reform and Revolution: Three Hypotheses about the Nature of the Regime Change." In *Lawful Revolution in Hungary, 1989–94,* edited by Béla Király, 33–59. Boulder, Colo.: Social Science Monographs, 1995.

Klaus, Václav. *Nemám rád katastrofické scénáře.* Ostrava: Sagit, 1991.

Kocáb, Michael. *Když nebyl čas na hraní.* Řitka: Daranus, 2009.

Kokošková, Zdeňka, and Stanislav Kokoška. *Obroda: Klub za socialistickou přestavbu.* Prague: Maxdorf, 1996.

Kotkin, Stephen, with Jan T. Gross. *Uncivil Society: 1989 and the Implosion of the Communist Establishment.* New York: Modern Library, 2009.

Koutská, Ivana, Vojtěch Ripka, and Pavel Žáček, eds. *Občanské fórum, den první: Vznik OF v dokumentech a fotografiích.* Prague: Ústav pro studium totalitních režimů, 2009.

Krapfl, James. "The Diffusion of 'Dissident' Political Theory in the Czechoslovak Revolution of 1989." *Slovo* (London) 19, no. 2 (Autumn 2007): 83–101.

———. *Revolúcia s ľudskou tvárou: Politika, kultura a spoločenstvo v Československu po 17. novembri 1989.* Bratislava: Kalligram, 2009.

———. "Revolution and Revolt against Revolution: Czechoslovakia 1989." In *Revolution and Resistance in Eastern Europe,* edited by Kevin McDermott and Matthew Stibbe, 175–94. Oxford: Berg, 2006.

Kraus, Michael, and Allison Stanger, eds. *Irreconcilable Differences? Explaining Czechoslovakia's Dissolution.* Lanham, Md.: Rowman & Littlefield, 2000.

Krejčí, Jaroslav. *Great Revolutions Compared: The Outline of a Theory.* New York: Harvester Wheatsheaf, 1994.

Kukral, Michael. *Prague 1989: Theater of Revolution.* Boulder, Colo.: East European Monographs, 1997.

Kumar, Krishan. *1989: Revolutionary Ideas and Ideals.* Minneapolis: University of Minnesota Press, 2001.

Larson, Jonathan. *Critical Thinking in Slovakia after Socialism.* Rochester, N.Y.: University of Rochester Press, 2013.

Lefebvre, Georges. *The Great Fear of 1789: Rural Panic in Revolutionary France.* Translated by Joan White. New York: Pantheon Books, 1973.

Leff, Carol Skalnik. *The Czech and Slovak Republics: Nation versus State.* Boulder, Colo.: Westview, 1996.

Leff, Carol Skalnik, and Susan B. Mikula. "Institutionalizing Party Systems in Multiethnic States: Integration and Ethnic Segmentation in Czechoslovakia, 1918–1992." *Slavic Review* 61, no. 2 (Summer 2002): 292–314.

Long, Michael. *Making History: Czech Voices of Dissent and the Revolution of 1989.* Lanham, Md.: Rowan and Littlefield, 2005.

Lukes, Steven. *Emile Durkheim: His Life and Work.* New York: Harper & Row, 1972.

Maier, Charles S. *Dissolution: The Crisis of Communism and the End of East Germany.* Princeton, N.J.: Princeton University Press, 1997.

Mareš, Miroslav, ed. *Etnické a regionální strany v ČR po roce 1989.* Brno: Centrum pro studium demokracie a kultury, 2003.

Margadant, Ted. *Urban Rivalries in the French Revolution.* Princeton, N.J.: Princeton University Press, 1992.

Maxa, Hubert. *Alexander Dubček: Člověk v politice (1990–1992).* Bratislava and Brno: Kalligram and Doplněk, 1998.

McAdam, Doug, Sidney Tarrow, and Charles Tilly. *Dynamics of Contention.* Cambridge: Cambridge University Press, 2001.

McRae, Robert. *Resistance and Revolution: Václav Havel's Czechoslovakia.* Ottawa: Carleton University Press, 1997.

Mejstřík, Martin. *Deník: Řekněte jim, že sametová. . . .* Brno: Computer Press, 2010.

Měchýř, Jan. *Velký převrat či snad revoluce sametová? Několik informací, poznámek a komentářů o naší takřečené něžné revoluci a jejich osudech (1989–1992).* Prague: Československý spisovatel, 1999.

Mihalík, Juraj. *Spomienky na zlyhania.* Bratislava: Príroda, 1993.

Možný, Ivo. *Proč tak snadno? Některé rodinné důvody sametové revoluce.* Prague: Sociologické nakladatelství, 1991.

Müllerová, Alena, and Vladimír Hanzel. *Albertov 16:00: Příběhy sametové revoluce.* Prague: Nakladatelství Lidové noviny, 2009.

Musil, Jiří, ed. *The End of Czechoslovakia.* Budapest: Central European University Press, 1995.

Nedvěd, Jan. *Cesta ke svobodě: Revoluční listopad 1989 v Karlových Varech.* Karlovy Vary: KMKK, 2009.

Newman, Simon P. *Parades and the Politics of the Street: Festive Culture in the Early American Republic.* Philadelphia: University of Pennsylvania Press, 1997.

Okey, Robin. *The Demise of Communist East Europe: 1989 in Context.* London: Hodder Arnold, 2004.

Ondruš, Vladimír. *Atentát na nežnú revolúciu.* Bratislava: Ikar, 2009.

Otáhal, Milan, and Zdeněk Sládek, eds. *Deset pražských dnů (17.–27. listopad 1989): Dokumentace.* Prague: Academia, 1990.

Otáhal, Milan, and Miroslav Vaněk. *Sto studentských revolucí: Studenti v období pádu komunismu—životopisná vyprávění.* Prague: Lidové noviny, 1999.

Ozouf, Mona. "De Thermidor à Brumaire: Le Discours de la Révolution sur elle-même." *Revue historique* 243 (1970): 31–66.

———. *Festivals and the French Revolution.* Translated by Alan Sheridan. Cambridge, Mass.: Harvard University Press, 1988.

Patočka, Jan. *Heretical Essays in the Philosophy of History.* Translated by Erazim Kohák. Chicago: Open Court, 1996.

Pecka, Jindřich. *Odsun sovětských vojsk z Československa, 1989–1991.* Prague: Ústav pro soudobé dějiny, 1996.

Perron, Catherine. "L'Emergence d'une nouvelle élite politique locale à Plzeň après 1989." *Transitions* 39, no. 1 (1998): 55–86.

Pešek, Jan, and Soňa Szomolányi, eds. *November 1989 na Slovensku: Súvislosti, predpoklady a dôsledky.* Bratislava: Nádacia Milana Šimečku, 1999.

Pilík, Sláva. *Sametový příběh rakovnické revoluce.* Nové Strašecí: Jiří Červenka-Gelton, 2009.

Pithart, Petr. *Devětaosmdesátý: Vzpomínky a přemýšlení.* Prague: Academia, 2009.

Pithart, Petr, Jaroslav Valenta, and Jan Vít. *Listopad '89.* Prague: Odeon, 1990.

Prins, Gwyn, ed. *Spring in Winter: The 1989 Revolutions.* Manchester: Manchester University Press, 1990.

Profantová, Zuzana, ed. *Hodnota zmeny—zmena hodnoty: Demarkačný rok 1989.* Bratislava: Ústav etnologie SAV, 2009.

Přibán, Jiří. *Dissidents of Law: On the 1989 Velvet Revolutions, Legitimations, Fictions of Legality and Contemporary Version of the Social Contract.* Aldershot, U.K.: Ashgate, 2002.

Pullmann, Michal. *Konec experimentu: Přestavba a pád komunismu v Československu.* Prague: Scriptorium, 2011.

Rachum, Ilan. "The Meaning of 'Revolution' in the English Revolution (1648–1660)." *Journal of the History of Ideas* 56, no. 2 (April 1995): 195–215.

———. *"Revolution": The Entrance of a New Word into Western Political Discourse.* Lanham, Md.: University Press of America, 1999.

Renwick, Alan. "The Role of Non-Elite Forces in the Regime Change." In *The Roundtable Talks of 1989: The Genesis of Hungarian Democracy,* edited by András Bozóki, 191–210. Budapest: Central European University Press, 2001.

Rogers, Everett. *Diffusion of Innovations.* 4th ed. New York: Free Press, 1995.

Rothmayerová, Gabriela. *Zo zápisníka poslankyne.* Bratislava: Perex, 1992.

Rychlík, Jan. *Rozpad Československa: Česko-slovenské vztahy 1989–1992.* Bratislava: AEP, 2002.

Řeháček, Jan. *Sametová revoluce v Pardubicích.* Pardubice: Klub přátel Pardubicka, 2009.

Sandford, Mariellen R., ed. *Happenings and Other Acts.* London: Routledge, 1995.

Saxonberg, Steven. *The Fall: A Comparative Study of the End of Communism in Czechoslovakia, East Germany, Hungary, and Poland.* Amsterdam: Harwood Academic, 2001.

Schuster, Rudolf. *Ultimatum.* Košice: Pressprint, 1996.

Sewell, William H., Jr. "Historical Events as Transformations of Structures: Inventing Revolution at the Bastille." *Theory and Society* 25, no. 6 (December 1996): 841–81.

———. *Logics of History: Social Theory and Social Transformation.* Chicago: University of Chicago Press, 2005.

———. *Work and Revolution in France: The Language of Labor from the Old Regime to 1848.* Cambridge: Cambridge University Press, 1980.

Shepherd, Robin. *Czechoslovakia: The Velvet Revolution and Beyond.* New York: St. Martin's, 2000.

Siani-Davies, Peter. *The Romanian Revolution of 1989.* Ithaca, N.Y.: Cornell University Press, 2005.

Skąpska, Grażyna, and Annamaria Orla-Bukowska, eds. *The Contemporary Moral Fabric in Contemporary Societies.* Leiden: Brill, 2003.

Skilling, H. Gordon, and Paul Wilson, eds. *Civic Freedom in Central Europe: Voices from Czechoslovakia.* London: Macmillan, 1991.

Slejška, Dragoslav, et al. *Sondy do veřejného mínění: Jaro 1968, podzim 1989.* Prague: Svoboda, 1990.

Smith, Simon, ed. *Local Communities and Post-Communist Transformation: Czechoslovakia, the Czech Republic and Slovakia.* London: Routledge Curzon, 2003.

Springerová, Pavlína. *Analýza vývoje a činnosti moravistických politických subjektů v letech 1989–2005.* Brno: Centrum pro studium demokracie a kultury, 2010.

Stein, Eric. *Czecho/Slovakia: Ethnic Conflict, Constitutional Fissure, Negotiated Breakup.* Ann Arbor: University of Michigan Press, 1997.

Steinberg, Mark. *Voices of Revolution, 1917.* New Haven, Conn.: Yale University Press, 2001.

Stokes, Gale. *The Walls Came Tumbling Down: The Collapse of Communism in Eastern Europe.* New York: Oxford University Press, 1993.

Suk, Jiří. "K prosazení kandidatury Václava Havla na úřad prezidenta v prosinci 1989: Dokumenty a svědectví." *Soudobé dějiny* 6, no. 2–3 (1999): 346–69.

——. *Labyrintem revoluce: Aktéři, zápletky a křížovatky jedné politické krize (od listopadu 1989 do června 1990).* Prague: Prostor, 2003.

——. *Občanské fórum: Listopad-prosinec 1989.* Vol. 1, *Události.* Brno: Doplněk, 1997.

——, ed. *Občanské fórum: Listopad-prosinec 1989.* Vol. 2, *Dokumenty.* Brno: Doplněk, 1998.

Suková, Irena, ed. *Proměny politického systému v Československu na přelomu let 1989/1990.* Prague: Nadace Heinricha Bölla, 1995.

Svobodová, Jana, ed. *Nezávislá skupina České děti (1988–1989).* Prague: Ústav pro soudobé dějiny, 1995.

Szomolányi, Soňa. "November '89: Otvorenie prechodu a jeho aktéri na Slovensku." *Soudobé dějiny* 6, no. 4 (1999): 421–42.

Šimečka, Milan. *Konec nehybnosti.* Prague: Lidové noviny, 1990.

Šišuláková, Mária, ed. *Anonymy: Výber z nepodpísaných listov bratislavským redakciám.* Bratislava: Digest, 1991.

Štefánková, Maria, and Marta Zisperová, eds. *Bratislava Symposium I: Ethics and Politics/Art against Totalitarianism.* Bratislava: Slovak National Gallery, 1990.

Šútovec, Milan. *Semióza ako politikum alebo "Pomlčková vojna": Niektoré historické, politické a iné súvislosti jedného sporu, ktorý bol na začiatku zániku česko-slovenského štátu.* Bratislava: Kalligram, 1999.

Tilly, Charles. *European Revolutions, 1492–1992.* Oxford: Basil Blackwell, 1993.

——. *Regimes and Repertoires.* Chicago: University of Chicago Press, 2006.

Tiryakian, Edward. "Collective Effervescence, Social Change and Charisma: Durkheim, Weber and 1989." *International Sociology* 10, no. 3 (September 1995): 269–81.

Tismaneanu, Vladimir. *Reinventing Politics: Eastern Europe from Stalin to Havel.* New York: Free Press, 1992.

——, ed. *The Revolutions of 1989.* London: Routledge, 1999.

Tížik, Miroslav. *Náboženstvo vo verejnom živote na Slovensku.* Bratislava: Sociologický ústav SAV, 2012.

Tőkés, Rudolf. *Hungary's Negotiated Revolution: Economic Reform, Social Change, and Political Succession, 1957–1990.* Cambridge: Cambridge University Press, 1996.

Tucker, Aviezer. *Philosophy and Politics of Czech Dissidence from Patočka to Havel.* Pittsburgh: University of Pittsburgh Press, 2000.

Tůma, Oldřich. "9:00, Praha-Libeň, horní nádraží: Exodus východních Němců přes Prahu v září 1989." *Soudobé dějiny* 6 (1999): 147–64.

——. *Zítra zase tady! Protirežimní demonstrace v předlistopadové Praze jako politický a sociální fenomén.* Prague: Maxdorf, 1994.

Urban, Jan. "Bezmocnost mocných." *Listy* 23, no. 5 (1993): 3–10.

Valeš, Lukáš, ed. *Rok 1989 v Plzni a západních Čechách.* Dobrá Voda u Pelhřimova: Aleš Čeněk, 2003.

Vaněk, Miroslav. *Nedalo se tady dýchat.* Prague: Maxdorf, 1996.

Vodička, Karel, ed. *Dělení Československa: Deset let poté....* Prague: Volvox Globator, 2003.

Vogt, Henri. *Between Utopia and Disillusionment: A Narrative of the Political Transformation in Eastern Europe.* New York: Berghahn Books, 2005.

Von Geldern, James. *Bolshevik Festivals, 1917–1920.* Berkeley: University of California Press, 1993.

Všetečka, Jiří, and Jiří Doležal. *Rok na náměstích: Československo 1989.* Prague: Academia, 1990.

Waldstreicher, David. *In the Midst of Perpetual Fêtes: The Making of American Nationalism, 1776–1820.* Chapel Hill: University of North Carolina Press, 1997.

Wheaton, Bernard, and Zdeněk Kavan. *The Velvet Revolution: Czechoslovakia, 1988–1991.* Boulder, Colo.: Westview, 1992.

White, Hayden. *The Content of the Form: Narrative Discourse and Historical Representation.* Baltimore: Johns Hopkins University Press, 1987.

——. *Metahistory: The Historical Imagination in Nineteenth-Century Europe.* Baltimore: Johns Hopkins University Press, 1973.

Wolchik, Sharon. "Czechoslovakia on the Eve of 1989." *Communist and Post-Communist Studies* 32, no. 4 (1999): 437–51.

Wolf, Karol. *Podruhé a naposled, aneb Mírové dělení Československa.* Prague: G plus G, 1998.

Worsley, Peter. *The Trumpet Shall Sound: A Study of "Cargo Cults" in Melanesia.* 2nd ed. London: MacGibbon & Kee, 1968.

Zajac, Peter. *Sen o krajine.* Bratislava: Kalligram, 1996.

Zatlin, Jonathan. "The Vehicle of Desire: The Trabant, the Wartburg, and the End of the GDR." *German History* 15, no. 3 (1997): 358–80.

Zatloukal, Petr. *Gaudeamus.* Olomouc: Univerzita Palackého, 1990.

Žatkuliak, Jozef, ed. *November 1989 a Slovensko: Chronológia a dokumenty (1985–1990).* Bratislava: Nádacia Milana Šimečku a Historický ústav, 1999.

Index

Note: References to the numbered photos between pages 110 and 111 are italicized.

strike committees: and OF/VPN, 116, 122, 124; student, 22n, 106–7; workplace, 16, 19–20, 84, 86, 114, 162–64, 182. *See also* Association of Strike Committees
Strýko, Marcel, 103n, 121, 126, 128
students: in commemoration, 30–32, 75, 211, 220–25; experience of, 40–41, 43, 55, 74, 82; formal organization of, 22, 81, 83, 86, 107, 128, 130, 137–38, 140; media production by, 4, 53–54, 77, 142–43, 147, 194–95, 197; as mobilizers, 12n, 14–16, 47, 53, 57, 59–60, 63, 114, 145, 155, 183, *6*; as "national guard," 64–65; as negotiators, 5, 17, 165, 195; as opinion leaders, 39, 67–70, 80, 82, 87, 90–91, 96–97, 100–102, 104, 144, 146, 149, 174, 177, 181; pre-revolutionary ferment of, 14n, 45–46; relations with civic movements, 20–21, 25, 89, 116–17, 125, 144, 192; relations with workers, 16, 53, 84, 163; and school administration, 23, 158–60, 174–76; symbolic actions of, 37–38, 56–65, 69, *8, 9, 11*; as symbols, 17–18, 43–44, 48–50, 52, 60, 67; as teachers, 92, 95, 156, 160, 162, 168–69
Suk, Jiří, 5, 113, 155, 187
Šumperk, 138, 195
Sweden, 92, 100

Teachers' Forum, 193, 207
television, 39, 66, 89, 148, 205–6; as discussion forum, 55, 76, 80, 90, 97–98, 117, 143; speeches on, 23–24, 144n, 178
"Ten Commandments of Our Revolution, The," 52–53, 91
Teplice, 14n
"Thank you, now leave!", 214n, 220
theaters, 12n, 14, 47, 76, 114, 144, 161. *See also* actors
Tiananmen Square massacre, 14n, 46
Tilly, Charles, 3, 11, 38
time, perception of, 43
Tiryakian, Edward, 71
Tiso, Jozef, 142, 147

Tocqueville, Alexis de, 110
Tomášek, František Cardinal, 119n
Topoľčany, 85, 101, 142, 147; VPN and OF, 114n, 166–68, 193, 207, 212–13
totalitarianism, 36n, 109; rhetoric about, 20, 129, 144, 180–82, 206; symbolic parting with, 38, 63, 68
tragedy: definition, 12, 27; as plot of revolution, 26–33, 177, 207, 214, 225–27; in revolutionary processes, 13, 218, 220
Train of the Gentle Revolution, 57, 59–60, *8*
Trebišov, 114n, 125
Trenčín, 114n, 194
Trend of the Third Millenium, 53
tricolors, 38, 55, 182, 221
Trnava, 30, 114n, 135–36, 197n, 206–7, 210
Trnava Initiative, 30, 210–15
truth, 18, 62, 65–66, 71, 75, 176, 226; demands for, 4, 42, 64, 68, 79n; as moral imperative, 27, 42, 55, 76, 83, 91, 178; understanding of, 51, 85
Trutnov, 135, 149, 190, 199–201, 211
turncoats, 67, 177, 182

Uherské Hradiště, 61
United States of America, 47, 66, 108
Urban, Jan, 31–32, 206n
urban rivalry, 57, 112, 121–22, 126–33, 139, 150–51

Vavroušek, Josef, 128–29
"Velvet Divorce." *See* dissolution of Czechoslovakia
violence, 12, 17, 119, 218; incidents of, 5, 14–15, 46–47, 82, 177; in revolutions, 11, 18, 32, 108; and symbolic differentiation, 36, 39, 47–53, 70, 102, *1*; tension with nonviolence, 9, 65, 68–70, 91, 181, 201; understanding of, 51, 66, 82–85, 96, 100–101, 109, 178. *See also* nonviolence; provocation
Vranov nad Topľou, 48, 52, 101, 114n, 125–26, 135, 169

Lightning Source UK Ltd.
Milton Keynes UK
UKHW020900181221
395724UK00001B/12/J